D1121698

HARVARD HISTORICAL STUDIES

Published under the direction
of the Department of History
from the income of the
Henry Warren Torrey Fund

Volume CI

Some of the Principal Inhabitants of y.ᵉ MOON, as they
Were Perfectly Discover'd by a Telescope brought to y.ᵉ Greatest
Perfection ſince y.ᵉ last Eclipſe; Exactly Engraved from the
Objects, whereby y.ᵉ Curious may Gueſs at their Religion,
Manners, &c.

John Toland and the Deist Controversy

A Study in Adaptations

Robert E. Sullivan

Harvard University Press
Cambridge, Massachusetts
and London, England
1982

Library of Congress Cataloging in Publication Data
Sullivan, Robert E.
  John Toland and the Deist controversy.

  (Harvard historical studies; v. 101)
  Bibliography: p.
  Includes index.
    1. Toland, John. 1670-1722.   2. Deism — History —
17th century.   3. Deism — History — 18th century.
I. Title. II. Series.
BL2790.T6S94   211'.5   81-7137
ISBN 0-674-48050-3   AACR2

Parentibus carissimis

Preface

In 1724 William Hogarth executed "Some of the Principal Inhabitants of the Moon: Royalty, Episcopacy, and the Law," a mordant caricature of the system by which Sir Robert Walpole and his fellow Whigs had brought stability to England. Of the three grouped abstractions which dominate the engraving, that of episcopacy is the most striking and complicated. Fixed between a coin-faced king and a mallet-headed judge, this gowned figure is topped by a mitered Jew's harp. The tongue with which it speaks is controlled by a rope weighted by a Bible and tied to the handle of a pump attached to a device resembling a steeple. Coins are raining from a pipe near its base into a commodious strongbox. The weather vane which caps the structure is motionless, but it is apparently capable of shifting to any position in response to the changing direction and velocity of the winds. For the present a light breeze directs it toward the crown. Although this onerous contrivance is working efficiently, it shows the roughness of novelty.

Turbulence ruled the preceding generation during which the elements of Walpole's regime had evolved. The political history of this period has been convincingly reconstructed. In contrast, its religious side has only begun to be explored anew. A series of theological controversies determined the character of the Georgian Establishment, but the deadness of all such past disputes has tended to impede further investigation. John Toland, who died in 1722, was an inveterate participant in these formative debates. My book has the modest intention of studying them through his contributions, as well as through the efforts of his teachers and his opponents.

During nine years of research and writing I have incurred a formidable variety of obligations, many of which I cannot acknowledge. Of the debts which I must own the public ones are easily expressed. I have been fortunate in being able to use the resources of the British Library, Dr. Williams' Library, the Lambeth Palace Library, and the Public Record Office in London; the Bodleian and Manchester College libraries in Oxford; the National Library of Scotland in Edinburgh; the Trinity College Library in Dublin; the Oesterreichische Nationalbibliothek in Vienna; the Henry E. Huntington Library in San Marino; the Spencer Research Library of the University of Kansas, Lawrence; the Sterling Library of Yale University; and the rare book room of the Boston Public Library. For permission to quote from manuscripts in their control, I owe thanks to the Board of Trinity College Dublin, the Managers of the Presbyterian Fund, London, the Trustees of the National Library of Scotland, the British Library, and Lady Anne Bentinck. I am grateful to the custodians of all these depositories for their courtesy and efficiency. Without the riches of three Harvard collections — the Andover, Houghton, and Widener libraries — and the cooperation of their staffs, I could not have written this book.

In recent years, many scholars have made remarkable contributions to our understanding of John Toland. I have depended on the works of Giancarlo Carabelli, Chiara Giuntini, Margaret C. Jacob, and A. B. Worden. As my notes suggest, some of the most important investigations of Toland and deism remain unpublished. The dissertations of Roger L. Emerson, Robert R. Evans, and Nola J. Wegman have offered me regular guidance.

Other obligations are at least equally important, even if they must sometimes be less exactly phrased. With graciousness and good sense John Clive has seen this text through its successive manifestations. Donald Fleming, Wallace MacCaffrey, J. G. A. Pocock, and George Williams have been enlightening critics, especially when they have disagreed with me. They have corrected many errors, and I alone am responsible for the ones which remain. Almost from the beginning Bill LaPiana and Karen Scott have helped me in countless ways to get on with Toland without taking myself too seriously. Madeleine R. Gleason has patiently but firmly applied her notable editorial skills to an often refractory manuscript, which also benefited from the thoughtful care of Camille Smith and Elizabeth Suttell as it went through press. In typing it, Sheila Barry and Janet Hickey showed uncommon resourcefulness and tolerance. J. Joseph Ryan has scrutinized the penultimate version with a medievalist's fine eye. Often doing for my sake much that they would never have done for themselves, Jack Ahern, John Boles, Michael Foster, Joe and Mark Fuller, Paul Ritt, John Sassani, Ruthanne Schwartz, and R. J. M. Sullivan have given more than they can appreciate.

Contents

In all human institutions, a great part, almost all regulations, are made from the mere necessity of the case, let the theoretical merits of the question be what they will.

Edmund Burke, "Speech on the
Acts of Uniformity" (1772)

Who, born within the last forty years, has read one word of Collins, and Toland, and Tindal, and Chubb, and Morgan, and that whole race who called themselves freethinkers? Who now reads Bolingbroke? Who ever read him through? Ask the booksellers of London what is become of all these lights of the world. In a few years their few successors will go to the family vault of "all the Capulets."

Edmund Burke, *Reflections on the
Revolution in France* (1790)

1 / John Toland: A Portrait

The Jacobite antiquary Thomas Hearne spent much of his last winter conjuring up the specters of some of the men who had crossed his path in life. His recollection of one old antagonist, safely dead for over a decade, was particularly splenetic.

Mr. John Toland was an Irishman born. He was a very ingenious man, but of most vile principles, which he took all opportunities of instilling into young Gentlemen and others. He did some mischief in Oxford, but more elsewhere. . . . He returned to Ireland, but was for his wicked books and principles quite drove from thence, . . . and then he came in to England again, where he continued his old cause of poisoning young men etc. . . . He was a man of Learning, but for the most part superficial.

Sensing that vilification was giving way to neglect, John Toland had had another judge in mind when, years before, he appealed to the wise few of future generations to "do justice to a man who dar'd to own his affection to Truth, the beauty whereof had set him above all fears and expectations."[1] Just as Hearne's treasured spleen suggests that Toland was not inconsequential enough for comfort, so Toland's overwrought appeal points to an inner disquiet at odds with his self-portrayal as a sage. John Toland was a singularly controversial man. He remains intriguingly complicated, more important in himself and in his relation to the public events and thought of his age than a representation of him as either a poisoner of the young or a walking, laureled bust would allow.

When Toland's acquaintance, Pierre Des Maizeaux, began a biography shortly after Toland's death in 1722, the materials seemed inadequate.[2] In the intervening two-and-a-half centuries, they have not improved. Toland habitually covered his tracks, and the bulk of his papers have been destroyed.[3] Coming across the order, "Burn this," on the charred fragment of a letter concerning Toland, a researcher must wonder how much has been lost besides.[4] Toland's own injunction, "If you would know more of him, search his writings," asserts the centrality of the public events and thought of his age for any effort to understand him; it also provides a means of delineating the contours of his life from disorderly evidence.[5]

Their delineation does not preclude recurrent uncertainty. The obscurity of Toland's origins, which he labored to intensify, is pervasive enough to have led to disagreements about the place and date of his birth. It seems probable that he was born on 30 November 1670 on Inishowen, the wild northern Irish peninsula, perhaps in the parish of Clonmany.[6] Later antagonists alleged that he was the bastard of a Roman Catholic priest. The vehemence of his denials, the absence of references to other family members in his letters, and the studied vagueness of his efforts to produce a pedigree are at any rate suggestive.[7] In attempting to obscure his origins, he even tampered with his given name. The strictness of the canon law governing Christian names makes it more likely that he was baptized Joannes Eugenius (Sean Owen) than Janus Junius as he would sometimes assert. Reared as a papist, he was a shepherd until his fourteenth year, when the first of the several changes in religion which punctuated his life occurred. Local lore attributed to him a juvenile anticlericalism. Whether or not this rebelliousness led to his Protestantism, his conversion brought him enrollment in a school in the neighboring town of Redcastle. He was developing an eye for the main chance.[8] His sponsors saw in him a potential missionary to other Gaelic-speakers. While he never lost his brogue, he proved sufficiently deft a pupil that, sometime in 1688, he was named an "Alumnus Academicus," a full scholarship student, in the College (later University) of Glasgow.[9] By his nineteenth year, he was a rootless, lonely, and bright young man with expectations.

The disorder of the college in which Sean matriculated reflected the disarray of Scotland on the eve of the Glorious Revolution. It would persist after the establishment of the new political order, for the ensuing change in the established religion from episcopacy to Presbyterianism created a demand for clerics, which swelled the number of students in all the Scottish universities.[10] Beginning as a homesick protégé of the bishop of Derry, he made advances to the archbishop of Glasgow but afterward associated himself with the waxing Kirk. In support of this new allegiance against the episcopally inclined magistrates of the city, he manned the barricades in 1689 for the only time in his life. As a candidate for ordination, Toland received a grounding in divinity and philosophy, more Latin, and at least some Greek.[11] He was growing to intellectual manhood on the regimen of theological categories and concerns that defined the endless sermons to which he was exposed. Through this exposure he matured from acquiescing in the general conviction that the orator was both guardian of truth and wielder of authority, to striving both to guard and to wield. Words expressed ideas, which at once represented and constituted reality. None of Toland's changes of view and occupation affected either his perception or his aspiration.

In late 1689 he decided to move on to the University of Edinburgh, which made him a Master of Arts at the end of that academic year. Although his formal curriculum continued to be unoriginal, it was apparently during this period that he first cultivated his enduring esoteric interests. Five years later he was remembered for having "set up there for a *Rosicrucian;* gave them the nick name *Sages* and printed a Book in French and English, with the title, *The Sage of the Time.*" This book, if it ever existed, does not survive; his "Rosicrucianism" depended on a repertoire of conjuring tricks that left him with some local notoriety. Such activities probably fostered the accusation that he had pledged in adolescence to make himself the head of a sect by the time he was thirty.[12] The character of his extracurricular activities in Edinburgh is irretrievably lost, but it is possible that his introduction to the world of secret societies, which fascinated him throughout his life, took place there.

John was neither the first nor the last Scottish-educated young man with expectations to trek south of the border in order to advance his fortunes. Shortly after arriving in London, he secured the patronage of an alderman in Clapham and with it entry into the prosperous dissenting circles of the city. In time, he became a tutor and, apparently, chaplain in the household of a wealthy widow, for it was as an ecclesiastic that he met Dr. Daniel Williams, the "Presbyterian Pope."[13] He may also have discovered London's radical political groups, connected by loosening ties of nostalgia with organized dissent. His acquaintance with them perhaps led to collaboration in several pseudonymous pamphlets that served their interests as well as those of the Dissenters. Toland's immediate opportunities lay not with political radicalism but with a Presbyterianism that had exchanged Calvinist rigor for Arminian suppleness under the influence of Richard Baxter's doctrine of "scriptural self-sufficiency." The tenuous union recently effected with the Independents was threatening to come apart because of the continued rigorism of most Independent ministers.[14] Williams proceeded to make a protégé of the young man who had competently defended him and scriptural self-sufficiency in the *Bibliothèque universelle,* the leading journal of Dutch Arminianism, and arranged for Toland to begin studies in

the autumn of 1692 at the universities of Leiden and Utrecht, the
citadels of that school of theology. His colleagues on the board of the
fund of the United Brethren agreed to pay £8 a year "towards the per-
fecting" of Toland's studies.[15]

Although two payments were made, Toland's name was never
entered in the register of students of either university. Presumably, like
most other English Nonconformists sent there, he neither registered
nor pursued a normal course of studies.[16] More variegated than Britain's, the theological environment of the late seventeenth-century
Netherlands played a considerable part in the development of his
mind. Frederick Spanheim the Younger, whom he described as "my
Master," was pursuing historical-literary investigations of Scripture
subversive of any literalism, while an unsettling materialism often
marked the widely circulating metaphysics of the later Cartesians. The
variety of Dutch freedom impressed Toland profoundly. Here was a
republic which, though in fact oligarchic, in theory honored an
aristocracy of talent and accepted intellectual novelty. For the rest of
his life he was to yearn for the achievement of such conditions in
England.[17] Even on the fringes of Dutch academic life, someone as
bright and iconoclastic as Toland would have been exhilarated. Once
he had tasted the thrill of challenge, he never lost his appetite for it.

Incapable of self-effacement, he gained a reputation in Leiden for
being inordinately desirous of celebrity. This desire was gratified in
part by meeting such men of substance as Benjamin Furly — English
Quaker merchant, intimate of John Locke, and factor of intellectual
novelties — and Jean Le Clerc and Philip Van Limborch, the Dioscuri
of advanced Continental Protestantism. All three would influence the
next decade of his life. Thus, Le Clerc became the guiding force behind
the *Bibliothèque universelle,* to which as to other Dutch journals Toland
contributed.[18] Since Toland later tried to inflate such connections into
intimacy, Le Clerc and Limborch could plausibly deny him as his acquaintance became inconvenient, or dangerous. On returning to
England in the summer of 1693, Toland carried a book of Le Clerc for
the inspection of the lord privy seal and works of Limborch for the
great Locke.[19] He had become a young man with prospects.

Renouncing the clerical career for which he had been trained,
Toland lingered in London for a few months. Christmas found him living in Oxford and cultivating local notables in order to induce something to turn up. He was already exhibiting many of the traits that were

to mark his later career. He grasped the reigning concerns of the learned and, for neither the first nor the last time, presented himself as sharing them. Encountering him as the compiler of an Irish dictionary, the keeper of the Ashmolean Museum became wary when Toland seemed to be pretending to more knowledge than he actually possessed. Earlier, he had approached the master of University College with a proposal to make a catalogue of the books and manuscripts of the English historians, but his reputation as a "Mocker of Camden" soon discredited him.[20] Toland did manage to find patrons: among them a fellow of All Souls', the principal of St. Edmund's Hall, White Kennett—the future bishop of Lincoln—and the fabulously learned John Aubrey.[21]

It requires little effort to imagine how donnish clerics viewed their protégé's conversation and conduct in the town's coffeehouses and taverns. In one of them he was "arraigned and convicted" by fellow revelers for burning a copy of the Book of Common Prayer. His behavior was usually less flamboyant. He whiled away the hours anticipating the themes of future books and pamphlets by "talking against the Scriptures, commending Commonwealths, justifying the murder of K.C. 1st [Charles I], railing against Priests in general, with a Thousand other Extravagancys." He did not escape notice. By the late spring of 1694 he was receiving anonymous warnings: "You are a man of fine parts, great learning, and little religion." Toland ridiculed the specific charge of Socinianism: "I could as soon digest a wooden, or breaden Deity, as adore a created spyrit or a dignified man." Had he cared to, he might also have answered the accusation of his monitor that he was frittering away his talent by courting "popular esteem and the applauses of a Coffee-house, or a Club of Prophane Wits."[22] By then, he was aspiring to a more secure reputation, which he sought to achieve through sustained attention to the written word.

His first project was "The Fabulous Death of Atilius Regulus." He suggested that his proof that the Roman consul had died peacefully rather than violently indicated that "there are a great many other histories as little question'd as ever this was, which we are very certain have not one quarter so much ground nor probability to recommend 'em for truth." Rumor had it that he was preparing to set off a tremor nearer the epicenter of current theological disturbance by completing "a piece with intent to shew, that there is no such thing as *Mystery* in our Religion."[23] Did this project lead the vice-chancellor to order him from the city? Or was it perhaps his ill-placed insinuations that "some great

men" were employing him "to act as a spy on the University"? Whatever the cause, by the winter of 1695 he had again transferred his base
of operations to London, whose entrenched, socially undifferentiated
literary world offered more opportunities for hire and greater security
against clerical surveillance and regulation. Later that year, he
published *Two Essays,* purportedly an afterglow of the recently blinding
controversy between Thomas Burnet and John Woodward about how
to modernize the geological history found in Genesis. In fact, Toland's
pamphlet exploited this dispute in order to combine a materialist
cosmology and arch reflections on ancient religion and mythology, including Christianity.[24]

Toland effortlessly secured a place among the politically and
religiously advanced thinkers who habituated London's cafés and
taverns. He had boasted to Oxford associates of his friendship with
Lord Ashley, Locke's student who became the philosophical earl of
Shaftesbury, and was apparently his pensioner. He had also become a
familiar in the circle of Shaftesbury's former teacher. His relations with
Locke's closest associates are comparatively well documented. He
described one of them, John Freke, as the "primum mobile of my happiness." With another, James Tyrrell, he scouted anti-Lockian sermons
on behalf of their target. His relations with Locke himself are more
obscure.[25] Although Locke later repudiated Toland, in these years the
philosopher granted him access to manuscripts, read his manuscripts in
return, lent him money, and accepted his assistance in the campaign
for the recoinage.[26] No letters from Toland survive in the extensive
holdings of Locke manuscripts in the Bodleian Library. Speculation
about the relations between the two men is profitless, but they were
probably much closer than Locke was ever willing to acknowledge.

Historians of deism have expended considerable energy in attempts
to determine which books directly influenced the work that Toland was
seeing through press in late 1695. It is important to conclude either that
Toland was aware of Locke's *Reasonableness of Christianity* while he was
revising the proofs of *Christianity Not Mysterious,* or that Locke had seen
one of Toland's drafts before writing the *Reasonableness.* It is at least as
important to remember that the basis of Toland's acquaintance with
Locke was their shared preoccupation with questioning received
religious and political opinions.[27]

Toland's dealings with the London Socinians, a group of radical
religious pamphleteers, were, on the available evidence, no less signifi-

cant. He knew Thomas Firmin, the philanthropic merchant who for a generation financed the publication of anti-Trinitarian pamphlets, and shared with him a keen interest in the manuscripts of proto-Unitarians like Servetus.[28] He was also acquainted with Stephen Nye, a beneficed minister of the established church who closed his service as Firmin's chief pamphleteer during the 1690s by becoming his admiring biographer. Finally, Toland's relations with Matthew Tindal, a fellow of All Souls' College, Oxford, who had made the exposition of Unitarianism a way station on the twisting course of his religious opinions, were palpably regular.

Not until the Licensing Act lapsed in the spring of 1695 did Toland venture to publish a book whose intent would, he recognized, be judged heretical. Fueled by an advertising campaign, *Christianity Not Mysterious* had appeared by Christmas of that year.[29] Anonymously, John Toland—waif, apostate, spoiled parson, habitué of taverns—had filed papers for citizenship in the republic of letters. Yet anonymity galled him, for it precluded the recognition he saw as the legitimate reward of his daring. By the late summer of 1696 he was allowing his name to be attached to what was proving to be a *succès de scandale*.[30] In a sense, all of Toland's subsequent troubles sprang from this act of vanity. Most earlier flaunters of orthodoxy had been evasive. Ever cautious, Locke tried to maintain public silence about his feats of literary paternity, and the Unitarian tracts had been similarly orphaned. In contrast, Toland presented himself to those who yearned to hunt heretics as a visible, available, and vulnerable prey. His acknowledgment of *Christianity Not Mysterious* almost coincided with its presentment to the grand jury of Middlesex, an action reported as far away as Dublin.

On returning to Ireland early in 1697, Toland was run to ground. Locke's change in attitude toward him during the next few months is remarkable. Locke's Irish friend, William Molyneux, had met Toland by the end of March, and wrote to the philosopher that he admired him as a "candid Free-Thinker, and a good scolar," but especially for his "Acquaintance and Friendship to you." Molyneux was, however, apprehensive about the intense hostility toward Toland in Ireland, particularly among the clergy. Locke's reply is revealing. Deserving well of Toland, he regretted that the younger man had failed to visit him and receive proper introductions before leaving for Dublin. But he was uneasy about Toland's vanity. "If the exceeding great value of himself do not deprive the world of that usefulness, that his Parts, if rightly conducted, might be of, I shall be very glad."

As if cued, Molyneux became alarmed. Locke's hints concerning "Mr. T——perfectly agree with the apprehensions I had conceived of the Gentleman." He was "irritating all the Parties" and, by using Locke's name very freely, implicating him in his own conduct. Molyneux was moved by pique rather than disagreement, "not so much by his Difference in Opinion as by his unseasonable way of Discoursing, Propagating, and Maintaining it. Coffee-Houses, and Public Tables, are not proper Places for serious Discourses, relating to the most important Truths." A letter of rebuke from Locke might lead Toland to mend his ways. Always wary, the philosopher took out his washbowl. Rinsing his hands of men dusting his chamber, Locke advised Molyneux against harboring any feeling of obligation toward Toland. Having decided that time spent on Toland was wasted, he did not propose to correspond with him. By then, Dissenters were clamoring for Toland's prosecution, and association with him had become dangerous.[31]

What had prompted this change? Molyneux shared in the general puzzlement about why Toland, who lacked "Fortune or Employ" but had "Subsistence," was in Ireland. Others thought they knew: he had come over in the advance train of John Methuen, the newly appointed chancellor, perhaps to serve as his secretary.[32] Toland's own actions tend to substantiate this hypothesis. Vigorously denying irresponsible conduct, he attributed his problems to the machinations of the chancellor's opponents.[33] Although Methuen had been appointed in January, he did not arrive to take the oath of office until June. If Toland's reckless assertion of a role in affairs even before the fact had nettled, it was not sufficiently provocative for him to be cast off.[34]

Christianity Not Mysterious seemed more outrageous in a provincial capital than in London, that theological cockpit. Commonly, Irishmen took it as a Socinian production, subverting belief in the divinity of Christ. This impression prompted the archbishop of Dublin to inspire a pamphlet which called on the civil arm to "suppress his Insolence."[35] Still, Toland's prosecution and subsequent hurried flight might have been avoided had the new chancellor's political position been secure. On the eve of Methuen's appointment the ascendancy had been roused by influential men like Molyneux and William King, then bishop of Derry, to one of their periodic spasms of Anglophobia. Their complaints included the state of the woolen trade, the maintenance of British troops on the island, and Westminster's abrogation of the second article of the Treaty of Limerick. The last grievance is incredible, since it presents the spectacle of Protestant bishops leading a fight to defend the rights of papists. Its very incredibility suggests that it and the others may have been pretexts for expressing opposition to the Whig clique that had dominated the administration since 1695. This opposition could only have been stiffened shortly after Methuen's installation by his decision against King in a long-standing property dispute.[36] When, at the end of summer, the chancellor's enemies considered a means of striking at him, his visible and controversial dependent seemed a convenient stick.

In September, the Irish Commons, acting on the report of an investigating committee, condemned *Christianity Not Mysterious* as heretical, and ordered that it be burnt by the public hangman and its author arrested and prosecuted by the attorney general. In England heterodox and orthodox alike interpreted this prosecution as a heresy-hunt, and later students have accepted their judgment.[37] Those close to the fray were of another opinion. Occasionally the lynx-eyed Bishop King decried the growth of irreligion. In his account of this parliamentary session he took note of three actions — all penal measures against Roman Catholics — which seemed to imply that the civil authorities were belatedly concerning themselves with religion. He did not see fit to mention the condemnation of *Christianity Not Mysterious*. As he was to write to the archbishop of Canterbury, Toland's prosecutors' real "design was against some greater persons, that supported him."[38] This underlying reality was of scant consolation to Toland, who was intimidated by the experience, particularly since English divines acclaimed the Irish for their action. He must have renewed his insistence — more often breached than honored — that prudence should be observed in theological controversy on board a packet crossing the Irish Sea in September 1697.[39]

While Toland's return to England saved him from prison, it did not end his troubles. As a recognized heretic, he became a pawn in the political struggle between the ascendant Latitudinarians and the emerging High-Church party for control of the Church of England. The insurgents, appointing themselves the church's defenders against both external and internal enemies, found in Toland a notorious figure whom they could identify with the most threatening of these foes.

Thanks to their efforts, he would throughout the nineties labor under the accusation of "Socinianism." He was not without resources in his effort to escape it. He was able skillfully to exploit the term's welter of implications by asking what it meant to be a Socinian. He could also point to the calculatedly ambiguous disavowal of his work offered by Stephen Nye in one of the late Unitarian tracts.

But suppose the Bishop [Edward Stillingfleet] had disarmed the Gentleman; what is that to us? do we offer this Book, against the Trinity of the Realists; was it written, with intention to serve *us* . . . ? We desire him to answer to the *Reasons* in our Books, against the Trinity of the Tritheists; but to these, he saith not a Word, but only falls upon Mr. *Toland's* Book: in which, or for which, we are not in the least concerned; nor do I think the (Learned and Ingenious) Author will hold himself to be interested, to defend that *Christianity Not Mysterious,* which his Lordship presents us with.[40]

In denying that he shared any of the positive teachings identified with early seventeenth-century Unitarianism, Toland was being strictly accurate. He had never embraced Arianism, which held that Jesus Christ, the Son of God, was a pre-existent agent who was not fully God, though as the creator of all other creatures he deserved worship as a secondary divinity who was not simply human. Neither was he ever disposed toward Socinianism, which held that Christ was a man miraculously conceived by the Virgin Mary. While his repudiation of both positions was honest, he did not feel moved to add that many of the English Unitarians of the 1690s eschewed them. Since his evasive reticence extended to an unwillingness to discuss particular Christian tenets, he was able to luxuriate in aggrieved innocence.

But there are a numerous Company of other Books that open'ly avow'd their Design, opposing the Doctrin of the Trinity, with several other Articles of the *Church,* expressly and by Name, som of 'em rejecting the *Scriptures* themselves; yet not a Word against any of these, tho in all Men's Judgments they ought to have preceded mine, whether we consider their Subject or the Time of their Publication.[41]

Despite his best efforts, he was on his way toward being made a Socinian cat's-paw with which the High-Church majority of the lower house of the convocation of 1698 could strike at the Whiggish and Latitudinarian upper house.[42]

Toland recognized the riskiness of "that dangerous suspition of being a Socinian." The last British *auto-da-fé,* the burning in 1697 at Edinburgh of Thomas Aikenhead, an adolescent medical student, for im-

pugning the Trinity and the authority of Scripture, demonstrates that
these risks were more than notional. Discreet Englishmen such as
Locke did not ignore Aikenhead's fate.[43] Because of the furor over some
remarks in the *Life of Milton* (1698), Toland was being compared with
Aikenhead. He had drawn an indiscreet conclusion from his assertion
of the pseudonymity of the *Eikon Basilike* attributed to Charles I:

I cease to wonder any longer how so many suppositious pieces under the name of
Christ, his Apostles, and other great Persons, should be publish'd and approv'd in those
primitive times, when it was of so much importance to have 'em believ'd; when the
cheats were too many on all sides for them to reproach one another, which yet they
often did; when Commerce was not near so general, and the whole Earth entirely
overspread with the darkness of Superstition. I doubt rather the Spuriousness of several
more such Books is yet undiscover'd.

His journey to Holland in 1699 was an act of prudence. Marking him
as "a notorious Socinian" and "Incendiary," the ministry had decided to
have his activities on both sides of the Channel watched in order to
discover his "Encouragers."[44]

Lockian circumspection proved to be contagious and had by then
spread to Toland's sanctuary. His English foes recognized that his
notoriety made him an embarrassment to all who had sympathized
with or shared his opinions. These erstwhile supporters were sufficiently
plausible in their attempts to distance themselves from him that
historians have accepted their revisions. Thus, the author of the most
thorough biography of Locke acquiesced in the assertions of both Le
Clerc and Limborch: that the one had met Toland only twice and had
snubbed him on the latter occasion, and that the other had no recollection of Toland.[45] In fact, Toland was the "homo Hibernus" whom Le
Clerc named as the English translator of his irenically undogmatic
Treatise of the Causes of Incredulity, which Locke's publishers had brought
out in 1697. If Locke and the Dutch Arminians had seen Toland as a
follower, they saw the prosecuted author of *Christianity Not Mysterious* as
a threat to their own respectability. Their friends within the Establishment agreed with them. When Gilbert Burnet was attacked for wobbli-
ness on the Athanasian definition of the Trinity, he wished to ensure
that Le Clerc, to whom he was both personally and intellectually indebted, was not maintaining indiscreet connections that could embar-
rass him. He was "very glad," he told Le Clerc, that "[you] put it in my
power to clear you of all correspondence with Mr. Toland." The trail of

Toland's connection with Limborch was more thoroughly cleared, but Limborch and Locke felt compelled to execute a *pas de deux* of disavowal as late as the summer of 1699. Toland escaped censure by convocation in 1698, as he would again in 1701, because of the bishops' unwillingness to tamper with prerogative powers, but his escape did not lead to a reconciliation with the man he considered "the greatest Philosopher after Cicero in the World."[46]

The Irish debacle separated Toland from his former ministerial Whig protectors as well as from Locke. If they had been his only available "Encouragers," he might have been forced to consider both the sources and the implications of his habitual indiscretion. The third earl of Shaftesbury and a number of other patrons provided a cushion against this necessity. Such inadvertent traces of his relations with Shaftesbury as he left were later marred, though not obliterated. In 1699, Toland published an edition of the young peer's *Inquiry concerning Virtue in Two Discourses,* a draft of the fourth treatise of the *Characteristics.* In a pious memoir the fourth earl, following his father's 1709 account, treated this publication as an act of piracy which had snapped their amicable relations. Actually, they were to continue to enjoy a close, if covert, friendship at least until the spring of 1705.[47] One of its consequences may have been Toland's introduction to Shaftesbury's family friend, Robert Harley, the leader of the Country forces in the House of Commons. Except for a lull between 1702 and 1705, Toland's complex dealings with this enigmatic politician were to be the obbligato of his career up to 1714. By the turn of the century Toland had gained a reputation as a "Commonwealthman," largely on the strength of his lives and editions of Harrington, Milton, Sidney, Denzil Holles, and Edmund Ludlow. Yet, that he produced his work on Harrington (1700) with Harley's aid implies that this label is not self-defining.[48]

Toland's other known encouragers during these years were diverse. Already a patron, John Holles, duke of Newcastle, a grandee of vaguely Court Whig disposition, sponsored Toland's publication of the *Memoirs* of his uncle, Denzil, who had been influential in both Commonwealth and Restoration. Newcastle continued his support for some years. Equally important was the sustained patronage of Sir Robert Clayton, a Whig director of the Bank of England, public creditor, and sometime lord mayor of London, whose nephew Toland had probably come to know at Oxford. The death of this heir in 1698 may have prompted

Toland to insinuate himself as a successor in the aging man's affections and fortune. Clayton's unsuccessful effort to persuade the City's aldermen to pay Toland for his edition of Harrington's works either resulted from or contributed to his dedication of the volume to the municipal authorities and his endorsement of the bank as the embodiment of the Harringtonian commonwealth. Toland consorted not only with financial supporters, but also with "Friends about Town," including William Stephens, a controversial Whiggish rector with whom he lodged briefly, Anthony Collins, an intellectually ambitious squire and friend of Locke, and Matthew Tindal.[49]

Whatever their differences of station and opinion, these men were all enmeshed in the "skein of tangled principles" which constituted Whig political thought in the 1690s. That the portion of the skein enmeshing Toland and his "Country" and "Commonwealth" associates was not peculiarly immune from tangles is suggested by Toland's own uncertain posture toward the Commonwealth ideal. If near the beginning of the decade he was publicly "commending Commonwealths," by its end he alternatively rhapsodized on their virtues and repudiated the very name "Commonwealthman."[50] His pirouettes — responses to the shifting foundations of his understanding of a commonwealth — also evince the tremors which caused their shift. The period opened with the hereditary Whig Harley joining obdurate Tories in invoking the old distinction between "Court" and "Country" in order to oppose the ministry in the name of "good management." Its progress saw him siding now with the ministry and now against it. It closed with him serving as the parliamentary "general" of a "motley band of Commonwealthmen and Whigs." A congeries of four issues dominated William's reign: the legitimacy of the Revolution Settlement; the connection between church and state; the extent of prerogative and royal influence; and the conduct and financing of foreign relations. When an aspect of either of the former two seemed pressing, Commonwealthmen, both self-styled and accused, tended to make themselves allies of Whigs, in and out of the ministry. When an aspect of either of the latter two impinged, they forged alliances with Country opponents of the ministerial Court party, which usually contained more than a sprinkling of Whigs.[51]

Toland's *Art of Governing by Partys* (1701) exemplifies this oscillation. After a fulsome dedication to the king, savior of Protestantism and liberty, he indicted both the arbitrariness of William's immediate predecessors and the corruption of his Junto ministers in trying to make him equally arbitrary. Toland's attempt earlier in the tract to construct a framework for his analysis by equating "Loyalist," "Court," and "Tory" and contrasting this equation with that of "Patriot," "Country," and "Whig" heightened confusion.[52] Like most political pamphleteers during these years, Toland was not a disembodied ideologue. Rather, he was a harried writer who tried as best he could to articulate general principles by examining inherited habits of thought and expression in the light of current circumstances and public concerns. He then sought to apply his formulations to these same circumstances and concerns by working out often quite personal arrangements with patrons and associates agreeable to his application, if not to his articulation. In the late 1690s, convinced that pressing political questions derived from the growth of prerogative and the unsatisfactory conduct of military and diplomatic affairs, rather than from threats to the constitution or clerical menaces, he and such friends as Molesworth and Shaftesbury usually pursued arrangements with politicians loyal to Country ideals.[53]

Notwithstanding these entanglements, some contemporaries thought that they had teased from the skein a strand binding Toland to a group of confederates. He and the other "republicans" who gathered at the Grecian coffeehouse in Devereux Court were behind a coordinated campaign against William III's proposal to maintain a standing army after the signing of the Treaty of Ryswick in September 1697. A few insisted that Toland and his cronies aimed at "promoting an English Commonwealth," if need be by revolution. At least one, that Grub Street perennial "Ned" Ward, claimed to have uncovered the existence of, and Toland's participation in, a related group, the "Calves-Head Club," radical litterateurs who frequented the Black Boy tavern in Newgate Street and marked the anniversary of the execution of Charles I with riotous festivities.[54] The attraction for Toland of London's coffeehouse and tavern society was inexhaustible. His role on this skirt, where "politicians, publicists, and their followings maneuvering in a world of common perceptions and symbols and seeking to interpret it for their competitive advantage" occasionally acted out their subplots, remains indeterminable.[55] So does the influence of these maneuverings on him.

For his part, Toland described how he circulated, discussed, and then revised drafts of his works before he published them, and the

Grecian provided a congenial environment for such virtually cooperative labors. It is self-evident that the opposition in the "paper war" over the ministerial plan for a standing army was not composed of monadic propagandists, but the extent of Toland's activity is unclear.[56] He may have collaborated with John Trenchard and Walter Moyle, also Grecian habitués, in composing *An Argument, Shewing That a Standing Army Is Inconsistent with a Free Government* (1697) and *A Short History of Standing Armies* (1698), or he may have written only the *Militia Reform'd* (1698). In any case, all the opposition pamphlets were products of a closely knit group variously inspired by Harrington's principles. Circumstantial evidence indicates that they coordinated their efforts with those of leading parliamentary opponents such as Harley.[57] Other questions suggest themselves. Is it, for example, possible to differentiate a coherent group of patrician "Roman Whigs," including Shaftesbury, Molesworth, Trenchard, and Moyle, meeting at the Grecian, who, though dismayed at abuses, accepted the 1689 settlement, from an often intermingling but nevertheless coherent group of "Calves-Head Whigs," including Toland, Stephens, and Tindal, who rejected it? Or was the Calves-Head Club merely a fantasy of the "unbalanced" Ward?[58] Whatever the answers, collaborating Commonwealthmen are unlikely to have exhibited greater unity and consistency than either their Country associates or ordinary Whigs and Tories of any known complexion.

Since Augustans could not separate theology from politics, it is no surprise that several of Toland's critics saw him engaged in secret societies whose subversive theological intent paralleled, or complemented, the political efforts centered on either Devereux Court or Newgate Street. As early as Toland's disastrous Irish expedition in 1697, one of them had descried his participation in a "secret Club, who set themselves with a great deal of Industry to destroy all Reveal'd Religion." A couple of years later, another was convinced that one of Toland's freethinking works was "very much magnify'd" by his friends, presumably including Stephens, Tindal, and Collins.[59] These magnifiers were seemingly less disinterested than Pierre Bayle had been in spreading the polemical argument of the *Life of Milton* or even Shaftesbury in encouraging Dutch acquaintances to diffuse the edition of Harrington.[60]

Toland was accused of "setting up for a Rosicrucian" while at Edinburgh, assiduous in studying and discussing the philosophy of Gior-

dano Bruno for almost half his lifetime, an eventual exponent of the
necessity of an esoteric theology, the recipient of the liturgy of at least
one secret society, and the concocter and publisher of that of another.
He probably cannot have avoided membership in some of the secretive
klatsches, clubs, and societies that enjoyed obscure, usually terminal
existences around 1700, as the European corporate structure began to
lessen its resistance to private activity outside the family. It is conceivable that Shaftesbury, Clayton, Methuen, Tindal, Collins, and
others of Toland's political and theological cronies were also involved in
such groups. Until this part of the subterranean world of the eighteenth
century has been better explored, its geography, let alone its ethology,
will remain even more difficult to describe than are those of its putative
neighbors, the Grecian and Calves-Head caves.[61]

The fact remains that neither individual patronage nor like-minded
society had made Toland prosperous. He consistently defaulted on his
agreement with the printer John Darby to produce translations at
regular intervals, and the effort to meet the payments on the bond he
had pledged against such defaults, or on its interest, proved burden-
some. Public employment, the ordinary means of escaping literary
penury, had long been his ambition. Accordingly, when his defense of
the Act of Settlement in *Anglia Libera* (1701) allowed Harley to secure
an invitation for him to accompany the "atheistical" Lord Macclesfield
on an embassy to present the act to the Electress Sophia of Hanover, he
unhesitatingly accepted.[62] Notwithstanding their common heterodoxy,
Toland and Macclesfield did not take to each other. From Toland's
relentless cultivation of the Hanoverian court, it might be imagined
that the ambassador had moments of doubt about who was the chief of
mission. Eventually the two men made up, and Toland's fawning
courtship of the presumptive heiress was successful enough that he
brought back to England "several gold medalls belonging to [the elec-
toral] family, and other curiosities to a considerable value." More importantly, his chief presented him to King William "and took off those
[hostile] impressions which might have been made upon him." His
denial the following year that he was a pensioner of the Dutch government suggests that tangible benefits resulted from this encounter.[63]
Clonmany must have seemed very distant and the future almost
secure.

Facing a responsible place in society in the last year of William's
reign, the youthful rebel was trying to transform himself into a not dis-

interested prop of the order of things in church and state, "no National Religion being less interested, or more rational; no other Common-wealth being now so free, or having so good a Foundation and Disposi-tion to attain all the perfections of Government." The English situation of frequent and easy social advancement contrasted with that under an "Arbitrary Government," where "most of the Inhabitants are for ever excluded from all Hopes of changing the Condition of their Birth by any certain or regular Steps." The word *moderate* was gaining a favored place in his vocabulary.[64]

Chronic insecurity could nurture imprudent aspirations. Bright prospects and the brisk sale of a recent publication enabled Toland not only to take Macclesfield's death in stride, but also to try unsuccessfully to have himself adopted for Clayton's pocket borough in the forthcom-ing general election. As a neophyte moderate, Toland had a past con-siderably more tangible than his future. In *Vindicius Liberius* (1702) he sought to redress this imbalance by laying to rest accusations of subver-sion in theology, accusations which had been renewed in convocation the year before. *Christianity Not Mysterious* had, he insisted, been a callow production. In March 1702, he assured the prolocutor of the last convocation that he had "firmly resolved never hereafter to intermeddle in any Religious Controversies." Unwilling to retract his early theological positions, he had to blame his adversaries, every one ig-norant, ill-disposed, or mercenary, for the controversy which sur-rounded them.[65]

The prospect of Princess Anne, a *dévote,* ascending the throne must have strengthened Toland's self-denying resolution about further theological work. His preoccupation with political affairs in these years was, at least in part, a token of maturity. In 1704, he described how logic could move a mind from Arminianism, through Socinianism, to deism, a form of materialism. He had long before made such a journey and therefore no longer spoke about Christianity from the inside, as one who regarded its speculative problems as more than exercises in in-significant speech. At the same time he did speak as one who accepted membership in the Church of England as an element of citizenship.[66] His position demanded that he wait out the reign of an ailing queen by serving powerful politicians whose purposes and principles would not unduly chafe him, rather than further endanger himself by writing about objectively unimportant matters. Implicit in his reasoning was the distinction between the simple truth accessible to a few enlightened men like himself and the ambiguous religion which disciplined a disorderly majority. Although it would be years before sustained reverses led him to disclose his theory that there had to be separate "esoteric" and "exoteric" ways of comprehension, since 1695 he had tried to act according to this premise. As long as he had prospects, Toland struggled to play for advantages more secure than attention.

No more than anyone else could Toland have foreseen the king's fatal horseback ride in late February 1702, but he knew the immediate risks which Anne's accession held for him. It was presumably as a kind of insurance policy that he had published in the last weeks of William's life the *Reasons for Addressing His Majesty,* in which he urged the Whig proposal that the aged dowager electress and her young grandson, whose preceptorship he sought, be invited to England and given their own civil list. With these chosen protectors close at hand, could he be fatally harmed? Since he had reckoned without Anne's feeling that she was to be more than a caretaker, this maladroit intervention led to his first brush with authority in the new reign. On 16 May 1702 the House of Lords condemned his pamphlet for its "Assertions and Insinuations, scandalous and dangerous, tending to alienate the Affections of the Subjects of this Kingdom from Her Majesty."[67]

This condemnation made a journey to Hanover expedient, and his preparations for it led him into a revealing encounter. On the strength of professions of regret for his earlier lapses and resolutions of attachment to the church and its teachings, including the Trinity, he secured an interview with John Sharp, the archbishop of York and Anne's principal ecclesiastical advisor. Toland proved equal to the occasion. He had already presented one of the archbishop's sermons to the electress, he said, and would buy the recent coronation sermon to deliver to her during this journey. Flattered, Sharp was moved to offer a copy. Toland disappeared before the prelate could consider the implications of the gift.[68] If he could clear himself with so ill-disposed and powerful a stranger, he must have had little doubt about his ability to conquer lesser beings.

What kind of reception awaited Toland at the Brunswick court? After his first visit the old electress judged him lacking in common sense but, despite his enemies' accusations, possessed of good intentions. His intentions did not make him less embarrassing to the Hanoverian cause in England, since his partisanship tended to alienate support for the succession and to irritate Anne. Reflecting these per-

ceptions, Leibniz, who devoted considerable time to examining
Toland's metaphysical problems, described him as an "homme d'esprit
et de scavoir." The accuracy of his reflections lends authority to the
philosopher's description of the calculating wariness with which the
electoral family received their self-invited guest. Warnings from persuasive voices that Toland, if not mad, was bad and dangerous to
know, had led them to ignore his fantasy of tutoring the future George
II. The decision of the elector's ministers to prevent the circulation of a
German translation of the *Anglia Libera* in his dominions can only have
added insult to injury.[69] Despite this unpleasantness, the aged
bluestocking, who had inherited from her mother a taste for
heterodoxy, received Toland with unfeigned pleasure.

Leibniz thought that Toland was the victim of the sort of mudsling-
ing which taints as atheists all who fail to conform to common prejudices.[70] The stimulus for Leibniz's protracted, if not always sympathetic, attention to Toland's work and person is unclear. The
presence of Rosicrucians at the Hanoverian court a decade earlier and
the possibility that Leibniz, too, belonged to such a group might suggest that Toland's ever elusive implication in the secret societies,
perhaps in an international network, is an element in this story. While
this suggestion may be appealing, until it is confirmed an older, more
pedestrian explanation must prevail.[71] Sophia was a forerunner of a
familiar type of eighteenth-century ruler, the Latitudinarian-Erastian,
whose tolerance extended so far as to divorce opinion from conduct and
make public indiscretion the only justification for government in-
terference with adventurous writers. In dealing with Toland, as in so
much else, Leibniz probably followed the line taken by his employer.
In any case, his mounting scepticism did not prevent him from corresponding with Toland until near the end of Sophia's life.[72] The
Hanoverian authorities were innocent of her attachment. Warned by
their resident in London not to ignore the damage to the electress
dowager caused by the hostility of the English episcopacy and ministry
toward Toland, they took measures to prevent further public indiscretion. In Amsterdam, Toland received through Spanheim, his old
teacher, an invitation from Sophia's son-in-law, the king of Prussia, to
visit Berlin. Conveniently, she would be powerless to ban him from a
court at which she herself was a guest. This stratagem was worthy of its
designer, the codiscoverer of calculus.[73] Once in the suburbs of Berlin
Toland disregarded the plan to have him lodge privately and instead

stayed in an inn frequented by courtiers. He did perform the part of the scenario that had him overtake the electress by surprise as she walked through the garden at Lützenburg and present her with the archbishop's sermon and letters from Spanheim and Clayton.[74] Playing at international intrigue was much more fun — and heady — than parson-baiting.

Toland remained in Germany until November 1702, paying court first to the electress and then to the Prussian queen, taking on local theologians, and intruding himself on any dignitaries who would receive him. His stay there unsettled Britons as diverse as the chaplain to Queen Anne's uncle and her own plenipotentiary in Berlin. Another concerted campaign seems to have been mounted against him, since it was at this time that Spanheim repudiated him after hearing the earl of Nottingham condemn him. Toland's later approximation of a persecution mania had warrant in his experience. So remorseless were his opponents that the electress professed to understand why he had defended cannibals in a debate. Since all of Christendom was against him, a time might come when he would have to rely on such savages for protection.[75]

The debates Toland had with sundry divines in Berlin were far-ranging and acrimonious. The most important began with the queen presenting him to her chaplain, Isaac Beausobre, as one "who questioned the basis of our faith," the Bible, and Toland seeking to vindicate his Christianity on his own terms. His opening thrust seems to have been to cast doubt on the acceptability of the canon of the New Testament, but by stages his position became so alarming that Beausobre questioned whether they had the same idea of God. Soon, Leibniz felt compelled to warn him against his appetite for paradoxes and for contradicting received opinion, lest he create an alternative dogmatism. When private warnings proved fruitless, a public admonition from the grand chamberlain followed. The electress eventually heeded Leibniz's advice to sever her connections with Toland. By early November, marking him as a continuing source of political problems in England, she had resolved not to see him again. Toland complied with her wishes and passed through Hanover on his way home without talking to anyone. Despite his loyalty to the Hanoverian cause, the animosities he had incurred in England and the lack of self-restraint which fed on his perpetual insecurity ended his open collaboration with the House of Brunswick. The following year, the electress ordered that autographed copies of his diatribes against the Tories be ignored.[76] Toland's second venture in international politics had done him more harm than good.

As Toland prepared to return to Britain in 1702, he described himself as "a stranger abroad and friendless at home," who "must needs have been in a very uncertain condition," except (inevitably) for "the high-born persons, under whose protection I then liv'd." Examining Des Maizeaux's collection years later, Canon William Stratford was appalled when he moved from this lament to the epistolary remains of Toland's connection with Robert Harley, who became the first earl of Oxford. As he wrote to the second earl: "I suppose your Lordship has seen the two volumes of Toland's posthumous Tracts. In the second volume I meet with somewhat to which I was not wholly a stranger, though I did not think it had gone quite so far. . . . I think it I own dangerous as well as improper for anyone to deal with such cattle, upon any terms or any occasions."[77] Had Toland not imbibed some of Harley's circumspection, the details of the most persistent and important traceable instance of patronage in his career could not have been kept from Harley's inquisitive chaplain.

How had John Toland, whose chronic intemperance had cost him all his "high born" supporters except Newcastle and Shaftesbury, obtained a position which uniquely offered a reasonable promise of security? In *Anglia Libera* he had lavishly praised Harley, but despite Harley's retention of the speakership in December 1701 and—perhaps because of—his partnership with Godolphin and Marlborough, Toland was not in contact with him after William's death. Interpreting the cabinet rearrangements following Anne's accession as Tory in design, Toland had used his friendship with Shaftesbury in an attempt to secure the patronage of Lord Halifax, the fledgling Maecenas of the Junto opposition.[78] Halifax did not give Toland the respectability which he would later bestow on Joseph Addison. Perhaps he shared the view of other Whigs that the author of *The Art of Governing by Partys,* an attack on all such groups, was both too partisan and too unstable to be useful. Certainly, Toland's sustained criticism while abroad of Marlborough's prodigious turpitudes had done little to serve the war policy to which Halifax and his allies were committed.[79]

Although rebuffed, Toland did not want for work. He was occupied in translating a French edition of Aesop, organizing the *Letters to Serena* from some of the philosophical papers he had read in Berlin, preparing a German travelogue, collecting his thoughts about the relation of the church to the state, and devising an attack on the notion of the originality of Hebrew religious practices. Yet he craved both the excitement of direct involvement in politics and official support. Casting about for expedients, he proposed complaisantly that he could best serve the government by serving the public, by starting one of the newfangled weekly newspapers of opinion. The patrons necessary for launching such an enterprise failed to appear. By late 1704, Toland admitted both that parties in religion and politics, however evil in theory, were inevitable and that prudence sometimes demanded alliance with the dominant force. If terms could be arranged, he no more than Robert Walpole scrupled at squinting in order to glimpse the butterfly of a nonpartisan administration emerge from its Tory chrysalis. Evasion about his overtures to Halifax was the least demanding accommodation he would have to make.[80]

Sidney Godolphin was instrumental in beginning these necessary arrangements. During the late summer of 1704 through the intercession of a mutual friend, William Penn, the lord treasurer secretly employed Toland to reply to James Drake's High-Church polemic, *The Memorial of the Church of England*. Drake's pamphlet was a tardy contribution to the dispute over one of the successive Occasional Conformity Bills, which Godolphin and Marlborough sniffed at as divisive even as they supported it. Toland's task was to defend them against Drake's charge of making "Trimming excuses." Critics of Toland's *Memorial of the State of England* were not slow to discern a secondary theme running through it: puffery of Robert Harley. Speakers of the House of Commons ranked only slightly below heiresses-presumptive in Toland's list of proper recipients of flattery.[81] Before long he made overtures to the object of this eulogy.

Toland had a reasonable chance of reconciling himself to that enigmatic politician. Because Harley retained his fundamental tenets, there was no real ideological incompatibility between the two men. Indeed, a few years later an observer thought he detected the former speaker's editorial work in that "extreme" restatement of the "Whig position," the *State-Memorial*. Among other clues its definition of a commonwealth (the mutual balance of the crown, the Lords, and the Commons) was distinctly Harleian. Although Harley had championed essentially Whiggish measures like the Place and Triennial bills, by 1705 his involvement with unambiguous Tories made him suspect to rigorists such as Shaftesbury, who seems to have taken umbrage at Toland's courtship of him. Toland's interest in Harley was not unreciprocated. Since the summer of 1704 Harley had been receiving reports on his movements.[82]

Arranging terms required bargaining. During the first half of 1705 Toland tried to secure an advantageous position by both obvious and devious means. He made sure that Harley knew that he was still sufficiently in favor with the electress dowager to be lodging with the Hanoverian resident in London; he also tried to demonstrate his influence with the Nonconformists, whose support Harley desired. Shortly after the appearance of the *State-Memorial*, Toland approached Edmund Calamy, a distinguised dissenting minister. He intimated "that he was able to drop several things in favour of Dissenters, to vindicate them from the narrowness they were charged with, which he said would come with more decency from such a one as he, than from among themselves." Calamy could see no advantage in having Toland associated with his cause. Equally unsuccessful was Toland's attempt to secure from other leading Nonconformists statements of support for religious toleration to refute the High-Church charge that dissent was less tolerant than weak. Checked, and having received no answer to his offer to act as a kind of agent in Germany, Toland again secured the aid of William Penn, who wrote to Harley at the end of August: "If you will not help him to help you what can he hope for? Do something I beg, after kind words and fair looks. He has hung too long upon expectations, and that is the plague of courts. Pray look kindly upon it to Lord Treasurer to-morrow. . . ."[83]

Twice in less than a year the Quaker leader had intervened to the "infidel's" advantage, and yet the sole certainty about relations between the two is that they were then amicable. From Thomas Clarkson onward, all of Penn's biographers have been silent about their association. Toland's connection with Penn was as important privately as it was publicly, but it presents an insoluble problem of weighing personality and ideas. The crucial questions—How had they met? Why did Penn interest himself in Toland? How did acquaintance deepen into friendship? Did either influence the other's thought?—remain unanswered and perhaps unanswerable. Some of Toland's critics saw him as sharing Socinianism with the Quakers, just as some of Penn's critics accused him of deism. Penn was more prone to heterodoxy on matters like the Trinity than most of his coreligionists. Moreover,

Toland's arguments occasionally appealed to Quakers well-disposed toward attempts at rationalizing Scripture. Beyond these hints only a few solid places are visible in a morass of puzzlement. Between 1701 and 1704, Toland's contempt for the sect and its leader had changed to admiration. He had come to depend emotionally on his older friend. This friendship proved, almost uniquely, to be powerful enough to thwart Toland's demonic inconstancy, for it endured until Penn's death.[84]

When Penn intervened in August, Toland was in dire straits. He had lost any capacity to bargain over terms of employment. With his creditors at his heels, he pleaded with Harley: "When you please to admit me *nearer,* I doubt not but to give full satisfaction as to all points, and if I have any learning or ability, I desire to be entirely directed by your orders in all I may do for the future: wherein it shall be my continual endeavour to recommend myself to your care by my diligence and fidelity." After conceding that his reputation precluded public employment, he went on to make a number of unprecedented confessions and commitments. He diagnosed his "chief misfortune" as having been "left at large to my own caprice and humours, without any certain patrons or settled business, and having neither estate nor relations to support me." It lay within Harley's power "to make me a new man without changing my old principles." In order to ease Harley's task, he had "by degrees broke off a great part of my tattling and mean acquaintances, frequenting no coffee-houses." Harley recognized an abashed spirit and must have sensed that he had acquired a tool to use as he saw fit. He began distributing copies of the *State-Memorial,* received letters of congratulation on his sensible patronage, and set Toland to work on another defense of the administration, which was never printed. During the next two years of probation Toland was Harley's dependent.[85]

The renewed striving after respectability that Toland's situation demanded faced the same formidable obstacle which had thwarted similar efforts. The perspicacious and perverse Francis Hare realized more clearly than Toland was then able to admit the implications of being labeled a heretic. To most Englishmen, it was

a Term, which there is a strange *Magick* in; though it has *no determinate Meaning* in the Mouth of the People, nor any *ill Meaning* in it self. 'Tis suppos'd to include in it every thing that is bad; it makes every thing appear odious and deform'd; it dissolves all Friendships, extinguishes all former kind Sentiments, however just and well deserved: and from the time a Man is deem'd a *Heretick,* 'tis Charity to act against all Rules of

Charity; and the more they violate the Laws of God in dealing with him, 'tis, in their Opinion, doing God the greater Service.

Anne's piety made a reputation for infidelity even more disadvantageous, and Toland was not alone in his efforts to assert his churchmanship. Charles Gildon, the "deist" Charles Blount's editor, had published what he hoped would be construed as a retraction of his heterodoxy under the imprimatur of that sulfurous nonjuror, Charles Leslie. As early as March 1702, Toland had asserted that, having "adhered to no peculiar society before," he now considered himself a member of the Church of England, "the best National Constitution on Earth, and admirably suited to our Civil Government." He had at that time promised the former prolocutor of convocation to publish the reasons for his conversion.[86]

In the apparent fulfillment of this promise, the anonymous *Principle of the Protestant Reformation Explain'd* (1704), Toland argued that the fallibility of every body meant that no subject could justify separating himself from the national church because he rejected one or another of its doctrines. In 1707, he flaunted his commitment to this argument by taking the sacrament, which he understood to be a "public Sign" of allegiance to the person and teachings of "the founder of our Religion," rather than "the means of conveying Grace." Later that year, he asked an acquaintance to present an undertaking of his good conduct to the archbishop of Canterbury. Perhaps hoping to duplicate the spell he had cast on the archbishop of York, he wrote to Tenison at least twice, assuring him of his sincerity and soliciting an interview, "to receive your paternal advice and directions, which next to the sacred precepts of the Gospel, I shall esteem the most obligatory rules whereby to frame the future conduct of my life."[87]

Although this performance was denied him, he was able to move sensible men professionally inclined to doubt his change of heart. One of them, a fellow of Queen's College, Oxford, tried to reassure Thomas Hearne: "I firmly believe him to be a man of Religion and of ye Faith of ye Church of England." This divine commented favorably on a draft of Toland's *Adeisidaemon,* which he took to be a defense of Livy's historical acumen rather than an attack on all religious prodigies, and went so far as to suggest that Hearne publish it. Toland was successful enough in refurbishing his reputation to avoid being linked in print with then modish infidels such as his friends Anthony Collins and Matthew Tindal. In time, something like respectability might have enveloped him, but he was still his own worst enemy. Once he returned to the Continent, where he mistakenly thought himself out of Harley's range, indiscipline resumed control. He ended what proved to be an entr'acte in his career by distributing copies of that callow book, *Christianity Not Mysterious*. [88]

A period of mounting irritation had preceded this lapse. After two years of docilely serving the ruling triumvirate of Marlborough, Godolphin, and Harley, and without regular income, Toland owned himself "disappointed." He had worked for them and was deserving "on many accounts not fit to be named," only to find other, less meritorious men better rewarded. Although his lack of family connections was an irreparable defect, he had succeeded in exuding enough of the odor of piety to put both church and chapel off his trail. Harley's failure to respond appropriately led him to fear that "it is an ordinary maxim with certain ministers to consider men no further than as they may be useful or hurtful to their own designs." But he followed this snap with a pledge "to run your good or bad fortune, for the future, and to have no other interest but yours."[89]

What did it mean "to have no other interest" but Harley's? As his contemporaries knew, the secretary was a dark man, who "generally either spoke so low in their ear or so misteriouslee that few knew what to make of his replys, and it would appear he took a secret pleasure in making people hing on and disappointing them. . . ." One political manifestation of Harley's inward-turning personality was that intense distaste for party which had led Toland to see him as a kindred mind and which he had made a fact of policy by 1707. Deviousness shaped his daily actions. Employing the author of *Christianity Not Mysterious* did not deter him from suggesting to Archbishop Tenison that, by using erstwhile Socinians like Stephen Nye, his grace strengthened the impression that he himself was susceptible to heretical influences. In hiring men to write for him, Harley chose a variety of authors, unknown to each other, to appeal to different audiences. Rarely during their overlapping periods of service to him did John Toland and Daniel Defoe address the same subjects.[90]

Though immensely cultivated, Harley saw his arrangements with pamphleteers as business transactions rather than acts of patronage. His treatment of Defoe exemplifies the pattern of his purchases: first he worked to foster dependency, and then apportioned assignments and payments so as to stave off disaster at the last minute and simultaneously to thwart security and independence. From the beginning Toland misconstrued his own position. Seldom wanting, his self-importance led him to obscure further the imprecise distinctions between adventurer and projector, and projector and man of letters. He fancied himself becoming a confidential advisor to the great man, one who could and did advise on matters high and low. In practice his tasks were less portentous. He hoped, for example, to capitalize on a propagandist translation of a sixteenth-century harangue against the French and receive a sinecure worth £400 a year. The pamphlet appeared, but the position did not. His effort to exploit the bibliomania which he shared with the secretary also proved illusory. While Harley was willing to trust Toland in procuring additions to his vast collection, he exercised a tough hand in dealing with his servant's recurrent flights from sound scholarship. His toughness did not keep him from subsidizing the Continental excursions that delighted and flattered Toland.[91]

Between 1707 and 1710 Toland spent more time abroad than at home. Even if the Harleian collection had been of Alexandrian proportions, it is improbable that these years were monopolized by dealers and librarians. The existence of Harley's uniquely efficient domestic and foreign intelligence system provides an entry into an obscure period. By the beginning of 1708 Lord Raby in Berlin was certain that Toland was visiting foreign courts "to inspect" and give Harley "the characters of the Queen's ministers abroad." Some months before, he had inquired of Harley whether "you admit him [Toland] into your conversation as he pretended to me," only to discover that Toland had seen this communication and informed a high Prussian official that he had reported on Raby's performance. Toland scrupulously maintained contacts in Europe, and fragments in Harley's papers suggest that, at least when he was in power, he regularly received information from Toland.[92]

Although Toland later recognized reality and confessed that he "was not design'd" to be a secret agent, he remained a willing, increasingly exposed player in Harley's multiple-ring cat-and-mouse game.[93] Harley had been disillusioned by Marlborough and Godolphin's rejection of a *pourparler* with the French at the end of 1706 and shared the queen's irritation at the threat which their growing dependence on the Junto posed to the still-setting centrist fusion of Whigs and Tories. In late 1707, he began to solicit fusionists from both parties for a new nonparty ministry. While Anne approved of Harley's project, her impatience with Godolphin excluded him. He and Marlborough proved, however, to be inseparable, and both resigned in early February. Harley, failing to recruit any Whigs except the duke of Newcastle — at once Denzil Holles' nephew, Toland's persistent patron, and his own son's prospective father-in-law — to a government to be headed by him alone, gave up a week later. Marlborough and Godolphin then returned to lead an effectively Whig grouping, which gained an absolute majority in the House of Commons in the general election in May.

For some time after the events of February, Toland remained loyal to his hard-won patron. At the German courts during the early months of 1708, he "spared nobody" but Harley. Arriving in the Netherlands at the beginning of summer, he was still busily at work in Harley's interest to the discomfort of Marlborough and Godolphin, who took it on himself to inform the queen about the sort of men her favorite employed. By the end of the year Toland was writing an anti-Marlborough pamphlet, and Godolphin proposed to have it seized. Whether or not Toland ever completed it, he carefully expunged favorable references to Marlborough from the second edition of the *Phillipick Oration* (1709). Perhaps in retribution, or in admonition, he received a severe beating from "some of Marlborough's ruffians."[94]

In this instance, Toland did not deserve his reputation for "charlatanism" and "untrustworthiness." If his sufferings on Harley's behalf riveted him to the sometime Country leader's cause, they did not change him into a less prickly client. A compulsion to prove his own importance led him to boast before casual acquaintances of his closeness to Harley, though even a whisper of such a connection never proved anything but embarrassing. Yet he tried, sometimes successfully, to be useful. However the secretary may have evaluated Toland's offer to report on acquaintances, associates, and friends in the literary demimonde, he cannot have been heedless of Toland's services during the delicate and protracted negotiations antecedent to his son's marriage to Newcastle's heiress. As with Toland's association with Penn, crucial questions of motive, nature, and influence remain unanswered and perhaps unanswerable. Necessity and convenience provide one approach to them. The ubiquitous Newcastle offers another. A third approach lies in the possibility that, believing that Harley alone had a reasonable chance of forging an enduring bipartisan ministry able to control the nation's natural Tory majority, Toland invested unique confidence in him.[95] It is, in any case, suggestive that that precociously mature cynic Robert Walpole moved at Harley's siren call not only in 1707, but again after the Tory triumph in October 1710.

When Toland set off for the Continent in the early summer of 1707 with his friend Anthony Collins, he was obliged to find a way of supplementing Harley's increasingly irregular payments. Although he moved from the Netherlands to Düsseldorf, on to Hanover and Berlin, then to Vienna and Prague, and finally back to Berlin, he made Amsterdam his base of operations. In Düsseldorf he risked his reputation as a defender of Protestantism and liberty against the international popish conspiracy by supporting the elector Palatine, whom he had once denounced for persecuting his Protestant subjects. Leibniz reported that the elector wanted something written in English to justify his policy to his allies, and his London minister proposed Toland as an available pen.[96] The result of this commission, *The Declaration Lately Published by the Elector Palatine* (1707), brought an invitation to the electoral court, where "an incident" Des Maizeaux found "too ludicrous to be mentioned . . . , oblig'd him to leave that place sooner than he expected." Despite his hasty departure, he extracted valuable presents from the princeling, together with a letter to the Electress Sophia, which gave him an excuse to visit her. While the Hanoverian ministers indignantly demanded an explanation from the elector, the old woman herself was so pleased at his reappearance that she received him alone for several hours a day.[97]

The immediate profitability of this enterprise must be weighed against the lasting damage it did to Toland's reputation. Throughout his past reversals, evasions, and outrages, he could have credibly maintained that he had been loyal to the Protestant idea of religious liberty with its dual emphasis on the inviolability of conscience and the duty of obedience to the government. Now, in less that fifty pages, he had provided men who required little evidence with proof that he was a simple mercenary.[98]

During this sojourn exigency again leavened Toland's braggadocio. Intimating that he could serve as an honors broker, he accepted a subsidy from a "famous French Banker" who aspired to become an imperial count. Thus fortified, he reached Vienna.[99] In the Netherlands, he had become an acquaintance of Eugene of Savoy, probably through his adjutant, Baron von Höhendorff. Once in the Habsburg capital, he moved in the prince's freethinking circle and found employment as his agent in some book purchases. For the only time in Toland's life, openly expressed heterodoxy proved to be compatible with favor from the powerful. While he could not exploit this access to the advantage of his client, he maintained amicable relations with both noblemen.[100] The nature of the "impenetrable negotiation" he undertook there at Eugene's behest cannot be discovered. He had fulfilled an undertaking.[101]

As 1707 drew to a close, Toland suspended discussions of Bruno and Hermetica, Spinoza's metaphysics, and noncanonical gospels and moved on to Prague for one of the more curious episodes in his lifelong grasping after respectability. In the course of an extended dispute with Pierre-Daniel Huet, an exotically erudite French bishop who had sought to demonstrate the Mosaic origin of all pagan parallels to ancient Jewish customs, the delicate subject of Toland's paternity was raised. In order to secure authoritative legitimation, he presented a genealogy to a convent of displaced Irish Franciscans there. The friars obligingly pronounced him to be of good family and offered him generous hospitality at the cost of a little dissembling.[102]

Still in great straits, Toland returned to Berlin in the hope of receiving "some medals" in exchange for the promise of a panegyric on the Prussian court. Presumably aware of the distaste for Germany that had trickled through a previous account, the authorities required a manuscript before they would oblige him. Reacting to the uncertainty of English domestic politics, he proceeded to display an almost systematic intent to outrage. After representing his inquiry of the court preacher about the prospects for a general Protestant union as a response to a royal suggestion, he was threatened with "ye Bastinado." He managed to offend Raby's fine sense of etiquette by first introducing a tailor to him as a gentleman and then securing a seat for the visitor; a seated Toland was apparently not offensive: "and upon my telling him that I wondered be brought him to me in that manner he did, his answer was that now in England a rich tailor was thought fit comparison for any nobleman, and that little or no difference was made between them." Raby had felt enough of Toland's charm to conclude that "the devil is not so black as he is painted." This conclusion did not deter him from acting to quash Toland's pretension to official status by securing a letter from the tottering Harley which affirmed "that it was true that some time he suffered him in his company, as a man reputed to have a good deal of reading, but that he was very far from ever having had any friendship for or confidence in him." Raby became assiduous in his efforts to discredit Toland, not only with the royal family but also with Leibniz. Already irritated by Toland's provocative comments on the relation between superstition and true religion in *Adeisidaemon*, Leibniz required little prodding.[103]

Toland's dalliance with like-minded men in the Netherlands during the more than two-year hiatus separating Harley's fall and return to power had less influence on his subsequent activities than did the political upheaval in England.[104] As late as 1709, the High-Church party seemed to be subsiding, and it could be expected to subside further when Sophia succeeded to the throne. Dr. Henry Sacheverell's emergence as the Josiah of its doctrines of passive obedience and nonresistance confounded these expectations. Persuaded that this recrudescence threatened the Hanoverian succession along with the entire Revolution Settlement, Toland became one of its most violent opponents. Like other observers, he thought the drubbing which the doctor had taken in the skirmish of the pamphlets following his provocative Guy Fawkes' Day sermon presaged both the success of his impeachment and the domestication of the Tory extremists.[105] Toland's growing alarm in the face of the Whigs' hollow victory in the trial and Sacheverell's subsequent public triumphs showed in his increasingly shrill pamphlets. The specter of the brutish masses pommeling the reasonable few, which had haunted him since his Irish condemnation, threatened to become tangible.

During the first months of 1710 a series of blows against the members of the Godolphin ministry culminated in a *coup de grâce* against the lord treasurer himself. Harley was appointed chancellor of the exchequer in August. In October, the once pinched Tories — an alliance of the church party and the chancellor's Country group — revived to achieve perhaps the greatest electoral success of the century. Toland found himself drawn into a cobweb spun from the fibers of his patron's machinations. He would eventually be entrapped in it and see his political ambitions recede further and further from his reach.

Formerly a target of the "church in danger" campaign because of his association with Godolphin and Marlborough, Robert Harley saw the Church of England as preeminently a means of social control. Throughout the Sacheverell trial he had engaged in an artful balancing act. As a sometime Presbyterian, supporter of limited toleration, and antiparty moderate, he was an improbable clericalist high Tory, but as

the political leader of Sacheverell's adherents and sympathizers, he inevitably exploited the electoral reaction the Whig mismanagement of
the affair provoked.[106] During the next four years he was forced to shift
his center of gravity in order to address the aspirations of the bulk of his
followers: securing peace with France on any reasonable terms and
bolstering the church against those marked as her enemies. Omi-
nously, among important Whigs only a handful, including his prospective kinsman by marriage, the persistent duke of Newcastle, joined the
new administration. The duke was dead by mid-summer 1711. As
Harley shifted, the ideal of a bipartisan administration which Toland
had shared with him faded into impossibility.

Whatever Toland's apprehensions, he did not reveal them in the
warm congratulatory letter he sent from Leiden on Harley's return to
office. Others who shared his views may have been more reserved, but
the lure of patronage was strong enough to dissipate their reservations.
Even as Robert Molesworth assured the new chancellor that his principles were unchanged, he pressed his claim for place and pulverized
"nominal" Whigs who stood aloof. Apparently rewarded for past services with a house at Epsom and disregarding the spa's fraying gentility, Toland himself took up those bucolic posturings that offered
distraction throughout the remainder of his life, first as he waited for
something to turn up, later as he waited for the end. Harley found
employment for Toland and office for Molesworth, but his indispensable allies on the right voiced suspicions about the impure of principle
approaching the well of patronage.[107]

It was less Harley's sensitivity to the demands of the church party
than his commitment to negotiations with the French which led him to
neglect and finally to cut Toland. The queen had recalled Harley to
office because she wanted to end the war, and her decision made him
the leading peace candidate in the October general election. Yet Anne
still despised party government and saw her new minister as a nonpartisan statesman who would conduct her business by striking necessary
bargains rather than by provoking endless party strife. Harley struggled to fulfill her incompatible expectations. His followers and the
"pure Tories" fused gradually between 1710 and 1714, and during the
interim he alone among government front benchers tried to advance
some of the points of the old Country agenda. In contrast, most of the
issues which Toland advocated during these years, such as converting
the war from an effort to secure the balance of power into an anti-

popish jihad and inviting the electoral prince to take his seat in the House of Lords, were, if anything, Whiggish. Nervously eying the developing terms of the Utrecht settlement at the end of 1711, he was convinced that both these positions were necessary props to the most secure article in his political creed, the Hanoverian succession.[108]

An appeal to the lord treasurer to purge the high Tories and become "the author of a happy Coalition between the true friends of their Country, which are the moderate Whigs and the moderate Tories," had been ignored. Despite the increasing difficulty Toland had in gaining access to Harley, the recently created earl of Oxford kept him attached with "repeated promises of the continuance of . . . protection." Toland mixed pleas for any kind of patronage — £200 a year would have been paradise, but at one point the advance of £20 would have sufficed — with attempts at what might have been called influence peddling, if he had possessed influence. He had also begun to act as an informer for the opposition.[109]

It was all to no avail. Harley had learned of Toland's double-dealing, and the infidel's name had been linked in print with his own. Pressured by his right wing as partisanship became more sanguinary, and using Swift to tar the Whigs with the brush of infidelity, he could no longer profit from even a tenuous connection with Toland. For once, penury and phantasy did not tempt Toland to self-delusion. His own ties to Oxford were irreparably frayed by January 1712, but a financially embarrassed Molesworth persisted in "fruitless expectation" until late that spring.[110] The remainder of Anne's reign would see estrangement turn to rancor.

Meanwhile, Toland fitfully occupied himself with peddling translations from Pliny and proposing a new edition of Cicero. His project failed to move a public whose critical expectations were being refined by Richard Bentley beyond an amateur's power to satisfy. In any case, his immediate interest lay elsewhere. Encouraged by anti-Oxford raillery from Continental correspondents, he sought in a series of pamphlets attacking the treaty to settle scores, separate himself from his recent associates, and gain a place among the supporting cast of a Whig revanche. His attempt to insinuate himself into the entourage of Lord Townshend, one of its potential leading players, did not succeed. He was, however, able to finance a last reconnaissance of the Netherlands and Germany early in 1714.[111] This excursion was brief. He recognized that only by staying in Britain and adding to the flood of printed outrage over the articles of peace would he establish the credibility of his separation.

Hallucinating from the Jacobite disposition of the Bolingbroke faction to a vision of a general conspiracy, the Whigs suffered a trauma in late 1713 and early 1714 unequaled in modern British political history until the Tories' breakdown two hundred years later. In this atmosphere Toland could ignore ordinary restraints and thrive. He unearthed an Irish papist-nonjuror plot against the Hanoverian succession: "swarms of these Locusts are spread over the Kingdom, sowing Treason and Discord in the Minds of the People, that it may lye brooding there till a proper season to reap the Fruits of it." He challenged Oxford "to make some signal *Atonement,* by offering at least an *expiatory Sacrifice*" in order to remove the suspicion that he had been a French agent since the days of King William. Toland's feeling that he would profit handsomely from such exercises does not prove him insincere. Not least among his strengths as a polemicist was his constant conviction of the integrity of his position, whatever it happened to be. Moreover, projection from his personal sense of betrayal to assurance of national treason must have been irresistible. He hit upon an ingenious technique, drawing a thinly veiled parallel between Oxford's conduct and that of General Monck after the death of Cromwell. Many Nonconformists resented the restorer of Charles II, and few Anglicans were eager to defend a traitor to the royal martyr. Shrewd observers thought that this device had damaged the treasurer's reputation among Hanoverian supporters.[112] Toland's success proved to be inconsequential. Almost tasted, the "luxurious Tranquillity" that had become his consuming desire evaporated with Sophia's death in June 1714: "Lord! how near was my old woman being a Queen! and your humble servant being at his ease!"[113] Save in choosing mistresses and attendants, Sophia's son had not inherited her taste for exotics.

Despite the Hanoverian allergy to filial piety Toland published a *Funeral Elogy and Character* (1714) of Sophia, in another effort to secure a part in the restoration of English life which he hoped the accession of George I would inaugurate. Elegies proved no more helpful than importuning assertions in unsolicited memorials that the king "will employ and countenance . . . men as will in time (under his benign influence)" advance such designs. As he had feared, the triumphant Whigs "shamefully abandoned" him because of his long adherence to Harley. By 1716 he was being singled out as one ignored despite his unbroken loyalty to the Protestant succession. His promises to correct misunderstandings about his past were as ever fruitless.[114]

While Toland remained an internationally notorious figure, notoriety did not pay his bills. After another flirtation with weekly journalism he resumed the theological publication which he had sought to avoid while courting respectability.[115] He retained his appetite for political polemic, too. Even though he joined in manufacturing the horror stories about menacing nonjurors that were staples of Whig propaganda, this enterprise was not as compelling as it had been in Anne's last months. It is uncertain how early he recognized what he admitted in 1720: his High-Church foes had suffered an irrevocable disaster. That he began for the first time to publish works on divinity under his own name implies that he felt that they would have scant effect on his acknowledged reputation as "a well-known Heretick" and "abandoned Free-Thinker."[116]

Supporting Benjamin Hoadly's Whig Erastianism in the Bangorian controversy allowed Toland to offer a salable consideration of religion and politics. When a bishop declared that God's favor depended on sincerity rather than creed, that Christ's supernatural laws were not subject to interpretation by any ecclesiastical body and that, consequently, the church had neither doctrinal nor disciplinary authority, then Toland's Anglicanism threatened to become plausible. Until 1716 he had shown no special interest in Hoadly, but after Hoadly published *A Preservative against the Principles and Practices of Non-jurors* (1716) Toland became a supporter and, effectively, an ally. The two parts of Toland's *State-Anatomy of Great Britain* (1717), which advocated the repeal of the penal laws against Dissenters, were taken to be contributions to the Bangorian controversy, and he soon found himself linked publicly with the bishop. While it is hardly surprising that Toland took this side in the dispute, his assurance in print that his support would not be disavowed is intriguing. It is impossible to know what sort of relations the two men enjoyed, but they seem at least to have shared an understanding.[117]

Toland did well out of this work, but within a year he was in uncertain health and lodging meanly in the carpenter's house in Putney where he would die. From the tangled record of debts which he incurred during these years and his railings against "the avarice of book sellers," it is clear that he never arrested his declining fortunes.[118] But had things ever been considerably better for him? What profit had he gained from being reviled as a "Heretick" for almost a quarter-century? While the surviving accounts of his earnings from his several score publications are incomplete, they allow plausible conclusions. A regular literary marketplace, the economic basis of his career, was a late seventeenth-century creation. In it "traders cultivated the demand for certain staple commodities and speculated on the chance of striking public favor with a novelty." These traders were publisher-booksellers who appealed to a political interest or a religious taste with productions of well-disposed authors.[119] Toland approached this marketplace with different wares at various times in his career. He could produce sober political tracts for specialized, dedicated purveyors like the radical Whig Darby, seek to exploit a lust for sensational novelty, cater to popular interest in things which he must have found nonsensical, or submit to the hackwork of repackaging a salable commodity until it became a drug on the market. Twitting conventional wisdom was doubtlessly exhilarating, but he cannot have believed in the "prophecy of Saint Malachay," a Renaissance imposture purporting to be a twelfth-century prediction of the eventual fall of the papacy, which he described in the *Destiny of Rome* (1718). Neither can he have found pleasure in making thrice-told tales from his impressions of the Hanoverian court. Still, both projects commanded customers who would be touched by someone else if fastidiousness restrained him.

None of the works he wrote for the printer Bernard Lintot over the years was spectacularly profitable. His most remunerative book, *The Art of Governing by Partys,* earned him £20. Of the ten remaining titles for which payment records survive, six were worth about £10 each, while each of the other four brought in less than £6. The significance of these figures is plain when they are contrasted with Lintot's payment to a fashionable preacher of more than £32 for a volume of sermons or his purchase of a half-interest in a set of Boyle lectures for about £22. Isaac D'Israeli, an avid student of such matters, once calculated that Toland made no more than £200 out of everything he wrote.[120] In light of his irregular production during the second spell of employment by Harley, it seems likely that he welcomed release from the fatigue of the marketplace.

Such dismal returns help to explain the preoccupation of this sometime spokesman for republican virtue with the price of South Sea Company shares between the summer of 1720 and the spring of 1721. A relatively tardy speculator, Toland borrowed money — he dealt in thousands — on the strength of the signature of his more sceptical friend Molesworth with the understanding that he would divide the profits when prices next rose. He followed the directions of Sir Theodore Janssen, a wealthy Tory public creditor, who promised vast success. His aim was to continue stockjobbing until he made enough to buy an annuity of £200-300 a year, the magic sum which would give him ease and independence. When disaster impended, Toland reacted with panicked credulity, indulging in recriminations against Molesworth, in whose power to arrest the fall he placed inexplicable confidence.[121] Notwithstanding his chagrin at the bubble's bursting, his later public comments partook of the detachment in adversity that he praised in ancient patriots. The knowledge that Molesworth, saddled with his debts, was leading the charge against the directors and the ministry may have made Toland more secure in his warnings against indiscriminate condemnations and in his attempts at judicious analysis.[122]

Toland's resignation had to withstand not just this calamity, however, but also years of sustained reverses. He perhaps last knew a measure of happiness in 1717. In addition to the good sales of the *State-Anatomy,* he was pleased with the composition of the sitting parliament and maintained the insider's air which always bolstered him.[123] Whether or not these intimations were any more accurate than charges that Toland served as a mouthpiece, he labored to associate himself with the modern Whig order. Sometimes his effort required acquiescence. He remained silent when faced with parliament's extension of its life from three to seven years in the Septennial Act of 1716 and did not protest the Mutiny Bill of 1718, which proposed to create a standing army. At other times his effort demanded support. He assessed the problems of landowners as if anticipating the grievances addressed in the "Black Act" of 1723, and supported the elements of the Peerage Bill of 1719 because of a "patriotism" that encompassed rejection of constitutional immutability. He may, in fact, have been involved in publishing *The Patrician,* a journal founded by Molesworth to support this effort to fix permanently the size of the House of Lords. His labors were not exclusively theoretical and propagandistic. His flattery of its chief proponent, the earl of Sunderland, at the time of the Whig schism of 1717 betrayed neither sympathy for the excluded Walpole faction nor lofty indifference.[124]

He did not persist in this association. Even before Toland and Molesworth were ruined by their financial debacle, the Peerage Bill had failed and the ministry's proposals for ecclesiastical and educational reforms stalled. Whatever their reactions to Stanhope's death and Sunderland's near-humiliation, they and their fellows were excluded from the scramble for position as Walpole began to consolidate power in 1721. No special powers of insight were necessary to foresee the establishment of a regime that would be more ministerial than parliamentary and concerned with pacifying the church instead of defending the rights of Dissenters. Faced with this situation, Toland began to publish materials that would reconstitute the history of a coherent Commonwealth-Country group whose present embodiment derived from the third earl of Shaftesbury's deputation of Molesworth as his agent in politics. He was appreciative of that rambunctious Country and freethinking journal, *The Independent Whig*. By the spring of 1721, with Toland preaching political apocalyptic, Molesworth himself had adopted a tone and tenor anticipating Bolingbroke's in *The Craftsman, The Country Journal*. In politically stable times, a law of excluded extremes comes into operation.[125]

If triumphant Whiggery had not restored Toland's political fortunes, its ecclesiastical complement, institutionalized Latitudinarianism, had transvalued neither his manner nor his reputation. Having fixed an impression as being too clever by more than a half by returning to polemical theology after 1714, Toland remained vulnerable to attack. This chapter in the history of his problems began when an old antagonist, Daniel Defoe, revealed the authorship of the *State-Anatomy* and proceeded to exploit Toland's bad reputation against his own Whiggish views: "would ever Men of any Forecast have singled out a Man scandalous among Christians, to have started their Friends' Cause into the world!"[126]

Abhorrence had private as well as public consequences. In the summer of 1718, Toland was rebuffed in his attempt to enlist the lord chancellor's patronage for further research on his long-projected history of the druids. Like an eminent antiquary whom he had approached for information three years before, the chancellor thought anything he dealt with that bore on religion would smack of infidelity. By this time John Toland was branded as an atheist, a brand which even those whose ideal was a church bereft of dogmatic authority dared not touch.[127] Other searches for patrons fared no better. Molesworth sought the by now Archbishop King's approval for a proposal to employ his friend in the campaign against a statute of 1720 denying the Irish House of Lords appellate jurisdiction from Irish courts. That realistic prelate gave a penetrating reply: "I wou'd not refuse even his assistance, if it might be useful, but I am assured his intermeddling will

be mischievous and it will be thought as sufficient answer to all he offer-
eth, that he is the author. . . . The notion of religion is so engrafted in
hearts of men, that the Generality will never have esteem for one they
believe has none, but he will be detested and abhorred."

Although King doubted the depth of Toland's knowledge of Irish
affairs, he did not object to using him, but only to using him publicly.
At length King conceded that Toland might work as a ghost if Molesworth were intent on having him. The *Pantheisticon* (1720) may or may
not have reflected Toland's membership in another secret society, but
its contention—that reasonable contemporaries, no less than reasonable ancients, were obliged to dissemble because of popular hostility to
the life of reason—amounts to a positive image of King's negative.[128]

That Toland could both remind himself of the need to despise "per-
ishable Honours, being to perish yourself in a short Time," and ironically refer to the inestimable value of his services to the High-Church
party suggests that in his last months he was grasping at a measure of
detachment, an appreciation that "Wisdom oft / Is nearer when we
stoop than when we soar."

So slight, this effort came too late. Abandoned and apparently
drinking heavily, Toland was unable to assert his long-obscured person
over its obscuring personas. A fatal affliction of kidney stones only
moved him to write a final pamphlet, this one denouncing physicians.[129] Bedridden in a cluttered room of another man's house since
Christmas of 1721 and "in want of Necessaries," he appealed to Molesworth, his oldest friend. Protesting friendship and a desire to help
("such small ones as I can afford"), the viscount seemed comfortably
distant from his plight. It fell to Toland's guide in the South Sea gam-
ble, the now disgraced financier Janssen, to meet his pressing needs.
Toland's account of his last torments is wrenching: "pains in my thighs,
veins, and stomach . . . total loss of appetite, hourly retchings, and
very high colour'd water." A supposed eyewitness recorded some dying
words: "The Pangs of Death were so strong upon him, (that as he had
no Inclinations, neither would Time permit for his being assisted with
the Advice of any Ecclesiastical Friend) he parted with his last Breath
with a Resignation peculiar to himself, and only said to those about
him, 'I thank you for your Care, but I am Poyson'd by a Physician.' "[130]

Thomas Hearne noted the passing of an "impious wretch" who had
loved novelty for its own sake. The press affected lapidary smugness:
"No man that wrote so voluminously against Religion, has ever done so

little mischief; 'tis a Question whether he was more pitied by the pious part of mankind, or dispised by his fellow Infidels."[131]

Finally out of the reach of critics, Sean-Janus-John was buried on 13 March 1722 in Putney churchyard under a Latin epitaph which, after describing his love of literature, truth, and liberty, as well as his lifelong independence, proclaimed: "His spirit was joined with its ethereal father / from whom it originally proceeded; his body likewise yielding to Nature, / to be again laid in the lap of its mother: / but he is about to rise again in eternity, / yet never to the same Toland more." Even in death, John Toland continued to tease.

If John Toland's writings cast flickers on aspects of his biography, they illuminate his character. The ideal Toland, whose lines he drew for his readers, was classically proportioned. He was a servant of God and of country, made for activity rather than solitude, daring the uncommon, defying the mean-spirited, and nourished by achievement, the solace of heroes. Although Toland's own dimensions may be unrecognizable in this survey, its distortion serves as a reminder of the tentative, shifting frontier between the early eighteenth-century's ideal cosmopolitanism and crude adventurism.[132] Insecurity persistently overspread and obliterated the boundaries Toland sought to draw between cosmopolitan aspiration and adventuristic reality in both his life and his work.

Whatever the truth about Toland's origins, he was an upstart in a society still more hierarchical than fluid, and neither could nor did forget the fact. A willingness to point to the similar beginnings of figures as diverse as Aesop and Cicero uneasily coexisted with promptings to hauteur. In "Hypatia" he dwelt disdainfully on the low births of the monks who persecuted his heroine. On other occasions he invoked his concocted genealogy, alluded to his well-staffed childhood home, and broadcast his familiarity in the counsels of the great. If the remarkable opportunities his abilities and interests presented were gutted by a burning self-assertion, this impulse was fueled by the same self-doubt which sustained his destructive indiscipline.[133] He seems to have held that by aping the *plaisir aristocratique de déplaire* he could persuade not only others but also himself of his own importance. His lack of discipline expressed itself in the improvidence which made him an habitual debtor who exploited the credit of those who tried to befriend him. Yet in order to survive as a performer in his society he acquired the gestures it demanded. His encounters with Archbishop Sharp and

Lord Raby testify to his personal charm, and he could exhibit manners sufficiently polished to commend him to fastidious men.[134]

His management of his performance demanded dexterity lest it tumble into farce. When he chose to denounce "this loose and sceptical age" or to upbraid the clergy for frequenting coffee- and alehouses, he risked losing his balance. In order to make his pretensions credible, he sought to disperse the weight of his learning. References to his Scottish degrees were infrequent, but his inevitable assertions of erudition frequently became intimidating displays of pedantry.[135] Since circumstances enforced servility, he relished opportunities to outrage the great, whether by making cheeky advances to the bishop of London or affronting Raby's sense of propriety. Contempt for conventions pervaded his career. He did not shrink from intercepting, altering, and publishing the correspondence of his opponents, perhaps because he knew that these respectable men were capable of returning the favor. Distributing copies of his *succès de scandale* after having repudiated it for years was a more dangerous game.[136]

If the public figure was defaced by insecurity, the private man did not thrive on it. Toland was gregarious. He craved companionship, and probably needed a love which he apparently never received. Lord Molesworth, nearly a faithful friend, was his social superior and intellectual inferior, a disproportion Toland could not ignore. Although Toland never married, references to amours punctuate his letters. None of them suggests that he sought a helpmate. His ideal mistress was "far from being the monster they call a Learned Lady," but rather "genteel without affectation, gay without levity, civil to strangers without being free, and free with her acquaintance without being familiar." There is a wistfulness in his contention that "the whole business of a woman" is to please one man.[137] Deprived of marriage and intimate friendship, Toland sought personal solace as well as intellectual stimulation in coffeehouses. Again the private man became a public performer. "I therefore hear and see every thing. I have the pleasure very often by cross questions or a seeming compliance, to draw that out of some people, for which they wou'd be ready to hang themselves, if they thought I rightly understood them. . . . Bantering and fooling, indifference and doubtfulness, are successful engines in this art of disburthening. . . . "[138]

His recreations afforded him slight opportunity for introspection. If he had a serious interest in either music or the plastic arts, he was uncharacteristically reticent about it. While spells of gambling cannot have fostered self-examination, escaping to the country to fish offered relief from the compulsion to display himself and perhaps occasions to consider the man he was.[139]

Whatever self-knowledge he achieved did not suffice to reveal to him that his disdain for contention owed less to a love for tranquillity than to the oracular quality with which he came to envelop his utterances. Such authority guaranteed that, despite buffeting, his opinions remained sound. He was too bright and too sensitive to ignore the judgments others formed of him. Perhaps an insight into his own adventuristic reality prompted him to translate Giordano Bruno's self-examination: "I know myself to be for the most part accounted a sophister, more desirous to appear subtil, than to be really solid; . . . a deceiver, that aims at purchasing brightness to his own fame, by engaging others in the darkness of error; a restless spirit, that overturns the edifice of sound discipline."[140] He never undertook a similar effort in his own voice.

John Toland the author cherished an ideal as cosmopolitan as John Toland the man.

Commanding Vigor shall my Thoughts convey, / the Softness seal the Truth of all I say: / I'll sooth the raging Mob with mildest words, / Or sluggish Cowards rouze to use their Swords. / As furious Winds sweep down whate'er resists, / So shall my Tongue perform whate'er it lists, / With large impetuous Floods of Eloquence / Tickel and Fancy, and bewitch the Sense; / Make what it will the justest Cause appear, / And what's perplext or dark look bright and clear. / Not that I wou'd the wrongful side defend; / He best protects who's ablest to offend. . . .

Toland's preoccupation with Cicero owed not a little to a conviction that his model had achieved these goals — and considerable worldly success. His caustic contrast of the honored state of the profession of letters in antiquity and its modern abasement served to rationalize the distance between his own expectations and performance and to cauterize the distress which it caused him. Insist though he might that he would not fail to perform "the Duties I ow *God* and the World," his principal task was often to write enough to survive.[141]

Requirements of daily survival combined with imperatives of temperament to lead Toland into compromises — in choosing topics, method of presentation, and on occasion viewpoint. There is nevertheless a risk that concentration on such compromises will foster neglect of the subjective and objective realities which both enabled him to aspire to—and sometimes clutch—cosmopolitanism and ensured his historical survival. Nothing he wrote manifests powers of the first order. Paradoxically, their secondary character, their essentially adaptive quality, explains both Toland's interest for the creative minds of his age and his importance to its thought. Because he was at the same time an unoriginal thinker and a man whose existence was defined by ideas and expression, he had to be attentive to dominant intellectual currents in order to survive: to move now with them, now against them. His premature anticipation of a confluence presaged a series of failures to chart an accurate course and his eventual entrapment in a backwater. No movement of adaptation is one-way. Plotting his choice of theological, philosophical, and political eddies indicates much about the main currents, which themselves sometimes show ripples from counterforces. More importantly, pinpointing the backwater in which he rested is central to any attempt to place the missed confluence.

Toland's career bridged the gap between daily demands and historical valuation. In order to ensure extended survival in early Augustan England, a theological controversialist had to be able to disperse his wares without piquing hostile authorities. It is unnecessary to accept the somewhat cabalistic interpretation of the late Leo Strauss to recognize that the threat of persecution influenced the art of writing in Toland's lifetime. In a sense, his experiences after 1697 form a monument to its reality. Toland's contemporaries were not as complaisant as those scholars who would take at face value all of his professions of conventionality. Pierre Des Maizeaux heard that Toland had learned from the Socinians that, in some circumstances, lying about one's beliefs was permissible. John Leland, the author of the first comprehensive survey of English deism, assumed that his subjects regularly used a variety of disguises.[142] Again and again Toland's critics saw a break between the stated intentions and the tangible effects of his works, though they themselves could fall prey to tunnel vision. One reviewer of *The Art of Governing by Partys* glimpsed secret intentions in that apparently pellucid tract. Yet Toland could be cited in support of this reading. Had he not written there that he possessed the "due regard which every one ought to have for his own preservation"?[143]

Only near the end of his career did Toland risk a tentative discussion of his method. In the preface to *Tetradymus* (1720), he described antiquity's distinction between exoteric and esoteric teachings and went on

to explain that persecution led authors to become "supple in their conduct," and "reserv'd in opening their minds about most things," even to
being "ambiguous in their expressions." These reflections nudged him
toward a rare hint of self-rebuke. "To what sneaking equivocations, to
what wretched shifts and subterfuges, are men of excellent en-
dowments forc'd to have recourse thro human frailty, merely to escape
disgrace or starving? And this very frequently on the score of
Metaphysical abstractions, or chimeras that never had any existence
out of the hollow noddles of waking dreamers." Pending complete
freedom of expression, intelligent men could not straightforwardly deal
with, say, transubstantiation or the Athanasian Creed.[144] Much less
could Toland give an unambiguous statement of his own pantheist
materialism, the esoteric theology whose insinuation became his
ultimate literary purpose.

The statute 9 and 10 William III, c. 32—whereby "any one who by
writing or speaking should deny any of the persons in the Trinity to be
God or assert there to be more Gods than one," was first disqualified
from holding public office, then deprived of his civil liberties and made
subject to imprisonment—was not repealed until the last years of
George III. Anthony Collins' insistence in 1717 that his publisher
neither keep on hand a large stock of his "Books of Freethinking" nor
publish them "in any public manner" indicates how remote security was
for suspect writers.[145] Whether as friends of truth or purveyors of
novelties, they had to find safe means of imparting their discoveries or
dispersing their merchandise. That Toland rose to this challenge is apparent in his ability to express coherent theological and political views
without following Aikenhead to the stake or joining Defoe in the
pillory.

Anatole France saw his task as the liberation of a bourgeois clientele
from their inherited prejudices. He cautioned his secretary: "Do not
tear away the veil of the temple. Pluck it off a little at a time. Riddle it
with sly little holes. . . . Leave to your reader the easy victory of seeing
farther than you." Working in less favorable circumstances than those
provided by the Third Republic, John Toland adopted a similar
method in order to accomplish what became the first of his subordinate
literary purposes, the criticism of received, objectionable theological
opinions. He knew his primary audience, the small reading public
drawn chiefly from the middling ranks, and appreciated that he had
both to stir their curiosity and to soothe their inhibitions. If he ad-

dressed them as "impartial lovers of truth" and they accepted him as sharing their aspiration, then they were on the verge of complicity in his plucking.[146]

When riddling, Toland used paradox like a sharpened needle. As he remarked in the insinuatingly titled *Christianity Not Mysterious,* the "deplorable condition of Our Age" compelled a seeker after truth either to remain silent or to "propose his sentiments to the World by way of Paradox." Although he later professed to be contrite for having used this device, his contrition did not include a resolution of amendment.[147] Other instruments were at his disposal: passing off a controversial pronouncement as if it were a matter of indifference or burying a hostile insinuation in a long digression. He also multiplied damaging, conjectural answers to a seemingly casual question. Why, he asked, had John Milton shunned public worship during his last years? "Whether this proceded from a dislike of [the clergy's] uncharitable and endless Disputes, and that hope of Dominion, or Inclination to Persecution . . . or whether he thought one might be a good man without subscribing to any Party, and that they all in som things corrupted the Institutions of Jesus Christ, I will by no means adventure to determine." And if a doctrine or practice found in the articles of the Church of England appeared comparable to a Romish imposture, if, for example, the Trinity seemed to resemble transubstantiation, then his readers could draw their own conclusions. Retailing the scorching opinions of unnamed "others" while tepidly dissociating himself from them was often as safe as noncommittally passing on the unsettling observations of defunct authorities.[148]

Toland fostered complicity, or at least acquiescence, among his readers as he moved from shared assumptions, through a stimulating observation, to a novel thesis. When opponents denounced the implications of his sly whispers, which may have eluded some readers, he could protest his innocence of the noxious opinions that they had inferred—and forced him to mention—or point to another as the real proponent of such views. Recognizing the solvent effect of doses of ridicule, Toland was not always genteel. His delighted contradictions of the doctrine of one father by that of another were relatively innocuous. He did not shrink from imputing thirty-nine articles of agreement to the customs of both the Jews and the Hindus, speculating about the state of Mary's hymen after the birth of Jesus, or asking what Moses' sentinels did under the cover of the cloud. For his part, he was appalled at contemporary license.[149] Whatever glint was to be found lay in his readers' eyes.

Besides providing suggestive analogies, the antipopery pandemic in England in its dual strains of hostility to "superstitious" Catholic practices and the "arbitrary" government they sustained offered a convenient repellent of those in close pursuit. Since his loathing for Rome was obvious, must there not be something suspicious about any foe whose pope-baiting was less prodigious than his own? He appreciated, too, that a refutation could serve more than one purpose. *Adeisidaemon* was nominally an answer to Bayle's charge in the *Pensées diverses sur la comète de 1680* that Livy was superstitious. Toland noted that Bayle's book seemed to favor atheism, which stood as Scylla to the Charybdis of superstition. In elaborating this contention, he diffused what he took to be Bayle's characteristic doctrines without defining the middle point between these two extremes. His vindications were equally protean. By undertaking Saint Paul's defense against his "Jewish Christian" critics, for example, he was able to indict the apostle's theologizing deviations from Christ's simple ethical teaching.[150]

Toland wrote a number of the political tracts in which he set out to accomplish what became the second of his subordinate literary purposes — the delineation of the English commonwealth and its purified, exoteric theology — at the behest of patrons whose views he had to represent. This pattern of interdependence further complicates the problem of unraveling a welter of insinuation and assertion. When did he mean what he wrote? When did he write what he meant? In the absence of a critical Urim and Thummim, two simple rules may prove helpful. First, it is necessary to consider the circumstances in which he wrote a particular work. Secondly, the acceptance of a given statement as his own depends on its consistency with what he wrote publicly and privately on the subject elsewhere. Their application provides evidence of coherent patterns of thought which, in turn, make the character of Toland's individual wares reasonably identifiable.

The question remains whether there was any accuracy in Toland's portrayal of himself as a disinterested seeker of truth. More precisely, in what measure did this professional polemicist for free thought in religion and against monarchical and clerical authority in politics possess the qualities of the learned with whom he sought to join himself? Toland dwelt outside the world of the *érudits*. For him, learning, far from being an end in itself, was an aspect of public life, something which he regularly resorted to rather than systematically pursued.[151] While his attitude did not entail hostility toward research, it did mean that his scholarship remained derivative and selective, that he lived off the patrimony of the *érudits*. Having appropriated their capital, he felt free not merely to draw on it to meet immediate needs but also to transfer it in ways that would have often surprised—and sometimes shocked—them.

Toland's attempts to discredit the canon of the New Testament rested on the Oratorian Richard Simon's *Nouvelles observations sur le texte et les versions du Nouveau Testament* (1695) and the first volume of the learned Jansenist L.-S. Tillemont's *Mémoires pour servir à l'histoire ecclésiastique* (1693). The *Letters to Serena* are a pastiche of understated and unacknowledged borrowings. The argument of the first letter, "The Origin and Force of Prejudices," was taken from Père Nicolas Malebranche's *Recherche de la vérité* (1674); the second, "The History of the Soul's Immortality among the Heathens," incorporated large sections from the article "Anaxagoras" in Bayle's *Dictionnaire historique et critique* (2d ed., 1702); and the third, "The Origins of Idolatry, and Reasons of Heathenism," drew heavily on the Dutch Anabaptist Anthony Van Dale's *Dissertationes de origine ac progressu idolatriae et superstitionum* (1696). These and other, more significant adaptations could not have helped him define the lines demarcating *haute vulgarisation* from gratuitous erudition on one side and prostitution of scholarship on the other. Though he casually referred to Dom Jean Mabillon's *De re diplomatica* (1681), he showed no appreciation of the monk's paleographical revolution. When the researches of the *érudits* did not buttress the point he was urging, he had few inhibitions about manufacturing the required support. He also accumulated piles of often marginal references in an effort to avoid confronting embarrassing arguments or conclusions and backed away from weighty antagonists like George Bull. While he ransacked Simon's work, an object of fear in England, he felt no compunction about dismissing it as ignorant whenever it proved an obstacle. His last redoubt was sheer, disarming brazenness. He passed off contentions top-heavy with implications and tottering on weak foundations as *jeux d'esprit,* worth whatever the reader chose to make of them.[152]

Even in the biographical and editorial works that constitute Toland's chief claim to independent scholarship, he was chronically unable to resist the temptation to make his thesis the end to which all else was subordinate. His lack of resistance often resulted in a palpable, and hence innocuous, tendentiousness. Toland presented a familiar Milton — a learned defender of liberty, who happened to have written poetry — and his treatment of Milton's life and art reflected this preconception. Similarly, though Toland produced, largely without benefit of manuscripts, an edition of Harrington's *Works* judged by their most recent editor, J. G. A. Pocock, as "on the whole" careful and honest, the biography he prefaced to them must, despite the unpublished materials he claimed to have consulted, be treated gingerly. Just because other lapses were better disguised, they are more extraordinary. Through learned and patient detection, A. B. Worden has exposed perhaps the greatest of them: Toland's re-creation of Edmund Ludlow, a regicide millenarian, as a secular Country-Whig gentleman of the turn-of-the-century. To recreate Ludlow for the *Memoirs* (1698), Toland had not only to rewrite completely *A Voyce from the Watch Tower* but also "to create and to inhabit a personality" quite unlike Ludlow's. However admirable as a work of imagination, this effort suggests that the few exasperated critics who dissected his scholarship had a sure intuition of his station in the republic of letters.[153]

Toland's inability to admit that criticism of him could derive from anything nobler than spite determined his response both to such dissections and to less responsible attacks: a fair-minded critic was by definition an impossibility. In his certainty he was a man of his age. As a group, Augustan pamphleteers seem to have been unable to separate themselves — or anyone else — from their ideas, but few other than Toland were sufficiently susceptible to autosuggestion to be directed by their own repeated assurances that they practiced "indifference in disputes." Despite his assiduous collection of critical remarks, *Christianity Not Mysterious* was the only book which he altered to answer objections. The detachment that filters through the early *Defence of Mr. Toland* all but evaporated as remorseless controversy made self-assertion the stuff of his survival. If he spoke with the voice of reason, then his opponents had to be moved by the base motives he imputed to them and thus stood outside the boundaries of civil dialogue. Did they not misrepresent questions, distort his position by paraphrases, selective refutation, and attribution of hidden motives, and draw illogical inferences? How could any reasonable man, how could John Toland, be expected to take them seriously? An *ad hominem* was his natural response. His critics were probably Jacobites. After all, their associates showed such tendencies. Like other eighteenth-century writers of every persuasion, Toland detected sinister conspiracies at work beneath the surface of great public events. At times of stress he was prone to the delusion that the monstrous popish and Jacobite intrigue against English liberties had marked him as its particular target.[154] Having pledged that "softness [would] seal the Truth of all I say," he was a victim of his insecurities, who reviled anyone challenging his occasionally whimsical construction of reality. Adventurism had again taken its toll.

In creating a style, Toland had also set up a cosmopolitan ideal.

For as every thing in the Universe is the Subject of writing, so an author ought to treat of every subject smoothly and correctly, as well as pertinently and perspicuously: nor ought he be void of ornament and Elegance, when his matter peculiarly requires it. Some things want a copious stile, some a concise; others are more . . . plainly handl'd: but all are properly, methodically, and handsomly exprest.

Since the "plain style" championed by Dryden was becoming fashionable, the Ciceronianism which Toland prescribed in this paraphrase of book one of *De oratore* was almost as anachronistic as the Commonwealth-Country publications of his final months. Sensitive to form, Jonathan Swift was to warn against the older style in *A Letter to a Young Gentleman Lately Enter'd into Holy Orders* (1721) because it appealed to the emotions.[155] What Swift disdained, Toland aspired to achieve: a classicizing, civic rhetoric. Toland proved no more obedient to his rhetorical ideals than to his political ideals. If he often tempered his aspiration in response to the pressure of inclination and fashion and contented himself with writing brisk English prose, he recurrently tried to confect a "copious stile." It was seldom happy. His attraction to the antithesis did nothing to restrain the temptation to divide reality into rational and irrational (or good and evil) compartments. Fusillades of apostrophes could obliterate his point.[156]

As his transformation of *A Voyce from the Watch Tower* into Ludlow's *Memoirs* suggests, he was a speedy and inventive writer. These gifts contained risks as well as opportunities. When writing at speed, he occasionally failed to argue plausibly or fell into inattentive confusion. The limitations of his inventiveness are clearest in some of his forays into translation. When confronted with a standard writer of silver Latin like the younger Pliny, he was frequently becalmed, unable either to steer ahead masterfully or to drift into another's mind and expression. Instead, he was kept fitfully moving by gusts of Latinisms.

Toland was not an Augustan wit, and his pages show only a limited capacity for sustained irony and satire. When he applied himself to the mockery indispensable to his ridicule, though, he could be funny. He described a prelate, "not very nice in other matters," as being "much better acquainted with the Mothers than the Fathers," and arraigned William Whiston, the Arian mathematician and theologian, for notionally assenting to the *Apostolic Constitutions* because he ignored their prohibition of shaving and haircuts. When these exceptions have been noted, it remains indisputable that, almost despite himself, Toland wrote English which is still readable. The critic who compared it to bottled ale ("Tho' *thin,* not clear; tho' *sharp* yet very *dull/Rage* without Strength; o'erflowing yet not *full.* ") was far of the mark.[157] Although Toland came no closer to realizing a Ciceronian ideal in writing than he did to living as a sort of walking, laureled bust, he achieved a measure of success as a stylist. Style need not always be the image of character.

2 / Latitude and Orthodoxy

After a century Leslie Stephen's *History of English Thought in the Eighteenth Century* remains the authoritative attempt to relate deism to its intellectual milieu. The outlines of his account are familiar: Archbishop Tillotson was both the primate and the most conspicuous of the Latitudinarians; in their tireless offensive against popery, these liberal divines "put forward arguments capable of being turned against themselves"; published near the end of the vague Trinitarian controversy, John Toland's *Christianity Not Mysterious* marked the return of this theological boomerang and started the deist controversy.[1]

The way to establishing historical periods is beset by pitfalls, and Stephen was not uniquely surefooted. Toland's *succès de scandale* was more an episode than a starting-point. Its title suggests that it was meant as a refutation of Robert South's notorious sermon of 29 April 1694, "Christianity Mysterious, and the Wisdom of God in Making It So." In writing his book, Toland may have sought to redirect a longstanding debate, but he was also announcing his involvement in it and his acceptance of its terms. He, his mentors, and his antagonists were creatures of the distinctive culture of early modern Anglo-Dutch Protestantism. Personal as well as theological ties bound them together. When Toland's teacher, Philip Van Limborch, wished to dedicate his *Historia Inquisitionis* (1692) to Tillotson, he sought the mediation of a mutual friend and Toland's future patron, John Locke. The archbishop delightedly consented to Locke's request and sent the Remonstrant a volume of his own sermons as a token of esteem. Within five years Toland, Limborch, the recently defunct Tillotson, and Locke were all being assailed as Socinians by a group of critics. *Christianity Not Mysterious* is an artifact of this culture, and it cannot be understood if it is approached as a freak.[2]

Sympathetic historians of seventeenth-century Anglicanism have acquitted it of intellectualism. Mistrustful of a system dependent "on a closely-knit logic," it was an ethos which imposed on both clergy and laity conformity instead of assent. Such mistrust, more than any characteristic tenets or methodology, united the Latitudinarians with their Caroline and Elizabethan predecessors. All of them partook of the Erasmian strain of piety, which in England was more deep-seated than the teachings of the magisterial reformers. It is unnecessary to interpret Erasmus as an unwitting modernist in order to realize that he believed the Scholastic application of philosophy to Christian doctrine to have been calamitous.[3] He was confident that the Holy Spirit would guide any pious and humble effort to assimilate the pure sources of Christianity, above all the New Testament. He held that, because uncorrupted minds are sensitive to natural truths, simple souls are most likely to succeed in the endeavor.

The faith of Erasmus pervades the Thirty-Nine Articles. The sixth affirms that "Holy Scripture containeth all things necessary to salvation: so that whatsoever is not read therein, nor may be provided thereby, is not required of any man, that it should be believed as an Article of Faith, or be thought requisite or necessary to salvation." The eighth imposes the Apostles', Nicene, and Athanasian creeds simply because "they may be proved by most certain warrants of Holy Scripture." The twenty-first denies conciliar authority apart from the Bible and finds errors in the deliberations of the early councils, "even in things pertaining unto God." From John Jewel through William Laud and William Chillingworth, Anglican theologians assumed that they could recover the meaning of the Bible, the religion of Protestants. It plainly and evidently presented every necessary truth and could be apprehended by a capacity present in all rational beings. Jewel, for example, was sure that, once given the texts in their own language, the Amerinds would become Anglicans rather than papists.[4] For three generations this assurance coexisted uneasily with the ninth article's assertion of the "fault and corruption of the nature of every man that naturally is engendered of the offspring of Adam."

In seeking to transmit Erasmianism to the Restoration church, Jeremy Taylor prepared for its transformation. Although reason was plural in object and form, its result was ultimately unitary: "it is reason that carries me to objects of faith, and faith is my reason so disposed, so used, so instructed." At the same time he disputed that one could conclude, " 'This is agreeable to right reason, therefore this is so in Scripture, or in the counsel of God.' " Instead, he insisted that in cases of apparent disagreement, "our understanding is to submit and wholly be obedient, but not to inquire further."[5] His vacillation reflected the conflicting demands of fighting on two apologetic fronts. When engaging the Socinians, he tried to humble the pretensions — or at least to assert the plurality — of reason. When combating Roman Catholics, he used his unequaled eloquence to magnify these very pretensions, to hint at the oneness of faith and reason in order to suggest the reasonableness of Protestantism.

Taylor depicted the first three centuries of the church as a golden age unblemished by internal persecution. His primitivism led him to deny that belief in the Athanasian Creed and all other formulas was essential to salvation. Since churches in every age inevitably modified dogma, none could hold itself infallible. Such considerations implied that Christian credenda had to be few. Religion was primarily a matter of moral obedience, so it could not be counted a sin if one, having "heartily endeavoured to find out a truth," remained ignorant or made an error. The fathers were contradictory, councils could only corroborate Scripture, and the existence of different versions of the Bible clouded its authority. Taylor maintained, therefore, that unity of faith meant the agreement of the living who chose to identify themselves as Christians.[6] In light of the depth and acrimony of Restoration religious arguments, the collapse of the consensus he defended must have seemed imminent.

Within a decade of Taylor's death one of his axioms, the Peripatetic notion of a plural reason, was becoming *outré*. Aristotelians had conceived of reason as part of the soul, the substantial form of the body and the agency directing all human functions. They had also distinguished between reason as a faculty partaking of the divine and reason as an activity. While their epistemology did not allow for innate ideas, they believed in inherent principles of the soul which enabled it to recognize both essences and the universals implicit in the data of sense. A popular manual of logic published in 1678 could still describe reason as a discursive faculty making complicated deductions. It presented this, however, along with several other definitions, one of which was becoming predominant. In a sermon dedicated to Robert Boyle and delivered three years earlier, the Reverend Thomas Smith, F.R.S., had accepted the identity of reason and demonstration, though he still insisted that there were varying degrees of probability in reasonings.[7]

Beginning with Chillingworth, Anglicans had opposed Roman professions of infallibility by maintaining that there were different, legitimate forms of reason, each capable of eliciting a characteristic kind of assent.[8] Seeking to steer a middle course between dogmatism and scepticism, these advocates of common sense allowed that human beings could reach either conditionally infallible certitude or moral certitude. While the former was effected by mathematical and certain metaphysical propositions, the latter, which amounted to probability, was the response of a sensible person to his evaluation of the evidence presented to him. In all the practical decisions of life — including that between belief and unbelief — men could aspire to no greater certainty. Although such prominent authors as Tillotson, Stillingfleet, and Locke continued to use this style of argumentation, their acceptance of neologism unavoidably affected it.

With the appearance of the long-gestating *Essay concerning Human Understanding* in 1690, the simplification of reason prevailed over common-sense probabilism.[9] Locke defined reason as a mental operation rather than as a faculty of the soul. He left it with only one of the functions that the Peripatetics had given it, ratiocination. While the data with which the mind operated were derived from the senses, its relation to the body was irrelevant, not least because it was inscrutable. The psyche lay in the mind, not in the soul. Earlier advocates of the common-sense theory had allowed for the persistence of reasonable doubt after the attainment of moral certainty, but Locke ignored this possibility. Instead, he held that the existence of adequate evidence gave assent the inevitability and lucidity of demonstration. The individual will could play no part in deciding it.

Whether from conviction, sluggishness, or fear, some writers clung to belief in inherent principles in the teeth of the new notion of reason. Yet even their intransigence was usually incomplete. Benjamin Whichcote's Platonism set him apart from the neologists, but he urged the redefinition of religion which, within two generations, the church would accept as a replacement for the vanished consensus. The "state of religion" consisted of goodness of mind and life, and its other elements were incidental. Christianity merely sought to restore humanity's connatural disposition toward true belief. While reason and faith were compatible, the human mind was better fitted to apprehend moral principles than the abstruse, secondary propositions that obsessed theologians.[10] John Tillotson was at once repaying a debt and affirming a creed when he eulogized Whichcote as "so wise, as to be willing to learn to the last; knowing that no man can grow wiser without some change of his mind, without gaining some knowledge which he had not, or correcting some error which he had before."[11]

Both Whichcote and Tillotson attended informal meetings of like-minded clerics and laymen which began in London shortly after the Restoration. Under the *de facto* leadership of John Wilkins, bishop of Chester and Tillotson's father-in-law, such diverse figures as Edward Stillingfleet, John Locke, Gilbert Burnet, and Thomas Firmin gathered frequently over a number of years to discuss theology. Whatever their differences, all of these men shared a distaste for dogmatism, a concern for morality, natural theology, and reason, and a flexible attitude toward the government of the church to which they conformed. Their moderation led scornful Calvinists to tag them as Latitudinarians and to accuse them of rationalism, Pelagianism, and laxity.[12] In time, some of them accepted the label as a satisfactory description of their effort to achieve a rational and inclusive exposition of Anglicanism. In their style of preaching, the divines who favored this enterprise exhibited their ideals. Eschewing appeals to emotion and the use of mysterious and obscure terms, they aspired to clarify Christianity by presenting it as a distinct set of teachings meant to affect human conduct.

As critics recognized, a contradiction vitiated their aspiration. It was impossible to be consistently rational and still remain doctrinally orthodox. In trying to square this circle, the Latitudinarians virtually reduced Christianity to morality, first by treating as natural what had always been seen as supernatural, then by ignoring, redefining, or eliminating all refractory elements. By the early 1690s, a few Latitudinarians were realizing the heterodox implications of their paradoxical undertaking, but most followed Tillotson in holding back, unable either to repudiate or to complete it. Their reluctance was short-lived.[13] By the end of the decade, the remnant of the original Latitudinarians, buffeted by remorseless, politically inspired attacks from the High-Church party, were bitterly divided between those, like Stillingfleet, who wished to reassert orthodoxy and those, like Locke, who upheld the primacy of reason. Although their struggle eventually subsided, it was never resolved.

Since even an attenuated Christianity can seem folly, the Latitudinarian search for a new consensus was challenged by thoroughgoing rationalists as well. Harried searchers were prone to accuse persistent challengers of atheism. While their use of this term was more commodious than precise, the existence of advocates of the hypothesis that all phenomena are explicable as permutations of matter-in-motion lent plausibility to their accusations. In opposing atheists, the Anglican rationalists depended on two apologetic tactics which respectively exhibited their rationalism and their moralism. Wilkins offered reasons for God's existence. Some of them were persuasives and depended on the alleged universality of the idea of God and the apparent finitude of the world. Others merely recapitulated the hoary argument from design, but Wilkins, influenced by the redefinition of reason as demonstration, outdid Aquinas and presented his arguments as proofs comparable in rigor to those achievable in mathematics. A number of the Boyle lecturers would intensify his scientism by dressing up the supposed proofs with a vocabulary appropriated from Newtonian physics. Suspicious of philosophical divinity, Stillingfleet sought to counter sceptics who denied the tenets of the religion of nature by treating them as victims of bad "manners." A campaign of moral improvement would dispose of them. Despite — or because of — its indirection, his proposed solution to the problem of doubt attracted supporters.[14]

Truisms can be revealing. Revulsion at the *odium theologicum* which had obsessed their fathers had left this generation with a marked distaste for passion and zeal, so intense that it contributed to their failure to accommodate the irrational. For Augustan divines, all worthwhile actions were grounded in reason, which in this instance meant the calculation of interests. Men believed because their knowledge convinced them that it was prudent to do so. In defending the veracity of the scriptural account of Christ's resurrection, Stillingfleet urged: "If *Credit* and *Interest* in the Hearts of People, might carry a Man on a great way in the Delusion, yet he would be loth to dye for it; & yet there was never a one of the Apostles, but ventured his Life for the *Truth* of this."[15]

An aesthetic bias also shaped the polemical objectives and tactics of the Latitudinarians. For them, simplicity was a sign of truth and complexity a mark of error. It followed that would-be simplifiers, whatever their indiscretions, were at least well-disposed, while those who were bent on complication were invariably malign. Tillotson's affirmation of the Christian character of natural religion ("the belief of a God and his providence; and of the immortality of the souls of men, and a state of rewards and punishments after this life") complemented his revulsion at the enormities of Romanism. Most churchmen followed Edward Synge, archbishop of Tuam in Ireland, and concentrated on attacking popery rather than answering Socinians. While Tillotson differed from the Unitarians on a few points of doctrine, he nonetheless praised them for having "managed the cause of the reformation, against the innovations of the church of Rome, both in doctrine and practice, with great acuteness and advantage in many respects." It seemed, moreover, that the papists had led the Socinians into their occasional deviations. Aghast at the critical researches of the Jesuit Denis Pétau and the Oratorian Richard Simon, not a few churchmen suspected that Romanists had determined "to keep their own People in ignorance, and pervert all those they call *Hereticks* to *Atheism* and *Infidelity,* that so having no *Religion* at all, they may be the better prepared again to receive theirs."[16] Gentleness was appropriate to fraternal correction, but combativeness had to inform warfare.

Scholastic theology was the machine the Roman church had employed to complicate the essential simplicity of Christianity. Only by destroying it could pristine truth be recovered. After all, Christianity was "a plain story of the life and miracles of Jesus Christ, and of his dying upon the Cross, and rising from the dead, and ascending into heaven; and a few plain precepts of life." In contrast, the Schoolmen had gratified their vanity by creating "Jargon and canting language." Believers had long been deluded into accepting it as an explanation of the Christian faith.[17]

For a generation and more, disdain for Scholasticism had been the common property of liberal Anglicans. Archbishop Laud's efforts to restore it to a place of dignity in the curriculum of Oxford had fared no better than his other enterprises, and it declined uninterruptedly at Cambridge. Few mourned the passing of the old system. Since physics and metaphysics seemed inextricably connected, the abandonment of Aristotelian natural philosophy dealt a fatal blow to the prestige of the theology identified with it. Anglicans did not undertake a concerted search for a defensible replacement. Most Caroline theologians were not professional academics, but rather busy parish priests and bishops who lacked both the training and the disposition to attend to speculative niceties. The mass of the clergy were increasingly well-educated, but their university studies were preponderantly belletristic. Whatever their technical deficiencies, theological controversialists tended to be inordinately confident of their powers of reasoning.[18]

Since men persist in thinking and questioning, there will inevitably be a need for theologians. These years were marked by unprecedented critical originality and scant apologetic creativity. When spokesmen of the church were pressed to explain what they believed, they awkwardly fell back on the only theological system available to them: the execrated categories and vocabulary of Scholasticism. Stillingfleet illustrated their dilemma. After having tried to describe universals in what he apparently intended to be the manner of Aquinas, he fulminated against "scholastic language."[19] Such inconsistency became habitual. As the patriarch of the Latitudinarians, he spent his declining years warding off objections to the Trinity from opponents who had not known the consensus of his youth. Unable either to formulate a new expression of the doctrine or to master the old theological idiom, he found himself adrift.

Antipathy to Scholasticism could also reflect suspicion — or fear — of thinking about religion. Many Anglicans wished to demarcate Jerusalem from Athens, as did Thomas Smith, in rejecting Aristotelianism because its excessive confidence in reason tended to promote heresy. Less subtly, Synge coupled a repudiation of dogmatic theology with a denial that controversy about religious articles could have an intellectual source. A frequent justification of such anti-intellectualism was the continued belief in both inherent principles and right reason, or even the confusion of these with innate ideas.[20]

Stillingfleet's works suggest that this hostility might have had an implicit basis as well. Along with others he realized that the force of national prejudice, historical and social, lay with Christianity, and hence with the Church of England. They were equally confident that prudence was ordinarily the criterion of faith. In a deferential society it was reasonable to move from these premises to a recommendation of silence in the face of doubt, particularly since learned men continued to believe. When addressing his social and intellectual equals, Synge simply contented himself with enjoining silence. Should prudence and prejudice prove insufficient inducements, the bishop of Worcester alluded to the threat which open doubt posed to public order: "Suspicion is a thing, which 'he that set Bounds to the Sea,' can set no Bounds to." An anonymous author was more direct:

I would desire the Gentlemen who either believe these [new opinions], or wish they may be so, to consider. . . . that taking away Religion is visibly contrary to their Interest: for it is by that they enjoy their estates, and are at leisure of discoursing and thinking; that they live a less drudging turbulent Life, then their Inferiors. . . . What would become of them if their Servants and Farmers, their Vassals and Dependents are of the same Opinion? There would soon be an universal uproar in the World; they would be forc'd to decide by Force and Blows, who should have the Use of any thing. As for *Property,* it would in a short time be distroyed.[21]

Having weighed the stakes, men would have had to be foolish or rootless to try to undermine the Establishment.

If divines sought to exact silence from sceptical men of property, they offered compensation in the form of easy terms of submission. Not only did their creed restrain the lower orders and thus help to maintain society, but it also gratified the ordinary expectations of responsible men: "Health of Body, Knowledge, and Understanding, and a Competency of Riches, Power and Authority," the "necessary Qualifications and Instruments for the better Performance of many of those Duties to which we stand obliged by God's Law." The pursuit of self-interest was more than barely compatible with godliness. In the view of many Latitudinarians, fulfilling the obligations imposed by the natural law — and likewise by Christianity — tended to advance men's worldly happiness.[22]

By disavowing the intellect and appealing to interest in order to justify religion, these clergymen were tempted to dismiss the possiblity of an honestly doubting mind. If they had so widened the gate, why did some persist in declining their invitation to enter? While Tillotson argued that evil habits sometimes kept men from accepting the truth, Stillingfleet dismissed the possibility of denying it for merely intellectual reasons.[23] Turpitude was usually the cause. John Williams was expressing what had become a platitude when he titled the fifth of his Boyle lectures "Immorality and Pride the Great Cause of Atheism." Such increasing dependence on *ad hominem* arguments hardly suggests forensic self-confidence.

Both the appeal to interest and the resolution of Christianity into good conduct depended on the view of the relation of church and nation general among Englishmen. From the Elizabethan period the Church of England had been seen as an expression of nationality. The conviction had united such diverse writers as Hooker and Milton, and it remained a watchword in 1700. Despite the trauma of 1689, the High-Church party did not abandon its longstanding belief in the comprehensiveness of Anglicanism, though its expression of that belief was idiosyncratic. Atterbury was willing to use the Occasional Conformity Act to compel the adherence of "such, as indeed have no Religion at the

bottom, nor any Notion of a Church," because he believed that to be
English was to be Anglican. Similarly, Archbishop Sharp treated *church*
and *nation* as interchangeable expressions. The notion retained its appeal to Dissenters, for the collapse of the Presbyterian-Congregational
union in the mid-1690s redirected the attention of Presbyterian leaders
to Anglican moderates.[24] For them, St. Stephen's, Westminster, was a
more powerful symbol than either Geneva or Edinburgh.

Tillotson, the chief Anglican moderate, was convinced that, by rejecting papal pretensions, Protestants had achieved fundamental agreement. His younger colleague, Humphrey Prideaux, thought that those
who had "drawn the abstrusest niceties into Controversy" bore primary
responsibility for perpetuating unnecessary rifts. No irreconcilable
differences about ecclesiology separated the two groups. For his part,
Richard Baxter, the doyen of Nonconformity, affirmed that Christ "intended to set up his Government in Power by Christian Princes, as soon
as his Word and Providence had ripened the Church for it." Divisions
had grown up within these national entities because of clerical ignorance
and immorality rather than dogmatic disputes. Baxter's Erastianism was
to be emphatically repeated by William Wake, a future archbishop of
Canterbury, in what became an influential treatise on church polity.[25]

Presbyterians were at least as suspicious of any dogmatic rigidity, including their own formulas, as Anglican moderates. Baxter's disciple,
John Humfrey, was convinced that theological disputes were for the
most part a "vein shew" directed by "Prejudice and Party." With candor
and minimal effort disputants could achieve reconciliation. For his
part, he refused to captivate his understanding to Luther, Calvin, or
the Westminster Confession. Humfrey could not have suspected that
Tillotson, himself a Presbyterian in his youth, sought to enthrall him.
That prelate never imagined himself infallible and believed that any
peculiar apostolic authority had ended with the death of the last apostle. In his denunciation of Roman pretensions, Tillotson maintained:
"there is no *visible judge* (how much soever he may pretend to infallibility) to whose determination and decision in matters of faith and practice necessary to salvation, Christians are bound to submit." In
moments of fervor, he was led to imply that uniformity of belief was
impossible, that "none could be guilty of unbelief but those who had
immediate revelation made to them."[26]

Here as elsewhere, Synge managed to order Tillotson's homiletic
randomness. He established three criteria for accepting a doctrine: it

must be intelligible, agreeable to "the self-evident Principles of Reason," and demonstrable by "solid Argument, either from Reason or Scripture." Like Taylor, Synge conceived of tradition as authoritative when it was unquestioned. That time having passed, it could no longer bind. Since only the powers of preaching and excommunication were "given to the Church immediately by God," all its other prerogatives and institutions were to be decided by the civil authority. He knew that "the Apprehensions of Men are so very different (especially in such things as, being remote from our Senses, are matter only of rational speculation)." Accordingly, in matters of opinion the right of excommunication had to be exercised with severe restraint. Because the church was comprehensive, the magistrate was unable either to inquire into or to coerce the consciences of individuals. Synge's position was representative. Sharing the universal revulsion at polemical divinity, Richard Willis was quick to assure Dissenters that the established church required of her communicants merely that they "examine the Truth of what she teaches by the Holy Scriptures" and reach their own conclusions.[27]

Although the Bible remained the religion of Protestants, developments in epistemology and hermeneutics were turning Chillingworth's boast into an incantation. For this generation the proposition seemed to have both a negative and a positive aspect. On the one hand it was impossible to admit affirmations about what Boyle termed "privileged things" without sufficient evidence. On the other hand it was probable that anyone who approached the Bible in a spirit of impartial searching and honesty would discover the essentials of faith.[28] The confidence of Jewel and Laud in an innate capacity which, under the guidance of the Holy Spirit, led men to grasp truth had been transformed.

While not unchallenged, the assumption of the accuracy of Holy Writ (or at least the decorous New Testament) remained general among churchmen. In 1675, for example, Stillingfleet, after cautioning the deists against reducing the Gospels to "a confused heap of indigested Stuff," proceeded from an argument based on their veracity to a set of hypotheses. He was left with the task of determining the exegetical means by which doctrines could be derived from texts, or rather how one of several possible interpretations might be imposed on them. He began with the bland pledge that interpreters were free to exercise their reason fully, since "the more we do so, the sooner we shall come to Satisfaction in this matter." Difficulties arose when he proposed his general rules. One had to accept that construction

(1) Which is most plain and easie and agreeable to the most received Sense of Words.

(2) Which suits most with the Scope and Design not only of the particular Places, but of the whole *New Testament;* which is, to magnifie God and to depress Man.

(3) Which hath been generally received in the Christian Church.

(4) Which best agrees with the Characters of those Persons from whom we receive the Christian Faith; and those are Christ Jesus and his holy Apostles.[29]

Since three of his criteria presumed assent to the traditional dogmas of the church (even in its corrupt medieval embodiment), their acceptability to all disputants was problematic. It was perhaps this consideration which led Stillingfleet to emphasize his first criterion. Synge was more realistic when he affirmed that "a sober and honest Enquirer" cannot "easily be mistaken" in interpreting the places in the New Testament which contain necessary truths. By implication, when responsible controversy about the intent of a passage arose, it ceased to contain necessary truths.[30] Once this exemption was admitted, the Bible presented fewer problems of exposition than it had a half-century earlier.

Insisting on the necessity of plainness and of ease of interpretation affected the Latitudinarians' conception of the nature and end of revelation. Tillotson saw it as the means "to inform the world certainly of the mind and will of God," to which purpose "the inspired penmen were so far assisted as was necessary." He remained cautiously vague about the extent of this assistance. Rejecting allegory, any "over-laboured and far-fetched interpretation," and other tools of a "lively imagination," he shared the first of Stillingfleet's rules: "all things necessary to be believed and practised by Christians, in order to their eternal salvation, are plainly contained in the holy scriptures." Tillotson's repeated insistence on the unofficial character of any doctrinal pronouncement "since the declaration of the gospel" was tantamount to a rejection of the other three.[31]

What did he mean when he declared the Bible's message to be plain?

Any man of ordinary capacity, by his own diligence and care, in conjunction with the helps and advantages which God hath appointed, and in the due use of them, may attain to the knowledge of every thing necessary to his salvation; and that there is no book in the world more plain, and better fitted to teach a man any art or science, than the Bible is to direct and instruct men in the way to heaven.

His explanation had serious implications for the content of a religion which purported to rest on one book. In order to become an official doctrine, a proposition had to be "clearly and plainly declared in the gospel," and recognition of such clarity and plainness need not always result from divine guidance. Confidence in the natural comprehensibility of revealed truths was not peculiar to Tillotson. As he realized, it was a corollary of the widespread assumption that truth and obscurity are antithetical. Besides dispensing with the agency of the Holy Spirit, such reasonableness tempted churchmen to flirt with the idea that Scripture should be read with the same critical presuppositions which applied in studying a profane text.[32]

Ecclesiastics of Tillotson's era increasingly relied on the miracles recorded in the New Testament as proofs of its extraordinary character. Since they failed to distinguish between public revelation and particular intervention, their reliance had a paradoxical consequence. In order to buttress its integral authority and to undercut the papist appeal to tradition, they came to insist that such intervention had ended with the death of the author of Revelation. Differentiating between the God of revelation and faith who both acts upon and is known to individuals through history and another God of nature and reason known to all men through logic, J. G. A. Pocock has described the implications of this insistence: "if there have been no revelations and no miracles since the lifetimes of the Christians who knew Jesus as a man, then the God who acts positively to rule and redeem his peculiar people is not immediately present to us now." The practical naturalism of the Latitudinarians shaped their appreciation of the achievement of revelation.

As for the *revealed religion*, the only design of that is, to revive and improve the natural notions which we have of God, and all our reasonings about divine revelation are necessarily gathered by our natural notions of religion. . . . But if any doctrine be proposed to him, which pretends to come from God, he measures it by those steady and sure notions which he hath of the divine nature and perfections, and by those he will easily discern whether it is worthy of God, or not, and likely to proceed from him. . . . If it is not, though "an Angel from heaven" should bring it, he will not receive it.[33]

The necessity of an act of faith, an individual's recognition and acceptance of an incarnate God, was the redoubt of the God of history in the Augustan religious sensibility. Latitudinarians by no means denied the necessity of faith, but their conception of it was also affected by the

new idea of reason. Adopting a tactic which would become commonplace, Tillotson defined any exercise of assent as fiduciary. His
definition in effect deprived the Christian profession of its singularity.
Standards of reason resembling those governing the acceptance of
scientific propositions should control religious commitment. In Tillotson's view, what had been seen as the exemplary case of stark faith, the
narrative of Abraham's attempted sacrifice of Isaac, was susceptible of
a tolerably reasonable construction. Insisting on both the fallibility and
naturalness of Christian assent tended to limit the range and efficacy of
the Spirit's activity. He had always to work within the confines of order
and propriety. As a result, Synge concluded, "the great and necessary
Truths of Religion" were "plain and evident to every sober and inquisitive Person."[34]

Since agreement on these verities had been unaccountably delayed,
men had to find a makeshift. Tillotson thought its essence lay in the
cultivation of sincerity, "a simplicity of mind and manners, in our car-
riage and conversation one towards another" and in devotion to God.
Among the signs of this attitude were a "constant tenor of goodness in
the general course of our lives" and an obedience to God which was
"uniform and universal, equally respecting all the laws of God, and
every part of our duty." Unlike theological propositions, sincerity presented evidence of things seen.[35] Having regularized the act of faith,
the Latitudinarians were on the verge of transforming Christianity into
natural morality.

The fate of virtuous pagans has been a problem for Christian
apologists since Justin Martyr. As Dante's consignment of Aristotle to
tranquil hopelessness in limbo was an unacceptable model, Anglicans
trying to cope with this embarrassment had two alternatives: damnation or bestowing baptism *honoris causa*. For clerics unsettled by Calvin's
influence on the Thirty-Nine Articles, promiscuous reprobation was
not an option. Once more Tillotson led the way. Those who were ig-
norant of the Gospel would be condemned "for sinning against the law
written on their hearts" rather than for any unbelief. Like their predecessors, the Anglican rationalists did not fail to appeal either to the
presumed existence of a universal set of moral principles or to an
innate religious faculty in an attempt to demonstrate Christianity's fundamental reasonableness. They were, however, more venturesome in
endeavoring to assert simultaneously that idiosyncratic Christian
teachings were true and that conformity to the discipline of natural

religion was sufficient for salvation.[36] It occurred to few of them that
their course might eventually change these doctrines into ornamental
vestiges.

The Latitudinarians' antipathy toward the systematic theological expression of their beliefs sustained their incomprehension. Willis spoke
for them when he disavowed the confusion of religion with "little
Tricks." It should be seen, rather, as "solid and substantial Goodness;
such as is for the Good of the World, for the Advancement of our own
Nature, and tends to make us pious and holy, and as like God as may
be." If Christianity was "beyond all subtlety of Disputation," more than
the satisfaction of "curiosity," a matter of "Faith and Obedience" instead
of "wit and cunning," then anyone who avoided evil and did good was a
Christian.[37]

Often epistemological lag and the vicissitudes of controversy
resulted in paradox or contradiction. Tillotson, for example, was
sometimes confident of the existence of a moral sense which led men to
imitate the good when it was presented to them. Yet on other occasions
he portrayed the acceptance of the tenets of natural religion as one of
the many acts of faith which filled his mental landscape. Notwithstanding such ambiguity, a vision of the character of natural religion and its
relation to Christianity informs his sermons. "Obedience to the natural
law" was normative, and the "positive rites and institutions of revealed
religion are so far from intrenching upon the laws of nature, that they
were always designed to be subordinate and subservient to them; and
whenever they come in competition, it is the declared will of God that
positive institutions should give way to natural duties." At root the two
dispensations were identical, since "the great design of the Christian
religion was to restore and reinforce the practice of the natural law, or,
which is all one, of moral duties." The sole advantage of the new order
was to make "our duty more clear and certain, by means of rewards
and the promise of assistance."[38]

The primary injunctions of natural law were clear: "That we should
behave ourselves reverently and obediently towards the divine Majesty, and justly and charitably towards men; and that, in order to the
fitting of us better for the discharge of these duties, we should govern
ourselves in the use of sensual delights with temperance and moderation." Only professed atheists formally rejected them by repudiating
their two props, belief in God and in personal immortality. Among the
secondary natural obligations to which Tillotson subordinated positive

institutions was the responsibility of mothers to nurse their infants. When considering the two great injunctions of the law, the love of God and of neighbor, which Christ had reaffirmed, he treated them as separable and maintained that "the second seems to have the advantage in the reality of its effects." As a result, "moral duties and virtues are the same with Christian graces, and with that holiness and righteousness which the gospel requires, and differ only in the name and notion." For Tillotson, the "greatest heresy in the world is a wicked life."[39] Having transformed grace from a divine gift into a human attainment, he never enumerated the lesser, culpable heresies.

Dryden distrusted the comfort of the emerging orthodoxy. Convinced that some divines had "too much exalted the faculties of our souls" by asserting the self-evidentness of the religion of nature, he suggested that its principles were "unattainable by our discourse." In parrying such thrusts, Tillotson and his epigones were able to cite endorsements of the creeds from their works.[40] But when confronted with the unavoidable question of the Gospel, "Whom do men say that I am?" and the resultant problems of original sin, soteriology, justification, and sanctification, they responded uncertainly. Even if they were unable to draw a logical deduction from their position, viz., that Christ, however admirable, was dispensable, others did not fail to do so.

When the Anglican rationalists alluded to the role of dogma, they were consistent. Having identified culpable heresy with wickedness, Tillotson rebuked those who were preoccupied with orthodoxy for obstructing the practice of true Christianity. Well-intentioned practitioners need not trouble themselves about these notional quibbles. To them he addressed a soothing exegesis of "If any man will come after me, let him deny himself, and take up his cross and follow me." He summarized his religion in the sermon "Of the Form, and the Power of Godliness," which includes a tirade against the figure who dominates the eleventh canto of Dante's *Il Paradiso*. St. Francis was

magnified scarcely for any other reason, but for saying and doing the most silly and ridiculous things. . . . As if nastiness was a Christian grace. These and many more such freaks which are related in his life, as instances of his great sanctity, save to no other purpose, but to render ridiculous to any man of common sense. As if to be a spiritual man, and a mere natural, are all one, and as if this is a good consequence, that a man cannot chuse to be very knowing in religion, because he is very silly in all other things; and must need have abundance of grace, because he hath no wit.

For Tillotson, paradise was not the "dry and sapless" beatific vision, but rather "the sum of all religion, the whole duty of man," a sort of eternal Society for the Reformation of Manners.[41]

The failure of either Tillotson or Synge ever to preach on 1 Corinthians 2:5 ("That your faith should not stand in the wisdom of men, but in the power of God") was consonant with their reluctance to stress the particularity of Christianity. Tillotson once ventured to describe the elements peculiar to the Gospel. Fundamental to it was the belief "that Jesus Christ, the son of God, was a person commissioned from Heaven and employed by God to bring men to eternal happiness." On this occasion his repugnance against "hard words" kept him from explicating the Incarnation. Whatever Christ's nature, his heavenly mandate required "an assent of the understanding" to everything which he "delivered to the world." In order to secure his benefits and promises, it was necessary to rely on him and to obey "all his laws and commands."[42]

Such flirtations with dogmatism were rare, and in his more congenial, irenic moods Tillotson maintained that the positive enactments of Christianity were limited to two sacraments and some elaborations of the natural law. None of them was very troublesome. At the moment of death the crucial factor in determining men's fates would be whether "our profession of the Christian religion hath evidenced itself in the virtue of a good life, in the constant course and tenor of an holy and unblameable conversation." Understandably, the greatest English preacher of the age ignored a stock figure of the homiletic repertoire, the good thief of Luke 23. Practice rather than conviction was the sum of Tillotson's religion. When the more thorough Synge undertook to list twenty-one tenets of gentlemanly Christianity, only the last, the existence of angels, was not implicit in Lord Herbert of Cherbury's five self-evident propositions of natural religion. Synge tactfully suggested that it was less than decisive. As he affirmed elsewhere, "God will never be offended" at a sincere "Error of the Understanding".[43]

The specific challenge "But whom say ye that I am?" perplexed the Anglican rationalists. At times Tillotson referred to "the depravation of our nature." Still, by failing clearly to relate the Incarnation to original sin and insisting that Christianity is compatible with ordinary reason, he blunted such references. He could paint so bleak a picture of man's natural condition that the weakest sign of rational or moral life amounted to a reflection of divine energy. As he neglected to shade his portrait with Calvin's contempt for every merely human activity, he managed to turn all helpful actions into tokens of divine favor. A coherent soteriology eluded him. Once the juridical events of Calvary were over, well-intentioned individuals were able to "aspire so much as is possible to become like" Christ in the assurance of receiving divine assistance in proportion to their own enterprise. Tillotson was vague about the role of a mediator in creating such aspirations. Notwithstanding his vagueness he was confident that the question contained little mystery. By identifying justification with "the whole Christian religion" after having reduced Christianity to the disciplinary promptings of the moral sense, he virtually guaranteed that he would achieve clarity.[44]

Despite his unrivaled prestige, the archbishop of Canterbury almost came to grief in his effort to construct a bark that would accommodate all who opposed papal pretensions. Try as he might, he could not escape the existence of ecclesiastical parties which were at loggerheads over theological questions. Less supple divines abhorred his willingness to relieve those who chafed under the doctrinal burden of the Thirty-Nine Articles. They were certain that the "Christian Religion is founded upon . . . Mysterious and Supernatural Truths, and the Principles of it are . . . paradoxical to the received opinions of Mankind," that mysteries alone give meaning to religious faith.[45]

When forced to discuss the Trinity, Tillotson could affirm that it "is still a great mystery, and so imperfectly revealed, as to be in a great measure incomprehensible by human reason." Such diffidence was as uncharacteristic as it was uncongenial. Elsewhere, he averred that "the Scriptures do deliver this doctrine of the Trinity without any manner of doubt." His distaste for mysteries was too fixed to allow him to do more than grudgingly admit that Christianity might contain them. In his mind, the disclosures of revelation conformed to the same standard of clarity and distinctness which typified the discoveries of reason: "the books of scripture are sufficiently plain, as to all things necessary to be believed and practised"; "no other doctrines which are not sufficiently revealed in scripture, either in express terms, or by plain and necessary consequence . . . are to be esteemed any part of that faith in religion"; "the scriptures are a perfect rule; and that all things are plainly contained in them which concern faith and life." By extension, principles of reasonableness had to control the interpretation of the Bible. God was innocent not only of contradiction but also of any other violation of reason. He did not expect men to assent to tenets they deemed absurd. In those few places where the Bible was uncertain, Tillotson implied that reason had to prevail.[46] His plea for a balance between the divine word and the human intellect was doomed. Other exegetes were multiplying instances of uncertainty and thus resorting more frequently to the arbitration of reason.

A variable standard came to govern the church's reaction to different kinds of exponents of this critical style. Positions that some of her communicants were proclaiming with impunity, a few of her lower clergy were inclined to transmit stealthily, and her leaders were learning to avoid. Sir Robert Howard, a privy councilor and Dryden's brother-in-law, maintained that since each man was bound to work out his own salvation, believers enjoyed a right of unfettered inquiry. Because of the clergy's usurpation of the privilege of defining the Christian faith, dissension had grown endemic. In order to subjugate a restive laity, priests had become specialists in devising and enforcing mysterious dogmas. Notwithstanding this bill of indictment, Howard presented himself as an Anglican in his *History of Religion* (1694). After selecting a tag from Archbishop Tillotson, he went on to pay obeisance to the commonplaces of Latitudinarianism: he repudiated Scholastic theology and defined culpable heresy as misconduct rather than as erroneous opinion. Unlike the primate, however, Howard went on to deny that Christianity could hold mysteries in the pagan sense of "divine secrets." Christ had sought to enlighten humanity, and so it was "a Matter of Astonishment that the Humour and Affectation of 'Mystery' should continue, when Religion and Faith were so wholly altered" by him.[47] Howard thus championed the distinctive position of the Socinians, but he died without forfeiting his offices. Among the gentility such secure heterodoxy was no longer anomalous.

While Arthur Bury, D.D., the rector of Exeter College, Oxford, was more cautious than Howard in explaining the implications of Latitudinarianism, his prominence in the citadel of the High-Church movement rendered the very effort foolhardy. He, too, began by upbraiding clerics, particularly those who adhered to Scholasticism, for having multiplied dogmas in order to dominate the laity. He went on to depict heresy as incorrigibility. It followed that once the essentials of Christianity had been rendered "clear and plain," sincere persons would be able to coexist despite their continuing differences. It was imperative "to turn Mens Minds from the study of Opinions and Speculations to Practical Piety."[48] Like Tillotson, he saw faith as an obedience which embodied a series of dispositions. Having rejected conciliar and other non-biblical authority, he proposed reason as the ultimate exegetical guide. He did so in order to ease a tension which plagued the Latitudinarians. In their hermeneutics they had tried to accommodate both the right of every individual to interpret the Bible as he saw fit and the insistence that articles of faith could only be established on the basis of express revelation and comprehensibility. Faced with a babel of interpretations, Bury turned to the one apparent principle of coherence.[49]

Although Bury shared the Latitudinarians' resolve to demonstrate that Christianity merely confirmed the tenets of natural religion, he disdained their judicious reserve toward apparently recalcitrant dogmas. If in "its largest Edition the Gospel . . . exceedeth not two Doctrines . . . Repent and Believe," then all other articles were either elaborative or superfluous. For him, the beliefs proposed by the New Testament invariably corresponded to the discoveries of unaided reason. Sometimes his judgments proved to be more curious than unsettling. The dogmas of the remission of sin and the resurrection, for example, were plainly stated in the New Testament because they were implicit in two of the self-evident teachings of the religion of nature, viz., providence and immortality. At other times he was recklessly provocative, as when he asserted that monotheism, which was known to all rational beings, associated Christianity with Islam. This common element was more important than any points of disagreement. He raised the problem of canonicity, another area which Tillotson had avoided, in order to provide a means of eliminating some conspicuous differences between the religions. The Bible had suffered from "Carelessness of Copiers, Fraud of Hereticks, or Dust of Time," as well as from deletions and emendations wrought by its interested custodians.[50] Armed with such a scalpel, his readers would be able to excise awkward texts.

The assumption that revealed religion presumed incomprehensible mysteries impeded the acceptance of his inclusive formula. Bury tried to uproot it. He found two meanings of the word *mystery* in the New Testament: "a Spiritual Truth wrapt up in a Sensible," and "a truth hidden from some Ages . . . but then 'made manifest': or from some 'Persons.' " Clerics had exploited the intrinsically harmless second definition to obfuscate and to dominate the laity. While conceding the existence of "a Mysteriousness, which, though it contradict not, Exceedeth humane Reason," he endeavored to make such mysteries intelligible. In his pursuit of this goal, he went so far as to assert that the dogma of the Trinity was implicit in natural religion. In order to vindicate this paradox he adopted a kind of modalism, resolving the three persons into properties of one God, mind, wisdom, and will. He considered the belief that "God might be *manifest* 'in the Flesh' " to be an instance of a "Spiritual Truth wrapt up in a Sensible." Censuring further inquiry into the Incarnation as fruitless and dangerous, he defined the object of Christian faith: "As therefore in the face of Jesus Christ we see more of the Father's goodness, so are we thereby obliged to higher strains of love to him and one another, which is the sum of Natural Religion."[51]

Had Bury's administration of Exeter been tranquil, his *Naked Gospel* would still have won him numerous enemies. As it was, the college was plagued by a rancor notable even by generous academic standards. In the summer of 1690 longstanding foes among his colleagues, abetted by the episcopal visitor, hauled him before convocation, which condemned the book. Admitting that he had intended to conciliate the Unitarians, Bury quietly dropped his analysis of mystery from the second edition.[52] While this act of tardy discretion may have postponed his fate, it did not save him. He was deprived of his university position in 1694, but he remained as a rector of Bampton, Oxford. Reduced to the state of an ordinary parson, he felt free to expand his original argument for the benefit of the deists.

Interest in Bury's plight extended beyond Great Britain. Jean Le Clerc's *Bibliothèque universelle et historique* had offered Continental readers a lengthy and sympathetic abridgment of *The Naked Gospel,* and Le Clerc himself appears to have written a defense of the book that was published in English in an attempt to forestall official action against it. His solicitude was understandable. From its beginnings as a self-conscious movement, Dutch Arminianism had been determinedly undogmatic, anticlerical, and anticonfessional. In some respects, its history parallels that of another legatee of Erasmus, the Church of England. Like the Anglicans, the Remonstrants were confident that, because of the natural human capacity for understanding Scripture, they would be able to reconstitute legitimate biblical Christianity. They sought at once to preserve inherited truth and to discard accumulated error. After they had been disappointed in their expectation, they embarked on a policy of doctrinal retrenchment. Le Clerc defined its principle: such arcane matters as Scripture had not determined and reason could not comprehend must remain moot.[53] Unlike the Anglicans, the Remonstrants disdained comfortable muddle. Their spokesmen were competent theologians who systematically pursued their objective.

Le Clerc's *De l'incrédulité* (1696), which Toland would translate in 1697, embodied many of the Remonstrants' characteristic themes. While it was "not necessary to have an exact and distinct 'Idea' " of a proposition before assenting to it, God did not make "Mysteries in Religion altogether incomprehensible only to humble Men," since "no body can believe what he understands not at all." The assurance that "his Disposition is good and conformable to Reason" allowed an individual to accept a doctrine. Because Le Clerc believed that common sense could guide any honest person to Christlike behavior, he was confident that all good men participated in true Christianity. Their conduct provided a statement of their religion more telling than the formal expression of mere opinions. For his part, he saw prudent doubt as both a desirable attribute of Christians and a rebuke to slothful prejudice.[54]

This pamplet was a cautious popularization of the technical works in which Le Clerc sought to apply Lockianism to the reconstruction of Christian theology. His effort was governed by a preconception: whenever the New Testament referred to a mystery, it did not mean something which was inherently unintelligible, but rather a truth which had been hidden or obscure before its revelation by Christ. He thought that he found in Locke's *Essay concerning Human Understanding* a way of purging Christianity of any mysteriousness. For him, the book's value lay in its analysis of intellection, which vindicated the thoroughgoing rationality of essential Christian beliefs. Although the first English edition of the complete *Essay* would be more tentative, the French draft that Le Clerc printed in the *Bibliothèque* in 1688 had emphasized the superiority of clear and distinct ideas over obscure and confused ones in the attainment of every form of cognition. Both simple and complex ideas could exhibit clarity and distinctness. These qualities marked any complex idea if its simple constituents were clear and distinct, and "their number and their order are clearly fixed and governed in the mind." Certitude occurred whenever the intellect formed such ideas, and, in Le Clerc's view, only certain propositions were able to command assent. Properly understood, Christianity offered no revelations which were contrary to the plain and evident findings of reason, and so its necessary articles were credible.[55] Le Clerc's redaction of Locke was distorted insofar as it rested on a selective reading of a draft whose completed form was richer and subtler. Although it avoided nuance, this version was plausible and influential. Not only was John Toland introduced to the *Essay* by it, but he appears also to have taken it as an authoritative interpretation of Locke's argument.

Limborch, the other leading Remonstrant theologian of the period, mirrored these notions. Two theses underlay his work. He maintained that anyone who grounded his life in Scripture would be immune to fatal error. At the same time he insisted that there was no single rule for interpreting it. Such permissiveness meant that even formal heresy was entitled to respect insofar as it was creative, though anything which partook of papal authoritarianism was of the Antichrist. Speculation over and above the ascertainable contents of revelation had to be avoided. The only necessity for salvation was belief in Jesus Christ, a standard that amounted to an invitation to ambiguity.[56]

But how was salvation achieved? In Limborch's view, "Justification is the merciful and gracious act of God, whereby he absolves from all guilt the truly penitent and believing soul, through and because of Jesus Christ apprehended by a true faith, or freely remits sins because of faith in Jesus Christ, and graciously imputes that faith as righteousness." Whether this proposition was to work to include or to exclude depended on the definition of a "truly penitent and believing soul" (*resipiscentem ac credentem*). Since Limborch believed that those who resisted the operations of divine grace (*qui divinae gratiae operationibus resistunt*) were damned, that not merely believers who faithfully obeyed God, but virtuous pagans as well, were saved, his conception of belief and penitence was apparently open. In a dialogue "between a Christian and a learned Jew" he discounted Christ's divinity as a speculation neither explicitly advanced in the New Testament nor essential to salvation. He could do so because he refused to identify the universal saving will of God, to which all who behaved morally owed their deliverance, with the sacrifice of Christ.[57]

The sentiments of Le Clerc and Limborch help to explain both the accusations of foes that they were Socinians and the compliments which English Unitarians paid them. Despite their compatibility, such judgments probably shed more light on the fears and desires of their authors than on the character of Dutch Arminianism. Still, it is indisputable that the Remonstrants regularly took up the cause of English theological liberalism, whether fashionable or unfashionable. The Unitarian tracts received at least their fair share of the attention lavished on foreign works of divinity in the *Bibliothèque*. Similarly, in 1708 when Matthew Tindal found himself charged with deism because of his obstreperous anticlericalism, Le Clerc defended him in print just as he had Bury twenty years earlier.[58] The Remonstrants may not have taught Toland that there were no enemies on the left, but their example must have intimated to him that they considered such foes to be few and far between.

Intellectual historians often seem to obey a finicking etiquette which prescribes that a first-rate respectability be segregated from a second-rate commonality. Professor Yolton, for example, has chastised the antideist scribblers for assuming that "the serious writers, such as Locke and Tindal, were advocates of frivolous doctrines like those held by the coffee-house frequenters."[59] Locke's preoccupation with separating himself from anyone who had become disreputable might almost seem to justify this procedure. Yet, as his treatment of Toland indicates, his efforts were more often recuperative than prophylactic. In fact, attempts to isolate Locke's concerns from those of lesser neologists, however discreditable, can distort the evidence. The gap in ability between Locke and Tindal was forbidding, but they can be mentioned together. Both Tindal and Toland were habitués of taverns. Like them and other reflective contemporaries, Locke was endeavoring to rebottle old wine. While his endeavor may have been singular in the brilliance of its conception and execution, his controversy with Stillingfleet suggests that, in some respects, it differed neither in kind nor in effect from theirs.

From his young manhood, Locke had found the multiplication of dogmas distasteful: "if schisms and heresies be traced up to their original causes, it would be found that they have sprung chiefly from the multiplying articles of faith, and narrowing the bottom of religion by clogging it with creeds, and catechisms, and endless niceties about the essences, properties, and attributes of God." Christianity had a particularly bleak record, and the pretensions and crotchets of its priesthood were "the cause of more disorders, tumults and bloodsheds than all other causes put together." Even though his early confidence in a religious *consensus gentium* would wear thin, he was firm in insisting that reluctance "to consult reason in the things of religion" had led men "into so strange opinions and extravagant practices . . . that a considerate man cannot but stand amazed at their follies." He wrestled with a dilemma. If the idea of God intervening in history was offensive to him, he was disinclined to allow that the uniform working of God in the realm of morals was intuitively knowable. His equivocal attitude toward both revealed and natural religion may have fed his abhorrence of nagging doubters. He sought to assist the progressive labors of "the builders" rather than the destructiveness of "the finders of faults, the confuters, and putters down."[60]

Celibate sociability moved Locke to try to realize his constructiveness by joining or founding a number of religious discussion societies. In addition to participating in the Latitudinarian meetings, he, together with Benjamin Furly, the expatriate Quaker who later befriended Toland, organized one in Rotterdam in the late 1680s. Its principles embodied the shibboleths of Anglican rationalism: credenda could be derived only from revelation; sincerity should animate all members, whatever their points of view; the essence of Christianity was moral, not speculative. In 1687, he cooperated with Limborch and Le Clerc in establishing another association in Amsterdam. While affirming the fundamentally ethical character of religion, its charter was more tolerant of the application of the intellect to belief. To be admitted, one had to produce "a good testimony from some of the society that knows him" and to affirm that "he loves and seeks truth for truth's sake; and will endeavor impartially to find and communicate it to others." Back in London after the Glorious Revolution he collaborated in the "Dry Club," which numbered among its members the Socinian William Popple.[61] These human connections at once manifested and fostered a congruence of outlook, which frequently received public expression. It is notable that Locke's publishers, the Churchills, were specialists in works of advanced divinity. In 1697 their catalogue would include Archbishop Synge's *A Gentleman's Religion,* Samuel Bold's crypto-Unitarian *A Short Discourse of the True Knowledge of Christ Jesus,* and Toland's translation of Le Clerc's *De l'incrédulité.*

The tension between the will to believe and the temptation to doubt which pervades Locke's religious writings makes it difficult to determine the nature of his mature opinions. At the end of his life he remained uncertain about some central theological problems. Nevertheless, it may be possible to ascertain at least a few of the occasions on which he passed from uncertainty and confusion to obfuscation. As he believed that the hostility of civil authorities had led Christ to be cautious—or to dissemble—and himself scrutinized contemporary cases of persecution, he had both precedent and warrant for a policy of reserve. He was, moreover, sensitive to the frailties of ordinary people. Had all men been reasonable, there would have been no need for revelation: "*Reason,* speaking never so clearly to the wise and Virtuous, had never Authority enough to prevail on the Multitude."[62]

Stillingfleet's reaction to his interpretation of Locke's views is as important for understanding the fragmentation of Latitudinarianism in the later 1690s as the views themselves. Recognizing the theological welter within the church and reluctant to aggravate disunity in the face of the popish menace, the bishop of Worcester had suppressed his reservations about recent speculation concerning the fundamental tenets of Christianity, particularly the Trinity. By the last decade of the century the situation had so far deteriorated that he could no longer remain silent. The Socinians had resumed publication, thereby violating the convention that respect "for the common interest of Christianity among us" should prevail over "mens busie and indiscreet zeal for their own particular opinions." Because of the climate of infidelity, unhappy disputes about " 'the Mysteries of the Christian Faith' " were threatening the survival of revealed religion. The success of the High-Church party in giving their political campaign against the Revolution Settlement the specious appearance of a defense of orthodoxy may also have helped to revive Stillingfleet. Disdaining the safe pursuit of small quarry, he joined the effort to run the great Locke to ground, to reveal him as an accomplice of the anti-Trinitarians.[63]

With considerable discernment Stillingfleet traced the present difficulties to the abandonment of the older, more inclusive definition of reason. Locke and lesser "Smatterers in Ideas" had erred. Far from constituting reason, certainty of ideas merely manifested its operation. Toland was faithful to Locke in insisting that, in order to acknowledge anything, one must first have a clear and distinct idea of it. Although the simple ideas which represented individual entities met this criterion, the complex ideas needed to represent universals did not. Their reality was, Stillingfleet concluded, uncertain. The implications of his conclusion were harrowing. It was now possible to deny the existence of a spiritual substance in man, for matter, whose nature remained unknown, might be capable of generating thought. Furthermore, considering universals as names and signs, rather than as realities, obliterated the distinction between nature and person which underlay the Trinitarian formula: "if there is nothing really, but an individuated Essence, then it must follow, that there can be no difference of Hypostases in the same Nature. For Nature individuated must take in the Hypostases; and Nature being taken as common is affirmed by you to be nothing but an Abstract and Complex Idea, and a mere Nominal Essence."[64]

In addition to these epistemological perplexities, Stillingfleet faced the erosion of confidence in Scripture wrought by the Unitarians' insinuations against the legitimacy of the canon. And if this burden were not heavy enough, he had also to manage the defense of his late friend, Tillotson, against charges of heresy, while simultaneously evading many of the fundamentals of the Latitudinarianism they had helped to create. His campaign lurched from irony to irony. In defense of the integrity of the Bible, he appealed to the discarded tradition of the church catholic. When discussing the problem of universals in order to explicate the doctrine of the Trinity, he awkwardly resorted to the idioms and technique of the execrated Scholasticism.[65]

The impossibility of Stillingfleet's position did not assuage Locke's embarrassment and apprehension at being linked with coffeehouse frequenters like Toland and the Socinians. He had one aim, to dissociate himself from them, and he pursued it doggedly: "Nothing but my Book and my words being quoted, the World will be apt to think that I am the Person who argue against the Trinity, and deny Mysteries, against whom your Lordship directs those Pages." By misconstruing Locke's mature epistemology, Stillingfleet had eased his task. In the *Essay* Locke neither advanced a clear-cut sensationalism nor denied that complex ideas were legitimate objects of knowledge. He was nevertheless careful to make his acceptance of the manifold "Faculties of the Mind" clearer in his rejoinder than it was in book 3 of that work. Studiedly ignoring Le Clerc as well as Toland, he insisted that he did not know at whom Stillingfleet was aiming his refutation of the proposition that " 'Certainty' [lies] only in 'clear and distinct Ideas.' " He had placed it "in the clear and visible Connection of any of our Ideas, be those Ideas what they will." He allowed, however, that clear and distinct ideas of things permitted better, fuller, and clearer "Discourse and Reason" about them.[66]

Before adverting matter-of-factly to the certitude produced by demonstration, Locke tried to show how his system provided for the reality of substance:

> by the clear ideas of thinking in me, I find the agreement of the clear idea of existence, and the obscure idea of a substance in me, because I perceive the necessary idea of thinking, and the relative idea of a support; which support, without having any clear and distinct idea of what it is, beyond this relative one of a support, I call substance.

It was impossible to demonstrate that human beings possess a spiritual substance which is immaterial. Even so, he was confident that he had sustained the principle that they possess a "thinking Substance" which is spiritual. Since he had proved the existence of God, the ultimate spiritual substance, by appealing to the principle of sufficient reason, his tentativeness about the existence of an immaterial element in man had no wider implications.[67]

If Stillingfleet blundered by taking Locke's analysis of the idea of substance as an assertion of the fancifulness of substance itself, Locke's procedure was no more graceful. He avoided reference to either his early, undifferentiated rationalism or to Le Clerc's adaptation of it. He would perhaps have been imprudent to have risked further attack by disinterring his own *juvenilia* and another's interpretation of them. He was certainly disingenuous in his attempt to dress up sufficient reason as a proof of God's being after having minimized all such metaphysical first prinicples as "trifling propositions" in the *Essay*.[68] Throughout their controversy both of these once devoted Latitudinarians manifested the rawness of dazed survivors.

Modern efforts to restore the primacy of religion among Locke's concerns form a useful corrective to the nineteenth-century portrayal of him as a general in the warfare between science and theology. In attempting to right this imbalance, however, they also risk distorting the nature of his theological enterprise. There is no doubting Locke's sincerity when, in a postscript to his *Letter* to Stillingfleet, he declared that "Holy Scripture is to me, and always will be, the constant guide of my Assent; and I shall always hearken to it, as containing infallible Truth, relating to Things of the Highest Concernment." As he knew from trying experience, the pursuit of truth was not always fruitful. Sometime during the nineties he compiled a little volume entitled *Adversaria theologica,* in which he listed biblical references bearing on the doctrine of the Trinity. While only two follow the notation "Trinitas," the heading "Non Trinitas" is amply documented. A similar imbalance marks the texts he collected for and against "Christus Deus." In the face of such ambiguity, Locke took comfort in the infallible truth of morality. Like the Latitudinarians with whom he associated, he wished to establish Christianity on so firm a foundation that only deluded or willful men could deny it. As the one first-rate mind among them, he must have early realized that the achievement of their purpose was irreconcilable with maintaining what had been seen as orthodoxy.[69] While divines like Tillotson were skirting dogmatic topics, Locke did not have to face the consequences of his realization. When at last Stillingfleet awoke to the fundamental incongruity of Latitudinarianism, he determined to stand with tradition, even if it meant forsaking the inclusive appeal of reasonableness. Locke, for his part, clung to the other half of the heritage of Anglican rationalism.

Locke's understanding of assent was confusing and, initially at least, confused. Although only something extraneous to the object of belief could elicit the assent of a person, before giving it one had first to grasp whatever he was being asked to accept. In the chapter "Of the Degrees of Assent" in the *Essay,* Locke had enumerated ten grades of probability, the lowest being "traditional testimonies, the farther removed, the less their proof." Truths discovered by "the knowledge and contemplation of our own ideas, will always be more certain to us than those which are conveyed to us by traditional revelation." At the same time he conceived of faith as more than a bare probability. It was "a settled and sure principle of assent and assurance, and leaves no manner of room for doubt or hesitation." There was thus an irreducible disproportion between the likelihood achievable by the cause of assent and the certitude which the act of assent created in the individual mind. Under Stillingfleet's prodding Locke came to distinguish between knowing and believing more definitively than he had in the *Essay.* His reluctant fideism entailed a thoroughgoing subjectivity. However certain a man's own faith might be, he could never communicate it to others, much less force it on them.[70]

Locke had been willing to admit the existence of a class of ideas above, but not contrary to, reason in order to allow for the retention of articles of faith. His earlier proclamation that morality was as "capable of demonstration" as mathematics overshadowed this concession. As if foreseeing his subsequent difficulties, he contrasted the inevitably ten-

tative conclusions and often hurtful effects of obsessive speculation with
the useful and tranquilizing results of attending to ethics. On a cau-
tionary note he urged that "it will become us, as rational creatures, to
employ those faculties we have about what they are most adapted to,
and . . . it is rational to conclude, that our proper employment lies in
those inquiries, and in that sort of knowledge which is most suited to
our natural capacities. . . . *Morality is the proper science and business of
mankind in general.*" There could be little doubt that people were most
secure in embracing the testimony of revelation when it confirmed the
conclusions which their minds had reached naturally.[71]

Stillingfleet blundered through an answer. Locke returned with a
reply. Stillingfleet answered again. Locke offered another refutation.
Only the prelate's death in 1699 snapped this self-perpetuating chain of
muddle and circumspection. In his original *Answer,* Stillingfleet had initially toyed with his favorite proof of God's existence, a naive assertion
that humanity possesses an innate idea of Him. He went on to rehash
the first of Aquinas' cosmological arguments, even as he continued to
denounce Scholastic language. Unwilling to concede that Locke had
managed to dissociate himself from heretics, Stillingfleet invited him to
settle the matter by subscribing to orthodox articles, including,
presumably, the Athanasian Creed which had vexed Tillotson. In
response, Locke once more asserted his innocence of dubious connections and reassured the bishop that his epistemology was directed
against none of those formulas.[72]

Aside from reproaching Stillingfleet for equating nonsubscription to
creeds with heresy, Locke ignored the invitation. His conception of
Christianity left him with no alternative. For him, a church was "a
voluntary society of men, joining themselves together on their own accord in order to the public worshipping of God, in such manner as they
judge acceptable to him and effective to the salvation of their souls."
God alone could determine which of these frequently competing
societies were orthodox. Locke extended the atomization of belief implicit in his analysis of assent to the internal authority of every church.
Because faith was a matter between God and the consciences of individuals, institutions were unable to dictate formulas.[73]

Stillingfleet's attack on Locke was the most poignant of the repeated
clerical attempts throughout the 1690s to defend the necessity of a
mysterious Christianity. Aimed at the Unitarians, the enduring opponents of this point of view, Robert South's "Christianity Mysterious"

also constituted an indictment of the supineness of much fashionable theology. Christianity was "an instrument to convey right conceptions of God into the soul of man," so far as its "finite," "weak," "slender," and "contracted" capacity was able to receive them. Man's frailty ensured that he could not grasp "the prime, fundamental matters" of Christianity, particularly the "unalterable, incomprehensible mystery of two natures united into one person, and again of one and the same nature diffused into a triple personality." After abandoning sound Christology, the Socinians had attempted to remake Christianity to "admit of nothing which the natural reason of man cannot have a clear and comprehensive perception of."[74] In doing so, they had repudiated the testimony of antiquity and the authority of dogma.

Against both Unitarians and Anglican rationalists, South maintained that the obligation to accept the "credenda" of Christianity was as strong as that to practice its "agenda." While the moral law might be comprehensible, articles of belief, as revealed truth, demanded an act of faith rather than of understanding. Every exorbitant desire for knowledge manifested that pride, induced by Satan, "by which man first fell from his original integrity and happiness." Salvation came from God and would remain, save for the "dim light of faith," all "riddle and mystery" to the believer. In one thing at least the obscurantist South agreed with such heretics as Bury and Locke: the preservation of mysteries depended on a vigorous priestly order. If clerics were again given due respect, "men would be less confident of their own understandings, and more apt to pay reverence and submission to the understandings of those, who are both more conversant in these matters than they can pretend to be, and whom the same wisdom of God has thought fit to appoint over them as their guides."[75]

South was engaged in an exercise in sour nostalgia, for a series of mental revolutions had despoiled the Anglicanism which he had embraced at risk in his young manhood. A turbulent generation would pass before the church found another consensus that would accommodate the new habits of mind of her articulate communicants. As a convert to the old Anglican ethos, South had good reason to fear the future: "What this may produce and end in, God only at present knows, and I wish the whole nation may not at length feel."[76]

3 / The Varieties of Socinianism

Writing as a contemporary historian, Gilbert Burnet noted that the period following the Glorious Revolution had been "unhappily disjointed in matters of religion." A sense of duty to his vocation may have kept Bishop Burnet from elaborating on his implication in a central manifestation of this disjointedness, the controversy over the Church of England's teaching on the Trinity. His private correspondence shows less reserve. Thus, he rebuked his old friend, Philip Van Limborch, for aiding the Socinians: "The leniency shown to the Socinians by the Remonstrants, who communicate with them, and minimize the difference between them, makes the worst impression here. For though civil toleration should not be restricted by any dogmatic bounds, ecclesiastical toleration has its limits."[1]

At the time, the bishop of Salisbury stood accused of Socinianism because of his partiality toward modalism. Such accusations made his familiarity with the Remonstrants, the most conspicuous international traffickers in liberal divinity, an embarrassment. Anticipating their conduct toward Toland, Burnet sought to dissociate himself from the Dutchmen and establish his orthodoxy in order to put off critics. Burnet's contretemps was one effect of the campaign which the High-Church party had begun during the convocation of 1689 to tar their political and ecclesiastical opponents with the brush of heterodoxy. John Toland's literary career overlapped this heresy hunt, which High-Churchmen sustained until George I checked them by proroguing convocation in 1717.[2]

Polemicists are rarely discriminating, and most hunters pursued the Latitudinarian party, of which Burnet was a leader, the Remonstrants, and the Socinians interchangeably. There is, however, enough evidence that the three groups shared elements of a common taxonomy to suggest that the pursuit was more than whimsical. Some of it is circumstantial. Archbishop Tillotson, for example, had occasionally left the nomination to an important lectureship to Toland's sometime friend, Thomas Firmin, the acknowledged paymaster of the Unitarians. Other evidence is direct. Burnet was not alone in recognizing that the Remonstrants had established close ties with Continental Unitarians, and Locke transmitted both information about the Remonstrants to inquiring English Socinians and Unitarian tracts to grateful Remonstrants.[3]

Contemporaries realized that in England the triune concept of God had been under attack since the appearance of John Biddle's works during the Commonwealth. Still, it seemed that the liberty to publish deviant theological opinion which James II had perversely fostered encouraged these assaults, which were more numerous — and menacing — after 1685. In the words of the nonjuror Charles Leslie:

> But of late *Years* these Socinians, under the name of *Unitarians,* have appear'd with Great Boldness, and have not only fill'd the Nation with their Numerous *Pamphlets,* Printed upon a Publick *Stock,* and given away *Gratis* among the People, whereby many have been Deluded: But they have Arriv'd to that Pitch of Assurance, as to set up *Publick Meetings* in our Halls in London. . . .[4]

While the volume of anti-Trinitarian publication increased after 1685, much of its content was unoriginal. As early as 1669 Edward Stillingfleet had shown symptoms of the concern with heterodoxy which was to dominate his age. In a pamphlet printed that year he had tried to differentiate the Restoration Socinians from their predecessors and maintained that their intensified effort to subvert the authority of Scripture would introduce deism into England. Twenty-seven years later he decided to republish the pamphlet without significant change. Since he had based it on a reading of earlier Continental texts, he apparently judged the arguments of that generation of English heretics to be either reiterations or developments of familiar themes. Other opponents of both the later Unitarian tracts and *Christianity Not Mysterious* were satisfied to reprint existing works. Many critics found the Unitarians' tactics as familiar as their arguments. Foes of the original Unitarians had concluded that they were working within the Church of England to undermine her teachings.[5] It would not have surprised them that the two most conspicuous figures of the Unitarian renaissance were Firmin, a conforming merchant, and Stephen Nye, a beneficed clergyman.

Apart from Firmin's patronage little is known about the circumstances of the five volumes of pamphlets which are the monuments of this renaissance. Although the last two volumes came from other hands than the first three, they were intended to form a series. The studied furtiveness of the Unitarian writers suggests that they were less secure in their churchmanship than the unselfconscious Anglicanism that has been ascribed to them would imply. Their quest for anonymity was so successful that even Nye did not know the identities of all his collaborators, and confident attributions of authorship remain impossible. Far from denying the continuity of purpose described by the orthodox, the pamphleteers took pains to establish their theological patrimony and to assert its diffuse attraction. Biddle's works were republished in 1691, and books of independent origin such as Arthur Bury's *Naked Gospel* appeared in Socinian collections. Perhaps mindful of the similarities between Matthew Tindal's *Letter to the Reverend the Clergy of Both Universities* (1694), one of the last Unitarian tracts, and *Christianity Not Mysterious,* Nye saw Stillingfleet's attack on Toland as an expression of his animus against Unitarianism. Despite their effort to claim the English Unitarian tradition, Nye and his confreres had, in fact, accepted only half of it. They were attentive to its rationalism but ignored its fervor, which survived among isolated, unpublished sectaries.[6]

Modern scholarship has only started to dispel this obscurity. Denominational historians have either ignored the Restoration Unitarians or skirted them in moving from Biddle to Priestley. Secular historians have adverted to them as possible forebears of the deists—some in order to affirm a connection, others to deny it. Disinclined to inventory a charnel of theological controversy, both sides have until recently neglected the contents of the Socinians' works. As Peter Gay has written, "there were a few Socinians (that is to say, Unitarians), but they were for the most part obscure." Still, pioneer scholars have made useful contributions. The late E. M. Wilbur, for example, recognized that Firmin's patronage extended to the proponents of various opinions, including Sabellianism, the assertion of a unitary godhead, which can exhibit itself in a number of modes; Arianism, the belief that God created a preexistent Word, through whom all other creatures came into being, and who was incarnate in Jesus Christ; Socinianism, the identification of Jesus as the Messiah miraculously born of Mary; and a straightforward Unitarianism. As a result, Wilbur concluded, the term Socinianism "when employed by the orthodox was used only as a term of reproach and contempt."[7]

While his verdict reflects the repeated denial by Unitarians of an attachment to Socinianism, it does not accommodate their assertion that they accepted reason as the one standard by which to judge a doctrine. Neither does it do justice to the range of interpretations of the movement offered by its foes. A few believed that those whom they called Socinians were just that and nothing else. Many drew on a repertory of abuse far richer than Wilbur imagined and did not flinch at charging the Unitarians with atheism.[8]

Extreme accusations more often serve to titillate an author than to convince his readers. Still, the tenacity with which Anglican traditionalists pressed the charge of deism against the Unitarians bespeaks a depth of conviction. For their part the tractarians labored to acquit themselves of the accusation. Identifying deism with an exclusive belief in natural religion, "which comprises all the parts of Religion that are general and in all times and junctures either necessary or requisite," Nye denied that he and his associates espoused such a creed. His subsequent affirmation that Unitarianism was congruent with catholic and orthodox teaching casts doubt on the credibility of his descriptions of his party's stance. It intensifies with an examination of his statements about the relation of Christianity to natural religion. His list of the self-evident principles which can be "deduced by undeniable, infallible consequence from sensible things" was almost identical with that offered by Lord Herbert of Cherbury. Nye thought that, in general, Christianity corresponded to them. Indeed, Christ, like the prophets, had worked to arrest the decay of natural religion by eliminating ritualism and other excrescences.[9] Despite Nye's efforts, the question of the relation of English Socinianism to deism remains open.

Bayle held that dissembling was intrinsic to Socinianism. Warned by the execution of Michael Servetus, Lallius Socinus, whose family had given its name to the movement, strove not to reveal "his thoughts but in a proper time and place, and behaved himself so dexterously that he lived among the mortal enemies of his opinions without being injured in the least." English Trinitarians found their own foes equally devious. The Socinians' professions — and practice — of conformity to the Establishment strengthened their critics' suspicions. Nye's endeavor in the books that he avowed to distance himself from the Unitarians and his fellows' recourse to a similar equivocation demonstrate that, for once, orthodox apologists were not merely striving for polemical advantage.[10]

Other obstacles stand in the way of determining a coherent list of English Unitarian ideas. Nye and his colleagues were never disposed to systematize. Because their efforts were critical and analytic rather than constructive and synthetic, their opponents were vulnerable to the fallacy of composition. By treating individual Unitarian writers as representative, they tended either to exaggerate or to underestimate the heterodoxy of the group. Notwithstanding the Socinians' hedging and randomness, they did form a body within the church, albeit one more often marked by shared presuppositions than by uniform convictions.[11]

Thomas Firmin belonged to an international movement that was more than a century old before he financed his first tract. Aware of this fact, the English Socinians tried to ferret out even more remote antecedents for what were apparently their most novel techniques and ideas. They pointed to the Ebionites or Nazarenes, the Jewish Christians "who were converted by the Lord Christ and the Apostles," as their first progenitors. Depending on St. James, "the brother of our Lord . . . these believed, that Christ was a Man only." The antiquity of the Nazarenes allowed their would-be descendants to conclude "that the Article concerning our Saviour's Divinity can be no longer defended." The destruction of Jerusalem in 70 A.D. had not caused a genealogical hiatus. There existed a kind of alternative apostolic succession:

But though the open and avowed Profession of the Unity of God (as 'tis taught by the *Nazarens*, or *Socinians*, and by the *Arians*) be supprest; yet 'tis observed, that not a few of the most celebrated and learned Writers of the Church, whether Catholic or Reformed, have certainly been either *Arians* or *Socinians*, or great Favourites of them; though they have used much caution in so expressing themselves, as not to lay too open to Expression, Envy, or Legal Prosecution.

Among its later members were Erasmus, Grotius, and Denis Pétau. Above all, the Unitarians looked to Erasmus, "who, 'tho he lived considerably before Socinus commonly interprets that way," as the first modern exponent of their position.[12] The English Unitarians thereby sought to demonstrate that they, too, accepted the Erasmian strain of piety.

While the title *Socinian* may be misleading, the immediate origin of English Unitarianism lay in Socinianism, which had begun in northern Italy and flowered in Poland and Hungary. Faustus Socinus' primary affinity with Erasmus lay in the assumption that the religion of Christ was ethical rather than intellectual. By denying the intellect a role in settling matters of ultimate concern, Socinus had committed himself and his followers to a particular metaphysical outlook. He had imbibed it from the Paduan and Bolognese Aristotelians of the early sixteenth century.[13]

Firmly anticlerical, they had insisted on divorcing theology from philosophy and rejected the Thomist domestication of Aristotle.[14] When considering the place of universals, for example, Aristotelians like Pietro Pomponazzi insisted that the human mind abstracted them from particulars. The philosophers also argued for the natural mortality of the soul, which they treated as a physical phenomenon. In addition to fostering a secular and human morality, such presuppositions gave a fillip to the materialism implicit in one reading of Aristotle. Because of his intellect man stood between the eternal and the transitory; he was the first permutation of an uncreated and indestructible matter. Nature itself obeyed uniform laws that admitted neither divine intervention nor demons and angels. Both determinism and pantheism easily followed from the Aristotelians' naturalism. Although the Socinians never elaborated a cosmology and an anthropology, few of them were unaffected by the implications of these propositions.

The Cisalpine Unitarians were selective in their Erasmianism. They did not emulate Erasmus' devotion to the fathers of the church. Instead, the Socinians sought to denigrate their authority by exploiting the researches of the Jesuit Pétau in order to show the imperfection of many patristic writings when judged by a later standard of orthodoxy. That *érudit* had no more foreseen their use of his patrology than Erasmus had their manipulation of his hermeneutics. In the view of the Socinians the right of private judgment was absolute. While conceding divine inspiration to the religious (i.e., moral) content of the New Testament, Faustus Socinus held that it often erred about other matters. Reason and morality provided the criteria for distinguishing truth from error. Because Socinus asserted the primacy of the law of contradiction, he thought that any passage in Scripture which appeared to contradict reason had, in fact, been misread and needed to be reinterpreted. Certain Hungarian Unitarians, whose radicalism the younger Socinus tried to moderate, were less restrained; they found confusion in authors as often as in interpreters.[15]

Gradually, some of the Polish Socinians came to abandon the Scholastic distinction between propositions *contra rationem* that could not be believed and propositions *supra rationem* that could. They suggested that, whenever revelation had manifested a truth, reason not only was capable of glimpsing it, but also had the power to comprehend it. An obscure revelation was useless. Applying this principle to the mysteries of religion, Johann Crell concluded that revelation enabled the mind to grasp them, even though they may have originally been inaccessible to it. Since Crell's theory presented revelation as an irregular intensification of natural capacities, it raised more questions than it answered. By the middle of the seventeenth century Joachim Stegmann had taken the inevitable step of positing that nothing in the Bible surpasses human understanding.[16]

Hungarian Socinians did not enjoy a monopoly on theological radicalism. While a few of them approved of a syncretism that could accommodate Islam, a group of "Socinian deists" were numbered among their Polish coreligionists. Perhaps responding to the perennial Marxist desire for a genealogy, recent Polish scholars have discerned anticipations of materialism in the works of some of these theologians. The fullest expression of the trend is the *Epitome* of the Colloquy of Raków of 1601, which was republished in 1966. Drawing on the familiar conception of the supremacy of reason in exegesis, the participants in the colloquy assumed a distinction between necessary moral teachings and extraneous mysteries. All essential truths are knowable by reason and the clear-cut information of Scripture. Conscience supplies access to both the dictates of the natural law and whatever revelation is essential for securing universal salvation. For most of the theologians at Raków, Christian faith consisted of the love and knowledge of God expressed by Christ, an exemplar and intermediary. Although they did not offer an elaborated cosmology, some of them held that matter is coexistent and coeternal with God. In arguing that the world could only have been created from preexistent matter and that man, as a material being, did not enjoy natural immortality, Faustus Socinus had pointed to their conclusions.[17]

The Socinians aspired to make their views more than the notions of an isolated sect. Amsterdam became their clearinghouse. Four years after the publication of Christopher Sandius' *Bibliotheca Anti-Trinitariorum* in 1684, the fundamental works of the Polish Unitarians appeared in eight volumes as the *Bibliotheca fratrum Polonorum*. By 1690 these works were circulating in England. Moreover, the Poles had for a considerable period sent their ablest young men to Western Europe to study and to diffuse their teachings. While abroad, the students observed the maxim that, as long as one preserved truth in his heart, one could join any Christian denomination. Such liberty was prerequisite to the exercise of wider influence. By the time John Toland was studying in the Netherlands, the views of the Eastern Europeans were well known. When, for example, the Calvinist Pierre Jurieu denounced the errors of the Socinians in 1690, he grasped some of their characteristic ideas: "Socinianism has created a religion unlike all the other religions of the world; a religion without mysteries, without obscurity and without shadow, a completely solid-footed religion, a religion in which nothing is believed because everything is seen; a religion in which reason alone dominates and faith has no place."[18]

The Continental legacy of the Restoration Socinians did not prevent them from sharing many of the concerns of the Latitudinarians. When the Reverend Stephen Nye sought to articulate the Socinians' aims, he could have been echoing Archbishop Tillotson. Divisions within the church were scandalous, and a formula had to be found to end them. Deists had long menaced Christianity, and Socinus — as well as any of his descendants — should be accepted as an apologist against the infidels. The transition from the statement of a constructive purpose to criticism was easy. By invoking the Protestant duty to undertake a free, impartial, and sincere inquiry into traditional notions of Christianity, the Unitarians played a motif alluring to even their most severe critics. The Unitarian insistence on the necessity of conducting such an examination sincerely had to be heard respectfully by a generation that had learned to take sincerity as evidence of truthfulness.[19] The parties in the Trinitarian controversy shared enough common ground to allow discussion.

Both sides saw the Trinity as the quintessential Christian mystery and often used *Trinity* and *mystery* interchangeably. Their debate inevitably came to center on the place of mystery in religion and, hence, on the adequacy and application of human language to depict God. As a contemporary theologian has written:

The meaning of theological concepts is always a mystery. The same must be said of theological propositions. To be more precise, in the case of theological propositions we have mystery at the second power. This is due to the very nature of a proposition, which is composed of two elements: two concepts and a nexus. Now, in theological propositions both elements . . . are wrapped up in mystery. For instance, . . . the proposition "God is triune." Here, we have a mysterious element in both concepts, and the nexus is also mysterious because we cannot see how God can at the same time be three and one. The connection between these two concepts, God and triune, cannot be verified by any human experience.[20]

Confidence in the reality of primitive truth, the foundation of the Erasmianism that Socinians shared with orthodox Anglicans, sustained their attack on the idea of a triune God. Like all Protestants, the tractarians saw early Christianity as more authentic than subsequent Christianity. Reformation was a metaphor resting on the myth of a simple, unselfconscious golden age which could be recreated: insofar as accretions are removed, men and their institutions will again be as they originally were. The Unitarians exploited this potent mythology to assert that Trinitarianism had caused the decay of Christianity and that only the shedding of it would restore purity. By adopting that dogma, the church had subjected itself to popery and the other enormities against which Englishmen struggled.[21]

At the beginning of the second phase of the controversy, some critics persisted in seeing Socinianism as no more than the denial of Christ's existence before the Incarnation. For their part, the anti-Trinitarians occasionally wrote about him with a deliberate ambiguity which suggested that they taught nothing else. In fact, their objections were more thoroughgoing. Many opponents knew that the Unitarian notion of Christ implied the denial of the fall and the inheritance of original sin. The last judgment and damnation of the wicked had, in Biddle's day, been controverted, but by Nye's time Unitarians who supported these dogmas had fallen silent. There were, nonetheless, certain doubts which the Unitarians eschewed. Nye was hardly unique in rejecting atheism, which he presented as a real menace. His defense of theism was compounded of horror at the chaos which would follow from denying God's existence and a pedestrian restatement of the cosmological arguments. The range of scepticism between Socinianism and atheism was considerable, and Stillingfleet thought the Socinian analysis of the contributions of reason and revelation to religious assent sanctioned virtually any incredulity within it.[22] Differing interpretations of the nature and implications of their rationalism heated the controversy.

Unitarians like Nye embraced the new definition of reason, and their foes were not backward in imputing the most advanced views to them: "The Great and General Principle of [Socinianism] is That nothing is to be believ'd, that is above the comprehension of Human Reason; or, That a Man is to believe nothing but what he can comprehend." In defending themselves, the Unitarians exploited the dependence of orthodox formularies on Scholastic and Aristotelian categories. Scorning faintheartedness, they presented their point of view as the culmination of the general rejection of Scholasticism. When Aristotle

> pretended to explain the Causes of the *Phaenomena's* of Nature, he gravely said, that they were *Occult Qualities*. It would have been better, sincerely to confess his Ignorance, than to return an Answer no more satisfying, than if he had said, "I know not." The Trinitarians follow the method of that Philosopher. We ask them, what they mean by three Persons in God? They Answer, they are three somewhats. Is it not better for them to confess that they know not what they are, since their Answer is an undeniable mark of their Ignorance?[23]

The relation between the epistemology of the Unitarians and that of John Locke, the most formidable English neologist, remains uncertain. They exhibit numerous similarities, and William Popple, Locke's Socinian intimate and future translator, was an early advocate of defining reason as a mental operation rather than as a faculty of the soul. Since these notions were becoming commonplace, it is uncertain whether such evidence indicates a pattern of influence or merely a series of convergences. In any case, by the 1690s some observers sensed that the flow of influence had reversed, that Locke's ideas were affecting the Unitarians. When the tractarians addressed themselves to the supposed debt, they were divided. In order to vindicate the self-evidentness of the articles of natural religion, Nye rebuked Locke for having denied the existence of innate ideas. Here, as elsewhere, he spoke for a minority. Most of his allies were ready to invoke so weighty an authority in support of their analysis of assent and to defend him when he was attacked.[24]

If the way of ideas was an element of the Unitarian analysis, a refined version of Socinian hermeneutics provided another and perhaps more important one. In attempting to describe this feature, historians have often reflected the tension about the relative valuation of revelation and reason which beset the Unitarian effort to frame rules of exegesis. One scholar, for example, has concluded that the Socinians were biblicists who sometimes upheld the supremacy of reason. Their understanding of the import of divine inspiration was apparently contradictory. While some of them maintained that ratiocination could not even establish the validity of monotheism, others were confident of the demonstrability of all the tenets of natural religion, the essence of Christianity.[25] It would take time for them to resolve their quandary.

The tractarians professed a unique devotion to both the letter and the spirit of the New Testament. Their eager rejection of unsettling biblical researches like those of Spinoza on the Pentateuch made such professions colorable. At the same time their repudiation of conciliar and patristic authority meant that, in order to justify their Christianity, they had to maintain the accuracy of their own interpretation of the Bible. The very claim of precision disposed their opponents to question their biblicism. Were they not guilty of forcing "improper and unusual Significations upon the words" and of a universal allegorizing? Could their teachings really be condemned as blasphemous only if they were characterized as such in Holy Writ? Some historians have seen merit in these doubts. D. P. Walker has suggested that from the beginning Unitarian hermeneutics attempted "the impossible task of a purely, radically rationalist interpretation of the Scriptures, impossible because, if it succeeded, it would only make the revelation superfluous."[26] The history of the exegetical efforts of the second phase of English Unitarianism is a success story.

Anglican apologists sometimes underestimated the radicalism of the Unitarians' enterprise. Thus, Archbishop Tenison found them exceptionable insofar as they denigrated typology, and Archbishop Synge consoled himself that their reinterpretation of Scripture did not entail a denial of its credibility. The persistence of such benign misunderstanding perhaps encouraged Stephen Nye, at once a subordinate of Tenison and the most industrious Socinian pamphleteer, to equivocate. When considering revealed religion, Nye was ambiguous. Though he admitted the authority of the Bible, he also confessed that its trustworthiness depends on "the fidelity of those Persons, who have transmitted [it] to us." Since their testimony could never constitute "indubitable evidence" like that offered by natural religion, it "has a greater certainty to us, than Revealed." Nye also maintained that the criterion of faith was the existence of proof. The adoption of this standard kept him from invoking the distinction between acceptable tenets *supra rationem* and unacceptable ones *contra rationem* and from discriminating between reasonableness and rationalism. In dealing with controverted questions of divinity which Scripture had not addressed, Nye held that reason, which he failed to define, was to play the determining role. Indeed, reason had to govern the content of revelation: "What is false in Reason, can never be true in Revelation, or by Revelation. So that whatsoever in Revelation doth seem to contradict Reason, can be nothing but our Blunder; our unskilled, injudicious, and too close Adherence to the mere Letter and Words of Revelation."[27]

Matthew Tindal, a fellow of All Souls, then a Unitarian, once a Roman Catholic, and later a deist, articulated the full implications of these premises.[28] For him, reason, or demonstration, set the limits of humanity's capacity to accept revelation. The teachings of Christianity and the discoveries of reason had to agree: "If Christianity is found contradictory to any thing the Light of Nature makes manifest, or should require of us to believe any thing of which we could form no Ideas, or none but contradictory ones, we should be forced so far to acknowledge it faulty and false." Whenever revelation seemed to conflict with reason, a figurative interpretation of it had to be employed. Remarkably for a seventeenth-century author dealing with the fundamentals of Christianity, Tindal sometimes used no scriptural citations. His practice offers a striking contrast to that of Toland in *Christianity Not Mysterious*, the work conventionally cited as beginning the deist controversy. Its pages are awash with proof texts. Straightforwardly rationalist, Tindal could dispense with Scripture: "Reason is as much the Word, the Will, and Revelation of God, as the written word itself, and without which the written word would be wholly useless."

How had the Unitarian vanguard succeeded in making revelation superfluous? Some of their critics thought they knew. First, the heretics had made "Scripture subservient to their ill Opinions and Designs," rather than making "it the rule thereof, in indeavouring to find out the true meaning of it." Secondly, they had followed Socinus in interpreting "Scripture merely by Criticisms upon the words, without any regard to the scope of the place, or the analogy of Faith." For their part the tractarians did not reject the second charge. They dismissed the analogy of faith, the reliance on language and concepts developed from God's Word to describe Him, as "the particular Opinion of the Party wherein one finds himself engaged," and as such a manifestation of "that particular Tradition, which we will not allow in the Church of Rome."[29] The Bible was never self-explanatory.

Had this anonymous writer been indiscreet, he might have profitably inquired into the significance of the analogy of faith for most churchmen. Tenison was not alone in preserving Tillotson's detachment toward traditional, patristic, and conciliar constructions of biblical language. It is only necessary to turn to the Boyle lectures of John Williams, bishop of Chichester, to understand how Anglican theologians had sapped the analogy of faith. Explicit revelation alone defined Christian doctrine, and most of the essential parts of Scripture were plain. Immersing oneself in the texts would inevitably make them more comprehensible, since God was obliged to enlighten any honest man with sufficient comprehension for his salvation. The results of such an effort were invariably personal. In the end, every individual was bound to interpret the Bible for himself.[30] Since Williams studied Scripture without applying rudimentary philological criticism or acknowledging the emerging historical method, he invited an unfettered subjectivism.

The bishop's neglect of exegetical innovations was symptomatic. For the most part, anti-Unitarians dismissed the precocious Continental development of critical techniques as a popish plot. Stillingfleet vacillated between trying to appropriate the new criticism and accusing the tractarians of deferring to Richard Simon, as if the Oratorian's name were itself an indictment. After Anglicans discovered deism, they tended to contrast the new heretics with the old and to assert that the Unitarians had allowed that "the holy Scriptures, as now in our hands, are genuine and uncorrupted."[31] Determining whether this reevaluation reflects increasing caution on the part of the Unitarians or a combination of opportunism and muddle on the part of apologists requires an examination of the tractarians' attitudes toward the nascent higher criticism.

Often the Socinians contented themselves with the apparent commonplace that, when read humbly and without presuppositions or prejudices, "as we should read the Proclamations of our Kings," Scripture expressed the whole will of God. Although compatible with the reigning legal and ethical view of religion, this dictum fostered solipsism more easily than it established credenda. Like most of his colleagues, Nye avowed that the anti-Trinitarians alone approached the Bible properly. When charged with alleging its wholesale corruption in order to dispose of stock Trinitarian references, Socinians answered that they received "into our Canon, all those Books of Scripture, that were received, or owned by the Church of *England*." Moreover, they denied that anyone could argue that the Bible was riddled by corruptions, since "the antient Manuscripts, the first Translations, the Fathers, the Historians of the Church, are sufficient Directors, concerning the authentick and genuine Reading of doubtful Places of Holy Scripture."[32]

In practice, they were less complaisant. Seldom referring to the works of Spinoza and Simon, they regularly insinuated or averred the

existence of systematic fabrication and distortion in the New Testament. To bolster such claims Nye undertook extensive, frequently
questionable reattributions of biblical texts. When dealing with passages whose authenticity he conceded, he favored a transparent tactic.
He accepted their verbal inspiration when they seemed reasonable and
allegorized them when they seemed extravagant.[33] In their attraction
to biblical criticism the Socinians were no less modern than the deists.

Uncertainty about the canon made urgent the task of explaining
how theological propositions were extracted from (or imposed upon)
the Bible. In considering the problem, the Unitarians arrived at their
principal theological contribution, viz., the insistence that in order to
give assent to a doctrine, it is necessary to have a clear and distinct idea
of its meaning. They derived the elements of their grammar of assent
from the commonly held Latitudinarian assumption that the essential
parts of Scripture had to be plainly expressed. Stephen Nye, eschewing
the possibility of a *"real* Clash between Revelation and Reason," stated
his school's version of the Latitudinarian postulate: "For we utterly
deny that the *express* Words, the *obvious* natural Sense of Holy Scripture, are on the Trinitarian side: we never fly (in these Controversies)
to a *Catachristical,* or harsh sense; no, nor have at any time need of a
Figurative Sense. . . ." Since the Athanasian formula assaulted reason,
"we cannot but profess ourselves surprized, that any should have the
Confidence to pretend, that there is *clear* and *express* Revelation, on behalf of the Trinity and Incarnation." Nye's insistence on the principle
"that 'tis necessary to interpret all both *Speech* and *Writing,* in Consis-
tence with Common Sense and our natural Knowledg" cannot have
diminished his surprise.[34]

In 1694 Tindal framed from Unitarian principles an indictment of the
credibility of revealed religion as forceful as any he would deliver a generation later as a deist.[35] Distinguishing between accounts passed on by
"tradition" and "original Revelation," things of which God "has given us
clear and *distinct* Idea's," he held that the latter were always more certain
than the former. Not only did the passage of time make any inherited
narrative dubious, but its initial reception was also plagued by difficulties. Did its recipients enjoy immunity to delusion? Had they accurately translated "Divine Speech" into human terms? Disputatious
Christians showed the precariousness of efforts to understand the alien
patterns of thought and expression that underlay even "the plainest
Texts." Knowledge was invariably preferable to belief. Yielding to the

temptation to invert this order "would destroy all the Principles and Foundations of that Knowledg God has given us, and render all our Faculties useless, and wholly confound the most excellent Part of his Workmanship, our Understanding."

Although Tindal's coherence was rare, his arguments were the common property of the Socinians. They tended to measure the worth of the Bible according to its ability to communicate clear and distinct ideas: "All the knowledge, which the Scripture affords us concerning God, was merely Moral and Relative to us, but no ways Metaphysical."[36] This criterion also determined the content of faith. The mind could conceive of divine attributes such as omnipresence and omniscience; "but to know whether there is an Immensity of Essence or of Operation, there are no Helps to the settling of my Confidence and Trust in [such ideas]. Therefore it is that Revelation does not speak precisely about this. Thus it is with the Unity of God."

If men could believe only tenets of which they were able to form clear and distinct ideas, then the Trinitarian faith that God was three persons sharing one substance was nonsense: "The Term of *Divine Person* made use of by the Trinitarians, is a *vain Sound, which produces no Idea.*" Nye trumpeted this proposition with an immediacy and vehemence unmatched by Toland: *"There is no Mystery at all* in any of the Properties or Attributes of God. They are no less *clear* in themselves, than they are *evidently* deduced from the Excellence of his *Works,* and the Methods of his *Providence.* The Mystery never lies in the Attribute or Property, but in the addition made to it by *fanciful* Men." While "it is the Nature of a Mystery to be wrapp'd up in Darkness," the Bible, the religion of Protestants, was essentially clear. Nowhere did that book assert "that [the Trinity] is an unspeakable Mystery, a Mystery that ought to be adored with a profound Humility, and cannot be explained."[37]

The word *mystery* appears several times in the New Testament, however, and as biblicists the Unitarians had to explain its meaning. Their explanation depended on two complementary arguments. First, they sought to expand on the general willingness to subject God to the law of contradiction. If a mystery could not be self-contradictory, it should not be allowed to defy any other law of natural reason. The notion of three persons in one Being was apparently a multiple offender. Secondly, since the authority of Holy Writ, indeed of all religion, rested on its conformity to rational principles, the task of revelation was to clarify rather than to obscure. No one could believe a mystery in the sense in which the orthodox used that term, because obscurity nullified clarity and distinctness, the prerequisites of belief. An examination of the New Testament texts containing the word *mystery* suggested that it had been used to characterize expedients provisionally applied until Christianity brought clarification: "It was a Mystery or *Secret,* before the Revelation of the Gospel; but since it was revealed, it ceases to be a Mystery or Secret: unless a Secret discovered is a Secret still." Christ was the abrogator of the mysterious, the imprecise and unintelligible.[38] For the Unitarians, Christianity held no mysteries.

Insofar as churchmen appreciated the Socinians' vision of a demystified Christianity, they found it troublesome. For many it constituted the essence of the Unitarian challenge. At the beginning of the journey which would take him from Sabellianism to orthodoxy in less than a decade, Bishop Burnet summarized his conception of their intent:

It is a question, whether those who plead for Mysteries, can believe themselves, after all their Zeal for them: since a Man can no more think that is true, of which he has no Idea, than a Man can see in the dark; for let him affirm ever so much that he sees, all other persons who perceive it to be dark, are sure that he sees nothing. It seems to be the peculiar Character and Beauty of the Christian Religion, that it is our *reasonable service,* or the Rational way of worshipping God.[39]

Despite their ingenuity, the post-Revolutionary Unitarians were embellishing familiar themes. Almost two decades before Burnet wrote, Thomas Smith had seen the object of his own Socinian opponents as the rejection of mystery. He assailed them for holding that they had to be shown an explicit Scriptural reference communicating a clear and distinct idea before accepting a doctrine. By the mid-1690s this judgment was threatening to become a truism. Stillingfleet described them as "great Enemies to all Mysteries of Faith, as Unreasonable Impositions on those of more refined Understandings, and of *clear* and *distinct* Perceptions." The Malebranchian John Norris maintained that the explanation "those of the Socinian Persuasion . . . give why they will not believe the Mysteries of the Christian Faith, is because they are above their Reason." A persistent though unhappy critic, Dean Sherlock accused them of holding that "all Divine Mysteries must be examined by our Natural Ideas, and what we have no Natural Ideas of, we cannot, we must not believe." More than a decade after the conventional end of the Trinitarian controversy, the indefatigable Charles Leslie gave this speech to "Soc." in a dialogue against the anti-Trinitarians: "How can any thing that is *Reveal'd* be a *Mystery*? It is a *Mystery* or *Secret* before the Revelation of it; but since it is Reveal'd, it ceases to be a *Mystery,* or *Secret.* Unless a *Secret discover'd is a Secret still.* "[40]

A general conception of challenge did not lead churchmen to develop a unified response. Robert South adopted what was at once the easiest and the hardest defense. He embraced traditional formulas, which required little creativity, and then proclaimed: "Credo quia absurdum est" — which, given the ascendancy of Latitudinarianism, demanded raw nerve. Although South articulated the emotions of the majority of the lower clergy who were to unsettle convocation for almost a generation, he had few theologically competent allies. Even High-Churchmen could find tradition onerous. Without attempting a restatement of the doctrine, Leslie hoped to discover a *via media* between traditionalism and neologism: "A Mystery is not that of which we know nothing at all. But that of which we know some part, but darkly and obscurely."[41]

As an unabashed Latitudinarian, Burnet had originally felt less inhibited. He ventured that a Gospel mystery can be explained to the extent of "shewing how it is laid down and revealed in Scripture," because Christianity had not sought to perpetrate arcana. His retreat to a more secure position may have been a measure of policy or a further manifestation of theological incompetence. Other divines were more adventurous, though equally maladroit. Sherlock labored to break new ground by arguing that the Trinity is made up of three eternal minds, two coming from the Father, which are one by reason of shared consciousness. He thereby unwittingly initiated yet another Trinitarian controversy within the Establishment: "Men may believe the Trinity to be an Incomprehensible Mystery, and yet speak of it in words which may be understood, which does not pretend to make the Mystery comprehensible, but to deliver it from Nonsense, Jargon, and Heresy."[42] In Sherlock's view, the abandonment of Scholasticism allowed for the deliverance of the dogma from nonsense and jargon. His endeavor led others to attack him as a Socinian. More seriously, his erstwhile friend, South, in a series of philippics published in the early nineties castigated his reinterpretation as tritheist. The appearance of virtually Socinian works by laymen such as Robert Howard aggravated the conflict.[43] The church was awake, groaning, and waiting to find its creed.

Partisans are seldom willing to identify religion with its theological presuppositions. In the short term at least, custom is more powerful than reason. Thus, the tractarians persistently styled themselves Christians even after they had transformed their critique of orthodox Christianity into an assault on the possibility of revelation. Like a once fashionable school of theologians who failed to realize that writing God's obituary might limit the demand for their own services, the Socinians did not connect theory and practice. For the most part, their critics were reluctant to force them to do so. As late as 1697, one author ascribed to them the belief that Christ was a divinely gifted man — a belief which must eventually lead either to idolatry or to the abandonment of the worship of Christ, and hence of Christianity. The persistence of such understated foreboding suggests that the tractarians' indisposition to write systematically worked to their advantage. As Leslie complained, "They dwell all in Generals. . . . They will not tell plainly what they would be at."[44]

Questions of Christology did not obsess the Unitarians. Aside from denying Christ's divinity, they only fitfully speculated about his character. Because of their reticence a reconstruction of their conception of the nature and mission of Christ must remain tentative. Although most of Firmin's authors were confident that God "will have all Men be saved," they were less certain that Christ was indispensable to realizing His universal saving will. The practice of a spiritual or ethical religion was essential to achieving salvation. For the majority of people, the light of natural religion sufficed to illumine the way. It also provided the standard for judging revelation, which

is given us to exalt and preserve among Men the Natural Principles of Morality and Religion, which Nature or the Universal Tradition has engrafted in their Hearts. And how could it confirm to us the Truth of those Natural Notions, and even strengthen them by a new Light, if the first Duty which it imposes upon us, did consist in calling into question our clearest Notions, and our most certain Principles?[45]

Like Arthur Bury, the Socinians found in Islam a powerful argument for the sufficiency of the religion of nature. Critics denounced them for either paving the way for Mohammedanism or being "Mohammedan Christians." The anti-Trinitarian William Freke asserted that nothing except the Athanasian Creed, "man's own invention," separated Islam and Christianity — which suggests that these charges were not factitious. Nevertheless, Stephen Nye was outraged when accused of reducing Christianity to theism by holding that "no more is required to make a Christian, but only that he believe, that 'Jesus is the Messiah.' " It was "a Christian's Duty to learn . . . all the other Articles of the Christian Creed." His outrage masked his evasion of the issue: Was Christ merely the Messiah? In one of the moments when Nye sought "to tell what he would be at," he described Christ as "the Messenger, Minister, Servant, and Creature of God." Unlike the Muslims, Nye was persuaded that, while the mother of Christ may have been blessed, she was not a virgin. The Holy Ghost was "the Power and Inspiration of God." The one "Almighty and Eternal" God was neither of these two.[46]

If belief in God's unity made Christ unnecessary, it did not in itself suffice as an explication of His attributes. While Nye and his colleagues agreed on no single account of God, at least some of them seem to have been successors of the radical Eastern European Unitarians. In 1698 Burnet was again warning Limborch about the Socinian menace. Mindful of the continuing relations between the Remonstrants and their anti-Trinitarian compatriots, he carefully, if inaccurately, noted that "the Socinians here depart strangely from [the faith] of their brethren abroad" because "they insinuate that God must have bodily form, and be bound by the laws of space; and that matter must be coeternal with him."[47]

Although Burnet treated their position as a novelty, a generation earlier, Henry More, the Cambridge Platonist, had written that the Socinians' "great mistake in Divinity" was "their incapacity of conceiving anything but Body or Matter." The notion that they taught a kind of materialism enjoyed wide and tenacious currency. As late as 1708 Leslie accused "the Biddlist-Unitarians" of having given God a body. In much the same way, John Toland had once slyly noted that the Cartesian principle that there is nothing in the universe except matter and motion had "gratify'd the 'Socinians.' "[48]

Apologists shared an idea of God that depended on the associated notions of eternity, immateriality, and miracle. They were convinced that the Unitarians' grammar of assent undercut its credibility. Thus Stillingfleet, who wondered how they could form a clear and distinct idea of eternity, maintained against Locke that immateriality was the precondition of both divine eternity and human immortality. Similarly, the capacity to work miracles was integral to God's omnipotence, since it guaranteed that He "has the same liberty of will, which we experience to be in our selves." If it were wanting in Him, then the universe must be an autonomous mechanism. The creation of matter *ex nihilo,* in turn, guaranteed the possibility of miracle, since it demonstrated that matter "may be again produc'd, or alter'd by the very same Power."[49]

Nye was aware of the association of these concepts. Ascribing their antitheses to contemporary disciples of Epicurus and Lucretius, he examined this point of view with the professed intent of refuting it: "All the possible Forms . . . will in length of time arise, from the perpetual changes of Figure and Place, that must happen to *First Matter,* by means of an Eternal Motion: and the Cosmical System or world being one of those possible Forms, we need only motion, or matter consider'd in a confused Motion, not a God to make the World." The tone of this examination was consonant with his restatement of Aquinas' five proofs and slighting references to a self-sufficient nature. Still, Nye conceded that "it has some faint appearance of likelihood, that in Infinite time, by Infinite Tryals and Changes, Matter or Bodies may undergo all possible Forms, and consequently this present which we call the World." He did not pass on to other matters after refuting Epicureanism. Instead, he restated it as the position of "the Stoicks and others." They

easily defend their Doctrine against these Exceptions [which he had raised]. . . . They say in short, that when Body or Matter arrives at such a determinate degree of tenuity, subtlety, or rarefaction, it *thereby* acquires Life and Thought: and with those *two* cometh of course, or in the nature of the thing, an *autokinesis,* or Self-motion, that is a power of arbitrary moving it self . . . for Body when so far subtilized that it gaineth Thought or Life, therewith the name of Spirit, Permeates all the gross and sensible Bodies; acts upon them, and is not acted on by them; it can move, or even dissolve them; they cannot move, or remove it, because it pervades them.[50]

Writing under his own name, Nye rejected both this position and the easy defense on which it rested. Nevertheless, his rejection might have inspired more confidence had he not also disavowed any connection with the Socinians.[51] It is striking that, having trained himself to avoid candor, he also reversed the procedure of controversialists, who begin with a strong statement of an opposing view, progressively weaken it, and end with a proclamation of their own opinion. His sentiments about the divine nature remain enigmatic.

In his anonymous Unitarian pamphlets, Nye described God as an "incorporeal, Omnipresent, and Omniscient" Being and denounced the idea that He "hath a Body, is like to Man." Although he had dismissed the Incarnation, he did not thereby exclude the possibility of a materialistic concept of God. Like the Paduan Aristotelians, the English Socinians accepted the existence of uncreated prime matter: "the most eminent Philosophers" had shown "that the 'Moles,' Matter or Substance of which the World is made, was from all *Eternity;* and that 'tis *immense* and *interminable.*" Some of Nye's associates declined to repudiate materialism, as for example the anonymous Unitarian who attempted to dispose of a number of misconceptions about his God. He carefully refuted charges of denying "His certain foreknowledge," maintaining that He was "omnipresent, not in his Essence or Person, but by his Knowledge and Power"; but on the charge of agreeing with "those Fathers [presumably Tertullian] who held God is a *Body,* not a Spirit," he chose not to reject patristic authority.[52]

Even the God of the public and Anglican Nye was less innocent of a hint of materialism than appearances might suggest. He was "a most powerful and wise *Mind* which at first contrived, and made the World, and will at last Account judge the *Rational Part* of his Creation." Nye's understanding of "Mind" proved, however, to be almost as Pickwickian as his use of "contrived and made." Eschewing particularistic interventions, his God worked through the mechanical order of nature, so that prayers of supplication to Him were useless. Nye refrained from urging the abandonment of such prayers, since they served as "an acknowledgment, profession and testimony, that our hopes and dependence are on him."[53]

It is useful to recall here that Nye's "Stoicks" did not deny the existence of mind, but made it the result of the *autokinesis* of uncreated matter, "of subtlety or attenuation." The phenomena which possessed it were simply exempt from the "Infulls of the gross Bodies of the World." There was no necessity of going back to antiquity in order to find an exposition of this view. A systematic modern statement of it appeared in the Paduan Jacobus Zabarella's commentary on the *De anima* of Aristotle. None of the Socinians limned an unambiguous materialism, though Tindal avoided listing incorporeity among the divine attributes.[54] Ill-disposed toward dualism, some of the tractarians at least seem to have felt the appeal of a mechanistic cosmology.

The sight of Thomas Firmin living as "a pillar of an Anglican congregation in the City" and Stephen Nye holding his glebe provides an indication of the Unitarians' success in separating practice from theory. In his biography of Firmin Nye explained their policy:

I did not wonder, however, that our Friend was so ready to embrace a reconciliation with the Church: for he was ever a lover of Peace, and always conformed as far as he could, according to that direction of the Apostle. "Whereunto we have already attained, let us walk by the same Rule." Which with the best Interpreters he understood thus, "Conform to the Doctrines, Terms and Usages that are commonly received, as far as you can; if in some things you differ from the Church, yet agree with her, and walk by *her Rule* to the utmost that in Conscience you may; or as the Apostle himself words it, "so far as (whereunto) you have attained."[55]

Firmin's solicitude for the Huguenot refugees from the persecutions of Louis XIV illustrates how the Unitarians treated what had once seemed to be fundamentals as incidentals. Although he disagreed with their Calvinism, he reasoned " 'Tis not the truth or falsehood of the Opinion, but the Zeal for God, and the sincerity to the dictates of conscience, that makes the Martyr." A sincere conscience expressed itself practically and ethically rather than abstractly and intellectually. Firmin was a Christian because, "like our Saviour, 'He went about doing good.' " For their part, his fellow Latitudinarians were accommodating. Acting as an Englishman and a Christian, "not more a Friend to the Liberties of the Nation, and to the present Establishment than he was an Enemy to Licentiousness," Firmin helped to found the Society for the Reformation of Manners.[56] Membership in the society justified his indifference to doctrine by proving its compatibility with active churchmanship.

Conformity did not prevent critics from stigmatizing the Unitarians as foes of the church and her ministers. In fact, even parsonical tractarians sometimes peddled truculent anticlericalism. As Nye wrote, "The truth is, were it not for *the Preachers,* there never had any Blood been shed." Distrust of the clergy shaped the Socinians' ideal of the church. It should exist to diminish ritual and to prompt obedience to the moral code. While the Unitarians admitted baptism and "the Lord's Supper," they held that the sacraments were merely symbolic and communal, not means of conveying grace. Good men were godly; "the true Heroes, Copies, and Representations of the Supream Being" were the ones "who most comply with those [natural] Laws and Obligations." The acts that made men evil, and hence ungodly, were obvious; "Lust, Riot, Excess, Covetousness" were proscribed because they "unfit us . . . for the service of God, and for that honest and honourable Discharge of our Station, whatsoever that is, in the Commonwealth."[57]

The association of divine obligation with citizenship strengthened

the determination of the tractarians to conform to the church in spite of
their idiosyncratic teachings. The task of religion was less to promote
individual sanctity than to foster civic virtue. An institution such as
Anglicanism was the necessary vehicle for attaining natural morality in
England. Conscious of the appeal of the practice of combining transparent heterodoxy and determined conformity, Anglican apologists
were occasionally disposed to label the Unitarians as Trimmers.[58]

In itself, the convergence of the ecclesiologies of some Latitudinarians and Socinians does not suffice to explain how the
Trinitarian controversy ended. It is puzzling that a conflict which
Burnet saw as furious at the end of 1694 could have subsided in less
than two years and remained dormant until the time of Joseph
Priestley. On inspection the transition from the Trinitarian to the deist
controversy appears to have been anything but sudden and clean. Firmin was still propagating his views in the autumn of 1696, and when
Stillingfleet tilted with Locke in the same year, his concern with Socinian teachings was undiminished. Of course, some orthodox writers in
this *annus mirabilis* did profess to believe that their dispute with the
Unitarians was over. Although the Reverend H. De Luzancy expressed such sentiments, he was still refuting the Unitarians in 1698.[59]
Presumably his belief in the closure of the episode derived from his
confidence in the invincibility of his arguments rather than from the
disappearance of his opponents.

The standard Unitarian bibliography for this period ends in 1700,
but it lists numerous pamphlets published during the later 1690s.
Many writers were oblivious of the alleged demise of Unitarianism. In
1703 John Toland observed that it remained dangerous to be identified
as a Socinian. Two years afterward the subject commanded enough interest to induce him to translate and paraphrase a tract by Le Clerc
which stated the group's teachings. Yet a change had occurred.
Burnet's remark of 1694 that deists had driven the Socinians to increasing radicalism prefigured the manner in which a variety of Trinitarians
came to describe their foes. By 1714 the Scottish divine, Thomas
Halyburton, was presenting the Socinians, and particularly Stephen
Nye, as "such of the *Christians,* who favour the *Deists* most." He did so
because both groups accepted the sufficiency of the principles of natural
religion. Controversialists persisted in making the connection through
the middle of the eighteenth century.[60]

Two problems remain. First, if the Trinitarian controversy did not end in 1696, what has led both denominational and academic scholars to choose it as a *terminus ad quem?* Secondly, how did contemporaries conceive of the relations between Socinians and deists?

The presupposition of ecclesiastical historians that there is a necessary connection between the institutional and intellectual aspects of the church suggests one answer. Tillotson seems to have hoped that the controversy would somehow disappear, but it became a matter of urgency to the hierarchy when Canon South sustained his attacks on Dean Sherlock as a tritheist. Almost effortlessly, the Socinians turned Sherlock's predicament to their own advantage and lured him to ever more damaging clarifications. Increasing divisiveness provided them with additional ammunition. After Sherlock's disciple Joseph Bingham—in a sermon at Oxford in November 1695—preached that there are three infinite, distinct minds and substances in the Trinity, the hebdomadal council rushed to condemn the doctrine as "False, Impious, and Heretical." Sensing the accentuation of an appalling internal dispute, Archbishop Tenison, Tillotson's successor, tried to stop preaching on the subject. He drew up for the king's signature a document forbidding the application of new terms to the Trinity and making obligatory the phrases contained in the Bible, the Thirty-Nine Articles, and the decrees of the first three ecumenical councils; it also reaffirmed the canons of the church forbidding public opposition between preachers. Shortly after William III promulgated the declaration, parliament passed an act penalizing anti-Trinitarian statements.[61]

Responding to these decisions, Sherlock undertook a grudging recantation, which appeared as *The Present State of the Trinitarian Controversy* in 1698. Meanwhile, Firmin's death in 1697 had deprived the Socinian movement of its organizer and ensured its fragmentation.[62] Administrative actions silenced South and Sherlock, limited challenges to the church's formularies, and persuaded historians eager to study the deist controversy to isolate *Christianity Not Mysterious* from its context. They extinguished, however, neither individual tractarians nor their characteristic ideas.

The second, more difficult problem did not even exist in the minds of many authors. They treated Unitarianism and deism as interdependent phenomena.

The evident and declared Design of the Socinians, is, to retain no Mysteries, but by forced Interpretation of Scripture to expound them all to their own, that is, to a new and absurd Sense; and it is but too plain, that there is a combined Design carried on between them and the Deists, who are contented to pass for Christians, with a Distinction, and without a Mystery: *Anti-Trinitarian* is a milder word than *Anti-Christian,* and Unitarian is but a different Name for Deist.[63]

This explanation was but one among many. In time Stillingfleet, who had been unwilling to assert such identity, would concede that the Socinians had aided in advancing deism: they had lessened the authority of Scripture, fomented anticlericalism, insisted on the priority of natural religion — thereby rendering revelation an indifferent thing — and supported various deists. For his part, Sherlock discerned a conspiracy. "Atheists and deists, men who are for no religion," had infiltrated the ranks of the Socinians in order to manipulate them. None of these hypotheses is verifiable, but it is suggestive that the early deists had distinguished themselves from the Socinians for a precise reason. Charles Blount, who paraded his dependence on the abhorred Spinoza, differed from them because he fancied that they worshiped Christ as a *deus factus.* His scruple would eventually prove to be needless. As Toland insisted, there were by the late 1690s no longer any real Socinians in England, and the Unitarians who had inherited that name held different views.[64]

Taken together, the uncertainty about the connection between Socinians and deists and the transformation of Socinianism into Unitarianism necessitate the reformulation of the second problem: Is there a persuasive way to end the Trinitarian and begin the deist controversy? Nye rejected efforts to amalgamate his party with infidels who failed to differentiate "between the *corrupted* and the *sincere* Parts of Religion." The atheist rejected all religion, but

the Deist, far more judicious, rejects hereupon only all positive and *revealed* Religion, and takes up with natural Religion, i.e. with the Belief of a God, whose Power and Wisdom he plainly sees in the *Structure* and *Contrivance* of the world, and with the Dictates of Reason, and our congenit and natural Notions concerning the moral and immoral, or good and evil.

Nye implied that the tractarians' creed was fuller, though he might have had difficulty in being more specific. Despite his reservations, other Unitarians wrote appreciatively of the deists' intentions and works. Nye himself was occasionally solicitous of some who had been branded as deists. Thus, while he asserted that *Christianity Not*

Mysterious was outside the Unitarian canon, he sought to ward off Still-ingfleet's thrusts against its "learned and ingenious author." He went so far as to affirm that "Mr. *Toland* does not know his own Book in the Bishop's Representation of it." Because Stillingfleet had misconstrued Toland's argument, he had failed to refute it. By then Nye's superiors had identified him as one of the principal tractarians, and he knew that he was a marked man. In his last years his appreciation of orthodoxy increased, and he bombarded Tenison with refutations of Toland's works.[65]

To Burnet's satisfaction, Firmin joined Nye's retreat before the counterrevolution of the High-Church faction and cut Toland.[66] Their actions proved opportune. Tindal's *Letter to the Reverend the Clergy*, pub-lished about a year before *Christianity Not Mysterious*, displayed greater asperity of tone and radicalness of method than that putatively deist work. No subsequent Unitarian tract could distill so thoroughly the as-sumptions which this party had come to accept. If tractarians like Nye were increasingly disposed to confine themselves to questions of Christ-ology, Tindal and others sought to preserve the whole legacy of Resto-ration Unitarianism. Gradually, they found themselves rewarded for their effort with the name *deists*.

Peter Browne, the perceptive bishop of Cork, maintained that he labored to refute "our modern Deists." Whether the objects of his po-lemics were direct descendants of Herbert and Blount or not, critics of the Unitarians absolved them of any dependence on the proto-deists. In contrast, they were chary of distinguishing the Socinians from Tin-dal and Toland.[67]

If their reluctance owed something to polemical truculence, it re-flected as well an inkling of both the premises and implications of the Socinians' theology. In their powerlessness to develop their intuition, Anglican apologists showed themselves to be creatures of a theological culture. For most Augustans, philosophical divinity meant natural theology, and they were either indifferent or hostile to the concomitant task of systematic theology. Beginning with those judgments of fact and value called doctrines, this specialty aims "to work out appropriate sys-tems of conceptualization, to remove apparent inconsistencies, to move toward some grasp of spiritual matters both from their own inner co-herence and from the analogies offered by more familiar human experi-ence." The Latitudinarians were unable to conceive that metaphysics is indispensable not merely to the understanding but also to the articulation of doctrines. As a result, most of them appreciated neither the character of the Socinian challenge nor their own vulnerability to it.[68]

They borrowed from Scholasticism in order to provide themselves with a natural theology. They made no attempt to imitate the late sixteenth-century Calvinists who fashioned a serviceable defense against Arians within their own ranks by grafting elements of the *Summa Theologiae* onto the *Institutes of the Christian Religion*. The novel effort of the mathematician John Wallis to explain the Trinity by geometrical analogies proved to be more curious than convincing.[69] Almost imperceptibly, liberal divines moved from professing what they half-understood to believing only what they found explicable. The neglect of systematics also affected the Socinians. Although they explored the logic of their doctrinal position, many of them did not realize the extent of their progress. Still, by 1695 a few adventurous writers had a clear idea of their achievement and were seeking appropriate and consistent ways of describing it so that others might better grasp it.

Any attempt to understand John Toland's theology must take account of the persistent conviction of most of his contemporaries that it was Socinian. Whether they read *Christianity Not Mysterious* as a rejection of Christ's divinity and the Athanasian Creed or as a series of vaguer, if disturbingly heterodox, insinuations, virtually all who attacked it shared the judgment that it was "a Branch of that bitter Root of Socinianism." Occasionally, foes sought to link the book with the works of the lay Anglican rationalists, but such efforts did not entail separating it from the Trinitarian controversy. Thus, when Edward Stillingfleet made a concerted assault on Locke and Toland, he professed to see nothing original in the intentions of either man. Both were contributors to that controversy; Toland's achievement had been to summarize and to elaborate the Unitarians' teaching. John Locke, in contrast, was reluctant to allow that his former client was merely a Unitarian. By hinting that *Christianity Not Mysterious* differed in intent from any of the Unitarian tracts, Locke sought to keep others from accepting the bishop of Worcester's damaging association. While Locke did not call Toland a deist, he tried to nudge his readers into including the Irishman among these notorious, if obscure, heretics. His enterprise was well founded. There were among the first critics of *Christianity Not Mysterious* some who asserted that the deists had welcomed it. Others, who called Toland a deist, were not denying that he had accepted anti-Trinitarianism, but were rather asserting that he had articulated its full implications: "the great Indifferency and Scepticism which reign among us have open'd a door to Socinianism, which is a sure Project for Deism.[1]

Until his death Toland would be treated as a Socinian. Although Defoe was a persistent advocate of this view, he was reluctant to accuse Toland of deism. Works as diverse as the *Life of Milton*, *Nazarenus*, and *Tetradymus* were decried as Socinian, and evidence survives that Toland's ordinary readers subscribed to this judgment. The flyleaf of the British Library's copy of the *The Art of Restoring* bears an inscription in an eighteenth-century hand: "This pamphlet was written by Toland ye

Socinian." It is understandable that one obituary presented hostility to Christ's divinity as the damning legacy of Toland's theological polemic.[2]

A common vulnerability may in part explain the mixture of approval and disavowal in the acknowledged Unitarians' published references to Toland. They recognized that their own opponents presented themselves as his opponents. Defensiveness alone does not elucidate their expressions of regard. Even in Stephen Nye's later, conservative period, when a desire to ingratiate himself with his ecclesiastical superiors led him to attack some of Toland's opinions, he was careful not to question the Irishman's Christianity. He went so far as to express his hope that the church was capable of reforming itself sufficiently to attract Toland. Nye was more inhibited than the unpublished Unitarians who wrote admiringly to Toland as an advocate of their opinions. No corresponding tributes from self-confessed deists survive among the Toland manuscripts.[3]

Toland's disavowal of the Socinians was at least as ambiguous as theirs of him. He differentiated these worshipers of a "Creature God" from the Unitarians whom he never repudiated, and artfully quoted Archbishop Tillotson's praise of them. Although he tried to separate himself from all parties in the second edition of *Christianity Not Mysterious*, he had originally intended the work to end the Trinitarian controversy. He realized that the very title gave offense, since it suggested not merely a refutation of Robert South's traditionalism, but also a rejection of the Trinity, which was seen as the uniquely Christian mystery. Like Defoe, Toland was alive to the danger of being labeled as a Socinian. It is notable that he ventured beyond disavowals of textbook Socinianism, which he knew had little to do with English Unitarianism, in order to defend anti-Trinitarians. He also praised individual Unitarians like Thomas Firmin and dismissed the tag Socinian as a slur used against anyone who "possesses more than ordinary *Learning* and *Judgment*." Despite his frequent professions of Anglicanism, only once, in an early letter that was published posthumously, did the clamor against him evoke the straightforward statement of belief in the Trinity which would have silenced his antagonists. Studied evasiveness characterized all of his later remarks on the subject. The piety with which he usually embellished them failed to satisfy his critics, who were sensitive to the Unitarians' facility with double meanings.[4]

Until recently historians of Augustan religious thought have disregarded the opinion of contemporary observers that the author of *Christianity Not Mysterious* was a Socinian. Initial attempts to correct this omission tended toward lumping and have thus prompted a reaction in favor of separation. Some scholars, not content with emphasizing the biblical predispositions and apologetic intentions of many of the Polish anti-Trinitarians in order to differentiate them from Toland, have assumed that the English Unitarians were distinguished by similar biases.[5]

More thorough investigators of the Englishmen have also posited a clear-cut distinction between them and Toland on the basis of their allegedly divergent intentions. Having concluded that Toland methodized the Socinian approach to mysteries and the Bible, one student went on to maintain that he shunned their "incessant quibbling over texts." Toland did so because the "Unitarian soul of the Socinians" had flown from his design. This argument is circular. It presumes that an identifying purpose animated the Socinian writers, offers a selective reading of their tracts in light of this presumption, and then derives from the reading the conclusion that Toland was substantially independent of the tractarians. The soul of the late seventeenth-century Socinians was variegated. Although some of their works dealt with texts and dogmas, others eschewed references to Scripture and skirted doctrinal matters in order to establish that "Reason is as much the Word, the Will, and Revelation of God, as the written Word it self, and without which the written word would be wholly useless."[6] A few Unitarians even flirted with materialism. While contemporaries recognized that Unitarianism was a conceptual portmanteau, they apparently linked Toland to the tractarians in the conviction that he had perfected their methods of sapping the mysteries of Christianity. In fact, Toland systematized the arguments of the Unitarians by grafting them onto a version of Locke's epistemology. Any attempt to subordinate their effect on him wants more persuasive evidence than the assertion that there was a peculiarly Socinian intention.

Every suggestion of intellectual influence is Janus-like. If it points toward a donor, it points as well toward a recipient. In order to ascertain the influences affecting a receiver of ideas it is necessary to avoid peremptoriness. A search for traces of influences in Toland's works must precede a conclusion about his intention, and, once made, such a judgment remains subject to revision in light of the discovery of additional obligations. Historians seeking to reassert Toland's independence of the Unitarians have failed to separate the question of purpose from that of effect in the writings both of donors and of recipient. They have assumed that establishing the existence of dissimilar purposes — or merely contending that two labels are meaningful and incompatible — vindicates the assertion of discontinuity. By taking the absence of identity as proof of a lack of influence, they risk denying causality a role in intellectual history. A familiar dictum of Arthur O. Lovejoy serves as a reminder of the way in which ideas often develop: "The seeming novelty of many a system is due solely to the novelty of the application or arrangement of the old elements which enter into it."[7]

Unless the intentions of the Latitudinarians, Remonstrants, and Unitarians who created the disorder that was Restoration theology are distinguished from the nature and implications of their characteristic ideas, it will be impossible to investigate how Toland adapted to and affected his intellectual environment. The consequences of the seventeenth-century redefinition of person for the dogma of the Trinity illustrate a way of making such a distinction and of attributing unintended influence. The Athanasian Creed required the worship of "one God in Trinity and the Trinity in unity, neither confusing the persons nor dividing the substance" (*neque confundentes personas, neque substantiam separantes*). In order to give precision to this formula, medieval theologians defined person as "an individual substance of a rational nature"; for them, a person was a subsistent relation. Descartes professed to be an orthodox Roman Catholic seeking to serve his faith through philosophy, but his decision to locate human identity in self-consciousness was to affect Trinitarianism. Whatever Locke's attitude toward the Trinity, he developed Descartes's insight and conceived of person so as to exclude the idea of a subsistent relation and render incoherent the Athanasian symbol. Although his concept of identity is elusive, he defined a person "as a thinking intelligent being that has reason and reflection and can consider itself as itself, the same thinking thing in different times and places; which it does only by that consciousness which is inseparable from thinking. . . . For since consciousness always accompanies thinking, and it is that that makes everyone to be what he calls self, and thereby distinguishes himself from all other thinking things." Despite his pious intentions it was the misfortune of Dean Sherlock to accept this definition of person and fall into tritheism. Unlike Sherlock, the Socinians sought to attack the orthodox formula, but they did so with the aid of the redefinition of person. Confronted with such incoherence, Toland was able to dismiss the consideration of person as a "trifle," presumably because, like the related notion of substance, it was unscriptural and belonged to the "barbarous jargon of the Schools."[8] The Trinitarian Descartes thus influenced not only the enigmatic Locke, but also the unwitting tritheist Sherlock, an anonymous Unitarian, and the dismissive Toland. Influence is not synonymous with identity.

If ideas can enjoy a measure of influence apart from the purposes of their exponents, judgments about an author's intentions must still be made. They will affect both the designation and appraisal of influences on his writings. Toland has acted as a magnet for discordant categories. He appears, for example, in the pages of a recent study alternatively as a deist and an atheist. Yet, there exist a number of suggestive attempts to explain the formation and execution of his thought. Aside from the stray fideist or Marxist reading, they may be separated into three classes: unsystematic, radical and divergent.[9]

Benefiting from an initial, magisterial statement, the first of these interpretations continues to enjoy learned support. Leslie Stephen presented Toland as a literary adventurer who brazenly appropriated and selectively developed some of the conclusions of the Socinians and Anglican rationalists, especially Tillotson and Locke. Although disdainful of Christianity, Toland was not arguing either for or against particular conclusions, but rather against the possibility of reaching conclusions. Stephen forestalled efforts to ascribe to Toland a positive teaching such as pantheism, and with it external sources, by dismissing *Pantheisticon* as "scarcely serious." Within the decade Stephen's thesis has received an erudite reformulation.[10]

Among the leading proponents of a radical interpretation of Toland's philosophical writings, one has assumed that he exhibited consistency of purpose, while another has described him as moving in an increasingly extreme direction. Conceding that Toland's religious opinions resembled those of the Socinians, Margaret C. Jacob has minimized their importance. As a student in the Netherlands, Toland had become acquainted with Hermeticism, and from Bruno's Italian dialogues he fabricated a rational expression of this point of view. Other subversive ideas, including those of revolutionary sectaries from the Civil War, Cartesian materialists, and Spinoza, affected him. Adhering to materialistic pantheism more determinedly than to republican ideology, he opposed a synthesis of Latitudinarianism and Newtonianism created by the Boyle lecturers. Although Chiara Giuntini, the author of the fullest study of Toland's thought, has offered a similar account of his mature attitude, she sees it as the product of his changing notion of how best to enlighten humanity. In his early days Toland had been an idiosyncratic follower of Locke and Le Clerc, as well as a republican ideologist. Introduced to Bruno in 1698, he became more radical theologically even as he grew more moderate politically in response to frustration at his inability to reconcile theory and practice. He transformed the mystical, theosophical presuppositions of Hermeticism into a vision that was at once modern and ancient. It was modern because it accommodated mechanism, ancient because it was intrinsic to the oldest — and hence natural — religion, though in an obscure form. Toland complemented his positive analysis with a polemic aimed at demonstrating that the history of religion is the story of its corruption. Antique sages had resorted to a double-truth theory in order to transmit their esoteric convictions without endangering themselves, but Toland did not seek to imitate their subterfuge.[11]

An explication of Toland's ideas must cope with the diversity of his writings. If Stephen's dismissal of *Pantheisticon* and the works which prefigure it exposes the vulnerability of his thesis, those who would ascribe to Toland a single-minded radicalism have resorted to another form of selectivity to similar effect. Professor Jacob has extended her depreciation of *Christianity Not Mysterious* by presenting the later works in which Toland developed some of its characteristic themes as monuments of antiquarianism. Her decision required that she ignore the invocations of Latitudinarian divines and professions of Low-Church sympathy which dot their pages. In effect, she has set aside many of Toland's publications in order to assert the centrality of a strain of argument absent from them. Dr. Giuntini has avoided this difficulty by creating one of her own. If Toland grew more radical after the appearance of his *succès de scandale*, he relied in numerous later efforts on the critical methods he had learned from Le Clerc to reach destructive conclusions. Giuntini's hypothesis depends, however, on an omission. In order to establish that Toland's radicalism was a relatively late development, she had to deny his authorship of *Two Essays* (1695), a more extreme work than *Christianity Not Mysterious* (1696). The case for attributing this pamphlet to him rests on internal as well as external evidence. Anticipating the *Letters to Serena*, its tag from Lucretius — *Edita doctrina sapientum templa serena* — became the first of the series of clues which he was to plant in one piece and then unearth in another so as to connect the two. He was also to recapitulate his attack on the historicity of the deluge, a fundamental argument of the pamphlet, a quarter-century later in *Pantheisticon*. Finally, the coda of the essay, *Jovis omnia plena*, projects his mature cosmology. While it is undeniable that Toland spoke in a radical voice, he did so at the beginning of his career and only periodically thereafter.[12]

For the most part, scholars trying to interpret the whole of Toland's thought have portrayed him as evolving into an exponent of divergent systems.[13] They have mistakenly dated the beginning of his publishing career from *Christianity Not Mysterious*, which they take to be either a statement of a sincere, if attenuated, Christianity, or an attempt at synthesizing a new position from deism and advanced Anglicanism. Toland did not remain committed to this synthesis. By the time he wrote *Letters to Serena*, he had become attached to a materialist philosophy, fearful of persecution, and sceptical of the capacity of ordinary people ever to think for themselves. He sought a means of propagating his ideas without inviting excessive risk. Champions of this view see in "Clidophorus" (*Tetradymus*, 1720) proof that the later Toland both paid lip service to an exoteric, vestigially Christian teaching and advocated an esoteric, materialist pantheism.

The notion that Toland was driven to speak in two distinct voices is suggestive, but it fails to account for his longstanding commitment to and equivocal use of both of them. He chose to teach esoterically and exoterically near the beginning of his literary career, years before he limned his strategy. Following the composition of *Two Essays*, he appears to have reconsidered his approach and reached a decision which affected everything else he wrote. Since he had avoided being connected with the pamphlet, he was perhaps moved less by concern about his own safety than by a desire to achieve acceptance. Despite its reasonableness, materialism would never supplant Christianity; it could persuade only a few and was, therefore, incapable of simultaneously advancing rationality and maintaining order.

Toland had to find a more supple means of promoting the cause of reason among the articulate classes without compromising his convictions. The protean quality of Socinianism offered him an example. If the Socinians had chipped at the most offensive features of Christianity and accommodated circumspect materialists, they also kept the goodwill of a number of weighty divines. Many of the leading Remonstrants had either countenanced or assimilated the characteristic notions of the

Unitarians and gone on to influence the Anglican rationalists. Even a projector less venturesome than Toland could have discerned in the fortune of Socinianism the possibility of transforming Protestantism. Toland never abandoned his effort to refine and to promote with intermittent discretion a metaphysics that eschewed the transcendent. Yet in *Christianity Not Mysterious* he cunningly forged from parts of liberal divinity an engine that would combat the irrational aspects of traditional belief and further a state cult in which any reasonable person could participate. His instrument was suitable for parry as well as for thrust. It allowed him both to present his esoteric teaching as circumstances or his own interests moved him and, when called to account, to point to his authorship of works suggestive of much fashionable theology.

Toland retrospectively defined the intention that underlay his writing from 1695; he analyzed after he had begun to write. In *Clito*, he offered the first tentative account of his purpose. "Adeisidaemon" (i.e., without superstition), his mouthpiece, sought "to teach Mankind those Truths which they mistake." Using "common words" in order to tell "vulgar things," he undertook to "make all Ideas with their Signs agree." Adeisidaemon differentiated the critical task from that of cosmology, which involved matters more rarefied than vulgar:

> Who form'd the Universe, and when and why,
> Or if all things are from Eternity;
> What Laws to Nature are prescrib'd by Jove;
> Where lys his chiefest residence above;
> Or if he's only but the World's great Soul;
> Or parts the Creatures are, and God the whole
> From whence all Beings their Existence have,
> And into which resolv'd they find a Grave;
> How nothing's lost, tho all things change their Form,
> As that's a Fly which is but now a worm;
> And Death is only to begin to be
> Som other thing, which endless change shall see;
> (Then why should men to dy have so great fear?)
> Tho nought's Immortal, all Eternal be.

More important than either of these projects was the pursuit of civic virtue. Above all Adeisidaemon was "the fatal scourge of slavery," who would reconcile squabbling parties to work for the good of England. For him, religion was morality, and patriotism the ultimate act of worship: "But they deserve and share his [the "one true all-perfect DEITY"] first Applause,/Who stake their Lives in their dear Contry's Cause."[14]

Not until "Clidophorus" did Toland elaborate the theory of truth encased in *Clito*. In the course of the essay he referred to "Varro's threefold Theology, the Mythical, Physical, and Political," used by poets, philosophers, and "particular nations respectively." Although this reference is late and brief, Toland must have been reflecting on such a division and its implications since his days as a theological student. The only surviving fragments of Varro's writings are those which Augustine quoted in *The City of God*. Varro conceived of truth as plural and sequential, rather than as an antithesis to error. His first theology, the mythical, contained "many fictions, which are contrary to the dignity and nature of the immortals." Augustine observed of it: "he is speaking, not concerning natural theology, not concerning civil, but concerning fabulous theology, which he thought he could freely find fault with." The second addressed cosmology, the domain of philosophy. In Augustine's opinion, Varro found "fault with nothing in this kind of theology which they call *physical*, and which belongs to philosophers, except that he has related their controversies among themselves, through which has arisen a multitude of dissentical sects. Nevertheless he has removed this kind from the Forum, that is from the populace, but he has shut it up in schools." Purifying inherited fable with the aid of philosophical speculation, the third took as its province the religion that every polity required. Augustine denounced it: "That theology, therefore, which is fabulous, theatrical, scenic, and full of all baseness and unseemliness, is taken up into the civil theology; and part of that theology, which in its totality is deservedly judged to be worthy of reprobation, is pronounced worthy to be cultivated and observed. . . ."[15]

Vico would transform Varro's scheme into a cyclical explanation of history which held that every culture passed during its lifetime from an age of gods through an age of heroes to an age of men. Whatever their other differences of interpretation, his predecessors had treated Varro as one of the late antique proponents of an erroneous allegorical exegesis of mythology. They had, accordingly, no inclination to take him as a guide in any current theological inquiry. Confident that reason was normative and compatible with faith, Le Clerc depicted allegorizing as the effort of embarrassed pagan philosophers to save their dubious religious heritage from the ethical and intellectual challenge of Christianity. The euhemerist analysis he favored revealed the history of paganism as the story of the degeneration of primitive truth. Notwithstanding his apparent fideism, Bayle was equally unsympathetic to allegorical theories, all of which ignored the simpleminded materialism that governed primitives. In his view, the gulf between belief and rationality was fixed and unbridgeable.[16]

Under Le Clerc's tutelage Toland adopted the idea of pervasive theological degeneracy, just as he was to exploit Bayle's hypothesis of an original materialism to his own purposes. Although he sometimes relied on euhemerism, he judged that even crude fables preserved elements of primordial truth and commended the attempts of classical demythologizers to uncover them. Believing that all religions exhibited a common morphology, he assumed the continuing necessity both of such investigations and of the kind of policy which had inspired the mythopoeism of ancient sages and rulers. Like their pagan counterparts, the founders of Judaism and Christianity had sought to mask their own moral and rational principles in order to gain the sympathy of the credulous many. It was Toland's intention to reconstitute their beliefs and to make them accessible to his contemporaries, who were attracted to enlightenment but still dependent on religion. With the aim of preparing for an exoteric theology, a set of politically necessary religious principles which had to remain distinct from his esoteric theology—philosophical truths about physical and human nature—he criticized mythical embellishments of Christianity. Classical sources informed Toland's sometimes wavering effort to associate these diverse goals. If he once proposed to imitate Plutarch's essay "On Superstition" and save the prevailing cult by mitigating its irrationality, he found in Cicero the precursor of his endeavor.[17]

Cicero had maintained that traditional religion, purified of the grossest superstitions, was essential to the preservation of the state. He "was not less tenacious of the Roman Establishment than we are of the English Establishment." Since belief in providence and in the immortality of the soul was indispensable to Cicero's political theology, it remained immune to criticism. As a true lover of philosophy, which "designedly shuns the multitude," Cicero doubted both the wisdom and the strength of the many. Implicit in his attitude was a measure of compassion for ordinary people, whose peace of mind was often disturbed by religious phantasms. Like many seventeenth-century Englishmen, Cicero identified religion with morality, and he labored to reveal the practical truths embedded in the Roman cult.[18]

Cicero's idea of a civil theology had, Toland thought, general applicability. Both privately and publicly, he maintained that "no nation or society of men can possibly subsist without some common Rule of life and manners." The majority in any society would adhere to customary conformity. Accordingly, while the sage combated superstition by differentiating it from true religion, he must remain silent in the face of harmless popular notions. Any great legislator, such as Moses, had to be careful to adapt his arguments to the capacities of his followers.[19]

Toland maintained that all Christian doctrines must be generally comprehensible, and he repudiated the proposition that any of them could possess both open and hidden elements. He did so not only to indicate the dependence of his exoteric theology on his critique of mystery, but also to demarcate it from his esoteric teaching. Toland meant *Christianity Not Mysterious* to oppose the vulgar faith by edifying the many, and he therefore avoided arcana in writing it. At the same time he held that, when one speaks commonplaces, "it is not always a sure rule that he speaks what he thinks," but when one expresses an unconventional opinion, it is prima facie evidence of honesty. This dictum contains a useful warning against taking at face value his subsequent portrayal of himself as a defender of the church; it also emphasizes the centrality of paradox in his theological method. To assert that Christianity could be relieved of mysteries was to project a task rather than a masquerade. Although he recognized that some might see his Christianity as idiosyncratic, he clung to the name Christian. As long as he lived, he sought to ensure that Christianity performed its mission of

reconciling God to sinners, of purifying the mind, of regulating manners, of directing conscience, of illuminating the understanding, of stating particular duties, of fixing the hopes of rewards to the good, of planting the fear of punishment in the wicked, of propagating mutual love, forbearance, and peace among all mankind, of improving, conducting, and supporting civil society.[20]

Convinced that "the universal disposition of the Age was bent upon a Rational Religion" and seeing the Latitudinarians as advocates of reason, Toland hoped for the success of *Christianity Not Mysterious*. Archbishop Tillotson provided him with a tag: "We need not desire a better Evidence that any Man is in the wrong, than to hear him declare against Reason, and thereby acknowledge that Reason is against him." Toland's selection of these lines reflected a shrewd estimate of the drift of English religious opinion. The desire for a comprehensive church was as widespread as the identification of the church with the nation. The Calvinism of the Thirty-Nine Articles, to which the clergy had to subscribe, was distasteful to both High- and Low-Churchmen, so that dissembling had become conventional, revulsion at dogmatic squabbles endemic, and uniformity of belief impossible. Suitably lightened, the burden of the Anglican past could be borne. As if to illustrate how judicious disregard of formularies might lead to the universal acceptance of Anglicanism, Toland seized on the casual suggestion made by Richard Willis, a Latitudinarian divine on his way to becoming a bishop, of a method whereby he could belong to the church without repudiating his own writings. Toland's pleasure in William III's episcopal creations is understandable.[21]

Reason imposed constructive as well as critical obligations, and Toland envisioned *Christianity Not Mysterious* as the first part of a trilogy, whose conclusion, *Christianity Restored*, would help to reform the Reformation. In the event, the sustained hostility evoked by the inaugural volume dissuaded him from prolonging a marked enterprise. By abandoning it, Toland did not forsake his attempts to end divisions about religion within the commonwealth, to reconcile churchmanship to nationality; rather he chose to work piecemeal.[22]

Toland was frustrated in his hopes for his civil theology because he had neither taken into account the sustained tolerance of the Latitudinarians for incongruity nor foreseen the general reaction against liberal divinity which the High-Church revival would provoke. For all his success in adapting, by fair means and foul, the characteristic dispositions and conclusions of a half-century of liberal English religious thinking into a systematic alternative to traditional creeds, he had reckoned without the persistent attraction of many of these formulas even after their intellectual props had been gutted. Moreover, as Locke's tortuous path to repudiating Toland suggests, the hue and cry against heretics which High-Churchmen raised in order to further their partisan interests forced exponents of theological liberalism to backtrack in an attempt to safeguard their political well-being. During Toland's lifetime a new reformation was powerless to be born.

The postponement affected Toland's perception of England's religious future. By 1705 he was subject to bouts of pessimism and optimism. His pessimistic moods had three symptoms: the conviction that disputes about religion are irreconcilable, the division of humanity into the reasonable few and the gullible mob, and the denial of the possibility of rational theology. When he was in this humor, he thought that it was the sage's duty to stand aloof and maintain indifference in disputes. Even in his last years, however, he did not become a proponent of an exclusively defensive double-truth theory. An optimistic mood always struggled for ascendancy. In one of his last books he insisted that, far from detaching himself, the sage was obliged by the fact of citizenship to "do all that can be done" to uproot superstition, and he retained his interest in demythologizing the vulgar religion in order to clear the way for a proper civil theology.[23] Even in frustration, John Toland remained the heir of Varro and of Cicero.

Toland's attack on the English poetical theology derived much of its legitimacy from his skill in playing on the national fixation with antipopery. By the end of the seventeenth century the Reformation had become as much a metaphor describing a set of values and prejudices as the designation of a series of events 150 years earlier. The omnipresent papist threat from across the Channel had popularized the expectation that undoctrinal mutual forbearance among Englishmen would lead to the establishment of a comprehensive national church. As a result, Protestantism itself now seemed to mean simply the rejection of the claims of the bishop of Rome — tyrannical pretensions supported by unchristian enormities designed to manipulate gullibility. Despite the suppleness of this reformulation, Protestantism, the Bible, and reason were still contrasted with popery, tradition, and mystery. If the new, vaguer understanding of Protestantism allowed Toland to identify himself with its cause, the persistent contrast enabled him to exploit antipopery. He defended his exposé of superstition as an effort to perfect the Reformation. When discussing the conventional idea of mystery, he used pejoratives which reformed apologists had developed in their struggle against Romish grotesqueries — gibes at transubstantiation being the most obvious.[24]

At the same time he felt obliged to explain why such a godly work had fared so indifferently. Because he at once shared in and exploited the universal taste for conspiracy theories, he found it easy to attribute the reverse to a plot hatched by the crypto-papist Archbishop Laud to "deform the Reformation." Toland went on to lash out at his critics for continuing the intrigue. Ironically, the imagery of antipopery was at once so vague and so pervasive that some of these critics attacked Toland as an agent of Rome sent to unsettle God's Englishmen.[25]

Toland brought considered epistemological assumptions to his attack on the Christian poetical theology. He seems always to have taken clarity and simplicity as marks of true propositions. He combined this preference with enmity toward custom and faith in novelty as the means for advancing truth. Custom was evil because it tended to habituate men to precarious and hasty conclusions. Only through determined effort would they recover their innate freedom. Because Toland believed that such a struggle was an imperative of human nature, he anticipated the Romantic interpretation of *Paradise Lost* as a Promethean allegory. The conviction also led him to follow his teacher, Limborch, and endow heresy with a creative purpose. Reason's initial task was critical; no subject was above investigation, and every subject had to be investigated. In place of Descartes's *cogito,* he asserted that "the unavoidable Supposition of our Existence [lies] in this very Proposition, 'I doubt if I am.' "[26] For Toland, to live was to doubt.

Following the Latitudinarians, Toland was prone to condemn philosophical divinity for fostering obscurity and deception. Still, he did philosophize, and later students have ascribed contradictory influences to the most systematic exposition of his thought, *Christianity Not Mysterious.* A commonly asserted debt has been to Locke, particularly—and mistakenly—to *The Reasonableness of Christianity.* Paradoxically, Locke's real legacy, the epistemology of criticism which, under Le Clerc's guidance, Toland extorted from the *Essay concerning Human Understanding,* has been denied. Locke himself disavowed any responsibility, but his disclaimers did not prevent observers more acute than Stillingfleet from repeating the charge. Although Toland would eventually do his old benefactor the favor of denying any dependence on him, his earlier statements were more candid and had the opposite effect. Had he not once singled out the *Essay* as "the most useful Book that was ever written in Philosophy"?[27] Since the Renaissance, logicians had sought to make human reasoning correspond with external reality by framing propositions that accurately represented it. While Toland later admitted that his adaptation of the Lockian epistemology in *Christianity Not Mysterious* was confused, he had relied on the *Essay* because, preeminently, it helped "Men to speak pertinently, intelligibly, and accurately, of all kinds of Subjects."[28] It also legitimated the criterion of assent he had borrowed from the Socinians.

The theme of Toland's work was straightforward: insofar as the human mind cannot discover and describe the intelligible reality presented by God, both creation and Creator are senseless. Like the Unitarians, he expanded the denial by orthodox theologians of propositions *contra rationem* to a denial of the attribution of propositions *supra rationem* to God. No true proposition can be a mystery. He held that four means of information are available to mankind. The first two are experiences of the senses and of the intellect which correspond to sensation and reflection in Locke's scheme; and the last are discoveries made by human and by divine authority, which Locke had termed human testimony and divine revelation. Collectively, the means of information constitute evidence, "the exact Conformity of our Ideas or Thoughts with their Objects, or the Things we think upon." An idea is the mind's object whenever it thinks, or the particular thought it employs to represent anything. For Toland as for Locke, the discoveries of authority are less certain than those of the senses and of the intellect; whatever value they have derives from the credibility of their source.[29]

Toland endued the mind with three faculties: perception, judgment, and affect. Perception is a passive process that allows for the receipt of ideas either by the senses or by the mind's consideration of its own activities. Judgment permits the affirmation or denial of relationships between ideas, and affect the formation of attitudes toward what has been perceived. His central concern, judgment, defines the scope of knowledge, which can be either immediate and intuitive (e.g., that of an individual's existence) or mediate and rational (e.g., that of God's existence). Knowledge of external objects is possible only by way of ideas expressed in words. Ideas are of three classes: first, images or representations of a body; secondly, sensations occasioned by a body; and thirdly, intellectual or abstracted thoughts. Toland admitted that limitations on the ideas a mind can form often result in probability, which is not knowledge. Yet, he distorted Locke's explanation of certitude and ignored both his insistence that sensory knowledge can never be certain and his effort to distinguish between the domain of reason and that of faith. In addition, Toland failed to explain *how* the mind attains certain knowledge from images and perceptions. Glossing over these failures, he maintained that "what is evidently repugnant to clear and distinct Ideas, or to our Common Notions, is contrary to Reason," which he synecdochially took to be the entire process of thinking.[30]

Construing the *Essay* as allowing the synonymy of intuition, to which Locke had given priority, with demonstration, Toland limited the operation of reason to mediate knowledge. He formally defined reason as that "faculty of the Soul which discovers the Certainty of any thing dubious or obscure, by comparing it with something evidently known." Coherence among ideas thus provided the standard for determining the correspondence of any single idea to the aspect of reality it allegedly expressed. Toland's definition did not keep him from investing reason, or reasonableness, with a number of connotations, some related and others discordant:

(1) that which is plain, simple, evident, or intelligible;
(2) that which is not mysterious;
(3) that which is not contradictory;
(4) that which is demonstrable from experience;
(5) that which is agreeable to common sense;
(6) that which belongs to ordinary experience;
(7) that which is actual rather than hypothetical;
(8) that which is theoretically possible;
(9) that which belongs to the natural faculties of man, the right use of these faculties, or the "Principle of Discourse in us."[31]

By accepting Locke's thesis that knowledge of a thing's properties does not entail knowledge of its essence, Toland stirred Bishop Stillingfleet from his nondogmatic slumbers. Locke had distinguished between a thing's real and nominal essences. Toland understood the former to be "that intrinsick Constitution of a thing which is the Good or Support of all its Properties," while the latter was "a collection of those Properties or Modes which we principally observe in any thing, and to which we give one common Denomination or Name." He borrowed this distinction not in order to exclude discussion of superempirical reality, but rather to use the concept of real essence without being obliged to concede that there is a mysterious element in cognition. His implication was plain. While men can know that God exists and form ideas of His properties, such as omnipotence, they can know nothing of His essence, that, for example, He is three coequal and coeternal persons in one substance.[32]

The violent opposition to *Christianity Not Mysterious* owed little to a consideration of its epistemology, which appears to have been nearly as incomprehensible to many of its critics as to the man in the pew. It arose instead from the book's implicit challenge to inherited theological predispositions, especially about the nature and discoveries of revelation. In his examination of both inspiration and mystery, Toland relied on Locke's *Essay* and the Unitarian tracts. Early in the book Toland had affirmed that irreconcilable differences among exegetes made reason the ultimate authority for dealing with scriptural texts and controversies about their interpretation. Locke had treated revelation as a unique means by which God discloses truths to men — hedging his declaration that "we may as well doubt of our own being as we can whether any revelation from God be true" with requirements so stiff as to call into question the claims of any of the competitors for the title of divine revelation. Toland simplified this treatment by presenting revelation as a "means of information" rather than "a necessitating Motive of Assent." In light of his conception of the New Testament as a "Prophetical History of the External State of the Church" containing "no new Doctrines," its importance as a means of information seems doubtful. Any assertion of revelation would have to be judged by the same tests of disinterestedness and probability as applied to data received on human authority. Having offered this principle, Toland piquantly rejected the allegation that the apostles were "transported with Enthusiastic Fits" and lacked "good Sense and a liberal Education."[33]

Toland admitted that "the Vulgar Faith" looked upon some mysteries, such as the Trinity and the Incarnation, as things imperfectly knowable "in the present state of our Faculties," and others, like "the *Prophecies* contained in the *Revelations*," as only imperfectly revealed. He proposed to turn to the New Testament to settle the meaning of mystery, but in doing so he was able to blend the Unitarian methodology with the demythologizing accomplished by the Latitudinarians and Remonstrants. In approaching scriptural references to mystery, he used the same assumption which governed his treatment of substance, viz., "nothing can be said to be a Mystery, because we have not an adequate Idea of it." Like the Socinians, he presumed that in the New Testament God's revelations are mysteries because of prior vagueness rather than present obscurity.[34]

He distinguished three uses of the word *mystery*: first, "the Gospel or the Christian Religion in general, as it is a future Dispensation totally hid from the *Gentiles* and but very imperfectly known to the Jews: Secondly, some particular Doctrines occasionally reveal'd by the *Apostels* are said to be manifested Mysteries, that is unfolded secrets. And thirdly, Mystery is put for any thing vail'd under Parables or Enigmatical Forms of Speech." He either dismissed recalcitrant texts as having "no reference to any thing in particular" or lumped them under his third rubric. In a calculated indiscretion toward the end of the book, he allowed a glimpse of his design: "either the Apostles could not write more intelligibly of the reputed Mysteries, or they would not. If they would not, then 'tis no longer our Fault if we neither understand nor believe them: and if they could not write more clearly themselves, they are so much less to expect Credit from others." During most of the rest of his career, he held that whatever mysteries Christianity might contain are negligible, because they do not serve its goal, the fostering of sound morals. Even his late declaration that endless disputes about the meaning of Christ's teachings suggest something inherently mysterious amounted to a restatement of the position that no man can be expected to believe what he cannot understand.[35]

Although Toland interpreted Locke as conceiving of faith as an "intelligible persuasion," he sometimes treated it as another form of knowledge. Thus, he would concede that assent "constitutes the formal Act of Faith," and then reassert the priority of knowledge in creating it. The reduction of faith to knowledge tended to make formal heresy a consequence of misinformation, for which no one could be held culpable, instead of the perversion of will envisioned by traditional theology. Yet in presenting the extirpation of error as a moral imperative, he indicted superstition as the single culpable form of misinformation.[36]

There were no exceptions to Toland's notion of faith as a form of knowledge. Even when he appeared to impart a tincture of spirituality to faith by defining its as "an internal participation of the divine nature irradiating the soul," he was using a circumlocution to restate his belief that the just live by works alone. The *locus classicus* of his intellectualist idea of faith in his exposition of the account in Genesis of Abraham's willingness to sacrifice Isaac. Archbishop Tillotson had contented himself with rendering the story tolerably reasonable. Toland went further. Maintaining that Jehovah must have given prior assurance of a satisfactory outcome, he asserted that there was in it nothing "but very strict Reasoning from Experience, from the Possibility of the thing, and from the Power, Justice and Immutability of him that promised it." St. Paul's verdict on Abraham—"He staggered not at the promise of God through unbelief; but was strong in faith, giving glory to God"—represents a hard statement of the demands of faith as alien to Tillotson's reasonableness as to Toland's rationalizing.[37]

Who was the God whose rationality Toland thought the patriarch presumed? How could His rationality accommodate the miracles ascribed to Him in the Bible? In response to charges that he was unorthodox about the Trinity, Toland outdid Locke's evasiveness and implied that his exoteric notion of God may have owed something to the Socinians. He had been artful in *Christianity Not Mysterious*. On the one hand he professed to censure paganism for fostering a view of life devoid of the transcendent and for explaining disorder in the lives of individuals as the consequence of ignorance rather than of sin. On the other hand he treated religion as an unchanging entity whose truth was judged by reason. His substantialism precluded the events in Eden, the inheritance of original sin, and a Redeemer. Understandably, he dismissed "curious questions about the Person of Christ" as having no bearing on the teaching of the New Testament. From his first major book onward, however, Toland adhered to something resembling the Lockian interpretation of the person and mission of Christ: the Messiah, who died for truth and the good of the race; who brought salvation by enlightening men, dispersing "those thick clouds of ignorance which from the Jews and Gentiles had much obscur'd the perfect truth" and engaging "his principal followers in the noble task of rescuing men from the tyranny of custom, fraud, and force"; who thereby restored the unchanging entity which is true religion. The impression that he saw Christ as a reformer is strengthened by his private musings on Christ's childhood, which were not reconcilable with the Christology taught in the Thirty-Nine Articles.[38]

Most of Toland's opponents accepted his theism, even when they saw him as "the most inveterate *Enemy* to reveal'd Religion." For his part, Toland was willing to publish a list of familiar qualities of "the one true God": goodness, mercy, justice, wisdom, power, and responsiveness to prayers. No evidence exists that he invested his own deity with any of these traits. He never recognized the existence either of a final cause (that because of which something is or becomes) or of spiritual substance (a permanent, underlying reality, as contrasted with transient things). He appears, moreover, not to have admitted a superintending providence in human affairs. He left neither meditations nor prayers, and no anecdotes survive that suggest that he believed in a personal God. In contrast, Voltaire is said to have gone down on his knees at dawn one day and proclaimed, "Powerful God, I believe!"[39] The implications of Toland's critique apparently were tangential to his personal beliefs.

Dr. Johnson's indignation at Hume's treatment of miracles in the tenth chapter of the *Inquiry concerning Human Understanding* suggests that for the Augustan sensibility the need—or hope—for them had become the redoubt of the God of Abraham and Isaac. Toland's deftly ambiguous discussion of miracles implies that the bestowal of personal attributes on the God of his exoteric theology manifested a desire for acceptance, rather than conviction. Ambiguity began with his efforts to define miraculous phenomena. For most apologists, a miracle was "an operation wrought by the immediate power of God, not by Assisting only, but Overruling the laws of Nature; not only by *hastning* and *accelerating* its Operations, but sometimes by an instantaneous production, by what is never to be effected by the united force of all natural causes." From *Two Essays* onward, Toland stressed the uniform working of the laws of nature, decried any attempt to introduce particularistic intervention in "the Machine we call the Universe," and rejected the account of the Noachian flood and mocked popular tales of miracles. When he framed his own definition, he ignored the notion that a miracle subverts the laws of nature, and maintained instead that it was an action "in itself intelligible and possible" which conformed to natural principles. He exploited the Latitudinarians' distaste for the supernatural, so that, *mirabile dictu,* the miracles of Christianity, which he never impugned, became proofs of its rationality. In turn, this maneuver allowed him to discount as fabulous most of the miracles related in the Old Testament and all those reported in post-Biblical times. He mitigated the damage of such limited concessions by holding that miracles offered no instruction about the content of religion.[40]

Because of the Latitudinarians' work, Toland could proceed in the confidence that at least the rudiments of his ecclesiology were familiar and in the hope that it would win widespread support. He recognized the lack of a generally accepted and coherent Anglican theory of the church. This vacuum freed him to urge the claims of his opinions, which he had formed "from the dictates of right reason, from my own observations on the best governments in the world, and from the Original Constitution of Christianity.[41]

What kind of church did he propose to construct from these sources? Two metaphors dominated Toland's thought on the subject: the existence of primitive truth and reform as a continuing search for it. In his view, the Reformation was a quest for the restitution of a natural right of inquiry. It was also an historical reality, and in interpreting it Toland, like the Socinians, adopted the argument of Bossuet's *Histoire des variations des églises protestantes:* variety of opinion was the effect of the Protestant rejection of Rome as the arbiter of truth. By placing himself in the line of intellectual descent from Luther, Calvin, and Zwingli, he connected his quest with the events of the sixteenth century.[42]

Toland shared in the primitivism to which his age was attached, but when considering the early church he used it primarily as a grab-bag for rhetorical devices. Throughout *Christianity Not Mysterious* he linked antiquity with simplicity and simplicity with truth. There was a pure religion, which could be recovered from the corruption that had resulted from cunning and greed. Notwithstanding his laborious inquiries, history scarcely affected his effort to restore the primitive constitution of Christianity. His definition of this pure state was apodictic rather than contingent. Since he assumed its nondoctrinal, moralistic character, he was free to dismiss—or ridicule—any of its dogmatic elements as perversions. His reliance on the genetic fallacy in presenting the history of the church complemented this bias. Having insinuated the aberrancy of various practices and articles, he was as concerned to obviate analysis of them as to preclude acceptance of them. Anyone who espoused views conforming to his conception of the natural and the reasonable was, by definition, faithful to pristine truth. Thus, he was confident that he could read Lactantius, the early fourth-century apologist, and separate integrity from debasement. Toland came closest to disclosing his real attitude toward primitivism on those occasions when he intimated that finite creatures' knowledge was cumulative and progressive. He invoked the psalmist to disparage "dark sayings of old," and his favorable references to the modernists Perrault and Fontenelle reveal his allegiance in the quarrel between the ancients and the moderns.[43] Of itself, even the most remote past enjoyed no automatic hold over living minds.

Protestantism also encompassed the rejection of the authority of ecumenical councils and the fathers. Given the attitude of the Latitudinarians, Toland's renunciation of conciliar authority required little justification, and his harshest critics did not fault him for it. Unlike the Latitudinarians, though, Toland grasped its significance. He maintained that there had never been a "constant System of Doctrine and Discipline" in the Church, and that without any adjudicatory body orthodoxy was a meaningless term. The church became a collection of individuals organized in national groups and "subject to prejudice, weakness, and error." No church had a guarantee of infallibility, so that the assemblies of individuals who constitute churches are susceptible to every kind of blunder. Informing Toland's discussion of institutions was the principle of an untrammeled conscience's right to choose what it cared to believe.[44]

Despite the devoted attention of Caroline divines to patristic writings, Toland was outspoken in his indictment of this source of authority. Besotted by priestly exclusivity and rapacity, the fathers were the progenitors of popish superstition. He also represented the High-Church party as their cadets. By doing so, he could implicate the whole group, which included his most relentless foes, in the enormities of popery. His contempt for the fathers had an additional motive: they exhibited a bewildering variety of opinion on crucial questions and an insatiable lust for gross credulities. The welter they had created doomed any effort to interpret the mind of the pre-Constantinian church on disputed questions, as surely as the renunciation of conciliar authority precluded attributing unanimity to the church after the Council of Nicaea. Toland disdained the notion that the fathers' proximity to the apostles entitled them to particular respect as exegetes. They had no fixed canon and relied on some texts which the church would subsequently reject. In playing on papist appeals to them, he went beyond innuendo to represent the doctrinal development which culminated in the medieval church as a tale of the clergy's uninterrupted accumulation of power.[45]

Anglicans had, of course, venerated patristic opinion before there was a High-Church party, and when confronted with evidence of such veneration in the twentieth article or in Hooker's *Laws of Ecclesiastical Polity,* Toland pursued a triple strategy. First, he invoked the biblicism of Chillingworth and his successors; secondly, he asserted that the fathers had only been historians; and thirdly, he maintained that their claims were inextricably bound up with the repudiated authority of general councils. This approach was a recapitulation of his statement of the necessary individualism of faith, the fallibility of all human opinion, and the right of a free intellect to choose its beliefs.[46]

In investigating the ante-Nicene fathers, Toland relied on the theories of the Socinians, much as they had relied on Pétau. With little effort he convinced himself that not only did the fathers' use of Scripture show gullibility, but also that their own texts were suspect. Imitating the labors of the *érudits* was, however, less attractive to him than formulating *ad hominem* arguments. He did not spare individual doctors. Jerome, for example, was a "raving monk." His choice invective was reserved for the theological heir of Athanasius, Cyril, whose followers murdered the philosopher Hypatia, the glory of fifth-century Alexandria's Neoplatonic school. Toland eulogized that distinguished woman in a tract which bore her name, and in its subtitle castigated the defender of the Homoousian for "pride, emulation, and cruelty." He capitalized on the abiding preference of broad-minded churchmen for honest heathens over devious clerics. The appeal of such anticlericalism was not restricted to sympathizers with William Whiston, the Arian disciple of Isaac Newton. *Hypatia,* Charles Kingsley's double-decker attack on the genealogy that his own High-Church opponents claimed for themselves, would merely embellish Toland's theme.[47]

Latitudinarianism had other, equally clear implications for the Church of England's institutions. Like Tillotson, Toland believed that there was no apostolic succession bestowing certain powers and privileges on the episcopacy, but here, too, he drew inferences which the archbishop had overlooked. Bishops had neither functions nor rights apart from those which the worshiping nation chose to bestow on them. Toland also recognized that the Glorious Revolution had profound implications for the church. By rejecting a sacred monarchy, Englishmen had virtually rejected a sacred episcopacy. It remained for them to assert their ancient prerogative of electing their governors. However they were selected, bishops enjoyed no *ex officio* supremacy over the laity. Synesius, Hypatia's student who gained a miter without abandoning Neoplatonism, exemplified the variety of belief—or unbelief—found among prelates and hence the lack of a peculiar episcopal teaching office. Toland expanded the Latitudinarian rejection of post-biblical prophecy into a denial that any living person possessed inspiration or vision beyond the ordinary powers of reason. His denial amounted to a reassertion of the supremacy of conscience. The props of extraordinary claims, ritualistic worship and an episcopally ordained clergy, were at once unscriptural and impediments to the reforming of the English Reformation, the achievement of individualism of belief.[48]

Explaining why the primitive truth of Christianity had suffered over the centuries was congenial to Toland. A mechancial view of human behavior enabled him to attribute action to the force of self-interest and to present theological perversity as the fruit of imposture and invention. He was convinced that the existence of a priestly caste inevitably led to superstition. It accounted for both the degradation of Judaism from its Mosaic purity by Christ's time and the subsequent divisions among Christians. The early church had known no distinction between clergy and laity; all believers had been literally and equally priests sub-

ject to the dictates of their inviolable consciences. Going beyond
ridicule, Toland's antipathy to the cultic expression of religion was
essential to his ecclesiology. He saw ritualism as the major instrument
of priestcraft and the greatest obstacle to the union of Englishmen in a
national church. Since ceremony was meant to foster mystery, it was
antithetical to Christianity. Toland adopted the Unitarians' sacramental system and admitted baptism as a rite of initiation and the Eucharist
as a simple remembrance. Nevertheless, he insisted that any effort to
complicate these two rendered them foolish.[49] His analysis of the clergy
and rites reinforced his conclusion that a church was nothing more than
a free association of those in any country who wished to identify
themselves as Christians.

Toland complemented his use of the minimization of the visible
church offered by the Latitudinarians by appropriating their emphasis
on sincerity in religion. In *Nazarenus* he elaborated a thesis that he had
long assumed. Priestcraft, the imposition of rites and formulas by an
exclusive clergy, both accepted and advanced personal insincerity.
Heathen and sacerdotal corruption had infected the primitive church
because, in their zeal to proselytize, its leaders had ignored the fidelity
of their converts. He exploited the vogue of sincerity to a more important end than historical explanation and invoked it to defend the truth,
i.e., the sincerity, of his own much controverted Christianity. There
was, he suggested, an antithesis between a legalistic religion which
does not elicit real assent and a heartfelt religion which does. The latter
always demands respect, however unconventional its tenets.[50]

Underlying Toland's belief in justifying sincerity was the in-
dividualist biblicism of the Latitudinarians: "The *Scriptures* have
engag'd me in this Error, if it is one; and I will sooner be reputed
Heterodox with these only on my side, than to pass for Orthodox, with
the whole world, and have them against me." The negligible role he
assigned to the Bible in forming religious opinions does not mean that
such protestations were bald subterfuges. In fact, his use of Scripture to
criticize Christian poetical theology suggests that he had turned it into
a tool for fashioning his civil theology. Professing to take the inspiration
of the New Testament for granted, he found in it no new doctrines,
only the revelation of "several wonderful Matters of Fact" and "Important Truths" inaccessible to unaided reason, including the creation, the
coming of Christ, the resurrection of the body, and the last judgment.[51]

Before one accepted a purported revelation, two conditions would have to be fulfilled. "Matters reveal'd by God or Man, must be equally intelligible and possible," and "the facility of the *Gospel* is not confin'd only to Method; for the Stile is also most easy, most natural, and in the common Dialect of those to whom it is immediately consign'd." He forged these criteria into an exegetical principle: the Bible must be easily understandable in all matters essential to salvation. Yet writing earlier without the aid of either the Socinian analysis of mystery or his own distinction between an exoteric and an esoteric theology, he had apparently taken the opposite tack: "The Sacred Authors themselves complied with this Humour of *Parables* and *Fictions,* the Holy Scripture being altogether Mysterious, Allegorical and Enigmatical; and our *Saviour* himself gave his Precepts under this veil." Even there, however, he had assayed the Bible's purpose—"to establish the true Theology and good Morals"—distinguished it from natural philosophy, and sought to refine it from the dross of obscurity.[52] Once he had stowed his combative libertinism and adapted both the analysis and the distinction, he was able to give a more felicitous statement of the same conclusion: only when the Bible is clear is belief in it essential to salvation, and it is clear only when it speaks of morality.

Toland usually dealt gingerly with the authority of the New Testament, but he had few inhibitions about attacking that of the Old. Indeed, he presented the Hebrew Scriptures as a series of attempts to use mystery to obfuscate. The ancient Jews were "expert in forgeries" and, like Orientals, disposed toward credulity. Popular xenophobia encouraged him to portray their habits as the source of superstitious accretions on Christianity. Three generations of textual scholarship— above all the researches Le Clerc, Simon, and, arguably, Spinoza— allowed Toland to question the received attributions of some of the books of the first part of the Bible in relative safety. The same findings encouraged him to delineate a tension between Greco-Roman reason and light and Hebraic superstition and darkness. Historically, the polarization had had grave consequences: "The *Jews* gave up their Arms to the *Romans,* and the *Romans* gave up their Understandings to the *Jews;* the nobler victory of the two."[53] In the years before Toland wrote, much Anglican opinion had pointed to such a dualism. Latitudinarians had shown a distaste for the Old Testament's enthusiastic and sanguinary tone and a hesitancy about defending it. Toland turned their aversion to his own end, the subordination of the God of revelation and history to the God of reason and nature.

His most sustained piece of biblical criticism was *Origines judaicae,* which he attached to *Adeisidaemon* (1709) and retailed in a cautious English redaction as "Hodegus" (*Tetradymus*). In *Origines* he denied that the Old Testament was the word of God or the production of His Spirit. Moses had not written the Torah, which was, accordingly, an uncertain authority subject to the errors besetting any human document. Toland dissected some of its misrepresentations. Moses was an Egyptian priest and provincial governor who led a confused and rebellious mob. Like any pagan legislator, he invoked the supernatural in order to legitimate his state, which was not a theocracy. Far from being a land flowing with milk and honey, Israel was barren. The religion that supported the Mosaic Republic was subject to the law of change which governs all the creations of men. Moses sought to insinuate an esoteric teaching differing from that which he promulgated to his followers. He thus set a pattern for the imposture that marked the subsequent history of Judaism. The oracles conveyed by the patriarchs and prophets were raptures and dreams, comparable to the hallucinations of other men.[54]

This indictment explains Toland's renunciation of allegorical and typological interpretations, his jabs at the association of the prophets and Christianity, and his determination to apply to the sacred classics the critical methods developed for studying the profane. Many of his contemporaries still insisted that it was impossible to divide the two parts of Scripture or to eschew a symbolic, prophetic interpretation of the Old Testament without undermining the divine mandate of the New. As Pascal had written, it is "Jesus Christ with whom both Testaments are concerned; the Old as its hope, the New as its model, both as their center."[55]

If Toland transformed the Latitudinarians' discomfort with the Old Testament into a wedge for separating it from the New, he turned elsewhere for implements for reinterpreting the Christian Scriptures. From French Catholics and High-Churchmen he appropriated researches into the history of the formation of the canon as a means of twitting the notion of biblical sufficiency. Following the Unitarians, he treated the Nazarenes as the original Christians in order to demonstrate that primitive Christianity had amounted to theism.

Realizing the growing doubts of English Protestants about the possibility of holding a chaste and coherent biblical religion, Toland adroitly managed his New Testament studies. Confident that his opponents, in their efforts to refute him, would reveal their own uncertainties and thus spread disquiet, he contented himself with hinting at the unspeakable. In "The Fabulous Death of Atilius Regulus," he concluded that the persistent misrepresentation of an episode in Roman history suggested that other histories accepted by "implicit-faith-men" were in reality "old-wives fables." Although some critics discerned an anti-biblical intent in *Christianity Not Mysterious,* four years passed before Toland publicly employed such analogical insinuation. In his *Life of Milton* (1698) he sought to prove that Bishop Gauden of Worcester, rather than Charles I, had written *Eikon Basilike,* which was the object of High-Church devotion. He ended by publicizing the hint contained in "Atilius Regulus": the success of this modern cheat explained the acceptance in antiquity of "so many supposititious pieces under the name of Christ, his Apostles, and other great Persons."[56]

In a sermon preached before the House of Commons on 30 January 1699, Offspring Blackall, a future bishop of Exeter, cited Toland's words as evidence that he denied the authenticity of the Gospels. Toland replied that he had not impugned the New Testament. As if to remedy the omission, he asserted that the received canon had been differentiated from heretical works only in the second century; he also undertook a survey of apocryphal gospels and tried to prove that the earliest patristic works were forgeries. He deployed no original scholarship in any of these efforts. While portraying himself as above the fray, Blackall awkwardly retracted his accusation, which he had made because Toland was held to be "a Person in high Esteem (as I had heard) with some Men for his great Parts and Learning." Whatever embarrassment the episode caused Blackall, Toland himself ought to have rued it, since others accepted the divine's construction of his words.[57] Even if Toland had invited such an acceptance, he had not anticipated the resulting furor.

Queen Sophie-Charlotte of Prussia may have had this contretemps in mind when she described Toland as one "who questioned the basis of our Faith," the Bible.[58] In the course of a debate with her chaplain, Toland refused to attack the authenticity of any part of the New Testament, but argued instead that the canon was suspect because books of dubious origin had been introduced into it at its formation. When pressed to elaborate, he maintained that the teaching of St. Paul seemed to exist independently of Christ's sayings in the received Gospels. In the heat of contest, Toland grew more truculent, and eventually dismissed the Gospels as fables containing the same quantity of incredible miracles as all ancient books. Although he had openly taken so extreme a position as early as 1702, he continued to be fascinated with the problem of the formation of the canon.[59] In his own mind at least, its resolution remained important to his critique.

By pursuing apocrypha and reconsidering the canon, Toland aimed to bolster his application of the Socinian thesis that the Nazarenes were the original Jewish Christians. He first suggested in *Amyntor* (1699) that they were the depositaries of the primitive truth of Christianity. From that time on, he was reluctant to attribute the corruption of pristine Christianity to rabbinical superstition; instead, he made Paul and his gentile converts the villains. Depending on the instinctive primitivism of his readers, he assumed that establishing the primacy of the Nazarenes invested his interpretation of them with authority in contemporary disputes. He added to the Socinian treatment an assertion, perhaps adapted from Isaac La Peyrère, that Christianity had always presumed a two fold dispensation, one for the Jews and another for the Greeks and the Romans. This ingenious addition allowed him to effect a verbal reconciliation of St. Paul and St. James, whose differing valuations of faith and works in religion perennially bedeviled exegetes. More importantly, it let him suggest that the modern Unitarians were the legitimate heirs of the Nazarenes, since the coexistence of Jew and gentile in the primitive church depended on the willingness of both groups to accept God's unity. In passing, he identified the Nazarene Christology with that of the modern Unitarians. Toland's flirtation with the anti-Trinitarians survived the publication of the last Unitarian tract. As his defense of William Whiston indicates, he sought to make common cause with them whenever he found it useful to do so.[60]

Toland's prize discovery during his researches into the apocrypha was the "Gospel of Barnabas"—a forgery made by an Italian convert to Islam not earlier than the fifteenth century—which he attempted to identify with an Aramaic "Gospel according to the Hebrews" mentioned by Jerome. In *Nazarenus* he contended that since the Muslims revered the gospel, it was proper to speak of "Jewish, Gentile and Mahometan Christianity." His contention served a number of purposes. Anglican apologists regarded Muhammed as the model impostor, and contrasted him with Christ. By linking the religions they had founded, Toland renewed the question of how any avowal or interpretation of revelation could be established. The boast that the Bible alone is the religion of Protestants presented at least as many difficulties — particularly how and by whom the canonical books had been differentiated from other contenders — as it settled. Moreover, he offered an ironic commentary on the taunt of the critics of the Unitarians that they were no more Christians than the Muslims: the simple monotheism they shared was actually normative for Christianity.[61]

The premises of Toland's early efforts were elaborated in his mature work. Reason and revelation were God's two means for informing men; they had to cohere; the plurality of interpretation and belief, however, made reason the ultimate guide to truth in religion. As true religion was changeless, it followed that revealed and natural religion must be one and the same.[62] After Toland had resumed insinuating his esoteric theology, he continued to criticize the errors of traditional Christianity and to adumbrate the principles of a new, exoteric theology. Throughout his career he saw insinuation, criticism, and adumbration as the concurrent tasks to which he had to devote himself.

He seized on the positive as well as the negative implications of the theological minimalism that captivated his generation. By emphasizing conduct and neglecting the systematic expression of Christian doctrines or even the doctrines themselves, the Latitudinarians had made morality the substance of religion. It fell to the Unitarians to devise a method that excluded the acceptance of traditional formulas by restricting assent to propositions of which the human mind could form clear and distinct ideas — a class richer in agenda than in credenda. More directly than either group, Toland reduced Christianity to morality. His criterion for evaluating human knowledge was always practical, so that goodness and sincerity became the tests of individual piety and obedience to Christ's "perfect Rule of Life," the mark of true Christianity. Thus he achieved credibility for his claim that he was furthering the search for an irenicon and justified his insistence that his discoveries were suited to the meanest capacities and conformable to the mandate of the church. Christ's mission had been to rediscover the moral law, and when his Apostles went forth, "they did not confound and mislead, but convince the Mind. They were employ'd to dispel Ignorance, to eradicate Superstition, to propagate Truth and Reformation of Manners; to *preach Deliverance to Captives,* (i.e.) the Enjoyment of Christian Liberty to the Slaves of the Levitical and Pagan Priesthoods, and to declare Salvation to repenting Sinners." Toland insisted that pristine

Christianity had sought to inculcate the unity of God and the practice of virtue. Never fastidious when evidence threatened a conjecture, he buttressed his interpretation by distorting a text of Justin Martyr in order to demonstrate that the fathers had treated virtuous pagans like Socrates as true Christians.[63]

Championing the semi-Pelagianism of Daniel Williams had been for Toland as much a matter of conviction as of interest. Although he deferred to the notions of the fall and of transmitted original sin in *Christianity Not Mysterious,* his later dismissal of the vexed question of justification as a scholastic aridity was a more honest expression of his mature attitude. Before succumbing to the debilitating fear of a primordial taint, mankind had sustained ethical autonomy. Disabused of the fantasy, it could do so again. Because Toland maintained that public order depended on the sanctions of religion, he avoided criticizing the traditional virtues of Christianity. Nevertheless, he did not identify ethics with Christian morality, and he ventured to describe the New Testament merely as *a* basis for conduct. Privately, he judged the Chinese to be the purest moralists and praised Cicero for having offered the best statement of human obligations in *De officiis.*[64] Toland's discontent with this aspect of the English poetical theology would spur his effort to endow his own exoteric theology with an autonomous civic virtue.

Like most Augustans, Toland professed to see the notion of the immortality of the soul as the chief sanction available to religion in its endeavor to bolster society. He regularly affirmed or implied that he accepted this belief, which was not the same as the Christian doctrine of the resurrection of the body. Like the Socinian mortalists, Toland treated the afterlife as a discovery of revelation. Since his critique pointed toward a denial of the capacity of revelation to establish religious truth, he would seem to have allowed no warrant for personal immortality. In letters of condolence he emphasized the necessity of behaving stoically in the face of death. He once chose as his model the *Consolation* which Cicero had written on losing his daughter, Tullia. Toland's choice was significant. Augustine had taken Cicero's work as an expression of the futility of the pagan view of death — and hence, of life: "Cicero, in the *Consolation* on the death of his daughter, has spent all his ability in lamentation; but how inadequate is even his ability here?" More telling evidence of Toland's rejection of personal immortality is available. He sided with those who disdained the most famous seventeenth-century defense of the Christian view of time and infinity, Pascal's wager argument:

It is at least a great piece of Imprudence, to hazard the losing of what he has, for the sake of gaining what he has not, and to venture what is certain upon the Prospect of that which is uncertain. For my part, I compare such a Man to the Dog in the *Fable,* who swimming, and holding a Piece of Flesh between his Teeth, let it go to lay hold of a *Shadow;* and by this means was frustrated both of that which he possess'd, and of that which he hop'd to catch.[65]

Whatever form civic virtue might take, it did not require the sanction of eternity.

In pursuing his critique, John Toland showed as much consistency as he did variety in his life. Throughout, he sought to collapse the vision of the city of God into that of a human community. He began his effort as early as 1694 in "Atilius Regulus." In *The City of God,* Augustine had seen a double import in the martyrdom of Atilius. It showed that "the gods do not secure the temporal happiness of their worshipers." In addition, it meant that the adoption of Christianity had not caused the sack of Rome, since similar calamities had befallen the city and her noblest sons under paganism. By denying Atilius' murder, Toland had undermined a prop of Augustine's apology, much as he would subsequently transmute the three elements which Augustine had identified as making up Christianity: creed, cult, and code.[66]

Had the Latitudinarians, Remonstrants, and Unitarians never written, Toland would have been unable to essay such a transmutation. They had repudiated Scholasticism without discovering a substitute and thus invited the wholesale revision of doctrine. The originality of *Christianity Not Mysterious,* the most complete statement of Toland's critique, lay in its selective adaptation, skillful organization, and tendentious application of dispositions, assumptions, and theses that were — or would become — commonplace. Anglican rationalists, Arminians, and Socinians anticipated his repulsion at superstition and Scholasticism, his deference to reason, his identification of reason with demonstration, his treatment of Christianity as the restoration of natural religion, his minimization of the church, and his preference for sincerity and morality over dogma. The Unitarians also provided him with his criterion of assent — the necessity of possessing a clear and distinct idea of a proposition before accepting it — as well as many of his exegetical techniques. With Le Clerc's help he acquired from Locke an epistemological justification of this standard. Yet most Latitudinarians and Remonstrants and a number of Socinians took offense at Toland's use of their attitudes and ideas.

Their discomfort presaged his failure. Toland discerned the hankering of his contemporaries for a rational approach to religion in the wake of the decay of the accord which Jeremy Taylor had defended. Equally acute was his decision to subordinate the libertine attack on Christianity that he had pursued in *Two Essays* to an attempt to transform it with a method provided by its supporters.[67] Nevertheless, his expectation that his effort would win sufficient approval to advance the refashioning of Christianity was unseasonable. He had anticipated neither the nostalgia for the decadent consensus which Swift would satirize in his *Argument to Prove the Inconvenience of Abolishing Christianity* (1708) nor the temporary retreat from theological novelty provoked by the High-Church movement. A generation would pass before churchmen framed a compromise which accommodated reigning Anglican attitudes and ideas without exacting of the Establishment institutional and doctrinal change.

5 / The Quest for Civic Virtue

A discussion of the types of immortal government — of Sparta, Rome, Venice, and the Mosaic Republic — led John Toland to confront an earlier political philosopher. In book 22 of *The City of God,* Augustine had disparagingly contrasted Cicero's vision of an immortal commonwealth populated by mortal citizens with the heavenly and eternal city for which Christians hoped. What Augustine condemned as a blasphemous fantasy, Toland saw as the intent of politics. By identifying man's existence with this world and denying that the life of every society had to end, Toland both repudiated the Christian idea of order and directed his own search for civic virtue.[1]

If autonomous, perpetual human institutions were Toland's goal, rationalism was the means by which he attempted to pursue it. Arguing that rational examination could yield infallible answers to individual problems, he depicted politics as a way of approximating ever more closely, and eventually achieving, a perfect social order. A state could measure its steps toward autonomy and perpetuity by its increasing material prosperity.[2] Toland may have been a visionary, but he was not deluded. He discerned formidable obstacles blocking his course. Tyranny was threatening enough, but it was simply a manifestation of the protean irrationality which misdirected human affairs. Custom — whether embodied in prejudice, superstition, or mystery — was the ordinary expression of unreason.[3] That Toland discerned all of these features in traditional Christianity was no coincidence. Had he been unable to characterize the church as the greatest impediment to progress, he would have been hard-pressed to find an alternate.

Toland necessarily presented this indictment obliquely, often in the guise of observations on ancient history. He made classical Rome a model of the possibilities of civic life. Intimating that the rise of Christianity had hastened the fall of Rome, he invited his readers to recognize the longstanding enmity between church and commonwealth. He seldom missed an opportunity to insinuate the parallel associations of Christianity with credulity and paganism with reason.[4] Charged with deviousness, Toland sought to defend himself by

multiplying lists of fixed principles which would reveal his championship of freedom. All of them mention religious liberty or toleration. Yet
in his hands advocacy of toleration could become a way of chastising
Christianity. Constantine the Great had been the betrayer of this liberty and Julian the Apostate its tragic paladin.[5] Toland's treatment of
modern history was often equally convoluted. Thus, he rummaged the
storehouse of convictions, prejudices, and fantasies which was English
antipopery, not to menace the papacy but rather to oppose the High-
Church party and plead for the reestablishment of a civil supremacy
over priests such as had obtained in pagan antiquity.[6]

The habit of convolution persisted when Toland treated specific
matters of political theory and practice. His writings are mazes of
inconsistencies. Some of them resulted from simple inadvertence, the
unsystematic character of his *pièces d'occasion,* or his virtuosity of suppleness. Others were responses to the necessity of exploiting commonplaces in debate. Thus, he invoked or scorned the conception of
national characteristics as circumstances dictated. He also relied on
means which were formally inconsistent in order to advance relatively
consistent ends. Whether Britain adopted a forward policy out of a
sense of being the leader of Protestantism or out of mercantilist self-
interest was a matter of indifference to him, as long as she did so.
Presumably, Toland was equally indifferent to whether the argument
from the innocuousness of opinion or that from the sanctity of conscience carried the day for religious liberty. Sometimes he appears to
have treated ends as chaotically as means. He disdained the word *Commonwealth* as an anachronism and proclaimed his desire to form such a
state. At different times he execrated and advocated party government;
he vilified a standing army and suggested a means of creating one; he
also championed frequent parliaments as a bulwark of liberty, only to
acquiesce in the Septennial Act, by which a sitting parliament doubled
its own life, and pleaded for both increased opportunities for upward
social mobility and the Peerage Bill of 1719, which sought to freeze the
size of the aristocracy.[7]

Such instability has not gone unnoticed. For the most part,
historians of Augustan political thought investigating Toland's
maneuvers have sought clues in his motives. He has been depicted as
"playing a shifting game," as taking out an "insurance policy" of sympathy with one side in a controversy, even as he catered to the opinions
of the other. More baldly, an aptitude for trimming his viewpoint ac-

cording to "inducements of fame and fortune" has been ascribed to him.[8] However intriguing psychologically, such attempts to extrapolate another's motives remain at best tentative, at worst projective. A cleft separates them from the available biographical data. In order to connect evidence and explanation another path of investigation must be opened.

Quentin Skinner has mapped one. He suggests the necessity for a reader to discriminate between an author's motives, a congeries of affections and desires, and his intentions, a combination of aims and verbal stratagems. Arguing that "the recovery of a writer's (illocutory) intentions" is a condition of interpreting his works, Skinner has offered two rules for their identification. First, a text cannot be understood in isolation from "the prevailing conventions governing the treatment of the issues or themes with which that text is concerned." Secondly, the world defining the mind of its author must be exposed.[9] Although Toland's biography furnishes a deep pond in which to fish for possible motives, every bite remains tentative. In contrast, his intentions are often accessible.

Paradoxically, the most obvious explanation of Toland's intentions is unsatisfactory. Depicting his inconsistencies as superficial effects of the pressure of contending motives, a few scholars have asserted that Toland's work exhibits fundamental unity because he intended to write as an ideologist, a partisan of a set of coherent, self-contained political principles. In a series of influential works, J. G. A. Pocock has cast Toland as a performer in the "neo-Harringtonian" act of the drama of English "civic humanism." Among its themes were the assertion of the rationality and virtue of the autonomous citizen, the acceptance of the House of Lords as a natural "intermediary between Crown and commons" in a balanced monarchy, and the dismissal of that "commonwealth of armed proprietors" which Harrington had taken to be historically inevitable. By engaging in a "polemic against patronage and corruption" and championing real property in a conflict with money, the neo-Harringtonians became proponents "of radical reaction in an era of devastating economic change." A. B. Worden has recently embellished this drama by making a distinction between a Grecian coffeehouse group, centering on Shaftesbury and attached to neo-Harringtonianism, and a Calves-Head tavern clique, including Toland, who only flirted with it. In Worden's version, Toland appears as an ideologist *manqué*.[10]

No simple ideological interpretation can accommodate so complex a writer as Toland. While Pocock has classified his Augustan civic humanists as exponents of an ideology, he has also hesitated at that word's rigid connotations. Their writings, he finds, often show them "employing a highly ambivalent rhetoric, replete with alternatives."[11] By describing neo-Harringtonianism in terms of rhetoric rather than ideology, Pocock has eased the task of reaching Toland's intentions.

The debate about the contribution of rhetoric to education and politics was a staple of early eighteenth-century intellectual life. Initiating it in the *Essay,* Locke took the negative, ultimately prevailing view. He denounced rhetoric for implanting wrong ideas, arousing the passions, and misleading the judgment. Inimical to the advancement of truth and knowledge, it was a perfect cheat. A half-century later Hume mounted a rearguard action in its defense. He justified rhetoric as a means of securing authority over mankind by engaging men's passions, rather than as a rational way of instructing their minds. For him, the orations of Demosthenes and Cicero were like "the rays of a meridian sun," outshining every other persuasive effort.[12]

Living through the early rounds of this controversy, Toland sensed that eloquence, as he styled rhetoric, was languishing, but he still found that among Englishmen the most eloquent man was generally the most considerable. By eloquence he meant more than speaking well and appealingly. For him, it was a way of life and thought. By calling for the repudiation of the language, matter, and method of the Scholastics in favor of the method and style of the ancients, Toland identified himself with what Paul Oskar Kristeller has termed the rhetorical tradition in Western culture. Its principle was the insistence that communication, at once a force for and an expression of human sociability, depended on persuasion more than on intellection. Rhetoric opposed, not the goods of the mind, but only all efforts to divorce them from the events of life.[13]

Toland sought models for his political aspirations in the republican theorists of antiquity, particularly in Cicero. Cicero was more than the historical figure preeminently worthy of imitation and the greatest expositor of civic ideals; he was the anticipator of Toland's own labors and disappointments, "who (making a due Allowance for Times and Persons) engag'd in the same work that I do now, yet expected so little goods Effects of his Indeavors. . . . " The unravelling of the intentions of Toland's politics must begin with Cicero's rhetoric.[14]

Cicero conceived of rhetoric as a practical study whose convergent ends were the winning over, instructing, and animating of men's minds.[15] The noblest eloquence provided a context for making decisions by joining particular purposes to general objectives; it was flexible because it was shaped in "the dust and uproar, . . . the camp and the fighting-line of public debate, . . . the daylight of reality." As a master of occasions, the conscientious orator had "to possess the intelligence, capacity, and skill to speak both *pro* and *contra*" on the topics with which he was concerned. Variety was an obligation, even though the mean-spirited might distort it into a warrant for deviousness.[16] The Renaissance civic humanists who transmitted Ciceronianism to Toland had drawn a reasonable conclusion about human existence from this vision of the public and specific nature of eloquence, the social science. For them, life was a succession of acts in response to circumstances.[17]

Cicero had in effect identified the orator with the statesman. He gave counsel, but his métier was uniting the republic and stirring it to appropriate action.[18] The civic humanists also relayed this emphasis to Toland. They were less interested in the possible contribution of institutions to the commonwealth's liberty and well-being than in vivifying the spirit of the governors and citizens who made and observed its laws. Such virtue expressed itself when individuals associated their particular desires with the general good, and the orator evoked it by first arousing and then channeling men into cooperation.[19]

A spendthrift trust did not encumber John Toland's inheritance of the Western rhetorical tradition. The strained couplets of *Clito* ("The Key") contain the clearest statement of his adaptation of it. The orator was able to unite eloquence and wisdom in order to address every question of religion, cosmology, and civil life, but as the paraphrase of a passage from *De oratore* that Toland used as a tag suggests, his emphasis was practical. In addition to giving advice on matters of public importance, the rhetorician was bound to speak compellingly, to rouse a listless nation to virtuous action and to dissuade it from vicious courses.[20] Once again Toland was expressing his preference for an active life over a retired one. He found in eloquence a means of directing such a life by culling thought from experience.[21]

In human affairs permanence was more the exception than the rule, states, like nature, being in a perpetual flux. Still, Toland thought that a nation could occasionally aspire to ever-greater stability and in time become an immortal government. The cultivation of prudence, the perfection of the ability to act, was essential to the success of this aspiration, indeed to all statesmanship. The prudent orator-statesman had, therefore, to choose his words and actions according to his situation, not his preconceptions.[22]

However much eloquence had to be governed by prudence, it could not remain oblivious to ideals. In whatever situation the orator found himself, he would offer his community a moral focus. The reciprocal relation between virtue and eloquence made the quality of his offerings inconstant. Toland assumed the venerable notion that rhetoric requires liberty, the fullest expression of virtue, in order to flourish. The waxing or waning of liberty affected, and was in turn affected by, the state of eloquence. If the principles underlying and issuing from rhetoric were eternally the same, the men whose situation controlled its practice went backward and forward in their fidelity to them.[23]

In order to fulfill his duty of teaching mankind the truths which they mistake, the orator had to think and speak clearly.[24] A view of history should inform his selection of means with which to pursue this double end. To deal with the living, he had first to converse with the dead. Toland believed that, taken as a whole, human experience was uniform: "Nature is ever the same." Man's character was immutable, and every possible expression of it had recurred over the centuries. Politics could, in fact, claim to be a science just because no sport existed to upset its taxonomy. Toland thus accepted the exemplar theory of history, which presented the past as a repository of those usable examples for present conduct without which a society was doomed. In introducing his scheme for a militia, Toland set rules for this continuing intellectual séance: "In this work I endeavor to copy the People whereof I treat, and will confirm my Subject with the most beautiful Passages of the Antients, as well as illustrate it by Modern Examples, both of the Dead and the Living."[25] He consistently aspired to an adaptive mediumship.

Toland's varying estimations of the task and possibilities of eloquence in his own day almost suggest that he had anticipated Sir Harold Wilson's view of the potentially epochal consequences of any political week. The impression that Englishmen were uniquely fissiparous led to the conclusion that they, like ancient Romans, were unable to endure either absolute liberty or absolute slavery. While his confidence in the efficacy of eloquence was great, it was not unlimited.

A stentorian voice might summon men to the defense of liberty, hasten their success, and promote civic virtue, but it could not uproot certain deep-seated patterns of belief and behavior. Acknowledging the formative power of the irrational in human affairs, Toland recommended the rhetorical education of antiquity because it had above all taught politicians to understand the customs, laws, and religion of their country. Prudence still required that they treat the people as infants. By "appearing to yield in all their childishness," the wise would be "better placed to conduct them insensibly toward more solid reasonings."[26]

The orator also had to respond artfully to the frequent displays of puerility by the masses about affairs. Eventually, reason might lead thinking men to hold uniform views, but in the meantime diversity of opinion would prevail. It was baleful if it touched fundamental principles. Yet, when it arose over either means or subordinate ends among the friends of liberty, religious toleration, and the Protestant succession, it worked to hasten the arrival of unanimity. Variety leavened the orator's offerings as he tried to meet the demands of an electoral system which forced candidates for public office to be all things to all men. The orator's fertile brain had to be prepared "new Terms [to] produce, / Or old Expressions [to] bring again in use."[27] He had, in other words, to be able to shift his language — and thus his position — according to changing conditions. Because inconsistency was inevitable, dealing with it became for Toland an aspect of political prudence.

Toland did not, however, reduce prudence to opportunism. In searching for a language from which to fashion new terms and cull old ones, he limited his own range of choice. Two families of political discourse were accessible to him. One was Tory and the other, Whig. Since the main Tory division displayed those monarchical and clerical tendencies which carried superstition, and the other divisions were at least susceptible to them, Toland never saw this family as an alternative. In his view, the cult of the royal martyr and the related High-Church revival were manifestations of a dominant trait, not mutations. Post-revolutionary Toryism admitted of a variety of branches, but they were as one in conceiving of the origin of government in terms of authority rather than consent.[28]

In many ways, Whiggery, the other accessible family of political language, offered a clear contrast to Toryism. Although the Revolution Settlement had only dented the theory that political and religious allegiance had to be coextensive, Low-Church Whigs interpreted it as amounting to a partial disestablishment. Moreover, their anticlericalism and political objectives inspired them to attempt to create a secular style of argumentation which appealed to history, reason, and natural law instead of divine mandate.[29] The first edition of Algernon Sidney's *Discourses concerning Government*, which Toland published in 1698, provided him and many other Whigs with the rudiments of a secular vocabulary. While Sidney was better able to undermine the presumptive force of custom than to offer a clear replacement for it, his insistence that legitimate governments were created and maintained by the consent of free men had an unmistakable meaning in the English context: it belonged to parliament to decide who should be king and to define the range of his authority.[30]

Toland's appropriation of Sidney's work seems to justify the familiar description of him as a Commonwealthman. At certain times during his career it was a label he chose to apply to himself. Thus, in defending his break with Oxford in 1710–1711, he sought to contrast his own integrity with Oxford's deviousness: "Such a Common-wealth'sman I only approve, as your Lordship formerly was, when you encouraged me to reprint *Harrington's Oceana*, tho' neither of us imagin'd the model it self to be practicable. For my own part, as I have ever been, so I still declare myself to be a Whig . . . by denomination as well as by principle, in the sense that I have explain'd in . . . *A Memorial*." Even when acknowledging the name Commonwealthman, Toland insisted that he was primarily a Whig. Together with every other Whig, a Commonwealthman accepted three propositions: authority depends on the consent of the governed and exists for their benefit; it is expressed in laws which restrain both magistrates and subjects; while many regimes could promote these ends, the English "mixed form of king, Lords, and Commons, the latter being purely elective, the second absolutely hereditary, and the first partaking of both" was best.[31]

When writing sympathetically about Commonwealth ideas, Toland portrayed them as the repristination of the Whig tradition. A Commonwealthman was distinguished by his devotion to the self-evident principle of liberty and his enmity to slavery and arbitrary power. His acceptance of the existing English government differentiated him from pure democrats. To bolster the last contention, Toland tried to forestall any invidious association with Cromwell's regime. By seizing power in 1653, Oliver had become a tyrannical usurper. Notwithstanding such denunciations, Toland labored for most of his life under the charge of being a republican. Those who favored this commodious expression as a term of abuse treated it as a synonym of Commonwealthman without thereby excluding Commonwealthmen from the Whig ranks.[32]

Such essays in guilt by association did not lead more respectable Whigs who abhorred republicanism either to discard the word *Commonwealth* or to shrink from Commonwealthmen. The disappearance of unambiguously republican aspirations and the blunting of pre-revolutionary issues perhaps strengthened them in their refusal to panic. During these years any critic of the constitution was vulnerable to the accusation of republicanism, so that the description of Toland as a republican says as much about the style of his rhetoric as its intention.[33] He found criticizing authority more congenial than presenting alternatives to it.

Toland's invocations of earlier examples and teachers of republicanism have to be read alongside his endorsements of the Revolution Settlement. In drawing parallels between Roman and English institutions, he not only sought to grade the constitutional arrangements of 1689 but also asserted their permanence. England already resembled Rome and would become even more like her. Toland made similarly discriminating use of republican theorists. While acknowledging his debt to Aristotle, Livy, Machiavelli, and More, he singled out Harrington for special tribute. If in *Oceana* Harrington had offered "the most perfect form of such a Government that was ever delineated," it remained impracticable. Harrington's utopian speculations nevertheless provided a standard for detecting the weaknesses and charting the progress of government. From Harrington's vision of a polity of armed freeholders, for example, Toland derived a lesson which intermittently affected his own political writing: "Such a Constitution, where all Persons are equally educated in Civil and Military Discipline, is never conquer'd by any Standing Armies, unless previously weakn'd by some intestine divisions."[34]

Appearing relatively late and to limited effect in Toland's writings, Commonwealth notions refined and directed his attack on the monarchical theory of politics. His opposition to every hint of a recrudescence of those royal pretensions which had marked the reigns of the earlier Stuarts was tireless and resourceful. Throughout the 1690s Toland dwelt on the crimes of Charles I. The *Memoirs* of Edmund Ludlow which he confected in 1698 only restated themes he had presented in the pseudonymous Ludlow letters at the beginning of the decade.

Charles had been guilty of invading the liberties and properties of Englishmen, undermining their religion and government, dispensing with parliament, and creating a peacetime standing army in order to over-awe his subjects.[35]

The contractual interpretation of the origin of government complemented this insistent polemic. Because such a theory denied to monarchical authority any role in the creation of the state, most Whigs found it suspect. The terms in which Toland explained the original contract owed more to John Locke than to any Commonwealthman: all men are born in the same condition within society, and at maturity they are equally free to dispose of themselves as reason shall direct them; they consent to belong to a polity, at first consciously, then, in subsequent generations, tacitly; their tacit consent amounts to a trust that binds them only if their rulers abide by its terms, which in England are reducible to the protection of their liberties and properties; violation of this trust dissolves the regime, and the society of individuals which remains is obliged to defend itself.[36] Toland's hostility to the superstition which he discerned in monarchism encouraged a capacious syncretism. He was prepared to befriend almost any enemy of his enemy.

Commonwealthmen may have given Toland a means for expressing his critical bent, just as Locke supplied an explanation of the linkage between consent and contract, but neither accounted for his versatility. Although all Whigs shared a political language, Whigs frequently split into two groups, the "Country" and the "Court," each of which had its own rhetorical themes and rules. Throughout his career Toland oscillated between them. It is now generally accepted that the lifeblood of the body politic during much of Anne's reign was the existence and conflict of two major parties, the Whigs and the Tories. Since this dualism solidified around 1702, it cannot be imposed on the politics of the preceding decade. During William's reign there were, of course, Whigs and Tories, but there were also Country and Court Whigs and Country and Court Tories. Issues were formulated, discussed, and fought out along either Whig-Tory or Court-Country lines. When attention shifted from the legitimacy of the Revolution Settlement or the connection between church and state to the extent of the prerogative and the conduct and financing of war, these secondary distinctions became dominant. Regularly under William and occasionally under Anne, some Whigs formed an identifiable Country element.[37]

At times the dichotomy of Court and Country has been taken as the reality underlying the appearances of political maneuver. Pocock, for example, has described the "dialogue between a Country interpretation which blended Machiavelli and Harrington with the ancient constitution, and a Court interpretation addicted to historical criticism and *de facto* empiricism" as "the constitutional debate of eighteenth-century England."[38] Whether or not such pervasive influence can be ascribed to these categories, they did have an identifiable content. While sharing assumptions about the nature and end of government, Country and Court Whigs had access to distinct vocabularies with which to formulate and express their disagreements.

The Restoration Country agenda originated in the camp of the first earl of Shaftesbury during the Exclusion Crisis, and it consistently displayed certain negative and positive features. The Country imagination fixated on a conspiracy against the freeholds on which English liberties depended. Corrupt ministers worked to subvert parliament through the use of patronage, and only the elimination of placemen and provision for frequent elections would thwart them. Both divisions of Whigs were partners in a shifting, symbiotic relationship. Countrymen defined themselves in opposition to courtiers, but courtiers did not invariably provoke their hostility. The third earl of Shaftesbury's changing evaluations are telling. At the beginning of 1709, when the Junto Whigs seemed to be consolidating a monopoly on office, he insisted on the reality and necessity of the Court-Country distinction. By the summer of 1712, faced with a Tory ministry led by the renegade Harley, he ridiculed the notion that a Whig cabal of courtiers could ever threaten English liberties.[39] Like his former protégé, Toland, Shaftesbury was a Whig before — and after — he was a countryman. As early as 1702, Charles Davenant had discerned Toland's way with Country words. In speaking of Toland as one "returned from the country," Davenant captured his efforts at that time to make peace with the ministry. Davenant also intuited the lack of commitment behind Toland's oscillations. While Toland often defended bridgeheads, he never burned bridges. In a characteristic act of projective self-disclosure, Toland had anticipated Davenant's analysis. "Ins," or courtiers, whoever they might be, behaved like ins, while "outs," or countrymen, perforce acted like outs. Throughout this period, government and opposition spokesmen recognized that just as every ministry was drawn to Court rhetoric, so dissidents were likely to resort to Country rhetoric.[40]

Although estranged politicians and writers such as Toland regularly availed themselves of this alternative, on three occasions during the half-century following the Glorious Revolution they used it to concerted effect: first, between 1698 and 1702 when Toland and others resisted the Junto Whigs' plan for a peacetime standing army; secondly, in the aftermath of the South Sea Bubble when Toland and Molesworth echoed John Trenchard and Thomas Gordon in baying at the disgraced ministers; and finally, between 1726 and 1734, when Bolingbroke worked to undermine the ascendancy of Robert Walpole.[41] Bolingbroke did not discover that the most effective way of tormenting a Whig ministry was to urge Whig principles against it. He merely appropriated an established Whig custom for Tory use. The essence of Country politics was hostility to the administration of the day phrased in a stylized language of excluded virtue opposing entrenched corruption. If this rhetoric was useless to Whig countrymen in their confrontations with Tories, its incompatibility with the constructive exercise of power made it no more helpful to them whenever they became implicated in government. When confronting Tories, they spoke in generally-accepted Whig terms. Once in office, they either fell mute or slipped insensibly into Court rhetoric.[42]

A reactionary undertone had always been audible in Country language. The political system which evolved after 1688 depended on a bureaucracy, ordered patronage, sophisticated government debt-financing, and a professional military. Insofar as these instruments reduced the citizen from independence to economic and political dependence on the state, they conformed in the minds of countrymen to the fixed pattern of corruption. For them, virtue was equally immutable, and the necessity of holding it up as a mirror to a degenerate age forced them to locate it in a cherished, imagined past.[43]

In its devotion to the Revolution Settlement and the Protestant succession, the rhetoric of the Court was as indisputably Whiggish as that of the Country, but it never became as formalized. The politicians who developed it were seeking a means, first, of justifying their determination to govern and, then, of accommodating their dominant perceptions of public life. A broadened franchise had heightened political instability and engendered conservative trepidation in many Whigs. At the same time a generation of warfare and commercial revolution had transformed the management of affairs and convinced these same men that flexibility was a defensible element of statecraft. Such considerations pointed to the necessity of a resourceful administration and the utility of a style of argumentation open to novelty. Court rhetoric was the creation of two groups of Whigs who, despite persistent tensions, generally worked together. Having combined in an effort to bind a reluctant king with fetters of indispensable support for his policies, the Junto peers learned to collaborate with Court M.P.s—a collection of individuals inclined to moderate views, deference to the monarch, and an appetite for office.[44]

The High-Church backlash after the Sacheverell trial helped to transform *frisson* into a program. Court Whigs now found congenial the Tory vilification of the mob, a volatile mass stirred up by demagogues and distinct from the people, the political nation. They increasingly based their tactics on three maneuvers: first, theorizing about the revolution had to be avoided; secondly, passive obedience had to be accepted and resistance allowed only in narrowly defined instances; thirdly, the support of the church rather than of dissent had to be cultivated. After the accession of George I these tendencies fused in a recognizable Court Whig language, whose core, borrowed from Sacheverell's defense during his impeachment, was the absolute sovereignty of parliament. The 1715 general election prepared the ascendancy of the Whig oligarchs who subscribed to this doctrine, and they proceeded to draft legislation that would perpetuate their hold on office. Although the Peerage Bill was to fail in 1719, the Septennial Act of 1716 allowed them to consolidate the regime which endured for almost fifty years.[45]

Unlike the language of the Country, the language of the Court could never sustain a purely rhetorical vision of politics. Accordingly, for all that Toland sometimes wrote as a courtier, in his heart he remained a countryman. The paradoxical combination of reactivity and inflexibility that marks his political thought testifies to this persistent sympathy. Notwithstanding his tactical resourcefulness, he was ill prepared to cope with, let alone adumbrate, orderly structural changes. Like the Renaissance civic humanists, Toland invested more trust in the vivifying contribution of the orator to the commonwealth's liberty and well-being than to any benefits derived from tinkering with structures. His writings contain musings on the institutions which would eventually serve an immortal government and abound in disparate responses to transitory polemical exactions, but they display little concern for the task of analyzing changing circumstances and adjusting government to meet them.

Successive controversies lured him into dealing with such intermediate adjustments. But whether he defended a proposal advanced by another, as in the case of the recoinage, or elaborated one of his own, such as the scheme for uniting the East India companies, his advocacy was as short-lived as it was vehement.[46] In these and similar cases, public attention pressed an issue which Toland addressed by manipulating the terminology he then favored. If neither the Court nor the Country division of the Whig political language determined his thought on fundamental matters like the primacy of reason, consent, and contract in society and the correlative supremacy of parliament, they regularly framed his choice of topics and mode of expression. More importantly, Country rhetoric allowed him to realize the implication of his rhetorical idea of politics and to treat public life as a theater rather than a factory.[47]

Toland returned from Ireland at the beginning of the standing army controversy, which occasioned his transformation from a suppliant of the ministerial Whig "college" into a Country pen. Shaftesbury was a central figure throughout this phase of the Augustan Country effort. At the turn of the century, as the campaign was slackening, Shaftesbury performed a series of lurches which not only epitomize the chaos of the preceding decade but also suggest the awkwardness of any effort to treat this language as an ideology or even an independent political variable. In April 1701, when the Tory majority in Commons sought to exclude Somers, the Junto Whig leader, from the king's counsels, Shaftesbury overlooked his support of the standing army and spoke of him as "our friend." Similarly, though Shaftesbury had started to dissociate himself from Harley in early 1702, by the end of the year he was still asserting that Harley "is ours at the bottom."[48]

During the early nineties the attempt of countrymen to restrain royal influence had enjoyed some successes, in particular, the establishment of commissioners of accounts charged with managing public expenditures and the limitation of parliament's term to three years. Nevertheless, the opposition of ministerial Whigs thwarted their proposal to reduce the number of placemen sitting in the House of Commons. Undaunted, Harley's New Country Party embarked in the latter years of the decade on an antiprerogative campaign. The political readjustments which followed the death of the duke of Gloucester led party members to abandon concerted action, and thereafter they began to go their separate ways. Thus, Harley underwent a slow and complicated evolution into the leader of Toryism. While remaining instinctively moderate and nonpartisan, he became bound to the Tories as Anne's reign wore on.[49] By 1711, old followers like Toland and Molesworth who had remained drawn to him by ambition and nostalgia were learning to shun Country archaisms and express themselves exclusively in Court neologisms.

The task of defining the mixed constitution informed the dialogue between Court and Country in Toland's writings. Since the Renaissance it had become a truism that liberty was most secure under a government which combined monarchical, aristocratic, and democratic elements. While the Italian humanists who appropriated this thesis from classical writers had given it a republican emphasis, its first complete English statement was *His Majesty's Answer to the Nineteen Propositions of Parliament*, drafted by Charles I's advisors in 1642. After the Restoration, however, even self-styled republicans came to accept it. In describing a real Whig, Robert Molesworth offered a summary of the Country understanding of the mixed constitution. It retained "the strictness of the true old Gothic constitution under the three estates of king (or queen), lords, and commons; the legislative being seated in all three together; the executive being trusted with the first, but accountable to the whole body of the people in case of maladministration."[50]

Toland's praise of this system was more straightforward than his explanations of it. In *The Art of Governing by Partys*, the most systematic presentation of his understanding, he maintained that while a commonwealth served the public good indifferently, an arbitrary government was essentially partial. A democracy was a popular commonwealth and an aristocracy a noble one, but England, like any mixed form of government, divided its supreme legislative power among the Commons, the Lords, and the supreme magistrate, the king. In their shared responsibility of legislating, these divisions each enjoyed distinct privileges and prerogatives and exercised a mutual check and balance on one another's oversights or encroachments. Nonetheless, Toland did not equate the mixed constitution of England with a balanced constitution whose parts enjoyed equal or concurrent powers, nor did he follow those Whigs, most of them countrymen, who portrayed it as ancient and immutable. He was, rather, a tenacious advocate of parliamentary sovereignty: "I am for an Arbitrary Power in Parliament, though I am against it in Kings." Toland flirted with republicanism because it located power in parliament, the sole medium through which the governed were able to consent to their government. Since one generation's laws could not control those of the next, development and change should be taken as symptoms of political health, not equated with degeneracy. In Toland's view, customary or prescriptive entitlements ultimately lacked standing in law.[51]

There is no hint that Toland ever entertained the suspicion of some of his contemporaries that investing the legislature with unrestricted power might threaten liberty. His sustained indifference to their fears suggests that, far from representing gross inconsistency or a simple oscillation between Country and Court languages, his eventual support for measures such as the Septennial Act and the Peerage Bill followed from his longstanding identification of the English mixed constitution with parliamentary sovereignty. Toland's conception of representation was also congruent with his devotion to legislative supremacy. If all citizens should enjoy access to the votes and proceedings of the House of Commons in order to fulfill their duty to discuss issues of the moment, their opinions need not decide legislation. Toland envisioned representation as more than delegation, and he sometimes portrayed the model legislator as that Country ideal, the independent gentleman.[52]

The only list of the functions and responsibilities of an M.P. which Toland prepared reads like a Country polemic. By simultaneously supporting the king's just prerogative and protecting the just rights and privileges of his subjects, the House of Commons would avoid the extremes of absolute monarchy and anarchy. In order to perform this balancing act, it was obliged to maintain due honor toward the executive and suitable respect and encouragement for those administering the laws; curb insolent and licentious ministers and ambitious and overgrown statesmen; advise the king in all matters of importance; legislate in order to preserve and improve the constitution; and control appropriations and scrutinize public expenditures. Toland's proposal to add to these tasks the responsibility of nominating the principal officers of state indicates that, for him, supporting the prerogative did not jeopardize parliamentary sovereignty.[53]

These sweeping charges amounted at the same time to a rejection of the kind of separation of the executive and legislative anticipated in the Act of Settlement and a blueprint for a state founded on untrammeled legislative supremacy. Toland's devotion to parliamentary sovereignty was compatible with his Country opposition both to the cabinet system practiced by the Junto under William and to the arrogation of powers by a prime minister. Since this same emphasis was pronounced in the emerging court rhetoric, it became a lingua franca that Toland used when passing from Country to Court.[54] He was free to reconcile his belief in the centrality of parliament with the objects of either form of rhetoric because, for him, both were primarily means of expression rather than sources of inspiration.

When writing as a countryman, Toland at least entertained projects for bringing parliament to a more responsible exercise of its power. On one occasion he proposed a thoroughgoing reform which included the creation of new seats for unrepresented commercial areas such as Leeds and Manchester. His expectation that their representatives would join the virtuous knights of the shires and suppress rotten boroughs assumed that landed and moneyed interests could cooperate to forge the political stability which England had needed for so long.[55] Yet Toland never repeated, much less promoted, this suggestion. His political writings are littered with other abandoned proposals, all of them testifying to his reluctance to pursue step-by-step institutional reform.

Although Toland did not disregard Country efforts to exclude placemen from Commons in order to liberate it, he was scarcely devoted to this cause. At the end of his first Country phase, he found it convenient to overlook the Place Act (1705), which relaxed the controls on placemen embodied in the Act of Settlement. He was no more constant in espousing frequent parliaments. In his last bout of Country politics, he trumpeted them as "the most essential part of our Constitution, . . . without which all the other parts are insignificant." A couple of years earlier, however, he had joined the clique at the Grecian coffeehouse in repudiating this item of the Country agenda by accepting the Septennial Act. None of these litterateurs undertook to work out the logic of their decision to push legislative supremacy to its extreme by eliminating every check on it.[56] Perhaps all of them, including Toland, had been concerned with parliamentary responsibility as a theme of Country rhetoric rather than as a complement to their devotion to parliamentary sovereignty.

In treating the monarchy, Toland responded to the varying demands of the political language which he was using. Thus, as a countryman he depicted the crown as an elective institution answerable to

the godlike popular voice, but as a courtier he located it somewhere between an absolute elective monarchy and an absolute hereditary one.
As Toland moved from Country to Court rhetoric, he took an increasingly benign view of the magistracy. The progress of his movement can
be traced in a series of changes of emphasis, some plain, others obscure. When writing for the Country, he treated the king as an executive whose principal tasks were to assure the nation's liberty and safety
by passively reigning. When writing for the Court, he eulogized the
monarch as the most important of the elements essential to the constitution. Already a tepid countryman, he sought in 1701 to confine the
Hanoverian heiress-presumptive with chains of restrictions: parliamentary advice would bind her in appointing the major officers of
state; a committee of Commons would attend her in order to discuss
matters of policy and monitor her actions; parliamentary approval
would be required for every treaty; any bill which parliament was determined to enact could survive her veto; parliament would control
military and naval affairs. Once George I had been enthroned, Toland, now a practiced courtier, shunned such instruments because his
vocabulary was unable to describe them. His evaluations of royal conduct display the same movement. He passed effortlessly from indicting
the offenses of James II as parts of a pattern of maladministration to excusing the infringements of George I as lapses.[57]

Though exhibiting comparable variety, Toland's descriptions of the
second estate defy explanation by reference to the conflicting demands
of Country and Court rhetorics. Depending on their perceptions of the
state of liberty, countrymen were equally prepared to agitate for
widened participation in order to forestall oligarchy or justify aristocratic privilege as a counterpoise both to the crown and to the mob.
Convinced of the superiority of a policy which sustained a virtuous
governing elite, Toland for his part abhorred democratic schemes of
government, distinguished liberty from leveling, and vindicated social
inequality. Republican Rome once more provided him with an example. Like Roman magistrates and tribunes, the governors of England
had to be educated to command through their words, bearing, and
prowess.[58]

The House of Lords was their normal arena. Toland's comments on
its place in the constitution, while virtually consistent, are so laconic as
to suggest that the subject bored him. He once tried to demarcate the
two houses in order to make the upper one a true judicatory, sitting

regularly without royal summons. This Country aspiration was consistent with his support as a courtier both for the Peerage Bill and for measures to augment the independence of the judiciary. Even if the fragmentary character of these observations defeats any interpretation of their near homogeneity, Toland's commitment to parliamentary sovereignty makes him an unlikely pioneer of the doctrine of the separation of powers.[59]

Strengthening the Lords gave urgency to the problem of deciding how to recruit an English aristocracy. Toland offered two irreconcilable solutions to it. As a countryman, he cherished upward social mobility as one of the clearest signs of freedom. Occasionally he contemplated abolishing hereditary titles because their bearers too often were unworthy of the power inherent in them. He was usually more restrained. Differentiating true nobility—the capacity to lead the people in peace and war—from accidents of birth, he insisted that honesty, prudence, and industry, rather than birth, estate, and credit, ought to recommend men to the ministry. Nonetheless, any man who possessed both social position and personal virtue was to be preferred to all others.[60] Even as a countryman, Toland was able to swell this concession into a version of the *thèse nobiliaire*. Because men of property had proved throughout history to be "the truest Lovers of *Liberty* which begets, enlarges, and preserves it," they enjoyed "a natural Right to share in the Government of any Place where they have such an Interest to secure." In this mood, he warned against elevating obscure men to office, lest they become creatures of irresponsible wirepullers. Toland's support for upward social mobility was never unqualified.[61]

Toland had few inhibitions about invoking the shibboleth of natural rights. At times he described the ideal of liberty as the gift of God and nature and presented specific liberties such as those of inquiry, discussion, and expression as natural rights. The rights of Englishmen offered him a standard for gauging the propriety of including among the rights of humanity an inclination or desire, and he went so far as to imply that this yardstick was absolute.[62] The progress of any people could be determined by their increasing ability to measure up to it.

Yet, Toland was not a coherent natural-rights theorist. As circumstances or pleasure demanded, he excluded one group after another from the full enjoyment of liberty. Thus, the almost congenital instability of Orientals had usually subjected them to a merited despotism, just as the inveterate popery of the Irish fitted them for subordination to the

English. Such wholesale exclusions of foreigners found parallels in Toland's willingness to limit or even abrogate the rights of certain Englishmen. While his insistent appeals to the authorities to silence his own
opponents may have been symptoms of exasperation, his call to neighbors to monitor one another represents more than a weakening of his
hostility to internal espionage. Like his readiness to defend religious
toleration by alternatively invoking the law of nature and mercantilist
self-interest, it shows him treating this theory as a means of expression
rather than a source of principles.[63] Toland appealed to natural rights
out of convenience, not conviction.

His idea of political participation would, in any case, have kept him
from embracing this system. As a countryman and a courtier, he denied that all men were entitled to citizenship by virtue of their humanity. A distinction between freemen, who have property or are able to
live of themselves and servants, who cannot subsist in such independence, was fundamental to his outlook. While landholding virtually ensured a citizen's autonomy, it was not the only means of doing so: "The
fairest way . . . is to make all those to be the Electors who pay to
Church and Poor." It was presumably Toland's concern to identify liberty with security of property, and the possession of property with the
maintenance of liberty, which prevented him from detailing the free-
doms of the servant class.[64]

The tension between the vocabulary of natural rights and the reality
of limited participation reflects the interplay of what Isaiah Berlin has
called two concepts of liberty in Toland's political thought. If on some
occasions Toland championed a negative notion by defining freedom in
terms of areas of personal choice and action from which the state was
excluded, on others he embraced a positive one by insisting that freedom allowed men to realize their humanity by participating in the
state. Considered abstractly, these two concepts of liberty imply a
series of stark contrasts. The positive notion required a particular social
basis, for example a numerous class of freeholders, but elements at
least of the negative one might be found in almost any society. Moreover, a kind of zero-sum theory regulated the participatory ideal: the
greater the number of possible participants, the less opportunity there
was for any individual actually to participate. Although this concept
did not allow that every person would eventually realize his humanity,
its countertype encouraged wider inclusion just because it conceived of
politics as a means rather than an end. In the negative view, the iden-

tity of the governors, or rather extending the opportunity to share in government, was less important than limiting the ability of a government to control its subjects. Since these two ideals precede both Court and Country rhetorics, it is impossible to correlate either of them with Toland's use of one or the other political language. When writing as a countryman, he sometimes advocated exclusion while on other occasions he committed himself to participation.[65] His responses to issues determined not only his choice of vocabularies but also his manipulation of assumptions.

Once again the unsystematic character of Toland's politics defies the application of easy categories. His writings do not reveal a consistent allegiance to either the negative or the positive concept in its abstract form. Examples of both recur in his work, and frequently they interpenetrate rather than coexist. He regularly exploited the presuppositions of one to support the conclusions of the other. Toland's ability to change emphasis while consistently identifying liberty with the rule of law exemplifies this pattern. He once described the freedom enjoyed by Englishmen in hallowed terms:

I live in a free Government where men may vent their thoughts secure from the dread of Informers, represent their Grievances, yet not be counted factious, and expect redress without claiming more than their due. We have known Rules and stated Measures of our Actions. Every Man has the same right to the Property as the Magistrat to the execution of his Office: And the meanest Countryman has his action and remedy at Law against the King no less than against any of his fellow Subjects. In these and the like privileges consists a great part of our Happiness above theirs who at no extraordinary distance from us groan under the yoke of absolute dominion.

This description seemingly expressed the negative concept of liberty. Participation in government consists of free discussion and that implicit consent which the people give to legislation enacted for the common good by their elected and closely-watched representatives. M.P.s exercise power in order to protect citizens in the exercise of their fundamental liberties, viz., freedom of thought, speech, property, and perhaps upward mobility.[66]

The positive concept of liberty was more complex than the negative one. If its hopes were grand, its fears were deep-seated. To the relatively few individuals able to participate in the life of the commonwealth, it simultaneously held out the promise of self-realization in virtuous times and the threat of purifying discipline in corrupt times. To the many who could not participate, however, it offered no similar balance. Their lot was to observe the reward appropriate to virtue and to endure the punishments due corruption.

Toland responded to this complicated range of possibilities by emphasizing the regulatory capacity of the law. As the director of the nation's life, it provided both citizens and subjects with a general standard and measure for their conduct. Its authority rested on a variety of deterrents and punishments. Intermittently applicable to participants, these sanctions were consistently necessary to regulate the mob, a category which, after Sacheverell's triumph, came to include for Toland, as for court Whigs, the majority of disfranchised, inarticulate Englishmen. "England is now so vicious and wicked, that it is of absolute necessity to put the several Laws strictly in execution, the doing of which tho' a seeming severity, yet is real charity; and no people will ever obey a Government that do not pay a ready obedience to the Laws." Toland was not slow to suggest ways in which the law might help to compensate for the corruption of Englishmen. Thus, he proposed harsh measures which anticipated the "Black Act" of 1723 in order to maintain the rural order and demanded that all who had escaped the fine mesh of restraints enclosing society ("Gypsies, Vagabonds, and Beggarly Strangers") be "taken up and severely handled." A presentiment of the vulnerability of the social fabric haunted adherents of the participatory ideal as well as courtiers.[67] Sometimes, in fact, the Court became the last refuge of repentant enthusiasts for the positive concept of liberty.

No such ambiguity marks Toland's ventures in political moralism. The warfare between liberty and corruption was a Country *idée fixe*, and when he wrote as a courtier he was free to dismiss it. The Renaissance civic humanists had diagnosed three elements which, if unchecked, corroded freedom: increasing private wealth, multiplying internal factions, and dependence on mercenaries. It fell to Machiavelli to generalize their diagnosis by defining corruption as a preoccupation with one's own interests to the neglect of the common good.[68] Harrington had adapted this generalization by providing it with a material emphasis. In order to participate in government, any individual had to be economically self-sufficient. He had to possess both arms and a freehold, and anything which challenged his possession of either amounted to corruption. Published in 1675, Henry Neville's translation of *The Famous Works of Nicholas Machiavel* gave a new lease on life to the moral interpretation of the relationship between liberty and corruption. Although influenced by Harrington, the Commonwealthmen's efforts to apply this analysis to Restoration politics tended toward moralizing. Molesworth, for example, in *An Account of Denmark* (1694) attributed the dissolution of the old, free Danish constitution to the combined assault of religious obscurantism, constitutional imbalance, plutocracy, and a professional standing army. He invited his readers to take warning. The authors of the anti-standing-army tracts did so. Unable to reconcile Harrington's deterministic analysis with the flux presupposed by his own rhetorical conception of politics, Toland accepted that tyranny was the result of sustainedly bad quality of both government and education.[69] This familiar terminology offered him a versatile tool to use to his own ends.

Whether conceived morally or materially, the description of politics as the conflict of liberty and corruption required an analysis of the relation between economics and politics. Toland's thoughts on this subject owed less to any interest of his own than to the requirements of debate. On first reading, his Country pronouncements on it seem to display rare uniformity of perspective, as if the effort which originality demanded was so unappealing that he contented himself with clichés. He located civic virtue in a bellicosity sustained by a militia composed of freemen nurtured in an agrarian regimen. Since M.P.s who owned land were uniquely secure in their independence, he contemplated establishing a precise qualification of real holdings for all of them. In addition, Toland effortlessly adopted the classicizing bias of Country rhetoric. By appealing to an age when Rome's "Consuls were taken from the Pruninghook, and her Dictators from the Plow," he was free to inveigh against the meaner statecraft of modern cityfolk.[70]

Notwithstanding such statements, Toland cannot be included among those neo-Harringtonians whose championship of the landed interest against Court Whig advocates of the monied interest Professor Pocock has reconstructed. No correlation between Country and land on the one hand and Court and finance on the other can do justice to Toland's excursions into the borderland between economics and politics. When writing as a countryman, he had praised the Bank of England, the foundation of the new economic order, as an approximation of Harrington's model state. As a courtier, he was to reject the very distinction between a moneyed interest and a landed interest. While visceral Country antipathy to corruption fed hostility to the new finance, neither Toland nor any of his contemporaries undertook the kind of sustained polemic against the financial revolution as the ultimate corrupter which was central to neo-Harringtonianism. Davenant toyed with this line, but its exposition fell to the next generation of country writers, particularly John Trenchard and Thomas Gordon.[71] After Trenchard died and Gordon became a government pensioner, Bolingbroke expropriated it.

Toland's choice of rhetorics nevertheless affected his economic pronouncements. Thus, when he advertised his practical model for an Irish National Bank as natural, public, and perpetual because it could be established without investment or interest, he sought to evoke a group of powerful associations in the minds of countrymen. For courtiers, his later denunciation of efforts to erect charity schools as a prodigious drain on the manufacturers and laborers was no less telling.[72] As his chosen audience required, Toland complaisantly urged measures calculated either to restrict or to encourage economic development.

One clue to the origins of Toland's convoluted economics lies in his longstanding association with the nonconformist Whigs who asserted themselves in the City after the Glorious Revolution. Early in his career Toland discovered both a community of opinion with this group and, in Sir Robert Clayton, one of its seniors, a desirable patron. By the mid-nineties, the Whiggish, Presbyterian financiers were growing more conservative, and they forfeited the support of London's inveterately disaffected radicals not to Country Whigs, but rather to Tories.[73] This development left Toland with the Hobson's choice of accommodating the changing views of his moneyed supporters or throwing in his lot with popular Toryism. His response was predictable. If the encouragement of these financiers did not always lead him to act as their spokesman, it usually kept him from opposing them, whether he spoke in a Country or a Court voice.

In this case, principle reinforced interest. Toland held that commerce furthered the growth of learning, so that economic expansion might serve as an indirect means of transforming Christianity into an acceptable cult. More importantly, he clung to the belief of the classical English republicans that Britain was a government for increase. Popular governments naturally tended, in Sidney's words, "to increase the number, Strength, Power, Riches, and Courage of their People, by providing comfortable ways of sustinence for their own citizens." While

Toland's statement of this proposition became more fervid in war, even in peace he insisted that, ideally, Britain should control the policies of other nations, receive their products, monopolize the trade of both Indies, and expand her own colonies. Only a growing economy could sustain such ambitions. The isolationist, nonbelligerent policy of Country Tories was better suited to perpetuating an agrarian society.[74] Because Toland saw England as a government for increase, he neither tied himself to the rural order nor stigmatized the financial revolution as a carrier of corruption until the explosion of the South Sea Bubble.

Toland's use of that other Country perennial, the insistence that factions had corrupted English liberties, was equally idiosyncratic. Superficially, *The Art of Governing by Partys*, his fullest consideration of this phenomenon, seems straightforward. Before the despotic Stuarts, England had been innocent of parties. James I and his heirs nurtured this "most wicked master-piece of Tyranny," so that their divided subjects would "the more easily becom a common prey to Arbitrary Power." Since only a government calculated for the interest of all the parties concerned guaranteed a healthy freedom, Englishmen would have to be brought into the same interest. It lay with the king to foster a unified national purpose by resolving neither to govern through one party nor to pit the parties against each other.[75]

Far from being the totem of countrymen, opposition to party was the common object of early Augustan political piety. Writers from every faction rushed to venerate it, even when they were being most partisan. Such widespread veneration raises the possibility that Toland's own nonpartisanship was merely formulistic. Other bits of evidence support this interpretation. He wrote as if a nonpartisan government were a reality in 1705, just as Harley, newly aligned with Godolphin and Marlborough, labored to isolate high Tories and evade the grasp of Junto Whigs. Toland berated standoffish Whigs whose addiction to their peculiar interests was sapping England's liberty and unity. It was not the first time, nor would it be the last, that he identified these benefits with Harley's goals.[76]

In fact, Toland's jeremiads against faction served one or another Whig interest with telling regularity. As his critics quickly noted, the *Art of Governing* itself was a reaction to the growth of Tory influence during the last months of William's reign.[77] Desiring to make ministerial changes in order to placate the Tories and High-Churchmen who were likely to dominate Commons, the king had appointed the arch-Tory

Rochester lord lieutenant of Ireland. Toland seems to have hoped to avert further concessions of this kind by raising the standard of nonpartisanship.

The key to Toland's Pickwickian sense of disinterested government lies in his conception of a unitary national interest. Only those who embraced the common good were worthy of public confidence and office, and all others effectively became traitors. Party distinctions were at least meaningless, and probably divisive, because there was one English party. In Toland's view, dissidents belonged to a French party. Whigs were congenital patriots: a true Whig was a man of principle rather than faction, a countryman rather than a courtier, and a patriot rather than a loyalist. A convinced Tory had, therefore, to be a man of faction, a courtier, and a loyalist, and a Tory administration hence inconsistent with the genius of the kingdom.[78]

Had Toland actually championed factionless government, he would in any case have found no hearing. To be active politically in late Stuart England meant opting for a party, not abandoning the parties. Toland sometimes mouthed the pieties of his Country days after his breach with Harley in 1710–1711 drove him into the arms of Court Whigs. More often, he aimed to separate the Whig sheep of liberty from the Tory goats of tyranny. This endeavor led him to a rare approximation of candor. He had belatedly discovered himself living in a period in which party distinctions were necessary because they preserved fixed principles. By the time of the accession of George I, Toland was urging a permanent Whig monopoly on office relieved by the exceptional presence of a pliable Tory. Even his vocabulary changed. Having once praised the Trimmers for their unwillingness to enroll themselves in some faction, he now scorned them as neuters.[79] His presentation of the national interest as a unity was as determined as his evaluations of party government were diverse. In the end, determination and diversity combined to keep him, even as a countryman, from offering a persuasive analysis of this corrupter of liberty.

In his considerations of a peacetime standing army, Toland managed both to provide a model Country analysis of corruption and to exhibit formal inconsistency. Resting on the thesis that tyrannies are supported by mercenaries and free governments by militias, *The Militia Reform'd* contained a project for levying Englishmen according to the Gothic pattern based on tenure that had been used by their German ancestors. Gothicism punctuates his discussions of military affairs, but his sneer at the English as "the progeny of barbarous pyrates and repeated mixture of several nations" suggests that he saw it as a literary convenience—or necessity. The exposure of this piece of disingenuousness would have been less embarrassing than was Defoe's disclosure of his later support for a peacetime standing army. In 1717, Toland anonymously proposed the establishment of such a corps but protested that, since it would be stationed abroad, it was not what it appeared to be. Taunted by Defoe, Toland lamely protested his own consistency. Like Molesworth, who took the same tack in the House of Commons the following year, Toland jettisoned this fixture of Country rhetoric in order to keep his place in the Court line.[80]

In the maze of Toland's expedient and rhetorical shifts there is risk of losing sight of his quest for a substitute for the Christian idea of order, the fixed object of his political imagination. The jumbled *pièces d' occasion* through which he pursued his various secondary concerns also reveal his struggles to present a serviceable alternative to Christianity. Although he entertained discordant proposals in various works, he accepted the conclusion of fabricators of ideal commonwealths and exemplary ancients that the survival of the community required the preservation of a popular religion cleansed of gross superstition.[81]

Toland was alive to the differences between Christianity and paganism, which had made demands that were abhorrent by modern standards. Longing for the renewal of antique virtue, he sought to reconcile his aspiration with the present reality. Shaftesbury's ethic, which Toland had previewed in his edition of the *Inquiry* (1699), seemed to him the liveliest contemporary representation of the doctrines of the ancients, one which preserved their very sap and blood. Despite later elaborations, Shaftesbury's purpose remained to vindicate the honor of humanity and of God by showing that men possessed an innate capacity to distinguish right from wrong.[82] While Toland never wrote an ethical treatise, his portrayals of the moral life exploited Shaftesbury's intuitionism to varying effects. In certain moods, Toland presented a starkly intuitionist ethic which depicted a sovereign light placed by the Almighty in every man's heart to guide his actions and moderate his passions. At other times he indulged in aestheticism, as when he insisted that contemplating the beauty, harmony, and reasonableness of virtue led people to act virtuously. Most often, he displayed an intellectualist bias: "He therefore that employs his Reason to the best of his Ability to find out religious Truth, in order to practise it, does all that

God desires. . . ." Toland granted that passions were integral to human nature, but he insisted that their subordination to the intellect was the hallmark of personal virtuousness.[83]

Intuitionism was doomed to be a subordinate part of Toland's effort to recreate the civic virtue of antiquity. The collective bias of this ideal was so thoroughgoing as to exclude the possibility of individuals persisting in goodness apart from a moral commonwealth. A merely private source of promptings and sanctions could not, of itself, ensure general morality. Toland thought that in the operation of self-interest he had found the necessary public and dependable governor. If the promptings of conscience might influence human actions, interest directed them. To Toland, it was evident that men could not be trusted to judge their own interests objectively, much less to pursue them peacefully. Only when they identified their happiness with the common good would they subordinate their interests to it. Toland counted more on the force of calculation than on the diffused impetus of the moral sense to foster such an identification. Several assumptions underlay his expectation: first, collective poverty was both distasteful and ignoble; secondly, a commonwealth's virtue and its prosperity were reciprocally connected; and thirdly, its economic interests determined the suitability of its institutions.[84]

Still, the commonwealth could not rely on material inducements to achieve social discipline. At a time when belief in the utility of divinely sanctioned oaths was giving way to confidence in materially self-interested guarantees, Toland affirmed the necessity of bolstering commonly accepted supernatural promptings. His suggestion that the law would better secure civil promises by restraining atheists is a token of his ambivalence toward religion. Although he fulminated against those who would lie to people in order to govern them, he was willing to tolerate a class of established superstitions which did not distort public life because he was convinced that spiritual self-interest complemented material self-interest. The art of living required that the wise adjust themselves to the customs of their society. Since every government depended on a national religion, its cultivation demanded special attention. This responsibility was all the greater in a free country like England because, in corrupt times, liberty might function as a moral centrifuge, decomposing the community.[85]

In his incomprehension of secularism, at least, Toland was faithful to the Commonwealth tradition. Attributing to Harrington a worldly idea of the political community, Professor Pocock has sought to trace a parallel between it and Toland's own understanding. Secularism is not, however, a univocal. Almost all seventeenth-century English thinkers assumed that political theory had to take account of man's relation to God. Harrington was no exception, and he endowed Oceana with a selectively tolerant cult founded on natural religion. Even in a democracy the government was the head of the body of people. Its proper functioning depended on an admittedly fallible system resting on the ministry of a popular clergy, the authority of "the Scriptures (or som other Book acknowledg'd divine)," the supervision of a "Directory . . . and a Council for the equal maintenance both of the National Religion, and the Liberty of Conscience."[86]

Toland's practice realized Harrington's theory. Undaunted by critics, he professed membership in the national church, which, he held, was bound to tolerate all dissenters except those, like papists, who sought to subvert it and secure a religious monopoly for themselves. Normalizing this private practice was a formidable task. In order to test the adequacy of any national church, he offered a practical criterion: the best religion taught the purest morality and the most useful doctrines. He articulated this standard more clearly than he ever did his conception of the proper relation between religion and politics. If he occasionally appeared to call for the separation of church and state, for the noninterference of the magistrate's tribunal with the minister's pulpit, he also baldly asserted that legitimate ministry consisted of inculcating patriotism. Tactics designed to move particular audiences, his appeals for mutual self-restraint by tribunal and pulpit did not disguise his certainty that religion and politics were inextricably connected. His answer to the inevitable question, "Who is to be Master?," was never in doubt, though he chose to deliver it piecemeal. Since national unity was paramount, anything which threatened it had to be neutralized. He devoted himself to trying to cope with the religious issues that divided the nation. After his various projects for broadening the Establishment came to nothing, he contented himself with urging occasional conformity as an alternative to unchurching Nonconformists.[87]

Even the proposal for creating a militia recognized and sought to exploit the social necessity and political possibilities of the established church. Following Machiavelli, Toland accepted that, since men habitually realized their social natures by sharing in military discipline and a common cult, the maintenance of civic virtue depended on providing for both. In the militia scheme, he set out to do so with utopian results. Promising to achieve the civic ideal, it presented a mass of details without scrutinizing their practicability. Men of all conditions between the ages of sixteen and forty would muster on the green for drill every Sunday after parish services and attend triennial camps of three weeks' duration. Initially, a veteran NCO was to live in each village and instruct recruits, who would compete for prizes. Drill became an extension of worship by other means. Officers were to possess estates in proportion to their ranks. While the lords lieutenant retained command of the levies from their counties, lower posts rotated. This regimen would necessarily bolster the tightly controlled, cohesive rural society on which its existence depended.[88]

Inseparable from the militia was proper education, to which Toland ascribed a regenerating capacity. For him, the desire that children should find learning pleasurable amounted to a perversion of nature, and he endeavored to counteract softness with obligatory doses of manly and martial exercises. Boys — his calculations did not include girls — were to be bred as soldiers and citizens. Perhaps the most formidable obstacle to any educational reform was the persistence of clerical dominance of the schools. As a first step toward their secularization, Toland developed a plan to reorganize the universities. Under lay direction their curricula would be changed so as to equip students to promote the nation's economic well-being.[89]

Although Toland refrained from proposing to disestablish the church, his suggestions for loosening its hold on education evidence a determination to redirect it. He never elaborated his conception of this new Anglicanism, and any effort to reconstruct it must be inferential and tentative. Earlier English republicans had judged Christianity too otherworldly to be the religion of a free nation, but Toland aspired to make Anglicanism an instrument for securing civic virtue. In attempting to reduce the church to the service of morality, Toland could invoke the authority of prelates as weighty as his erstwhile opponent, Stillingfleet. They, too, conceived of the end of religion as fostering moral instruction and general peace, order and happiness. Once directed by true virtue and understanding, the cult could promote a just society, in which "sufficient food may be provided without violence, venery without force, the sick and aged reliev'd, and madmen and idiots taken care of." Bishops were not exceptional in their attraction to this sort of religion. Having plausibly transformed Edmund Ludlow from an oracular millenarian into a moralizing gentleman, Toland was convinced that the literate classes were more comfortable with decorum than enthusiasm.[90]

It is one thing to recognize a current of opinion, another to navigate it. Toland's explorations of the relation between Judaism and Christianity suggest how he expected to move Anglicanism. He maintained that the religion of the Jews applied only to their own nation and republic insofar as it embellished the natural tenets of the unity of God and the moral duties of men. In depicting the birth and growth of Christianity, he exploited the revered metaphor of reform to his own purpose. The church had begun as reformed Judaism, free from the ceremonial and legal peculiarities which had marred the synagogue, and it was obliged always to be reforming, constantly to be returning to its first principles. Much that was achieved during the last response to this imperative, in the sixteenth century, had been lost to a recrudescent paganism. Unless the labors of the reformers were renewed, Anglicanism was likely to degenerate into Romanism.[91] Having appealed to the raison d'être of Protestantism and insinuated that pristine Christianity had been an approximation of natural religion, he left it to his readers to draw their own conclusions.

By invoking the commonplace of natural religion, Toland apparently hoped to win a hearing, if not sympathy, for his essay in reform. This summary of allegedly self-evident beliefs exercised so irresistible an attraction that, by and large, Anglican apologists who refused to identify Christianity with it came insensibly to presume its normativeness. Much of their effort sought to demonstrate that revelation, properly understood, merely elaborated the discoveries of reason. For his part, Toland anticipated that the preponderance of lay readers would be no less reasonable than these divines. Personal immortality was to have no place among the formularies of the new cult. Shaftesbury's ideal of a self-sufficient virtue implied that actions based either on hope of reward or fear of punishment, both on earth and in heaven, were amoral. Despite Toland's sympathy for this point of view, he was dubious about the unassisted capacity of ordinary people to do good and avoid evil. He rejected the idea of hell as a priestly artifice, but he was too much a man of his time to trust individuals to behave decently unless the threat of extralegal sanctions hung over them. Convinced that a law of reputation, the human desire for fame, reputation, and honor, worked to form the conduct of men and women in face-to-face societies, he sought to extend and intensify its effect by making it posthumous. Virtuous ancients had striven to deserve the respect of posterity. The hope of glory and fame had moved the few to great achievements, just as aversion to forgetfulness and silence had impelled the many. Toland's militia plan ultimately depended on these same incentives to inspire both leaders and rankers. Omitting personal immortality from the tenets of natural religion presupposed faith in the survival of the government.[92] Only an enduring state could so educate its citizens in patriotism that, whether in war or peace, they always acted with confidence that their reputations would last as long as the commonwealth itself: forever.

Affronted by the way England was coming to be ruled in 1722, Toland once more resorted to Country language in order to express his public and private discontents. For all that the government being fashioned by Sir Robert Walpole favored aristocratic stability and Erastianism, Toland diagnosed in it an essential perversion which condemned it to remain a parody of a commonwealth. His rhetorical cast of mind had stunted his political imagination as surely as it had encouraged his tactical resourcefulness. Although he accepted variation, he effectively denied the possibility of originality. He could only hope to restore in England the civic virtue of pagan antiquity. No more than any of his contemporaries did he discern the contours of the modern state in the emerging regime. Yet, long after Walpole's system had become the object of learned curiosity, Britain had developed into a state which disdained transcendent supports and whose magistrates enjoyed a sovereignty restricted only by the liberties granted to its subjects. If Toland's shade retains both his principles and his eye for the main chance, it may even now waver between surprise and pleasure at such a novelty.

6 / The *Philosophia Perennis*

A straightforward esoterism would scarcely deserve the name. It is, accordingly, understandable that, when considering John Toland's esoteric theology, scholars have shown less agreement than in their discussions of either his critique of traditional Christianity or his political ideas. In their puzzlement, they have followed a pattern established by Toland's contemporaries. Not only did perceptive readers sometimes arrive at contradictory interpretations of the same text, but Toland's own acquaintances were often uncertain about his real beliefs. Augustans were, however, better able to cope with an elusive author than are moderns. In the eighteenth century, there was a general recognition that advocates of unconventional religious opinions tried to disguise them. For their part, Toland's foes regularly accused him of dissembling by resorting to hidden or double meanings, but it seemed to them that they need only clarify his assumptions in order to discover his purpose.[1] Like some historians, they were frequently tempted to take studied evasiveness in a writer as evidence that he was engaged in wholesale cryptography.

As an advocate of clear and distinct ideas, Toland denied that it ever occurred to him to dissemble in his theological writings. Yet he held a theory of the social responsibility of learning which at once presumed and justified such dissembling. Almost all women and the majority of men were incapable of pursuing the truths of philosophy, much less of living by them. They could, therefore, never be expected to share fully in the truth. Intellectual progress depended on the efforts of an enlightened minority; but if its direct influence was confined to this group, its effects could be much wider. Toland's belief that truth was plural, differing in content according to the circumstances of those who were to receive it, explains his ability to balance two competing convictions. Such pluralism enabled him at once to insist on the correctness of his own opinions and to judge their appropriateness by evaluating their disruptive consequences.[2] Because this standard required that he not broadcast his whole system, it led him to articulate a civil theology. Men were entitled to such knowledge as they could grasp without abandoning social restraints. By fashioning a state religion which eschewed dogma and bolstered morality, he sought to advance the cause of popular enlightenment. Men were, however, incapable of abiding absolute knowledge. The end of his esoterism was to reveal to the worthy few doctrines which could not be disseminated safely among the dangerous majority.

The disparate interpretations of *Pantheisticon* (1720) illustrate the difficulty of making sense of this aspect of Toland's thought. Perhaps because he felt that Toland's mind was too facile to admit of real conviction, Leslie Stephen dismissed the book as a *jeu d'esprit*. In doing so, he freed himself of the burden of dealing with Toland's secret teachings. While a few later scholars have presented more subtle statements of this theory, most have seen a consistent materialism as the key to Toland's mature position. Reviving a notion current during Toland's lifetime, some historians have gone so far as to read *Pantheisticon* not as a philosophical essay but rather as the revelations of the prophet of a syncretistic religion.[3]

Even if that work and the volumes which had anticipated it are taken seriously, the problem of connecting their doctrines with the dissimilar contents of books like *Christianity Not Mysterious* remains. It will persist unless contemporary scepticism about the possibility of an intelligent and serious early-modern writer holding formally inconsistent views is abandoned.[4] The determination with which Toland pursued his critique of inherited beliefs along lines suggested by the Socinians and Anglican rationalists presents an obstacle to any attempt to minimize it. A progressive interpretation of his thought which presents him as having become increasingly heterodox is no more satisfactory.

On the evidence of *Two Essays Sent in a Letter from Oxford* (1695), Toland had embraced the elements of materialism and was aware of precedents for the indirect statement of such radical ideas before he undertook either his analysis of the Christian poetical theology or his explorations in civic theology. In this pamphlet he argued that from the time of the ancient Egyptians there had existed a tradition of "mythologick theology," which sought to veil esoteric truths from the gaze of the vulgar. For such antique sages as Moses, the belief that God was corporeal and that the cosmos was His body had been the central mystery. Toland was careful not to profess this point of view. Rejecting as nonsensical the account of creation given in Genesis, he refrained from offering a detailed alternative. Still, his invocations of "the

Plastick Power," and his conviction that living things had been spontaneously generated, suggest that when he proclaimed "Jovis omnia plena," he spoke literally: everything was full of God, who was in everything.[5]

He had written *Two Essays* in defense of Thomas Burnet's *Sacred Theory of the Earth* (1681-1689) against the attacks of John Woodward. Since multiplying fossil evidence had exposed the scientific deficiencies of the poetical narrative of Genesis, Burnet endeavored to reconcile the underlying truths concerning creation and the flood contained there with modern discoveries.[6] The earth had originally been a smooth, upright globe with uniformly fertile soil, the proper environment for a golden age. The accelerating immorality of mankind had led to a comparable natural calamity, the Noachian deluge. Subterranean waters had burst through the earth's surface, tilting it on its axis and creating its present irregular topography. These events had not resulted from God's direct agency, but rather from the operation of the correspondence between moral and physical nature which He had decreed in the beginning. Describing the universe as a mechanical clock, Burnet maintained that it had been formed gradually by the action of matter and motion. Primordial history pointed to the eschaton, when the surface temperature of a disordered globe would rise until a conflagration occurred.

Criticized from all sides for impiety, Burnet proceeded to restate his theory in greater and more provocative detail. In *Archaeologiae philosophicae* (1692), he rejected Aristotle's theory of the eternity of the earth in favor of Epicurean atomism, an equally unpalatable thesis. Burnet was as unfortunate in his supporters as in his exercise in self-vindication. Charles Blount, a notorious infidel, took up his cause in the *Oracles of Reason* (1693), a posthumous collection of essays. Disregarding Burnet's sincere intention of modernizing the biblical account, Blount seized on the negative message of his labors: "the whole rather seems to have been but a pious Allegory, which *Moses* was forced to accommodate to the weak understandings of the Vulgar." In the course of the controversy the issue had become the credibility of the Bible. Although Woodward was late in entering the lists, his *Essay towards a Natural History of the Earth* (1695) was the most elaborate attempt to explain the plethora of fossils without abandoning a straightforward reading of Genesis.[7] The remains of extinct creatures proved that the whole world and everything in it had been dissolved in the flood. As the waters subsided, debris had sunk into the earth according to their specific gravities, the heaviest resting at the lowest depth.

Toland's putative defense of Burnet took up where Blount had left off. Moses had demonstrated his preeminence as a legislator by his ability to adapt "his *History* of the *Creation* and *Deluge* to [the Israelites'] capacities." If the deluge had really been universal, then providence, as manifested in the orderly processes of nature, would be meaningless. In fact, creation itself reflected the rule of natural law rather than miraculous caprice. Throughout his work Toland was concerned to acquit Thomas Hobbes of the charge of atheism. The term itself was a red herring and, even if it were more credible, it could not be applied to Hobbes's notion of the corporeality of God. Moses himself had held the same view, though he had expressed it in a suitably enigmatic and parabolic fashion.[8]

Despite the priority of his esoteric doctrine, Toland did not choose to give it pride of place on his literary agenda. His discovery that, by adapting the critical arguments of the Socinians, Remonstrants, and Anglican rationalists, he might succeed in transforming Christianity into a reasonable civic religion suggested a more promising approach. Only when he was frustrated in his desire to diffuse his two exoteric theologies, did he turn again to the exposition of his esoteric theology. Thus, the *Letters to Serena* (1704) and *Adeisidaemon* (1709) were responses to the ordeal which had begun after the publication of *Christianity Not Mysterious* (1696), and which at length convinced him that the arduousness of attempting to refashion Christianity meant delay. In much the same way, his sense of political impotence in the face of sustained official neglect after 1717 led him to subordinate the quest for civic virtue to the elaboration of esoterism in *Pantheisticon*.[9]

Whatever role such considerations may have played in moving Toland to recur to his third theology, they cannot account for its content and form. He agreed with most of his contemporaries that the investigation of the nature of certainty, not of being, was the first task of philosophy. Once he decided that Locke had provided a satisfactory map of the human understanding, he felt free to grapple with the three secondary questions which most seventeenth-century philosophers set themselves: explaining the natures of substance, space, and time. His Lockianism necessarily shaped his perception of and solutions to these issues. Because Locke's way of ideas was a description of the operations of single minds, it implied a kind of psychological atomism. Although

Toland's insistence on the centrality of clear and distinct ideas in the creation of knowledge enforced this bias, it did not relieve the problem of describing individual identity which he had also inherited from Locke.[10] Toland had to struggle with the ancient dilemma of trying to reconcile the one and the many.

Toland was, however, to turn Locke's agnosticism about the character of substance to his own very different purposes. For Locke, it was an unknowable and changing substratum with no necessary connection with perceivable and changing phenomena. If men could not know the real constitution of a thing, they had to content themselves with attributing to it a nominal essence, the complex idea of characteristics which it seemed to share with other individuals of its species. Toland appears to have followed Locke in concluding that "the abstract *idea* for which the name [of a species] stands and the essence of the species are one and the same thing." In the same chapter of the *Essay* in which Locke made this observation, he warned against confusing the "sensible ideas" of qualities which are observed in a thing with its real essence.[11]

Locke conceded that there "may be" a chain of being extending from God down to the "lowest and most inorganical parts of matter." He could say no more, because unlike some medieval philosophers he was unable to affirm that the substance of every creature was the composition of a potency for being and a divine act which gave it existence. For Christian Aristotelians, this view of reality had pointed to total dependence on God; it was "in the creature itself and not only in someone's thoughts about the creature." Spurning Locke's reserve, Toland tried to develop a cosmology which met his criterion for certitude. As Leibniz recognized, he was a convinced sensationalist. In his comments on Bayle's article on the Hellenistic philosopher Dicaearchus of Messene, Toland hinted that he saw an all-embracing materialism as the inevitable correlate of his epistemology.[12]

Locke's friend and protégé, Anthony Collins, understood Toland's intention in the *Letters to Serena,* the first extended treatment of his cosmology. Before its appearance Collins described the physical basis of Toland's system for the benefit of his aging mentor: Toland sought to prove that motion could exist in matter independently of an external agent. He had framed this book in 1702 in Germany, where he had gone after the House of Lords had condemned *Reasons for Addressing His Majesty.* Severe criticism from Leibniz persuaded him to delay publication in order to tighten his arguments, but its title was a tribute to the circumstances of its composition: "Serena" was Queen Sophie-Charlotte of Prussia.[13]

With a few exceptions Augustan apologists were convinced that treating motion as a constituent of matter made God unnecessary. Thus, Samuel Clarke denounced

> those men . . . who, merely through a vanity of Philosophizing, have been tempted to embrace that Opinion, without attending whither it would lead them; ought not, indeed, to be directly charged with all the Consequences of it: But 'tis certain, that many under that cover, have really been Atheists; and the Opinion it self (as I before said) leads necessarily and by unavoidable consequence, to *plain Atheism.*

Understandably, he and his fellow Boyle lecturers felt a special obligation to prove the natural immobility of matter. Like most of their contemporaries, they were sure that the notion of dependent being, and hence the existence of an independent divine causality, required that motion be treated as a continuing gift whose bestowal was reserved to the deity. To do otherwise would be to subject creation to the rule of "mere Chance and Accident."[14]

Toland rejected such arguments. In his view, "activity" was of the essence of matter, and matter expressed itself in motion. A particular body was only "a certain Portion of Matter, made up of many simple Substances." These bodies were "but several Determinations or Modes, existing and perishing by their several Causes." The "Motion of the Whole" alone properly deserved the name, and all local motions were "only the several changeable *Determinations* of the Action which was always in the Whole." Impenetrability and extension were the other characteristics of matter. Place, or occupied space, was therefore "either the relative Position of the thing with respect to the circumstantial Bodys or the Room it fills." In *Pantheisticon,* he would elaborate his account by describing "Prime Matter or First Bodies, or the Elements . . . most simple, and actually indivisible, infinite too in Number and Species."[15] The uniqueness of these atom-like entities lay in their having real rather than nominal essences.

Two competing metaphors inform Toland's descriptions of his ontology. On some occasions he spoke organically, as when he portrayed everything in nature as the fruit of "its own seed." Elsewhere, he rejected hylozoism and relied on mechanical tropes which implied that an inevitable causation was at work throughout the universe. In this mood, he excluded the fortuitous and unpredictable circumstances that regularly attend organic growth. His unwillingness to imitate the attempts of some like-minded contemporaries to draw a detailed blueprint of the cosmic machine suggests the limitations of his own mechanism.[16] Despite his materialism, he resisted making a decision against vitalism.

He was confident, however, about his ability to offer a general description of the universe. There was no such thing as incorporeal space, and local motion affected only the interconnected permutations of matter called bodies, not matter itself. Toland denied as well the existence of gaps such as vacua, thereby placing himself in conflict with the best scientific authorities of his time. Sir Isaac Newton, for example, accepted the existence of three-dimensional vacua. Toland's denial also suggested that his primary scientific debts were to the Paduan Aristotelians or the Cartesians, the most conspicuous opponents of a void. Divines like Samuel Clarke, who sought to invoke the authority of the new science in defense of their opinions, were neither slow to recognize the reactionary quality of Toland's teachings nor reluctant to try to turn it to advantage. To them, it seemed that if vacua were, in fact, possible, Toland could not argue that matter was necessary. Such objections failed to shake Toland's confidence in the accuracy of his general description of an infinite, eternal universe whose unity and order derived from the harmonious and ceaseless movement of its contiguous and indestructible parts.[17]

Attributing motion to matter and treating the universe as an exclusively material entity had implications for anthropology that were at least as unsettling as those which it had for divinity. By denying the immateriality of the intelligence, such a theory seemed to most Augustans to snap the link which connected the individual human being to God and thus to constitute atheism. It also precluded the idea of the immortality of the soul. Apologists probably devoted more time to the defense of this tenet than to any other save the existence of God. Without doubt, flesh and all other matter were as "grass which withereth." Nothing that Locke wrote had aroused so much hostility as his casual observation in book 4 of the *Essay* that God might be able to confer the power of thought on matter.[18] In excluding the possibility of an immaterial thinking substance, Toland went much further, and the vehemence of his critics was correspondingly greater.

Leibniz had been severe in his criticism of the draft of the fifth of the

Letters to Serena ("Motion Essential to Matter"). He held that Toland had failed to explain how, if the soul was only a "concurrence of corpuscles," matter had succeeded in achieving both movement and order. At that time Toland had apparently been chary about professing a completely mechanistic materialism. He had insisted, though, that under certain circumstances the unchanging essence, matter, acquired the accidental characteristic of thought in the same way that in other situations it took on the quality of roundness. When these circumstances disappeared, matter ceased to be thought. Although Toland allowed that the soul's essence was unknowable in itself, he believed that it was comprehensible through the senses as it functioned in the body. He went on to assert that the "Ego" — or soul — was the result of the impressions which other material things made on the brain, and that each species had a brain which dealt with such sensations in distinctive ways.[19]

Toland never managed to deal with Leibniz's objections and develop a more systematic account of individuation. Indeed, his efforts to elaborate his theory were almost circular, with matter being explained by reference to mind and mind by reference to matter. If he did not deny individuality, he nonetheless presented particular forms as the concurrent operations of specific parts of the universe that were ultimately inseparable from the whole. He depicted individual bodies as mere mental abstractions of "limited Systems, or particular Quantities," which did not exist apart from "the Extension of the Universe." Insofar as Toland treated particular material objects as epiphenomena of the mind, he was obliged to explain the nature of the human intellect. He never undertook to fulfill this obligation directly, but there is enough consistency in the hypotheses that he rejected to suggest the form which his own might have taken. By refusing to view the brain as the organ of thought, he sought to dispose of the notion of individual thinking substances. Intellection was only the "peculiar Motion" of the central nervous systems of human forms. All ideas were reducible to a purely external corporeal process, and all human actions were explicable by an analysis of motion.[20] His failure to undertake such an analysis did not, of course, diminish his faith in its possibility.

In *Pantheisticon,* Toland adorned his atomistic explanation of human understanding with references to "Ethereal Fire" — a kind of mind-matter more "subtil," or lighter, than other forms of matter — which suffused the entire universe and provided it with harmony. While he implied that large concentrations of it were present in the human central nervous system, their existence did not undermine his conviction that human thought and action were mechanically determined operations of matter. Like Descartes, Toland was convinced that animals were machines, but he did not follow the philosopher in completely separating humanity from the rest of animal creation. If the brutes were mankind's fellows, man was also a machine.[21]

For once, Toland had justified the worst fears — or fondest hopes — of Anglican apologists. He had adopted a remorseless materialism and dismissed every supposed manifestation of immaterialism as an illusion. His procedure did not require him to explicate the presuppositions of his system. Thus, he prudently refrained from denying the immortality of the human soul. His sneering account of the origins of the notion sufficed to confirm the opinion his foes had drawn from his denial of the soul's immateriality.[22] He did not believe that personal identity — whatever it was — survived the dissolution of the human form.

Unlike Augustan polemicists, modern scholars have been reluctant to ascribe atheism to any eighteenth-century sceptical writer. For Toland's contemporaries, the word *atheist* had two compatible meanings: a person who formally denied the existence of either a Supreme Being or teleology in the universe; or one whose speech or habits displayed no reference to a personal deity. Because the presence of speculative atheism was at once more ascertainable and less common than that of practical atheism, Christian apologists only infrequently accused sceptics of the intellectual offense. Nevertheless, for some theologians Toland's cosmology provided evidence that he conformed to their definition of speculative atheism.[23] But is it sufficient to prove the charge?

In the *Letters to Serena,* Toland portrayed the infinite universe as a unity in which "every material Thing is all Things." At the same time, while he denied that God is the prime mover, a being apart from the cosmos on whom it depended, he was unwilling to do more than hint that He could be identified with it. Indeed, he sanctimoniously reproved those who had "made Nature or the Universe be the only God," even as he rebuked clerics who accused them of atheism. They "did firmly believe the Existence of a Deity," so that, if "their unwary Zeal refin'd him into mere Nothing, . . . the Goodness of their Intention ought to secure 'em with all men of Candor from the Charge and Consequences of Atheism." Toland's reproof becomes even more curious in light of his failure to refute those who took the universe as their God, his offhand affirmation of the creation of matter-in-motion, and his

decision to relegate his acceptance of God's immateriality to a coda to
the last of the *Letters*.[24] Such a performance was scarcely calculated to
mollify his numerous and determined foes.

As circumstances and his own inclinations moved him, Toland intermittently attempted in the years after 1704 to elaborate the
chiaroscuro that resulted from this effort to sketch his esoteric theology.
His first task was to create a satisfactory vocabulary. When he coined
the word *pantheist* in *Socinianism Truly Stated* (1705), he meant by it one
who recommended indifference in theological disputes on the grounds
that they were inconclusive. He was willing to describe himself as a
pantheist in this sense, but he only alluded to the "system of
philosophy" that underlay his attitude. He first used the word in what
has become the accepted metaphysical way in the Latin tract *Origines
judaicae,* which he appended to the *Adeisidaemon* (1709). He was not slow
in translating it into the vernacular. By 1710, he was referring in his
correspondence to "the Pantheistick opinion of those who believe in no
other eternal Being but the Universe." Nevertheless, he postponed
openly identifying himself with this opinion prior to *Pantheisticon*
(1720): "Finally, the Force and Energy of the Whole, the Creator and
Ruler of All, and always tending to the best End, is GOD, whom you
may call the Mind, if you please, and Soul of the Universe; and hence
it is, that the Socratic Brethren, on a peculiar Term, as I said before,
are called Pantheists." Toland's aim was to eliminate both the separation of God from the universe and the distinction between a supreme
intellect (or soul) and the natural activity of matter. While it was possible to speak of God as the mind of the universe, or as the force and
energy of the whole, in reality such expressions were merely a sort of
shorthand for the principle of individuation. Operating through the
laws of motion, it allowed for the differentiation and description of
transitory aspects of the totality. By the time of his death, a French
polemicist had created the abstract noun *panthéisme* to describe the
opinion, and English writers were regularly using *pantheist*.[25]

Toland was understandably loath to identify his pantheism with
atheism. Not a few scholars have shown a similar reluctance. Attempts
either to convict or to acquit him of the charge are probably fated to
degenerate into a wrangle about semantics. Still, it does seem ill-ad-
vised to try to vindicate him by treating his references to the existence
of "Force and Harmony" in the universe as expressions of the traditional idea of providence concealed in a "secular" philosophy. When

used indiscriminately, the concept of secularization can obscure the extinction of meaning. For Toland, attributing force and harmony to the universe was only another way of describing its fixed order. Its mechanical regularity was not tantamount to the purposiveness required by the theistic idea of general providence. Moreover, it could not even accommodate the Christian belief in particular providence, the divine justice which allows that each man receive his due. Toland's mechanism could not accommodate the presence of such a bond between humanity and God; nor could it admit that by charity every man might enter into a sort of friendship with Him. In Toland's view, nature contained its own self-ordering and autonomous principle which precluded divine guidance of individuals through prescience, loving care, and intervention.[26]

The effort to stave off accusations of atheism preoccupied Toland. In *Adeisidaemon*, he suggested that there was a mean between atheism and superstition and, without defining it, implied that his own system embodied it. Later, in *Pantheisticon*, he distinguished his teachings from those of the "Epicureans" or "atheists." By this time, however, he was candid enough to admit that "Use that great Master of Language would have it otherwise." Most of his contemporaries were obedient servants of use. As early as 1709, Leibniz was becoming sceptical about the sincerity of Toland's disavowals of belief in the Godhead of the material universe, and after Toland's death many of his critics did not hesitate to reject his disclaimers of Epicureanism.[27]

Toland's apprehension about being labeled as an atheist seems to have had a more complex origin than fear for his own safety. Like most of his contemporaries, he was convinced that religion was as necessary an expression of human sociability as government, so that a commonwealth of atheists was an impossibility. Moved by the same conviction, Locke had excluded atheists from his generous provision for toleration of belief. Although Toland thought that superstition was more dangerous to public order than atheism, he saw complete disbelief as enough of a menace to concede that the civil authorities would be justified in penalizing it.[28] The validity of esoterism did not relieve its adherents of the obligations which fell on them as social animals.

By portraying himself as the heir and expositor of the authentic meaning of the most ancient theological doctrines, Toland sought to justify the piety of his esoterism. Primitivist motifs recur in Toland's writings, but he was far from simply assuming, first, that the primitive was usually the closest approximation of the natural and, then, that the natural was invariably true.[29] He nonetheless shared in a theological culture which deferred to primitivism, and was himself affected by its premises. The Latitudinarians were eager to establish the compatibility of Anglicanism with natural religion. Their desire resulted from the conjunction of traditional Erasmian primitivism and an Arminianism that was sometimes nearly indistinguishable from Pelagianism. If the consequences of original sin were negligible and the normativeness of antiquity presumed, then the search for religious truth would have to be extended as far back in history as possible.

The determination of the Anglican rationalists to show the naturalness of Christian beliefs rested on a dangerous assumption. If the truth of Christianity was vindicated when it was shown to be congruent with the elements of mankind's primordial religion, then this core became the standard for judging the suitability of religious opinions. In fact, should the norm be reconstructed, was there need for any further elaboration? Toland presumably thought not, for he presented his own esoterism as the modern expression of the religion which was common to "all wise men." He was laboring to restore forgotten truths. Not only was he confident that the ancient sages had been able to understand the nature of things, but he was also sure that he could reason as they had.[30]

In order to recapture their real opinions, it was first necessary to clear away the manifest nonsense which often surrounded them. Because Toland's hermeneutics rested on his conviction of the accuracy of his own point of view, it tended to foster syncretism. To the extent that an author, whether ancient or modern, had taught a doctrine which seemed to anticipate — or at least be reconcilable with — Toland's understanding, he belonged in the ranks of wise men. Examples of intractability, error, or superstition in another writer could, therefore, be dismissed as manifestations of circumspection or partiality. Esoteric teachers had perforce to mean more than a casual reader might gather. In the case of ancient texts, there was, moreover, always the possibility that monkish bigots had mutilated the manuscripts in copying them. Since groups as diverse as Pythagoreans, Academics, and Brahmans had mythically embellished pantheism, their real doctrine, Toland could compile a formidable list of remote intellectual progenitors.[31]

Despite his partiality for Greek and Asiatic sages, Toland was far from exclusive in compiling his genealogy. He noted, for example, the "atheists" of antiquity, who had asserted the existence of a unitary God. They resembled the "most ancient Egyptians, Persians, and Romans, [and] the first Patriarchs of the Hebrews" in grasping "the simplicity of the Divine Nature" and judging "an indifference of Place and Time to be the best expressions of infinite Power and Omnipresence." From 1704 onward, Toland sought with progressively less discretion to demonstrate the identity of what would come to be called pantheism with natural religion.[32] It had been the esoteric theology of the founders of the great cults of antiquity.

Armed with this theological master key, Toland felt free at once to attribute chronic mystery-mongering to the Egyptians and to present their priests as sages who had secretly held an essentially Copernican cosmology. The Egyptians were less important to Toland in themselves than as the teachers of Moses, the "Egyptian philosopher" who had founded the Jewish commonwealth. *Origines judaicae* had as a principal object the defense of Strabo's theory that Moses was a pantheist. In *Pantheisticon*, Toland singled him out among Old Testament figures as an object of respect for just this reason. Contemporary German anti-Semites had taken a similar line in order to establish the Jewishness of Spinoza's heresies.[33]

Toland's concern to identify pantheism with natural religion helps to explain his preoccupation with derivative researches into the beliefs and practices of the druids. The suggestion that Toland's esoterism included a kind of vestigial, druidic sun worship is improbable, but it points to the cause of Toland's solicitude for the reputation of the Irish hierophants. Like the modern pantheists, his compatriots had been a self-conscious fraternity dedicated to pursuing truth and to protecting it from the fatal gaze of the vulgar. For all their extravagances, they had held the "two grand doctrines of the Eternity and Incorruptibility of the Universe and the incessant Revolution of all Beings and Forms."[34] By rehabilitating these notoriously superstitious and cruel pagans, Toland not only bolstered his case for the universality of pantheism in antiquity, but also emphasized the degeneracy of the majority of his fellow-Irishmen.

The attempt to demonstrate that pantheism was the natural religion carried with it the melancholy task of describing how the polytheism with which ancient sages had ornamented their wisdom had gradually distorted and eventually crushed it. In the first of the *Letters to Serena*, Toland undertook to explain the origin and progress of superstition.

While he emphasized the euhemerist theory of mythology, he did not hesitate to use the alternative allegorical interpretation. Many of the ancient gods were mortal kings and heroes whom priests had deified to impress on the unlettered the grandeur and power of the one God. Others were poetical representations of "the Elements and Qualities of Matter" or the "effects of Nature"—both aspects of the one God—which the vulgar had deified under the benign gaze of their priests. Insensibly corrupted by the offerings of votaries, the sacerdotal class abandoned the jealous defense of their esoteric theology. The slide into forgetful confusion proved to be irreversible. The successors of these errant sages were as credulous as the multitude. Perhaps because Toland's theogony was a coherent synthesis rather than a one-sided analysis, it dominated European writing on the subject for almost two generations after his death.[35] Judged by the standard of tenacity and extent of influence, Toland's account of the origins of the gods was his most important contribution to the republic of letters.

He considered the "incessant Revolution of all Beings and Forms" to be as essential to his esoteric theology as the deification of the universe. If the cosmos was a closed and self-sufficient system, it could not undergo "real Innovation" in any of its sections except "the sole Permutation of Place." Since rest itself was only a "motion of Resistance," the pantheist could be certain that every part of the universe was in constant, uniformly "equinoctial" motion. Toland repeatedly chose to present such mechanistic principles through organic metaphors: "All the Parts of the Universe are in this constant Motion of destroying and begetting, of begetting and destroying." The opposition of contrarieties maintained the rhythm. Because changes in parts of the universe led neither to mutations in the whole nor to the loss of any particle of matter, all configurations would, over infinite time, inevitably recur. Human forms were not immune to this rule, so that the experiences which individual forms underwent were also recurrent. This constant motion controlled the history of man as well as the history of nature.[36]

Toland rejected as "thread-bare" arguments for the "newness" of the world from the supposed lateness of human culture. None of the various tragedies and comedies which made up history was original; all of them were acted out again and again during the eternity of time. With Ecclesiastes, he argued: "The thing that hath been, it is that which shall be; and that which is done is that which shall be done; and there is no new thing under the sun." This rhythm made the study of the past a worthwhile enterprise. Every kind of government followed a cycle of birth, growth, perfection, decay, and destruction. Learning and the arts conformed to a similar pattern, with periods of light alternating with periods of darkness, though neither light nor darkness was ever absolute. Because the nature of human forms was consistent, learning amounted to a constant attempt to recover forgotten or half-remembered truths.[37]

Belief in periodic cycles did not lead Toland to despair. On the contrary, he saw them as confirmation of the purposiveness of the universe, because they showed that ordered permanence underlay the appearance of random change. The certain recurrence of every instant gave all of them eternal meaning. In much the same way, the inclusiveness of civic virtue systematized the often apparently random lives of individuals.[38] Just as the succession of the variable but interconnected periods of history were incorporated into the stability of the whole, so the inconstant actions of each citizen were merged into the order of the commonwealth.

Toland's materialism would seem to have had obvious implications for his conception of human conduct. Inhibited by convention from admitting—perhaps even to himself—the import of such decisions as denying the autonomy of mind, he avoided dealing systematically with fundamental ethical problems like the nature of evil. Still, he hinted at the rudiments of an esoteric ethic which differed from that of either the Christian poetical theology or his own civil theology.

Although critics erred in accusing him of the blasphemy of trying to separate morality from religion, they thereby showed an inkling of the paradox of a mechanistic materialist trying to elaborate a civic religion. Try as he might, Toland was unable to reconcile all the presuppositions of his esoteric and exoteric teachings. He could, for example, propose a consistent hedonism which ascribed to the human form an innate attraction to pleasure and a corresponding repulsion from pain. While his civil theology required that he describe such feelings as manifestations of the will, his esoterism implied that they were no more than the regulators of a mechanism. Even so, he could continue to profess his faith in a moral law whose dictates men knew connaturally and to equate obedience to it with religion. Some of the tenets of his public doctrine were, however, resistant to such neat translation. Despite his hopes, his third theology could not easily accommodate bestowing a disciplinary function on rhetoric and the judgment of posterity.[39]

Generalizing from his own painful experience, Toland created the figure of an isolated sage which came to haunt his esoteric writings. Not only were most people too weak to pursue and follow truth, but they also envied and feared its devotees so much that they regularly conspired to restrain or destroy them. The sage was often a man apart, whose isolation virtually became the precondition of his search for virtue.[40]

At least one prolific antideist thought this motif paradoxical: how could a writer insist that the principles of religion had to be universally accessible and still assert that the mob was incapable of knowing truth? Put another way, were the deists not guilty of the very outrage for which they berated priests, viz., denying that ordinary people could aspire to full human dignity? Toland might have answered this question by rebuking his critic for superficiality, for being simultaneously too pessimistic and too optimistic. If traditionalists underestimated the ability of common men to live in rational community and clung to inherited fables, they also ignored the impersonality of the cosmos. Ultimately, a would-be sage had to confront the universe alone and to accept with indifference his own suffering and eventual extinction. These realities were so austere that Toland himself was sometimes moved to palliate them by depicting nature in maternal images.[41]

In order to sustain himself, the sage had to achieve moral autonomy; and to that he could aspire only after he had liberated himself from custom. The process entailed abandoning traditional language and its attendant metaphysical delusions and, through recognition of the relativity of all habits and usages, transcending his native culture. When he had reached such maturity, he would begin to appreciate that in the knowledge of truth lay his primary support. By accepting the reality of a mechanically determined, self-sufficient, and exclusively material universe of whose infinity he was a transitory speck, a wise man could be freed from the terror of death.[42]

Toland saw nothing grim in such acceptance. Virtue depended on an understanding of causes precisely because it alone supported resignation in the face of mortality; only if one was certain of dying peacefully could one live serenely. Virtue might, therefore, be said to be its own reward.[43] By practically denying the reality of the problem of evil, Toland's determinism entailed a kind of cosmic optimism. The most immediate evidence for the reasonableness of such an attitude was the release from the burden of priestly tutelage which awaited the wise man. He was bound solely to his conscience, his conscious participation in the working of the whole.

In discussing the social obligations of the sage, Toland cast further light on his esoteric ethics. He maintained that what was commonly regarded as atheism included suspension of belief in moral absolutes and the adoption of a practical morality. Of course, pantheism was not atheism. While pantheists enjoyed complete freedom of thought and action, they eschewed licentiousness. Toland's cosmology clarifies his distinction. By licentiousness he seems to have meant persistence in the delusion that one can act as one wills, while by freedom he meant action informed by knowledge of the necessity of reality. Toland knew the truth, and it had made him free. As a true Epicurean, the pantheist behaved temperately, because the contemplation of nature had impressed on him the regularity which was its first law. There existed, in other words, a parallelism between the orderly behavior of particular human forms and the regularity which prevailed throughout the universe. Just as there was a single set of cosmological laws, so there was only one standard of human action for a particular situation.[44] For Toland, the real was the right.

Individuals acceded to this standard by acting prudently. Self-restraint was essential to prudence, and it could often make oppressive exactions. In order to fulfill his duty as a citizen, for example, the pantheist would have to conform to the commonwealth's established religion. Not all the responsibilities of prudence were inhibitory. Even though it made life pleasant, conviviality belonged to morality. Scattered through Toland's writings are intriguing comments which seem to imply that he viewed sexuality as an extension of conviviality and accorded it a dignity greater than that of mere passion. Thus, at the conclusion of *Clito* he depicted the love between man and woman as the token of a final self-transcendence which would transform the sage's confrontation with the universe into participation.[45]

Such comments, however piquant, remain insinuations. They are neither numerous nor clear enough to warrant the conclusion that Toland thought that he lived in an age partial to "disinhibition," much less that he himself intended to further this cause.[46] Prudent restraint in defiance of habit and, if need be, inclination, was a consequence, as well as a cause, of intellectual liberation. Toland's confidence that he had recovered the perennial philosophy never tempted him to forget the responsibilities of citizenship.

Scepticism enjoyed less support in the half-century before the publication of Hume's *Treatise of Human Nature* (1739–1740) than it had at
any time since the Renaissance. Toland shared in this neglect. It is
easier to depict a solitary individual confronting the universe than it is
to be such a person. He seems never to have undergone a sceptical crisis as cathartic as that through which Hume would pass. Indeed, he
dismissed the "silly Sophism of the Sceptics" because it confounded the
possibility of error with error itself.[47] Almost effortlessly, he managed
to insulate himself against the destructive potentialities of his esoteric
theology. Toland's conviction that he had recovered the truth delivered
him from a harrowing personal experience, just as it protected him
against the more threatening implications of his esoterism; it was more
than a trope. Far from seeing himself duty-bound to revolutionize
mental habits, he believed that he was conserving a creed known to the
best minds of the past. Since he held that such wisdom had to remain
the possession of a minority, he struggled to avoid straining the majority's limited tolerance for reason. Within the limits of his mercurial
temperament, he was faithful to his double task of conservation.

Although Leibniz had a low opinion of Toland's philosophical competence, he took his views seriously enough to attempt to correct them.
As he recognized, Toland was dealing with weighty issues which also
engaged the leading minds of the age. The substantially derivative
character of his own efforts was far from being an embarrassment to
Toland.[48] Since he felt that he was laboring to restore the beliefs which
were common to truly wise men in every period, he freely appropriated
and modified the ideas of other thinkers, often with little or no acknowledgment. If his syncretism helped to admit him to discussions more re-
condite than his unaided talents might have otherwise allowed, it complicates any attempt to identify the sources of his esoterism. Unless the
search for his intellectual antecedents is narrowed, it risks becoming an
idiosyncratic epitome of the history of ideas. Fortunately, there exists a
manageable catalogue of possible sources. Toland sometimes owned
his debts, both directly by praising an author and obliquely by correcting another's deviations from the primordial truth. He tended to make
his direct statements privately and his indirect ones publicly, but he
frequently neglected either kind of courtesy. Besides considering the
creditors whom Toland acknowledged, both his contemporaries and
later scholars have sought to remedy his negligence by suggesting additional candidates.

Without knowing that Toland had written the *Two Essays*, Leibniz maintained that his cosmology was Hobbist. Though the philosopher may have simply been clutching at a familiar label, his surmise was nonetheless acute. Hobbes had exerted a formative influence on Toland's mechanism. The assiduity with which the young Toland had defended him was tantamount to an endorsement of his ideas. Differentiating between natural and civil philosophy, Hobbes insisted that both of them were concerned above all with establishing the causes and attributes of material bodies. Motion was the "one universal cause" of all forms: "the variety of all figures arises out of the variety of those motions by which they are made." Motion was invariably local motion. He also dismissed the concept of an incorporeal or spiritual substance as "insignificant speech." It followed that, in applying such terms to God, men were only trying to evade admitting His incomprehensibility. Far from resigning himself to agnosticism about the divine nature, however, he held that God is "a most pure and most subtle corporeal spirit" possessing extension. In natural philosophy, mathematics was identical with reasoning, and it permitted the discovery of the chain of universal, necessary causation. Both time and space were phantasms arising from the working of motion.[49] Hobbes was, in other words, a consistent materialist and mechanist.

After the *Two Essays*, Toland never again referred to Hobbes, an omission that has puzzled historians and would seem to call into question the assertion that Hobbism continued to influence him.[50] Yet might not his determined silence be as important for solving the mystery of his intellectual antecedents as was the failure of the Baskervilles' hound to bark in Conan Doyle's story? Although Toland had decided before the end of 1695 to change direction by laying aside combative libertinism in favor of the less exceptionable approach of the Socinians, he did not thereby abandon his belief in an essentially Hobbist materialism and mechanism. He would develop this point of view by mixing it with hylozoic and vitalist elements, but he never repudiated it. It surfaced with increasing distinction in the series of publications which runs from the *Letters to Serena* to *Pantheisticon*.

Hobbes was one of three writers whom Anglican apologists held in horror on account of the aid which they had supposedly given to atheism. Toland referred to Descartes and Spinoza, the two other offenders, if only to belittle the former as a dabbler in "philosophical romance" and to correct the latter. In contrast, he never chose to pay Hobbes even such an oblique compliment. The Channel has repeatedly offered cultural as well as military protection to England. Just because Hobbes was an Englishman, his countrymen found him more troublesome than any European heretic. By the end of the seventeenth century the effort to confute his ideas had almost become an obsession.[51] When Toland decided to pursue a three-fold theology, he must have found it imperative to distance himself from an association which would be especially encumbering. The self-discipline which he showed in avoiding so much as a hint of indiscretion was unique in his literary career.

For the first Boyle lecturers, Descartes was the original modern exponent of the impious attempt to frame a cosmology solely on the basis of matter-in-motion. Acquiescing in this thesis, some historians have contended that Toland owed to Cartesian physics his ascription of motion to matter and his denial of the existence of vacua in the universe.[52]

There are a number of similarities between Descartes's physics and Toland's pantheism. For Descartes, matter was an indefinitely extended unity which was differentiated by the speed and direction of motion. It made up a closed universe, everything outside of which was indeterminate and inert. Although he presented motion as unified, in practice he distinguished three manifestations of it: metaphysical, which accounted for the existence and condition of particular bodies; kinematic, which allowed for a theory of bodily change; and dynamic, which explained physical causation. The circular movement of the whole resulted from the instantaneous responses of its parts to varying circumstances. Their motion was susceptible of geometric analysis. Notwithstanding Descartes's insistence that God was the ultimate cause of motion, first *philosophes* and then philosophers have discerned in his system the elements of a coherent pantheism. But did Toland share their interpretation? In themselves, Toland's objections to Descartes's rationalist epistemology do not disprove some degree of intellectual dependence, for his metaphysics and physics could be separated. Two other considerations do, however, militate against attributing systematic influence to Descartes. Unlike some other seventeenth-century philosophers, he did not allow that motion was intrinsic to matter. Recognizing this omission, Toland also criticized him for having made extension the primary quality and expression of matter and for having failed to demonstrate the infinity of the corporeal universe.[53] Although Toland may have viewed Descartes as one of the sages, he refused to defer to the philosopher.

Cartesianism was, however, a movement which included original thinkers besides its founder. The greatest of these was Spinoza, and the late Rosalie Colie has attributed to him a profound effect on the English deists, including Toland. This theory must contend against even more obstacles than faced the attempt to connect Toland with Descartes. In addition to the difficulty presented by their divergent epistemologies, Spinoza's effort to solve the mind-matter problem by presenting these two alleged substances as correlative attributes of a single component was incompatible with Toland's straightforward materialism. The indissolubility of Spinoza's system would have hindered easy reconciliations. More immediately, in the fifth of the *Letters to Serena*, Toland set out to refute Spinoza—or at least to undermine the vision of him as the exemplary modern atheist presented by Bayle and the Boyle lecturers. For various reasons, a few scholars have accepted the sincerity of his undertaking. Yet in that work, Toland had not so much repudiated Spinoza as reproved him. He objected to the *Ethics* because he believed that its author's refusal to endow matter with motion undercut its cosmology. On its principles, one could neither make the finite intelligible nor explain the origins of matter. Familiar with the technique of insinuating Spinozism under the cover of refuting it, churchmen were disinclined to mitigate their suspicions about Toland's design.[54]

Since Toland did not object to either Spinoza's method or his pantheism, their wariness was probably justified. Advertised as a sweeping condemnation, the fifth letter had shrunk by its conclusion to a few specific objections. For all that Toland sometimes used *pantheist* and *Spinozist* interchangeably, the attempt to interpret him as a disciple of Spinoza remains vulnerable to the objection which prevented the ascription of such tuition to Descartes. From the Revolution onward, a number of English writers who were seemingly unblemished by Spinozism held views which were virtually indistinguishable from those which connected Toland with Spinoza.[55] During Toland's lifetime the impulse to merge man into the universe and to deify the result was too widespread to warrant singling out Spinoza as its primary source.

In contrast to these tantalizing parallels and conjunctions, Toland did owe an unmistakable debt to Cartesianism. He once observed that his confidence in his own cosmology depended on the researches of modern scientists, particularly astronomers, who had attained certainty in their descriptions of nature. He singled out Alfonso Borelli because he had "evidently shown" that the universe worked "mechanically or mathematically." Borelli (d. 1679), whose works Toland may have come to know while a student in the Netherlands, had tried to synthesize the teaching of the Italian Aristotelians and Descartes in an inclusive mechanism. Like the later seventeenth-century Dutch Cartesians, Borelli was less a mathematician than a mechanist. Viewing the task of science in Aristotelian terms, such savants aimed to achieve a certain understanding of things by explicating their necessary causes. They struggled to preserve the dominance of pure rationalism over natural philosophy.[56] The *Principia Mathematica* offered a divergent program, and by the turn of the century it seemed to be carrying the day.

Besides converting Locke's epistemology into a thoroughgoing sensationalism, Toland sought to exploit his prestige by using other of his ideas to limit the damaging impression caused by the clashes between his own esoterism and the physical theory of Isaac Newton. By denying that man could know the nature of substance, Toland explicitly invoked Locke's authority in support of his notion of matter. Such professed agnosticism did not, however, prevent him from trying to describe the composition of bodies. In fact, Toland's esoteric writings display a pattern wherein his practical assertiveness bursts through the master's theoretical modesty. Both men rejected the Newtonian concept of absolute space, but while Locke restricted himself to an examination of the human understanding of this kind of complex idea, Toland could not forbear speculating about the illusive character of space. In much the same way, he declined merely to repeat Locke's analysis of motion as an instance of an undefinable simple idea.[57] Once more, Locke could have reasonably been vexed at Toland's self-assertive discipleship.

For one as self-consciously modern as Toland, there could be no possibility of repudiating Newton's authority. Notwithstanding their disagreements about such fundamental matters as the existence of absolute time and absolute space, Toland styled him the "greatest man in the world" and insinuated that their positions were reconcilable. Whether or not Toland meant such comments to be taken seriously, the presuppositions of his cosmology owed little to Newton's system. He was at Edinburgh before the *Principia* entered its curriculum, and his Dutch experience offered nothing to dissuade him from embracing Hobbism. It remains to be seen to what extent Toland's esoterism represents either a reaction to the ascendancy of Newtonianism or an attempt to separate its mechanics from its metaphysics.[58]

Toland's rhetoric does not sustainedly reflect the influence of the scientific revolution, with which he sought to identify himself. His acquiescence in the divines' monopoly on the tropical uses of gravity and inertia may indicate his evaluation of the immediate contribution of modern science to his esoteric theology. Despite his endorsement of the application of mathematics to the study of nature, he seems to have been oblivious to the significance of Newton's quantification of mechanics. Newton rejected Cartesianism because it blocked the development of the mechanical philosophy, which entailed the "estimation of forces in nature by geometrical calculation in terms of matter-in-motion."[59] In contrast, Toland's orientation remained tenaciously qualitative.

Notwithstanding the distance between his own point of view and that of Toland, Newton apparently worked to avert any confusion of the two. Margaret C. Jacob has argued that he drafted the twenty-third query of the 1706 London edition of the *Opticks*, which affirmed the inherent passivity of matter, in order to counter Toland's position. At first sight, Newton's sensitivity might seem unreasonable. He treated motion as a relation (the rearrangement of atoms in space during time) rather than a property; and following the publication of Toland's *Letters to Serena*, he maintained that only an active metaphysical principle — more precisely, the will of God — could account for it.[60]

While it is unquestionable that Toland was prone to attack Newtonian theologians, he was inveterately deferential to Newton himself. When he could invoke Newton, he did so ostentatiously, and he expressed his disagreements with him in a regretfully tentative way. Once more Toland's eclecticism seems to have prompted him to hope for an accommodation. There was no denying Newton a place among the sages, and his occasional mistakes were amendable. Toland may not have endeavored to lift Newtonian science from its metaphysical foundations, but he cannot have ignored Newton's theological flexibility. After 1717 the great man began to materialize motion. The rift between the relational and attributive concepts of motion was not erased by his discovery that God's omnipresence required that He be substantially present in the universe. Still, his literal belief that "in Him are all things contained and moved" now balanced his insistence that God was incorporeal both in His substance and in His operation.[61]

Some of the Boyle lecturers dismissed the idea that their most radical opponents were indebted to any modern school of natural philosophy.

Thus, John Harris maintained that they offered "only the Arguments of
the Ancients a little varied and embellished"; the Epicureans were their
teachers. Toland meditated on the physical theories of antiquity, which
provided more convincing precedents for his esoterism than his fanciful
reconstruction of the druids' lore. Indeed, Aristotle had defined the
issue that dominated Toland's physical speculations: "But those who
say that there is an infinite number of worlds, some of which are in process of becoming while others are in process of perishing, assert that
there is always motion (for these processes of becoming and perishing
of the worlds necessarily involve motion), whereas those who hold that
there is only one world, whether everlasting or not, make corresponding assumptions in regard to motion." Although Toland sometimes
praised Democritus, he was eager to demonstrate that Cicero, his
revered mentor, had held doctrines which anticipated the very truths to
which contemporary pantheists adhered. In this effort he once again
displayed his uncanny ability to determine the real meaning of virtually
intractable texts. With remarkable consistency Cicero's import coincided with Toland's own views.[62]

The expansiveness of the list of Toland's putative sources, whether
classical or modern, points to the Janus-faced quality of his physical
analysis. The ancients had conceived of physics as an inquiry into "the
nature of things and their inherent properties rather than their behavior and relations."[63] Democritus, Aristotle, and Cicero would,
therefore, have understood Toland's insistence that motion was a property of matter. Despite its decreasing appeal, their attitude survived
into the eighteenth century. The regularity with which Toland invoked
modern authorities testifies to the waning of this point of view. His eclecticism has proved strong enough to thwart every attempt to demonstrate that a single thinker or school provided the physical foundations
of his pantheism.

In recent years yet another proposed source of Toland's esoterism
has come to occupy pride of place. Beginning with the recognition that
many of his ideas parallel elements of Renaissance vitalism, an elaborate genealogy has evolved, which presents him as the heir of a "Hermetic tradition." Frances Yates, who has been primarily responsible for
the contemporary notion of Hermeticism, has sought to trace the use
which European thinkers from the later Middle Ages onward made of
the congeries of Platonic, Neopythagorean, Stoic, and Oriental notions contained in the *Corpus hermeticum*.[64] The authors of these assorted

texts, which date from the first through the third centuries A.D., had pursued *gnosis*, the ultimate wisdom, which they thought they could discover by first contemplating the universe and then reflecting on their own efforts. The *Corpus* is at once the record of the results of such contemplation and an incentive to its continuation. Although earlier devotees had been drawn to this collection because they saw in it a system of natural magic, their successors experienced progressive disenchantment. The magical aspect of the movement did not survive the failure of the attempt of John Dee and the continental Rosicrucians to transform the *Corpus* into an alchemical handbook. In the later seventeenth century, the remaining adherents of Hermeticism continued to desire *gnosis*, though their choices of aids in finding it were usually as various as their interpretations of it.

For Miss Yates, Giordano Bruno was the architect of the modernization of Hermeticism. It was his achievement to realize that the magical aspirations of this vision required that man become the manipulator, rather than the subject, of nature. Interpreting Copernican astronomy as a purification of the heavens which presaged the reform of earthly society, Bruno succeeded in the improbable task of connecting the old magic to the new science. He was drawn to Copernicanism because it vindicated the divinity of the universe and thus offered a deepened *gnosis*, but he proved to be an unwitting prophet of the seventeenth-century mechanization of the cosmos. At one time or another, Bacon, Descartes, and perhaps even Newton came under the influence of Hermeticism, in part because of its affirmation of the potency of knowledge.[65]

Yates's thesis has received widespread interest, much sympathetic and some critical. Three related problems have occupied its critics: the possibility of reconstructing a coherent tradition of Hermetic and natural magic; the role of Hermetic ideas in the life and thought of Bruno; and the Hermetic character of such notions as extended spirits and powers which survived into the later seventeenth century as alternatives to corpuscular mechanism. In effect, these scholars question whether it is necessary to introduce an external, Hermetic element to account for the various nonmechanical opinions of the early-modern thinkers who have been presented as the continuators of Hermeticism. Since its presuppositions were essentially Neoplatonic, there would seem to be no reason for trying to identify it as a phenomenon independent of the revival of Neoplatonism which began in the fourteenth century. Aside from Raymond Lull, Yates tended to ignore medieval precursors of Bruno in an effort to establish that he derived his ideas from primarily classical sources. Yet Bruno showed some affinities with Nicholas of Cusa, a decidedly non-Hermetic figure. Moreover, his use of the *Corpus* did not keep him from abandoning some of its fundamental doctrines, and his interest in the infinite owed more to his ethical concerns than to scientific curiosity. Because of Bruno's exclusively theoretical interest in magic, his peculiar mixture of rationality and credulity, and the religious quality of his idea of reform, he emerges from the pages of the most recent study of his natural philosophy as an isolated, unsystematic thinker who neither belonged to nor founded a school. In the case of later alleged adepts, it has been argued that their deviations from mechanism can be explained by the vestigial appeal of Neoplatonism.[66]

The debate continues, but an investigation of the extent of Toland's indebtedness to Bruno need not await its resolution. His habit of reading other authors as he chose was too ingrained to dispose him to try to reconstitute and adhere to the assumptions of any external tradition. Toland was familiar with the supposed inspiration of the Hermetic legacy. He kept the *Corpus*, which he called the *"Trismegisti Opera,"* in the room where he died and occasionally referred to its contents. In some respects, the collection anticipated his characteristic teachings. Its authors were given to portraying the cosmos as the image of God, eternal, infinite, and unmarred by vacua or voids. The indestructible stuff of the universe was matter, in which motion inhered, and individual phenomena were the results of constant changes in matter. Such anticipations did not undermine the proof that the *Opera* were Gnostic rather than ancient Egyptian works nor palliate their stubborn animism, so that Toland, who discerned their Platonism, was unwilling to accord them any particular respect.[67]

If Toland had little use for the Hermetic *Corpus*, he admired and promoted the writings of Giordano Bruno. By 1698 he was in possession of some of Bruno's works, which he judged to be among the most obscure he had ever encountered. Notwithstandng his own interpretive perplexities, he thought *De l'infinito, universo e mondi* of sufficient importance that he produced an English abridgment of it. He essayed translating other of Bruno's works as well, but he was fascinated by the *Spaccio della bestia trionfante*. It offered a model for every proponent of esoterism, because its teachings enlightened the wise and eluded the vulgar. Toland had been distributing fragments of the Italian original throughout Europe for more than a decade before he published a translation — perhaps his own — in 1712. The pained reactions of eighteenth-century writers to Bruno and the *Spaccio* suggest that Toland may have overestimated his elusiveness. Divines excoriated him as an atheist, and the *Spectator's* heated expression of contempt for the book was a token of the fear it inspired in proper minds.[68]

Seldom an appreciative legatee, Toland was demonstrative in his gratitude to Bruno. Confident that an age of light was dawning, Bruno based his theology on the repudiation of orthodox Christianity, including the Bible. Destruction was not, however, an end in itself. As Toland appreciated, Bruno's analysis of motion was the tool with which he constructed his cosmology. Defining change as movement and all movement as local motion, he concluded that variation was merely displacement, while locomotion was integral to matter. Even though the whole was immutable, its separate parts were constantly moving. In accepting the idea of a plurality of worlds, one was obliged, he thought, to view the universe's motion as infinite and without a central source. He had no need of an unmoved mover. Because corporeal beings were moved by an intrinsic active power, they participated in infinity and possessed immanent divinity. Contrariety was at once the source of universal movement and the principle of individuation. The diversity of the cosmos was not limitless, for all its constituents passed through a cycle.[69]

Bruno had little patience with the concept of a vacuum, which he saw as a denial of the unity and infinity of the universe. His efforts to describe the stuff which composed the cosmos were nonetheless inconsistent. On the one hand, he catalogued its attributes: it was a "composable, divisible, manageable, contractable, formable, mobile . . . unannihilable" substance. On the other hand, he gave a reassurance that matter existed under "the dominion, power and virtue of the soul." Such inconsistencies resulted from his adherence to a set of assumptions which thwarted his monistic intentions. Thus, his invocation of the soul coexisted with his contention that, since the oneness of the universe partook of "the Unity of the Divinity, which is in all things," the whole was perfect in itself and nothing could be added to it. The continuous interpenetration of the parts of the universe manifested its perfection. Although Bruno's retention of the Aristotelian categories of form and matter and act and potency kept him from elaborating a purely materialistic immanentism, he accorded matter greater dignity in his natural philosophy than his contemporaries did in theirs.[70]

For Bruno, true morality was exemplified by an inward reformation founded on an ideal law immune to the ravages of time. The study of cosmology was crucial to achieving the good, for it enabled the adept to internalize the universal order and so preserved him from any fear of death. Once freed from such irrational dread, he could begin to understand the nature of things. In time, he would reach resignation, which was itself a badge of magnanimity.[71] As a part of the eternal whole, man was indestructible: he had become Jove.

Bruno's contempt for the many was deep-seated. He was convinced that because the study of cosmology was desirable, it was closed to the majority of men. His attitude exposed him to the predicament which would later beset his translator, John Toland. Sometimes he pointed to republican Rome as the exemplar of a civic ethic that rebuked the asceticism which he identified with Christianity; sincerity was intrinsic to this code. At other times his fear of the mob became so intense that he advised separating belief from conduct and even expression, and insisted that the social necessity of religion justified external, hypocritical observance of conventional practices. In addition to expressing a desire for security, his protestations that his teachings endangered the authority of neither the church nor the state may have betokened an appreciation of his quandary.[72]

If it is clear that Toland found inspiration for developing his esoterism in Bruno's doctrines, there were nonetheless certain incompatibilities between the two systems. Intellectual changes during the seventeenth century made such differences inevitable. Confident that mere empirical knowledge could not produce certitude, Bruno discriminated reason from the simple ideas gathered through the senses. His concept of reason was symptomatic of an essential dissimilarity between his outlook and that of Toland. Unlike Toland, he appears to have been subject to raptures that influenced his philosophical speculations. He saw, for example, the interpenetration of the parts and the whole not merely as a physical phenomenon, but also as the reflection of a World-Soul in which each individual soul participated. Transmigration was the way in which spiritual quanta changed their perceptible forms. His drive to be united with the cosmos was alien to Toland's more mundane sensibility. Nevertheless, as his references to the "Plastick Power" and the spontaneous generation of living things in the *Two Essays* suggest, Toland was uncomfortable with the stark mechanism of Hobbes. He appears to have seen in Bruno's vitalism the necessary corrective to Hobbism's explanatory deficiencies. Toland, therefore, took exception to Bayle's portrayal of Bruno as a precursor of Spinoza not because it linked the two as advocates of a materialist pantheism, but rather because he was convinced that Bruno, unlike Spinoza, had accounted for the self-sufficient activity of matter.[73]

There may have been one more point of contact between Toland and Bruno. Drawing on Bruno's insistence that natural philosophers ought to be subordinate to "gentlemen astrologers," Frances Yates has theorized that he led an association of such adepts. For all that Toland must have found Bruno's terminology quaint, he might have recognized in it an anticipation of his own belief that conservators of esoteric theory were superior to practitioners. Moreover, he considered the conservation of esoterism to be a social task. In the *Pantheisticon*, he described the organization, tenets, and liturgy of the "Socratic Society," a dining club whose members were dedicated to the candid discussion of all philosophical issues. Despite their differences, its members shared a religion which was "simple, clear, easy, without Blemish [of superstition], and freely bestowed."[74]

The society's liturgy was a *pasticcio* which drew on sources as various as Horace's "Centennial Hymn" and the Book of Common Prayer. Toland's own testimony strengthens the impression of adolescent playfulness offered by this concoction. Like many of his contemporaries, he used the word *Rosicrucian* as a synonym for obscure nonsense. In addition, on the eve of the appearance of *Pantheisticon*, he referred to the book as "this foolery." Repeatedly in its pages he seems almost to be winking at his readers, as if to confirm that he wished to be taken literally when he proclaimed, "Let Jokes and Mirth be our pleasures." Yet Toland's mirthfulness does not in itself establish his lack of participation in one or another secret society. Although he showed characteristic scorn for the *disciplina arcana* so precious to such groups by publishing the ritual, he also evinced an initiate's fascination with it.[75] Once more Toland may have been consistent only in his paradoxicalness.

A number of facts have fed various hypotheses about the nature of the body (or bodies) to which Toland may have belonged. By the middle of the seventeenth century secret societies had begun to prosper in England. While still a student at Edinburgh, Toland was accused of

Rosicrucianism, and Sir Robert Clayton, his sometime patron, belonged to a kind of Masonic lodge that may have been related to the dining club in which both men participated and whose members used Greek pseudonyms when addressing each other. Toland occasionally styled himself "Adeisidaemon," and he received letters from a variety of acquaintances who used similar aliases.[76] Pierre Des Maizeaux, who knew Toland and became his biographer, accepted his assertion that the Socratic Society flourished and had branches throughout Europe. Later students have gone on to argue that Toland was somehow implicated in the origins of Freemasonry. Early twentieth-century statements of the thesis were informed by the obsession of generations of French writers with the conjecture that the Revolution had Masonic origins. In turn, critics were not slow to point out that similarities between Masonic practices and those of the Socratics do not suffice to establish their identity.[77] Despite such reservations, the thesis has been reformulated in a more sophisticated manner.

The Socratic Society appears to have vanished without a trace, the contention of the "British Circle of the Universal Bond" that it was founded by Toland in 1717 being unsubstantiated and probably groundless. If there is no justification for supposing that his organization survived independently, it is suggestive that eighteenth-century Masons had a lively interest in one of Toland's more arcane pursuits: the effort to rehabilitate the druids. Still, the available evidence for linking him with English proto-Masonry remains ambiguous. There are several superficial parallels between the procedure described in *Pantheisticon* and the order of the annual feast of the English Grand Lodge, which was functioning by 1717. The beginnings of Masonry lay in the creation of autonomous lodges by nonprofessionals who had earlier joined bodies of craftsmen. These secessionists transformed the trade secrets of operative masons into their own rites, of which Toland seems to have been unaware. Their identities are unknown, but Toland's name does not appear on any of the surviving lists of later members. More importantly, the doctrine of the first Masonic catechisms was untouched by pantheism, so that official historians of English Freemasonry have absolved it of any share in Toland's esoterism.[78]

The possibility that Toland's real affinity lay with continental Masonry, which has always been less staid than its English counterpart, cannot be excluded. In the decades following its publication, *Pantheisticon* generated considerable interest in France, where it was immediiately translated and widely diffused. With resourceful ingenuity, Margaret C. Jacob has labored not only to document Toland's involvement in such European bodies, but also to establish their connection with an archaic, radical English Masonry. She has reconstructed the activities and doctrines of a group called "les chevaliers de la jubilation," which was centered in the Hague. Toland at least possessed information about it, and during his intermittent residence there between 1710 and 1713 he was acquainted with Jean Rousset de Missy, a member who went on to help found Dutch Freemasonry. In Jacob's view, Toland exported to the Continent a determinedly subversive Masonic organization. Its initiates were partial to a materialist cosmology which would prove to be abhorrent to the worthies of the Grand Lodge.[79]

Because Professor Jacob has chosen to describe the Dutch club as "the earliest Masonic group" in Europe, her hypothesis has been greeted with scepticism by Toland's most recent biographer.[80] Two separable theses are involved in the dispute. Toland may well have been associated with the *chevaliers* sometime during his career, but the society itself need not be termed Masonic. Although members of the group in the Hague may have turned up later as Masons, it would be anachronistic to style it Masonic on the basis of their subsequent affiliation. In light of the available evidence, individual participation in both circles may be more prudently seen as coincidental than as proof of continuity.

While Toland's Dutch associates may have shared his attraction to a radical style of freethinking which accommodated materialism, it would be rash to try to enmesh him in any kind of official doctrine. Throughout his life he was too recalcitrant to submit to the discipline of prolonged membership in any organization dedicated to an ideology. If he felt that the wise in every age had a grasp of eternal truths, he knew that his own was uniquely firm.

Elucidating Toland's involvement in the murky world of the early eighteenth-century secret societies will, in any case, have even less importance for understanding his esoteric theology than a final verdict about his participation in a Hermetic tradition. Unless his bibliography is expanded in an unforeseeable way, the outlines of this aspect of his thought will remain clear. Throughout his literary career, he held a coherent pantheism, but he never sought to expound it as he did both his critique of the Christian poetical theology and his civil theology. Along with the other teachings which constituted his esoterism, it was to be insinuated for the benefit of the discerning few. Originally inspired by domestic sources, his materialism grew to be an adaptive interpretation of Bruno's ideas. Although mechanist inclinations, derived principally from the writings of Hobbes and Spinoza and other Cartesians, served to offset Bruno's hylozoic and vitalist emphases, Toland resisted deciding between these competing points of view. Instead he used them as complements, much as modern physicists do the wave and particle theories of light.

In its essentials, Toland's esoteric theology is a strand of the monist tradition which, beginning in the Hellenistic age, runs through the history of Western philosophy.[81] Like his analysis of the universe as matter-in-motion, his repeated calls for resignation in the face of inexorable natural processes point to the ultimate dominance of his thought by a vision of totality. Even if he failed to deal convincingly with such central problems as individuation, his straightforwardness in coining the word *pantheist* to describe himself stands in sharp contrast to his refusal either to call himself—or to allow himself to be called—a *deist*.

7 / The Elusiveness of Deism

John Toland's commitment to a pantheist esoterism has not deterred many historians from placing him in the front ranks of deism. For the most part, their efforts have proved to be ambiguous, if only because the diversity of Toland's thought strains the confines of such a category. Scholars who have characterized him as a deist have usually enveloped the label with a patchwork of qualifications and elaborations: "he was certainly in later years an evolutionist Unitarian. That he was a critical Deist is certain. . . . Toland was also a constructive Deist, his *Letters to Serena* including a cosmological system of matter, motion, and intelligence; a fusion of neo-Stoic and Newtonian principles."[1] While such an abundance of modifiers may do justice to Toland's intellectual variousness, it tends to leave the reader puzzling over the meaning — and perhaps the analytic value — of a deism which is supple enough to be compatible and coincident with both Unitarianism and pantheism. An investigation of whether deism suitably describes any of Toland's three theologies might begin with the semantics of the word. How did early modern Englishmen define deism? What was the intention of Toland's contemporaries who chose to call him a deist? What has moved certain historians to follow their lead?

In 1621, Robert Burton used the word *deist* to describe a group of infidels rather than a peculiar form of infidelity:

> with many such vain cavils, well known, not worthy the recapitulation or answering, whatsoever they [libertines] pretend, they are *interim* of little or no Religion. Couzingermans to these men are many of our great Philosophers and Deists, who though they are more temperate in their life, give many good moral precepts, honest, upright, and sober in their conversations, yet in effect they are the same (accounting no man a good Scholar that is not an Atheist) *nimis altum saprunt,* too much learning makes them mad. . . . a peevish Generation of men, that misled by Philosophy, and the Devil's the rest, hold all Religion a fiction, opposed to Reason and Philosophy, though for fear of Magistrates . . . they durst not publickly profess it.

That the *Oxford English Dictionary* should have excerpted the opening sentences of Burton's account to buttress its definition of a deist — "one who acknowledges the existence of a God upon the testimony of reason,

but rejects revealed religion (The term was originally opposed to atheist, and was interchangeable with *theist* even in the end of the seventeenth century . . .)" — suggests that the confusion which originally
surrounded the term has persisted. Although Pierre Viret, who had
coined the word *déiste* in 1564, sought thereby to distinguish a group
who were neither Christians nor atheists, later French authors used it
commodiously rather than narrowly. Writing three years after Burton,
Marin Mersenne indicated that he, too, thought that a *déiste* was a kind
of infidel; his primary concern was, however, to refute Giordano
Bruno's *De l'infinito, universo e mondi* (1584). Throughout the eighteenth
century many English writers would continue to use *deist* "as a term of
reproach with little or no precise meaning."[2]

When the word *deism* became current, the form of infidelity to which
it referred was distinguished from atheism. As early as 1660, Pascal
was using *déisme* to describe the opinions of men who believed in a religion that could be achieved by reason apart from Christian revelation.
Although Dryden had presented deism in 1682 as adherence to "the
principles of natural worship," over the next hundred years Englishmen often identified it with Unitarianism. While the two definitions are
not necessarily irreconcilable, they are by no means synonymous. In
the Arian Samuel Clarke's second set of Boyle lectures (1704), he presented the deists much as later textbook writers would:

They see that things generally go on in a constant and regular Method; that the Frame
and Order of the World, are preserved by things being disposed and managed in an
Uniform manner; that certain Causes produce certain Effects in a continued Succession, according to certain fixed Laws or Rules; and from hence they conclude, very
weakly and unphilosophically, that there are in *Matter* certain necessary *Laws* or *Powers*,
the Result of which is That which they call the *Course of Nature*, which they think is impossible to be changed or altered, and consequently that there can be no such thing as
Miracles.

The matter-of-fact precision of Clarke's account offers no hint that after
his death observers would still be identifying deists and anti-Trinitarians much as some of his contemporaries had.[3]

Others who wrote during Clarke's lifetime chose to postulate the existence of an association between deism and Unitarianism rather than
to identify them. Although many who did so failed to differentiate the
opinions which joined the two movements from those which separated
them, a few attempted to be more rigorous. Nonetheless they could

sometimes fail to discriminate between a tendency toward deism and its actuality. Bishop Browne, for example, portrayed Socinianism and deism as adjoining points on a curve descending from orthodox Christianity to atheism; he went on to assert that deism was a new religion blending Socinianism and Arianism. If Browne never precisely defined deism, he offered a more incisive analysis of it than most antideists. He concluded that the Unitarians' primary contribution to the deists was a theory of language which restricted meaning to words which communicated clear and distinct ideas. When applied to religion, this rule would eventually dissolve all traditional formulas. For their part, less sophisticated advocates of an association theory were likely to contend that the Socinian method of interpreting Scripture linked deism with Unitarianism: both subordinated Holy Writ to human reason. Even Augustans who sought to distinguish the two positions could not agree on any event or book as a boundary. Just as late seventeenth-century divines saw deism as a menace prior to the appearance of *Christianity Not Mysterious,* so their Georgian successors reckoned anti-Trinitarianism to be a force in 1722, the year of Toland's death.[4]

When writers whom contemporaries judged to be deists discussed the meaning of deism, they frequently treated it as implying coolness toward revelation. Sometime after Matthew Tindal stopped contributing to the Unitarian tracts, he became a professed deist. Indeed, he numbered himself among the "True Christian Deists" who maintained that a morally convincing religion would have to be available to all men in all ages. Since a creed achieved such universality only when it was obtainable by unaided human reason, it had to be independent of revelation. Tindal therefore made the tenets of natural religion — though not necessarily the five articles which Herbert of Cherbury had presented in *De Veritate* (1624) — the essence of his Christianity.[5]

Numerous antideists had anticipated him in seeing the denial of either the necessity or the possibility of revelation as the note of their foes, but not a few of them had also maintained that it derived from the Socinians' biblical researches and theories. If most of those who were characterized as deists did not follow Tindal in adopting the name, they nonetheless thought that antipathy to the idea of divine inspiration was central to deism. When Toland mentioned the heresy, he often held that it amounted to rejecting "the Authority of *Divine Revelation.*" Similarly, Anthony Collins saw the deists as impugning revealed religion. He never admitted to being a participant in the enterprise. Rather, like the Unitarians and Toland, he depicted himself as laboring to restore primitive Christianity "as deliver'd in the Scripture." In contrast, while Peter Annet was a confessed deist, he reported that he had abandoned "rational Christianity" because he no longer believed in the divine inspiration of the Bible.[6]

At first sight such conflicting testimonies might suggest that there is an ascertainable distinction between dissembling deists on the one hand and candid deists on the other. An examination of Tindal's reservations about revealed religion does not indicate that such a clear-cut dichotomy accommodates him. In fact, the central objections which he raised as a deist to any scheme of revelation were those which he had urged as a Socinian tractarian, or logical consequences of them: since scriptural texts were often either obscure or corrupt, they could not be automatically invested with binding doctrinal authority. Other Unitarians were also disposed to paint deism as the renunciation of biblical religion. Perhaps because the Reverend Stephen Nye grew more theologically conservative with advancing age, he was never accused of deism. Attempting to prove his antipathy to the new heresy, he published *A Discourse concerning Natural and Revealed Religion* (1696). In that work he described the deists' characteristic doctrine as an exclusive belief in the articles of natural religion, which meant the denial of the existence — and perhaps the possibility — of divine revelation.[7]

This was a harsh, though clear interpretation of the point of view of such recent allies as Tindal, but such exclusivity was rarely taken as the peculiar attitude of the deists. For example, some of Locke's critics deemed the effect of *The Reasonableness of Christianity* to be the denial of revelation, even if they were reluctant to call him a deist. Moreover, a few theologians doubted that the deists had gone as far as Nye maintained. While conceding that they "expressed a mean Esteem" of the Bible, Edward Stillingfleet was confident that they respected it as the best statement of the moral law, which they accepted.[8] In doing so, the bishop attributed to the deists an idea of biblical religion virtually indistinguishable from that presented in the tracts which Nye had edited. Nye's interpretation may, therefore, say more about his later opinions than it does about the differences between Unitarians and deists.

Convinced that the deists' critique of religion was more far-reaching than an attack on the Bible, other observers insisted on describing them in terms which recall Burton's. For his part, the Arian William

Whiston judged the deists to be atheists who had been so abashed by Richard Bentley's Boyle lectures that, after the mid-1690s, they confined themselves to undermining revealed religion. More orthodox writers often shared Whiston's impression of the essential radicalism of these men. Bentley himself thought that, since the ranks of atheism included all who denied God's creation or government of the world, they included the deists; those who adopted the less offensive title were attempting to disguise their real allegiance.[9]

Since Bentley was writing in 1692, he may have had Charles Blount, the author of *An Account of the Deists' Religion* (ca. 1686), in mind. Blount had anticipated Bentley's definition of atheism; he, too, thought that it was the denial of God's existence or His providence. If Blount did not take umbrage at the imputation of deism, he was eager to refute the accusation of atheism. Despite Blount's efforts, antideists were not alone in repeating Bentley's identification. Toland, for example, sometimes used the words *atheism* and *deism* almost interchangeably. On several occasions he presented deism as equivalent to "Indifference about Religion," or belief in a God "so impotent that He could not, or so malicious that He would not reveal himself," and rejection of personal immortality. For many, such opinions amounted to practical atheism, a category commodious enough to include all who declined to take part in public worship or neglected to observe religious rites in their homes. It did not take Toland's critics long to realize that they could exploit such commodiousness to his disadvantage. For some of them, it was a matter of indifference whether he was labeled as an atheist or a deist, for they were certain that there was no substantial difference between the two sets of infidels. In turn, Toland the critic of the Christian poetical theology exploited their indiscriminateness by pointing to the implausibility of accusing him of atheism as a self-evident refutation of charges of deism.[10]

Until Toland coined the word *pantheist* in 1705 and his foe Elié Benoist made it an abstract noun seven years later, Europeans who wished to describe thoroughgoing materialists or deifiers of the physical universe could only style them atheists or deists. The two most notorious materialists of the late seventeenth century, Hobbes and Spinoza, were regularly treated as deists. Their example prompted some observers to generalize. William Popple, Locke's Socinian friend, defined deists as "those who deny immaterial beings"; he thought that they were indistinguishable from atheists. Ironically, Locke's critics

used this definition when they accused him of deism because of his unwillingness to accept the demonstrability of spiritual substance. Besides
strengthening the impression that when Toland called himself a pantheist, he was only using a neologism to announce that he was a deist,
the *Letters to Serena* intensified the feeling that the deists were champions
of materialism. Antideists were convinced that when deists

> speak of the *Divine* Nature, or the Divine *Being,* or God, or the Existence of God, or of
> the Great God, they only mean Universal Nature, or the whole Universe of that one
> only Uncreated Substance of Matter, which, according to their Doctrine, is infinitely
> extended, and hath existed from all Eternity; and which Acts as a necessary Agent [pro-
> ducing] all things by various Modifications, or Collections of Modifications, of, and in
> their Eternal God, the Universe of Matter.[11]

The inability of Augustans to agree on any single principle as typical
of deism did not deter them from lumping individuals together as
deists. Nevertheless, an examination of some of their groupings reveals
the inconsistencies implicit in their lack of both an agreed concept of
deism and intelligible criteria by which to judge an individual's acceptance of it. After the appearance of *Christianity Not Mysterious* writers who
set out to refute Toland or other deists depicted their targets in a variety of ways. Such authors
    (1) postulated the existence of a deist movement whose most
prominent members were Spinoza, Blount, and Toland;
    (2) believed in such a movement and cited only Spinoza and
Toland as representatives;
    (3) included Spinoza among its spokesmen, but omitted Toland;
    (4) compiled exhaustive catalogues of deists without including
Toland;
    (5) viewed Toland and Spinoza as atheists and Lord Herbert of
Cherbury as a deist;
    (6) wrote of Blount not only as a philosophical descendant of
Herbert, but also as the most conspicuous recent English deist;
    (7) treated Blount as both a deist and a Socinian, as if the two
heresies were indistinguishable;
    (8) included Spinoza and Blount in a list of atheists without men-
tioning either Toland or deism;
    (9) named Toland and Blount as the most notorious English
deists;
    (10) equated Toland's opinions with those of the Socinians or

treated him as a Socinian rather than as a deist;

(11) presented Toland as an atheist in some ways, but as a deist in others.[12]

Their confusion seemingly justifies Professor Yolton's dismissal of the Augustan manipulation of theological characterizations: "Labels of slander which had accrued to terms like 'Socinian,' 'Unitarian,' and 'Deist' . . . were meant and understood as synonymous with 'atheist.' "[13] However tempting, such curtness ignores the laboriousness of some apologists. If churchmen merely saw deism as a convenient pejorative, it is difficult to understand why many of them labored to define — or at least to refine — their idea of it. As early as 1704, Samuel Clarke scrupulously divided the deists into three groups. There were those who believed in nothing save "an Eternal, Infinite, Independent, Intellectual Being" and attributed to Him the creation of the world, primarily to separate themselves from Epicurean atheists. There were others who endowed Him with the governance of the universe, though they denied that the words *good* and *evil* had objective meaning. Finally, there were those who had at least a partial idea of God's moral perfection, but persisted in denying human immortality. Clarke seems to have directed his Boyle lectures to the last group, because he thought that, but for their rejection of the immortality of the soul, they were almost Christians. Yet he was either unwilling or unable to name a single writer as a member of any of these divisions. His reticence was not peculiar. In 1732, William Berriman, another Boyle lecturer, introduced the distinction between critical and constructive deism with which Leslie Stephen sought to order his discussion of the phenomenon in the *History of English Thought in the Eighteenth Century*.[14] Unlike Stephen, Berriman did not try to establish which deists belonged in each subdivision.

From time to time students have tried to account for the general failure of eighteenth-century divines to address the ideas of individuals in their polemics against deism. Thus, T. E. Jessop, the editor of Berkeley's antideist tract, *Alciphron,* recognized that the bishop seemed to be refuting arguments which none of his contemporaries had ever published. In an effort to reassure readers that Berkeley had not stooped to caricature, Jessop postulated the existence of two kinds of deistic opinions: the decorous teachings which found their way into print and the less seemly discussions which went on in coffeehouses.[15] While his theory may account for Berkeley's imprecision, it remains unprovable because such distorted reflections are the only vestiges of these allegedly radical manifestations of deism.

Throughout the eighteenth century, observers placed themselves in the paradoxical situation of presuming that deism was a meaningful term, even though they could neither adequately define it nor agree on a list of its advocates. As often as not, later writers continued to treat the word as a convenient pejorative. Within eight years of Toland's death one churchman printed a catalogue of deists which included Collins but ignored him. Inclusiveness could lead to as much confusion as exclusiveness. At mid-century Philip Skelton presupposed a kind of deist anti-apostolic succession which began with Herbert and Hobbes and included not only Toland, Tindal, and Collins, but also Hume. Skelton did not think pantheism was inconsistent with deism. In his view, the deists were linked by the denial of revelation, which was more important than any differences among them. All of them held that "the light of nature is sufficient to discover to every man, without instruction, all that is necessary or expedient for him, as a moral agent to know." It followed, he concluded, that every deist at least acquiesced in the Herbertian articles of natural religion.[16] Skelton failed to consider that Herbert's axioms were incompatible with the assumptions of a consistent materialism.

Skelton was afflicted by an imprecision extreme even by the generous standards of the age. John Leland, whose three-volume *View of the Principal Deistical Writers* (1754-1756) influenced future students of deism, was more disciplined. He, too, saw rejection of revealed religion as characteristic of the deists, but he did not thereby infer that they all accepted the articles of natural religion. Toland belonged to this school insofar as he had helped to undermine belief in the New Testament, but Tindal was more radical because he had mounted the most thoroughgoing attack on the authority of revelation. Leland's failure to discover uniformity of opinion did not lead him to conclude that any of the deists had repudiated the articles of natural religion. Still, whatever the deists' intentions, their efforts had introduced "an universal scepticism and indifference to all religion."[17]

The inconclusiveness of earlier attempts to define deism and to enumerate its adherents has not kept scholars from trying to use it as an analytic term. A distinguished historian of the Enlightenment has recently organized an anthology of deistic writings on the principle that there was a group of English writers beginning with Herbert who shared certain basic ideas. Even when scholars have clashed over the interpretation of deism, they have clung to it as a concept. For the most part, they have either amplified or qualified the classical definition offered by G. V. Lechler almost 150 years ago: "Deism is essentially an elevation of natural religion, supported by free examination, to the norm and rule of all positive religion." In their efforts, however, they have been less inclined to adhere to the often inapplicable philosophical and prescriptive interpretation of the word than to search for an adequate historical and descriptive one.[18] The normative construction entails an understanding of God's relation to the created order that denies that He is either present or immanent in the world and limits His role to the act of creation and the establishment of laws which have since ruled the universe. In contrast, historical deism is seen as a phase of the theological rationalism which originated in the seventeenth century and dominated the eighteenth.

Those who have attempted to follow a descriptive approach in studying deism have stressed the reputations and intentions of individual authors, the presence of a distinctive style in their works, or their acceptance of a few general ideas. Thus, Roger L. Emerson has proposed four criteria for identifying a writer as a deist: his contemporaries had to have applied the label to him; he himself must have attacked revelation, disparaged miracles, and implicitly or explicitly rejected Anglican formulas; his writings should have worked to subvert organized religion "in the hierarchical and quasi-political sense"; he ought to have conceived of himself as a deist, free-thinker, or reformer of Christianity in a manner favored by professed deists.[19] Such standards are flexible enough to accommodate not only figures like Blount, Toland, Tindal, and Collins, but also many others who today are rarely styled deists. If they were accepted, it is difficult to see how many of the Socinians, John Locke, and Bishop Hoadly could be absolved of the charge of deism which was frequently laid against them. They also undermined Anglican formulas and minimized particularistic intervention, sought to weaken religious institutions, and used a reforming language which resembles Tindal's.

Yet the quality of Blount is indisputably different from that of Locke, and in this case style may be all. A recent student of Blount has endeavored to describe his deism:

In Blount are all those features of deism that characterize a man like Toland. There is his anti-clericalism parading as an attack upon popery; there is the same childish sense of humor and gift for cynical parody, able to condemn clerics in little ditties and bad rhymes, able to scorn Christians for their inability to live up to their professed standards. Blount expressed that combination of cajolery, invective, wit and reason which was to distinguish the freethinker of the following century.[20]

The adoption of such a stylistic emphasis would require shortening most of the existing lists of deists. Even if Toland's self-defeating indiscipline could divert him into boisterousness, he often succeeded in speaking in a temperate voice. Aside from Thomas Woolston and Peter Annet, most of the other English deists seem almost straitlaced. The sober pages of Herbert of Cherbury are free of both invective and wit, and Tindal was more often pedantic than outrageous. On occasion Collins was sharp, but he seldom descended to anything as vulgar as cajolery. Chubb's earnestness was anticipatory of the high seriousness of a Victorian free-thinker like John Morley rather than evocative of the ribaldry of a Restoration libertine. If Blount, Woolston, Annet, and perhaps Toland were the only deists, then the importance of deism has been consistently exaggerated.

Concerned with the nature of ideas instead of the character of authors, other scholars have avoided epitomizing the qualities of supposed deists in order to try to determine the intellectual components of historical deism. Arthur O. Lovejoy's essay, "The Parallel of Deism and Classicism," is now over a half-century old, but it remains an intriguing attempt to inventory the mental baggage of eighteenth-century rationalists, including the deists. "Taken for granted by most philosophers," the ideas he described there governed the "opinions, on all manner of subjects, of the majority of educated men for more than two centuries, in so far as they were emancipated from tradition and authority."[21] This congeries included nine principles: reason is common to all men and its conclusions are uniform; they are discovered, however, by individuals without the aid of tradition or external authority; only beliefs that are shared by the whole race can be normative; special pretensions to truth are inadmissible; neither particular revelation nor original genius is a trustworthy source of fundamentals; the comprehension of the ordinary person defines the limits of acceptable complexity in necessary matters; anything that surpasses it is inadmissible; essentials have been known since the dawn of human history; all changes thus tend to be degenerations. Whether deism is understood as the denial of the possibility, necessity, or originality of revealed religion or the affirmation of the sufficiency of some kind of natural religion, it shows all of these assumptions.

Because a variety of Augustans relied on such notions, Roland Stromberg has denied that Lovejoy provided an adequately specific analysis of deism: if historical deism amounted to nothing more, it would seem to be indistinguishable from contemporary manifestations of nominal or rational Christianity. For his part, Professor Stromberg contended that the identity of deism rested at least as much on the repudiation of particular revelation as on the assurance of the competence of unaided reason. It was, in other words, negative as well as positive in intent. Earlier he had maintained that the deists aimed to republish the articles of natural religion, though he failed to establish consistency of opinion about any of them among the supposed representatives of this point of view.[22]

More recently, Günter Gawlick, a productive German student of the phenomenon, has tried to reassert the priority of constructive intentions on the deists' agenda: "What characterized all of them was the aim of making a clean sweep of superstition and priestcraft, intolerance, and religious persecution by placing morality on a footing independent of revelation. Rationalism was a means to this end no more."[23] In his view, advocates of deism embraced a coherent group of practical objectives and exhibited tactical suppleness in pursuing them. Even if they are separated and fuzzy, the traditional images of deism as the rejection of revealed religion and the proclamation of self-evident religious or moral verities survive in one form or another in the principal modern expositions of it.

The inability of both Augustans and historians to agree about the meaning of deism does not eliminate the late seventeenth- and early eighteenth-century writers who identified themselves as deists. They adopted this name in order to describe either their coolness toward revelation or their adherence to some kind of natural system of belief and practice.[24] In many cases, they seem to have believed in religious principles which resemble at least some of those that Herbert had offered in *De Veritate*. Sometime before 1730 Tindal had become a professing deist, but neither Toland nor Collins ever made such a profession. Since the careers and reputations of the three men were linked, the effort to determine whether deism can be reasonably attributed to any of Toland's theologies might begin with an examination of their opinions on the possibility and nature of revelation and the five articles of the Herbertian creed. Such a comparison must have reference to the works of others who either confessed deism or have been perennially charged with it.

Toland never denied either that divine revelation might be possible or that Christianity's claim to it might be warranted. Nonetheless, his epistemological assumptions were irreconcilable with allowing divine inspiration a role in the creation of humanity's religious opinions. His conviction — that, should God use this means of information, the intelligence He conveyed would have to conform to the canons of human reason by presenting clear and distinct ideas, rather than mysteries — precluded any discoveries. Toland had other ways of undermining the authority of Scripture. If he sought to depict his preoccupation with textual problems as a token of his desire to reestablish the integrity of the Christian revelation, his foes saw it in a different light. To them, it was a painfully effective way of sapping respect for the Bible, the religion of Protestants. When Toland's position is compared with those of other deists, it seems to fall in the middle of a wide range. At one end stands Herbert of Cherbury, who was so far from doubting the possibility of revelation as to insist on it as a validation of truths which individuals had perceived through introspection. At the other end, men like Thomas Woolston undertook a concerted attack on the Bible and scorned insinuation in favor of ridicule.[25]

When dealing with revelation, Blount, Collins, and Tindal sometimes used similar techniques and frequently reached compatible conclusions. Despite such similarities, neither their approaches nor their judgments were identical. Although Blount's approach was unsystematic, its implications were unsettling. When he dealt soberly with the topic, he avoided textual researches in favor of raising fundamental issues such as that of the possibility of validating any assertion of exclusive revelation. He was sensitive to the double problem of ascertaining how human beings could identify divine interventions in mundane affairs and also comprehend their significance.[26] To him, it seemed indisputable that supernatural truths must be communicated to men through the same means by which they acquire every other kind of knowledge.

For their part, theologians recurred to scriptural miracles and prophecies to establish Christian claims. Blount sought to undermine such alleged evidence. He translated Philostratus' third-century life of the Neopythagorean Apollonius of Tyana in an effort to demonstrate that paganism had relied on similar tales of heavenly favor to its saints. In addition, he repeatedly drew parallels between the beliefs and practices of the ancient Jews and those of their heathen neighbors. If there were no way of proving an individual's assertion that he had received divine inspiration, then every person was free to use his own judgment in evaluating such contentions. With greater sophistication Toland would rehearse many of these arguments, but in the English works which he owned after 1695 he was usually more subtle than Blount. His decision in *Christianity Not Mysterious* to employ the demythologizing, developed by the Socinians and increasingly favored by the Anglican rationalists as the complement of their moralism, rested on a hopeful calculation. He believed that Christians, some of them heretics and some of them apologists, had provided a way of transforming the church into a proper civil religion. If he sometimes relapsed into the raillery which punctuates the *Two Essays* and was often willing to prepare his readers to reach damaging conclusions, he was less concerned to trumpet the improbability of the more extraordinary passages of the New Testament than to explain them rationally. In neither his critique of traditional Christianity nor his esoteric theology did he cultivate Blount's self-consciously outrageous style.[27]

In his expressions of attachment to the elements of primitive Christianity "as deliver'd in the Scripture," Collins resembles Toland rather than Blount. At the same time he differentiated such teachings from those which had been fostered by popish and priestly craft. When he set out to recover the primordial truth, Collins, as if by instinct, appropriated many of the themes which dominated Latitudinarian discussions of the Bible. Like them, he insisted that Protestantism was a reasonable religion whose foundation was scriptural. While his enterprise went beyond making explicit a tendency implicit in the hermeneutics of earlier liberal theologians, he was able to exploit their work to his own ends. In his most systematic critique of traditional exegesis, *A Discourse of the Grounds and Reasons of the Christian Religion* (1724), he denied that Old Testament prophecies were literally fulfilled in the accounts of Christ's life recorded in the New Testament. He defended his work—not implausibly—as a logical extension of Hugo Grotius' biblical researches.[28]

Grotius had indeed tended to moralize religion, favored an exemplary rather than a penal notion of Christ's atonement, and adapted the techniques of philological criticism to exegesis; but he had mitigated his disposition to rationalize by insisting that scholars must take account of ecclesiastical tradition when forming their conclusions.[29] Whether or not Collins decided that Grotius was guilty of inconsistency, he himself made no pretense of conforming to the church's inherited interpretations. If Latitudinarian exegetes were, for the most part, less straightforward than he in abandoning tradition, they often did not differ markedly from him in practice.

Like Toland, Collins treated reason and Scripture as twin means of information. Besides excluding the Bible as a motive of assent in itself, his attitude required that it be read as an historical document rather than allegorically or typically. Although he did not devote much attention to the idea of natural religion, Collins was confident that the unaided human intellect could somehow discover the elements of true religion. His deep-seated reservations about the credibility of the Bible's authority had left him with no alternative. The variety of possible manifestations of revelation meant that reason alone could decide among them; the Christian version would have to conform to the standards of coherence and veracity which reasonable men applied before accepting any book. Collins borrowed Toland's thesis that Moses had depended on Egyptian religious practices in framing the Jewish cult. Such parallels are recurrent. If Collins was disinclined to labor over either the Old Testament or arcane textual problems, he had nevertheless shouldered a burden of proof. In order to support his thesis that the number of contradictory readings and the late establishment of the canon undermined the unique status of the Bible, he had to expropriate the researches of the *érudits*.[30] It remains impossible to determine whether Collins was sincere when he asserted that he wrote as the heir of seventeenth-century Protestant exegetes. In any case, he never published the repudiation of revelation which has been taken as the distinguishing feature of deism.

In writing about Scripture, Tindal raised Toland's fundamental question in another form: how can one choose among a multitude of competing claimants to the status of authentic interpreter of an external revelation? Less ambiguously than either Toland or Collins, he designated natural religion as the standard by which the claimants should be judged. He never denied that revelation was theoretically possible, but rather asserted that this criterion alone offered an intuitively self-evident means of information. Tindal thought that conflict between reason and revelation, though often apparent, was not inevitable, and his avowed purpose was to reconcile the two. Any legitimate act of revelation could only make known "the Unchangeable Will of a Being" who himself was always the same.[31]

While the communications of self-styled prophets were riddled with inconsistencies, the decrees of reason were always and everywhere the same. Therefore, a creed which came from God would have to be immutable, as He himself was. Throughout history, humanity had shared a vision of the moral life that provided a tangible way of judging the truth of any religion. When Tindal measured the conduct of the principal bearers of the Hebrew revelation, the patriarchs and prophets, against his universal standard, he found it deficient. It was unlikely that God would have chosen as His agents men whose writings contravened the laws which He had promulgated to all. The burden of Tindal's writings was that the only credible achievement of the Bible was to confirm the discoveries of reason. He insisted that Christianity "has existed from the Beginning."[32]

Unquestionably, these men, whom historians have termed deists as regularly as did their contemporaries, held opinions about the Bible and the nature of Christianity which would have outraged both Archbishop Laud and the Puritan William Ames. The ribald anticlericalism and libertinism of Blount appalled Latitudinarians like Tillotson, and they were uncomfortable with the ruthlessness with which Toland, Collins, and Tindal maintained that morality was the sum of religion and that the validity of the Christian revelation depended on its conformity to the discoveries of human reason. Yet Unitarians such as Tindal writing under Firmin's patronage had been no less consistent in maintaining these propositions, and many Anglican rationalists espoused them, though usually in an indirect fashion. If the incendiarism of Blount was shunned by Toland and his contemporaries, these later deists articulated the assumptions held by many churchmen and went on to extract some disconcerting implications from them. In his more sober moods Blount had embraced Herbert's "Catholick or Universal Principles," but his obstreperousness tended to vitiate the benign impression of his endorsement.[33] Collins, Tindal, and even Toland—to the extent that his inconstant temperament allowed—tried to avoid being thus confounded; but was their relative sobriety merely the result of greater discretion or changing fashion, or might it represent a deliberated approach to the reconstruction of belief? To phrase the question more precisely: did they cap their criticism of revealed religion with a commitment to something resembling the Herbertian principles of natural religion?

Students who have depicted the deists as advocates of the five articles of natural religion framed by Herbert have found support in the testimony of self-described deists. Tindal and Annet, like Blount, adopted variations of Herbert's articles. Such testimonies in themselves were not necessarily badges of a distinctive affiliation. By the end of the seventeenth century, admiration for the supposed proto-deist was becoming general. Because Herbert had never repudiated Christian revelation, even such exemplary clerics as Richard Baxter could present his work as an aid to Christian apologetics.[34]

Perhaps out of deference to Herbert's emergence into respectability by the early eighteenth century, a few scholars have assigned the paternity of deism to Restoration libertines. In many ways, the case of Blount would seem to justify their decision. Not only did he ransack the works of authors from Epicurus to Spinoza in search of arguments against orthodoxy, but he also played the role of the adversary against Bishop Burnet in the fight for the soul of John Wilmot, second earl of Rochester, the model libertine.[35] Sustainedly destructive, Blount's writings only indicate glimmers of the positive aspirations which underlie both Toland's critical and civil theologies and mark the works of Collins and Tindal.

Blount was concerned to connect his own positive beliefs with the religion of primitive antiquity in order to establish their naturalness. To this end, he adopted Herbert's antithesis between truth and simplicity on the one hand and error and complexity on the other; the archetypal creed had been simple before wily priests introduced perverting complications. While some later deists tried to prove that the contrast meant that early Christianity had been compatible with the tenets of natural religion, Blount had been indifferent to the possibility of reestablishing the Christian creed on a rational basis. Tillotson could not have gainsaid their conviction that the object of religion was to lead men to behave morally, but advocacy of what was becoming a truism was not tantamount to endorsement of the particulars of Herbert's system.[36] It was possible to assert the normativeness of an essentially moralistic religion without embracing the doctrines of natural religion.

The effort to determine the deists' views on Herbert's first article ("There is a Supreme God") is more complex than the brevity of the proposition might suggest. It requires ascertaining whether Toland and his alleged confederates shared an epistemology which would have allowed them to achieve a common vision of God. While Herbert's scheme of natural religion presumed that there were valid forms of a priori knowledge, most of his putative heirs were disposed toward empiricism. All of them rejected Aristotelianism and, either explicitly or implicitly, accepted the idea that reason was equivalent to demonstration. They were nonetheless often more concerned to show that there was a conflict between reason and tradition and to assert the presumptive advantage of the novel over the customary than to address epistemological problems. Thus, when Collins spoke of freethinking, he did not mean so much a particular set of opinions, or even a method, as a willingness to question conventional theological formulas whenever they appeared to rest on defective argument or evidence. Although both Blount and the generation of deists which followed Toland lacked an interest in—or perhaps an aptitude for—epistemological investigations, both Collins and Tindal shared Toland's concern and allegiance. They too were Lockians. In contrast to their laborious efforts to explicate, defend, and apply Locke's system, a writer like Annet was able to content himself with declaring his attachment to it.[37]

The acknowledgment of a debt does not reveal its dimensions. Tindal was almost as attentive to epistemological issues as were Collins and Toland. At times his Lockianism seemed as thoroughgoing as theirs:

All the ideas we have, or can have, are either by sensation or reflection; by the first, we have our ideas of what passes, or exists without; by the second, of what passes or exists within the mind: and in the view, or contemplation of these consists all our knowledge; that being nothing but the perception of the agreement or the disagreement of our ideas.

Elsewhere he strayed from the way of ideas by insisting on the existence of self-evident propositions which men can know through intuition:

Those Propositions which need no Proof, we call self-evident; because by the comparing the Ideas, signify'd by the Terms of such Propositions, we immediately discern their Agreement, or Disagreement: This is, as I said before, what we call intuitive Knowledge, and is the Knowledge of God himself, who sees all Things by Intuition; and may, I think, be call'd *divine Inspiration,* as being immediately from God, and not acquir'd by any human Deduction, or drawing of Consequences: This, certainly, is that divine, that uniform Light, which shines in the Minds of all Men.

Tindal's fitful efforts to reconcile these positions were unavailing. In contrast, while Collins admitted that certain manifest truths provided "the foundation of our Reasoning," he never ventured to expound an intuitionism at odds with the argument of book 1 of Locke's *Essay*.[38]

Although Toland's fellow deists did not share an interpretation of how men know, they were consistent when discussing what was unknowable. Since they conceived of reason as demonstration and assigned it the decisive role in creating assent to doctrines, they were loath to allow the credibility of mysteries that were defined as eternally incomprehensible propositions. In fact, the deists rejected mysteries of religion as uniformly as the Unitarians had, and some of them did so for similar reasons. Blount summarily dismissed "*Divine Mysteries*" as antithetical to "*Common Reason*." Collins decided that Socrates had done good—and thus been religious—without knowledge of mysteries. Tindal declared that person happy who would "suffer no Mysteries, or unintelligible Propositions" in his creed. Chubb scorned all mysteries as things "which we do not understand," and Annet reached the same conclusion. It is noteworthy that, in rejecting mysteries, Collins and Tindal, like Toland, adopted the anti-Trinitarian insistence that assent could be given only to propositions which produced clear and distinct ideas in the mind.[39] In contrast, Blount, who had written most of his tracts before the outbreak of the Trinitarian controversy, never mentioned the criterion.

There are other indications that the Trinitarian controversy which flared up after the Glorious Revolution influenced most of the supposed deists. Blount had expressed his preference for the religion of the "Arians" over that of the orthodox, but in his single-minded negativism he seems to have been oblivious to the possibility of turning the characteristic arguments of the anti-Trinitarians into a justification for a rational and moral religion. If his attitudes had been fixed during the reign of Charles II, most of his younger contemporaries who were labeled as deists were drawn to elements of the Unitarian analysis. On becoming a deist, Tindal did not repudiate his Socinianism; neither did he fail to express a continuing sympathy for that heresy and its spokesmen. Going beyond respectful allusions to his former colleague, Nye, he repeated the Unitarian indictment of the Incarnation, the hypostatic union, and a triune God as the cardinal irrationalities of traditional Christianity. Moreover, his deist critique of Scripture depended on the premises which had informed his Unitarian examination of it. Collins stood apart from the movement sponsored by Firmin. Though he owned a large collection of Socinian tracts and dealt ironically with the dogma of the virgin birth, he was as careful as Toland to keep his distance from organized Unitarianism. Thus, even as he defended William Whiston's freedom of expression, he devoted most of book 2 of *A Discourse of the Grounds and Reasons of the Christian Religion,* to attacking Whiston's use of the Bible.[40] Collins' posture of sympathetic detachment is reminiscent of the attitude his mentor, Locke, struck when facing the Socinians.

The later deists tended to imitate Tindal more often than they did Collins. Beginning as an exponent of Unitarianism, Chubb persistently used arguments which had first appeared in the tracts edited by Nye. Morgan developed intellectually much as Chubb had, and throughout his career he pursued the same object which had attracted the Socinians, viz., a completely articulated religion with moral goals. Even Annet pointed to the hypostatic union as Christianity's principal absurdity.[41]

The deists also drew on the theories of more respectable theologians. For the most part, Augustan divines thought it axiomatic that the easiest way of knowing God was to observe His workings. They did not agree on one description of them, but many Anglican rationalists were coming to favor the "clock metaphor"—the image of the physical universe as a great mechanism whose detached maker was God—which is a feature of every textbook account of deism. Significantly, Toland used it sparingly in all of his theologies, though both his esoterism and his exoterism assumed that creation was governed by predictable and regular processes rather than by God's particular and irregular interventions. Toland conformed to a pattern followed by most of his fellow deists. While they seldom used the metaphor, they were hostile to miracles and other anomalies. Their antagonism, however, admitted of degrees. Some contented themselves with maintaining that God generally worked through the course of nature, while others flatly rejected the possibility of miraculous occurrences.[42] The more cautious position was not inconsistent with the desire of many Latitudinarians to end God's interventions in His well-ordered creation at the conclusion of the apostolic age.

The deists' disagreements about how God came to be known and how He worked foreshadowed their often ambiguous discussions of His nature. Blount exemplified one of the most persistent of these ambiguities. Though he assured Richard Bentley that there were no real atheists, he also insisted that matter was eternal and infinite. Anticipating Toland, he defined providence as the operation of materially determined natural processes. Most contemporaries suspected that atheism was the concomitant of such opinions. Blount's scattered references to the relation of God to the universe can only have aggravated their suspicions, for he was intrigued by the notion of a world soul, which he occasionally seemed to imply was an aspect of the Godhead. In *Anima Mundi* (1679), he sought to trace the concept of the human soul to the cosmology of the "ancient philosophers," which had presumed the immanence of the deity. Without defining what would become known as pantheism, Blount quoted the same tag from Vergil — *Jovis omnia plena* — with which Toland was to close his anonymous *Two Essays* sixteen years later. Despite this parallel, the two writers made different uses of the Stoic doctrine of God's identity with the universe. In examining Varro's thought, Augustine had cited Vergil's line to support his contention that the belief that "God is the soul of the world, and that this world itself is God" was fundamental to the philosopher's third, or philosophical, divinity. When Toland decided to elaborate his own three-fold theology, he made the same principle the basis of a systematic esoterism. Although Blount would again advert to the notion in the posthumously published *Oracles of Reason* (1693), he had no more interest in explicating it than he did in reformulating Christianity as a rational creed. Like Charles Gildon, his editor, Blount was indifferent to the distinction between an immanent and a transcendent theology. He was attracted to pantheism as a weapon with which to attack the hiddenness of the God of Christianity and did not espouse it.[43] Presenting God as an intelligible being obviated consideration of His nature.

By and large the later English deists were more straightforward than Blount in rejecting pantheism. Not only did Collins deny that there were any real atheists, but he also spurned the notion that God was one with the cosmos. In his view, He was "a being distinct from the universe, which we call immaterial." Yet Collins' attitude toward the deity remains a matter of controversy. In trying to establish that His attributes and those of mankind were univocal, Collins sometimes treated Him almost anthropomorphically. Despite Collins' apparent belief in a supreme being, David Berman has recently offered a tentative justification of Berkeley's charge that he was a crypto-atheist. Berman maintained that the key to Collins' real position is the argument that self-existent matter must contain all perfections because the idea of

God's perfection depends on the observation of the attributes of material beings. From this premise, Berman reconstructed a hidden proof of atheism: if God were immaterial, His identity would be inconceivable; inconceivable things are meaningless, and the conceivable attributes of a spiritual deity are necessarily contradictory; but a meaningless or contradictory God cannot be said to exist. Since Berman's thesis rests on extrapolations and conjectures rather than direct testimony, it is unproved — and perhaps unprovable. It remains possible that Collins was sincere when he described God as an immaterial being, even though he might have thought Him unique.[44]

No such ambiguity surrounds Tindal's concept of God. He alone among the first generation of English deists fashioned a theology whose centerpiece was the great artificer found in most summaries of deism. None of his statements about God imply that he was sympathetic to pantheism, anthropomorphism, or atheism. Commonly, deism is alleged to have postulated an absolute separation of a Creator-God from His creation, and hence to have been antagonistic in principle to pantheism. Nevertheless in his esoterism Toland, who appears in every catalogue of the English deists, rejected such a dichotomy. While all of the deists espoused Herbert's first article, they did not hold a common interpretation of its meaning beyond excluding Trinitarianism.

Herbert inferred that the existence of a supreme being meant that He deserved to be worshiped. Although the deists' disputes about God's nature may suggest that they were unlikely to defer to Herbert's second article, to the dismay of their foes many of them followed Toland in professing loyalty to the Establishment. If they were not separatists, they nonetheless held divergent interpretations of the meaning of the church's articles and formularies. The failure of most of them to match Toland's elaborate discussions of ecclesiology makes it difficult to establish their points of view concerning the nature of the church and the obligations of Anglicans. Still, it is notable that they frequently sounded the same themes on which he depended in his critical theology. They also professed to be laboring to return to the pure sources of Christianity, and saw popery as the quintessence of corrupt religion. Virtuous pagans and Muslims could more properly be termed Christians than could papists.[45]

Few of these writers were as preoccupied with the evils of clericalism as the sometime Roman Catholic Tindal, but they all considered priestcraft to be the mark of popery and a menace to true religion.

Those who wrote in the midst of the attempted High-Church counter-revolution shared Toland's habit of treating the counterrevolutionaries as crypto-Romanists. A regular corollary of this attitude was the denial that a priestly caste could determine the beliefs of church members. Since assent was of its nature a personal action, efforts to fix religious belief and practice were manifestations of the clergy's lust for power. In a catalogue to which Tillotson could not have taken exception, Tindal rebuked the groups that had historically craved such gratification: fathers, councils, and bishops lacked binding authority.[46] Whatever the Anglicanism of the deists meant, it bore scant relation to that which churchmen were sworn to uphold.

Like Toland, Tindal and Collins had recourse to the only possible means of forestalling the atomizing of the church implicit in their denial of corporate belief. They also made the church the instrument of the state. Though assent was an individual matter, the magistrates were obliged to defend the interests of society, and to that end they could curb opinions such as atheism which threatened public order. National churches were the logical units of worship; and as each of them was "a perfect Creature of the Civil Power," it lay with the government to regulate church polity and determine clerical duties. Far from championing the modern ideal of a secular state, the deists sought to ensure that the magistrates controlled religion. While both Tindal and Collins presented the Netherlands as a model for the ordering of relations between church and state, Tindal was willing to press Erastianism to an extreme conclusion. He agreed with Toland that the Commonwealth was a proper object of piety, much as the Greek city-state or the Roman Empire had been in antiquity.[47]

However intriguing such aspirations for a civil religion might be, they were tentative and subordinate parts of the deists' treatment of worship. Other elements were no less interesting and considerably more important. From Blount to Tindal deists relied on the idea that personal sincerity was proof of devotion to truth. Even if their use of what was a shibboleth of the emerging theological consensus was self-justifying, it provided them with a point of intersection with Anglican rationalism. As Tindal once wrote, sincerity is "the only way to discover true Christianity."[48] Liberal churchmen were too attached to the notion that subjective conviction legitimated belief to abandon it because of the unsavoriness of such exponents.

Though less thoroughgoing than Toland, both Collins and Tindal tried to turn such intersections into a conjunction with the dominant Latitudinarian party. Often they presented themselves as the continuators of that theological liberalism whose contemporary English manifestation was Latitudinarianism. In tracing his own intellectual lineage, Collins foreshadowed the argument of Lord Dacre's essay on "The Religious Origins of the Enlightenment." He was convinced that opposition to dogmatism defined freethinking; from the time of Erasmus, its first modern exponent, the struggle had been carried on successively by such thinkers as Grotius, Chillingworth, Falkland, Herbert, Whichcote, Cudworth, Le Clerc, and Locke. Tindal was less detailed in his genealogical researches, but he, too, invoked the authority of Jean Le Clerc. The erudite Remonstrant was not only the most conspicuous living Erasmian, but also one of Tindal's more reputable defenders. Moreover, both Collins and Tindal were as assiduous as Toland in paying their respects to the memory of Archbishop Tillotson. Collins, for example, eulogized him as one "whom all *English Free Thinkers* own as their Head, and whom even the Enemys of *Free-Thinking* will allow to be a proper Instance to my purpose."[49]

Subsequent Latitudinarians influenced the deists' conception — and facilitated their continuance — of membership in the church. Samuel Bold, one of Locke's most prominent clerical defenders, provided Collins with the substance of his ecclesiology. Moreover, notwithstanding his dispute with Samuel Clarke, Collins deferred to him as one "whose authority is equal to that of many others put together." The deists realized that they owed a more immediate debt to the Latitudinarians. Because many of their opinions clashed with the dogmas enjoined on them, these divines were habituating the church to accept diversity of belief about fundamentals. As a result, it seemed reasonable to infer that those who chose to worship as Anglicans were free to construe the church's formulas as they wished. Although Tindal would eventually receive an annual pension from the court, he became more outspokenly utilitarian in his attitude toward the church as he grew older.[50] Unlike Annet, however, he never felt that the principle of sincerity required that he separate himself from its ranks. With Toland and Collins, Tindal was willing to accept membership in the church as long as it entailed only a profession of attachment to the Establishment and acquiescence in its rites. The nature of one's worship remained one's own concern. Insofar as Toland, Collins, and Tindal had a coherent notion of a worshiping church, it rested on a plausible set of deductions from assumptions and practices which had been gaining ever-wider support among Latitudinarians since the 1670s.

In his third article, Herbert argued that "the connection of Virtue with Piety, defined in this work as the right conformation of the faculties, is and always has been held to be, the most important part of religious practice." By the 1690s such moralism was becoming ax-iomatic to the majority of articulate Englishmen, including suspected deists. Nevertheless, the heretics held inconsistent opinions about both the sources of ethical dicta and their relation to religion. Most of them interpreted religion as exclusively a matter of morality. Tindal, for ex-ample, identified his Christian deism with the pursuit of virtue.[51] If Tindal was more forward than either Collins or Toland in styling himself a deist, they shared his certainty that religion at base was equivalent to morality. Instead of alienating like-minded readers by raising the banner of deism, they labored first to expose positions which they shared with liberal churchmen and then to elaborate some embar-rassing implications of this point of view. Although increasing numbers of clerics accepted — or at least acquiesced in — moralism, for the most part they were vexed by the appearance of these unwanted and taste-lessly single-minded auxiliaries.

The deists sought to establish a tangible standard with which to evaluate a doctrine. Most of them agreed with Blount's assertion that determining an article's moral content or goodness was the best way of judging its truth. His standard rested on two commonplace premises. First, the proper division of mankind was between the moral and the immoral, not between the orthodox and the heterodox. Secondly, since human nature was unchanging, all legitimate ethical teachers held the same views. The deists were thus persuaded that, insofar as Socrates and Confucius had taught honestly and lived morally, they might prop-erly be spoken of as Christians.[52] Tillotson had often taken a similar line, though he neither explicated its presuppositions nor searched for non-Christian exemplars.

Despite their belief in universally accepted moral principles, the deists failed to agree on an interpretation of the origins of morality. In addition, their several explanations occasionally manifest internal in-consistencies. In his positive moods Blount, for example, could assert that he was cooperating in the search for a religious irenicon and describe his contribution as a theology derived exclusively from self-evident moral principles. He was confident that his effort would command support because such rules were "extant and operative in the hearts of all men." Though his gnomic phrase might have been read as the expression of an apriorism at odds with his rejection of intuitive knowledge, he never bothered to explain it, much less to attempt to reconcile the apparent contradiction.[53] In much the same way, the oscillation between denying and affirming innate ideas that Tindal displayed when treating the ways of knowing God, intensified when he tried to account for the operation of the human conscience.

Tindal's often fussy attention to epistemology precludes the defense from indifference which might have been invoked for Blount. Here was an author who, notwithstanding his positive intention, had seemingly elected to publish contradictions. Without repudiating Lockianism, he insisted that God "had implanted in our Natures a Sense of Piety, and a Desire of being belov'd, in order to oblige Mankind to treat one another kindly" and continued "daily to imprint it."[54] Tindal's purpose in thus expounding incompatible theories of knowledge must remain a matter of conjecture. Whether he was torn between an inherited ethical vocabulary and a novel epistemology or merely trying to accommodate a deep-seated prepossession, he gave no indication of seeking to propagate a starkly naturalistic morality.

Collins' scattered remarks suggest that he possessed a more nearly consistent etiology of morals than the other deists. Like Toland, he hinted that ethical conduct was a consequence of man's ability and need for social life, and that the virtually mechanical operation of self-interest in human affairs made society possible.[55] While Toland's attraction to Shaftesbury's *Inquiry* occasionally led him to adorn or complicate similar hypotheses with an aprioristic rhetoric, Collins was faithful to his understanding of Locke's empiricism. Perhaps his inclination toward naturalism convinced him that an exposition of his moral theory would be injudicious.

On those occasions when Toland's fellow deists chose to discuss their image of the moral life, they, like him, offered a mixture of conventional affirmations and novel insinuations. Their insistence on portraying the exercise of reason as a primary moral activity implies that they held a dianoetic theory of the good. Since reasoning had negative as well as positive obligations, they made criticism of received opinions — what Collins termed freethinking and Tindal pulling down — the gate through which all who sought to enter into a fully moral life had to pass.[56] At the same time his predisposition toward criticism did not lead Collins to intimate that he had reservations about the code of duties which more and more of his contemporaries took to be Christianity, let alone to suggest an alternative.

Tindal was almost as circumspect, but Blount anticipated Toland's intimations of sympathy with an unconventional moral vision. Thus, when Blount alluded to ancient philosophy, he was careful to differentiate "true" from "brutish" Epicureanism. His precision seems to have been the result of his own intellectual disposition rather than chaste scholarship. Epicurus' surviving fragments imply that his hedonism was pulled between an ideal of autarchy and the fact of human dependence; he sought to relieve the tension by emphasizing friendship. Blount's effort to link morality with feelings of affection may reflect a desire to cope with a similar tension in his own thought. If Tindal longed for the reestablishment of antique virtue, he was more obscure in expressing his desire than Blount. He did not choose to rehabilitate any pre-Christian moral system. Yet, his comments on changing judgments about the propriety of usury indicate that, despite his appeals to uniform moral intuitions, he was as sensible of the advantages of progressive utilitarianism as Richard Baxter, the model of Protestant worldly asceticism. For his part, Tindal rejected any morality that enjoined self-abnegation—even if it professed to be Christian—and did not fault the rationality of prudent hedonism.[57]

The deists were as confident as Pope that "Order is Heaven's first law," but they resembled Toland in skirting the ethical implications of their political ideas. It appears that none of them held a pluralist theory of power; once realized, their common desire to deprive the church, the only available check on the state, of an independent role would have made the civil authority omnipotent. For the most part, they were reluctant to explore such a prospect. Only Blount urged the raw naturalism of Hobbes. The deists' failure to agree on a coherent theory of politics did not, however, keep them from reaching the same answers to a number of current questions. Tindal and Collins, no less than Toland, accepted the necessity of a hierarchically ordered society, rejoiced in the impeachment of Sacheverell, and championed the Hanoverian Succession. Tindal was partial to natural rights equalitarianism and presented the social insects as exemplars, but neither he nor Collins approximated Toland's sustained attention to political analysis.[58] There is no more evidence that the deists shared a vision of public life distinct from that held by all staunch Whigs than that their moral attitudes differed markedly from that of any *anglican du monde.*

When Herbert asserted that men's vices and crimes had always filled their minds "with horror" and must therefore "be expiated by repentance," he was elaborating his intuitionism. God was a legislator whose law was morality. He had given men consciences as justices of their internal peace, charged with bringing them into conformity with His law by convicting them of violations of it. In their portrayals of the moral sense, later deists aggravated the confusion which marked their analyses of how men know right from wrong. While Blount, with characteristic inconstancy, invoked right reason from time to time, Tindal insisted on the centrality of such a faculty to the moral life of humanity. As both writers had weakened the epistemological foundations of Herbert's theory of conscience, repentance in response to its promptings may have entailed for them little more than a change of behavior in the face of sanctions.[59]

In contrast, Collins sought to treat freethinking as the effective medium of conscience; for him, man could not be good without searching for the truth. Yet Collins also confronted a gap between his epistemology and his rhetoric. Like Toland, he held a materialist view of consciousness, which he then went on to elaborate into a rigorously determinist concept of human behavior.[60] Such a theory made conscience a periphrasis and freethinking an oxymoron: how could a mechanically determined permutation of matter be said to be other than figuratively capable of reflection or agency?

The fifth article of *De Veritate* ("There is Reward or Punishment after this life") disclosed a fundamental motive of repentance. Herbert's heirs proved to be as hesitant about the cause as they had been about the effect. Toland's sly observations on the prospect of individual immortality help to explain why many antideists were sceptical of their foes' loyalty to this tenet. Blount had anticipated Toland's evasiveness. Besides artfully balancing insinuations against the notion with affirmations of his own belief in it, he offered a history of its origins which was unlikely to reassure its proponents. Ancient legislators had first inculcated the idea of life after death in order to strengthen their control over the masses. Moreover, Blount was as diligent as Toland in setting forth precedents for conceiving of immortality as an infinite series of transfers of forms rather than as personal survival. He made book 3 of Lucretius' *De rerum natura* the basis of a long and ambivalent exposition of the "pagan" conception of the afterlife: "As when by death the Body

and Soul are parted, the Man they thought was gone, but the Spirit remain'd in its Original, and the Body in its Earth from whence it came:
and they when wrought again by Nature separately into new mixtures,
entered into a new state of Being which they supposed in no way concern'd or related unto the former."[61]

It is noteworthy that both Tindal and Collins shared Lucretius' concern to liberate men from their terrors about the hereafter. Tindal's
professions of assent to the fifth article, though numerous, were often
perfunctory. Collins' most recent biographer was persuaded that his
subject accepted the truth of personal immortality, but Collins could
describe Seneca as a "religious man" immediately before referring to his
rejection of everlasting life.[62] Whatever the actual opinions of the two
deists about the existence and character of life after death, they were
less fervent advocates of the concept than either Herbert or the
Anglican rationalists.

If their differences were so numerous and deep-seated, if these
writers were even more diverse in their affirmations than in their
criticisms of orthodox Christianity, then attributing a characteristic
deism to them would seem to be a matter of convenience rather than an
aid to analysis. There remains, however, the possibility that they
somehow envisioned themselves as engaged in a common enterprise.
Toland, Tindal, and Collins knew each other and studied one another's
works. Perhaps Toland and Tindal had become acquainted under the
aegis of their patron, Firmin; in any event, Tindal felt concerned
enough about Toland during his tribulations in Dublin in 1697 to seek
information about him from Locke. Although they frequented the same
coffeehouses and took the same side in many political contests, little
can be concluded about their ideological relations.[63] Accordingly, a
verdict of insufficient evidence would seem to be justified in the question of their concerted action.

Toland's intellectual and personal connections with Collins are better documented. One of the targets of Collins' first book, *An Essay concerning the Use of Reason* (1707), had been an early critic of *Christianity Not
Mysterious*. Moreover, some contemporaries were so certain of the
closeness of the ties between the two men that they thought Toland had
had a hand in writing the *Discourse of Free-Thinking* (1713). In addition
to dedicating two works to Collins, Toland corresponded with him and
was his houseguest at Baddow Hall. Toland was, however, Collins'
suitor. For his part, Collins was sufficiently embarrassed by the

association that he scrupulously avoided actions which might have encouraged Toland. Enduring collaborations are seldom so one-sided. At various times during his career Toland was closer to Jean Le Clerc and William Penn than he ever was to either of his supposed confederates. Moreover, he never indicated that he was conscious of belonging to a longstanding movement. In his publications and surviving manuscripts, he apparently referred to Herbert only once — and then as an historian rather than a philosopher or theologian; after the *Two Essays* he never made even indirect allusion to Blount.[64]

The omission of Blount is remarkable, for he alone of the earlier deists had so much as entertained opinions which resemble the content of Toland's esoterism. Since Blount's references to the Stoic belief that God was identical with the universe did not constitute an endorsement of that point of view, Toland was under no obligation to him. In the *Two Essays* he apparently echoed some of the themes with which Blount had toyed. Like him, Toland advanced a self-serving defense of Burnet's cosmology and intimated his approval of Hobbes's mechanistic materialism. By essaying a three-fold theology — critical, exoteric, and esoteric — Toland ended this brief connection. Blount had scant interest in the subjects on which Toland relied both in his critique of the Christian poetical theology and in his civil theology. In addition, Blount's style marks him as a child of an earlier generation. If he sometimes professed to take Montaigne as his example and affected sceptical fideism, his enthusiasm for twitting orthodoxy vitiated this impersonation. Blount's hankering for *bouleversement* was too ingrained to allow him to work to establish any kind of system.[65] Toland, by contrast, not only endeavored to criticize received opinions, but also sought to effect a reconstruction. Contemporary Latitudinarians, Remonstrants, and Socinians contributed more substantially to his undertakings than libertines such as Blount.

Although the traditional definitions of deism do not apply to the works of Toland, Collins, and Tindal, the two treatments of it which now enjoy scholarly attention credibly describe the purposes of these writers. Yet both Lovejoy's complex of nine ideas and Gawlick's combination of a struggle against superstition, priestcraft, and intolerance and a desire to establish morality on a basis independent of revelation were also typical of many early eighteenth-century authors who professed to oppose deism. They thus fail to delimit the individuality of the deists.

When *Christianity as Old as the Creation* appeared in 1730, reaction to it was nearly as furious as that which had greeted *Christianity Not Mysterious* a generation earlier. On examination, however, much of the opposition to Tindal's book seems paradoxical. Thus, in *The Usefulness, Truth, and Excellency of the Christian Revelation Defended,* James Foster, an eminent Baptist preacher, set out to refute what he saw as a deistic attack on "the *truth* of *Christianity,* and its *usefulness* as a divine revelation." Foster maintained that the Christian revelation offered "momentous discoveries, and *discoveries that were so much needed,*" but his list of its principles suggested that they were elements of a restoration instead of a new dispensation. Christ had taught "the unity of God, the rational and acceptable method of worshipping him, and the truths of natural religion." Foster conceded that he shared two assumptions with Tindal: the immutable, self-evident principles of true religion "cannot be superseded, alter'd, or contradicted by an external revelation," and all *"positive institutions"* had to be "entirely subservient" to "the *religion of nature."* Foster nonetheless took issue with Tindal insofar as he had been equivocal in admitting Christianity as a necessary revelation.[66] In attempting to counteract the deist Tindal, the Christian apologist Foster relied on most of the ideas which Lovejoy thought characteristic of deism, and proved to be as hostile to irrationality and as convinced of the morality and naturalness of legitimate religion as any of Gawlick's deists. Because Foster was exceptional only in his lucidity, his effort raises another problem. If the numerous divines and laymen who sought to controvert men such as Toland during the half-century after 1696 were not combating deism, what were they about?

John Toland may not have belonged to a coherent deist movement, but any attempt to deny the reality of an intense deist controversy would seem doomed to founder on a reef of antideist pamphlets, tracts, sermons, and books. Although historians have acknowledged the existence of this dispute, they have differed in their interpretations of it. There are four principal versions of the end of the deist controversy. One holds that the deists, while anticipating some of the conclusions of the nineteenth-century rationalists, failed to offer an intellectually serious challenge to Anglicanism. Their refutation was a foregone conclusion. The second sees deism as less a theological than a spiritual menace. Its critique was turned back, but only the preaching of Wesley and Whitefield relieved the dessication it had wrought in "the heart of the people." In contrast, some scholars have maintained that these sceptics were never answered. Far from being vanquished, deism presented such strong objections that would-be apologists ended by adopting them. Finally, Mark Pattison doubted that the controversy ended in victory for either side. He believed that deism was an identifiable phenomenon, but he was convinced that its primary assumptions also moved its critics: "The Churchman differed from the Socinian, and the Socinian from the Deist, as to the number of articles in his creed; but all alike consented to test their belief by the rational evidence for it." In Pattison's view, Anglican rationalists, Socinians, and deists came to form a quarreling extended family.[1]

An estimate of Toland's immediate influence requires an evaluation of each of these accounts. A Toland beneath notice must be viewed differently from a Toland who managed to convert his critics. A Toland who, having adopted premises which were familiar when he began to write, reached conclusions, many of which would become platitudes, must be seen in yet another way. If the assumptions of *Christianity Not Mysterious* proved to be inexplicable apart from the ethos of late seventeenth-century Anglicanism, theological developments within the church in the generation after 1696 determined the fate of Toland's thought. Christian apologists were confident that they were writing against deists, but they frequently seemed perplexed about who these men were and what kind of doubt characterized them. As a rural vicar complained near the middle of the century: "I wish a single Article of the Creed could be named (the first only excepted, which asserts the Being of 'a God, the Maker of All Things, whether in Heaven or in Earth'); excepting that, I say, I wish a single Article could be named, which has not been openly disputed and denied." If doubt was both so extensive and so intensive, if deists were so pressing a threat, it is remarkable that those in authority, prelates like William King and Peter Browne, should have paid so little attention to them in their private letters. It is no less remarkable that Sir Robert Walpole's ecclesiastical major-domo, Bishop Gibson of London, was so dilatory about trying to deal with them. In fact, when Bishop Warburton advised a correspondent in 1741 that a recent publication of the deist Peter Annet was more safely ignored than publicized by refutation, he could have invoked the solid weight of precedent.[2]

A reading of the early Boyle lectures, which have often been presented as definitive statements of the Anglican case against deism, does not reveal the coherency which might be expected in a campaign waged against a definite foe. Rather, the lectures seem to embody the diverse concerns of a number of ambitious younger clergymen. Richard Bentley, the first lecturer, was preoccupied with speculative atheists and those who denied a superintending providence in the universe; he took the latter to be deists. Richard Kidder sought to convert the Jews. With equal amounts of vigor and imprecision, Offspring Blackall applied his lash to Jews, atheists, papists, and deists. Before continuing Bentley's hunt for speculative atheists, John Harris endeavored to prove that they were not a species of theological unicorn. By implicitly making deism in its philosophical sense (a watchlike universe and its detached maker) a form of speculative atheism, Samuel Clarke became the first Boyle lecturer to exploit the tactical potentialities of combating this elusive target. Confident of the strength of the prejudice against practical atheism, the denial of a personal God, he played on it by presenting a stark choice between atheism and a theism which, despite consistent dogmatic suppleness, drew on the vocabulary and forms of traditional Christianity.[3]

Clarke was moved by the same desire to achieve plausible generalization which led most of the lecturers to avoid dealing with the thought of individual atheists, excepting the inevitable Spinoza and Hobbes. In turn, Harris's effort to prove that speculative atheists actually existed may explain the vacillation of Toland's critics between accusations of deism and atheism. While Augustans could cope with the psalmist's fool speaking his heart, they had grave difficulties in coming to terms with the idea of an intellectually coherent atheism; at the same time, they could not deny the existence of a deliberate attack on some of the church's fundamental teachings. Theologians thus faced the problem of defining a category which, while it accommodated the boisterous neologism of writers like Toland, did not stigmatize the undogmatic, practical religion increasingly attractive to the articulate Englishmen whose allegiance they had to retain. Whatever its form, the designation had to be more convincing than, and hence at least verbally distinguishable from, speculative atheism. Churchmen thought they had found this category in deism.

The lassitude of men like Gibson, King, and Browne owed something to the recognition that social realities limited the appeal of scepticism. As an urban phenomenon, freethought did not seem to threaten a quite rural England guided by custom and ruled by an alliance of clergy and gentry. Like Locke and Toland, most Anglican apologists were convinced that the bulk of mankind would remain illiterate. Moreover, they saw the sceptics themselves as gentlemen, who presumably viewed their inferiors with a mixture of dread and contempt. Swift's insistence that no real gentleman could be guilty of such impropriety suggests a rebuke rather than a description. None of the deists of this period had to work with his hands to earn his bread. Thomas Chubb, probably the lowliest of them, occupied a higher social position than would Thomas Paine. Two uneasily coexisting implications followed from these facts. First, gentlemen of this persuasion were unlikely to disappear, so that it seemed expedient to accept the permanent existence of a disaffected minority.[4] Secondly, it was impossible to tolerate widespread sceptical proselytizing, for if the growing numbers among the political class who were tempted to reject traditional formulas swelled the ranks of the minority, then the cooperation of manse and manor on which the church depended would be undone.

To forestall such a catastrophe the political class had to be convinced that it could guarantee the docility of the lower orders only by quarantining them against the contagion of scepticism. Apologists would devote considerable attention to this endeavor, and a universally held axiom strengthened their hand. For most Augustans, it seemed self-evident that the governors of a hierarchical society were competent to set standards for the governed in most matters, including religion. Churchmen did not hesitate to seek to assist in the enterprise. For example, in *A Gentleman's Religion* (1695) Archbishop Synge counseled his readers on ways of instructing illiterates in the Scripture in order to preserve them from both enthusiasm and novelty. Neither was the plight of the middling orders — those who were increasingly evading inherited discipline without sharing fully in power — neglected. Most antideist tracts were written to be read by those literate only in their mother tongue.[5]

There were other incentives to episcopal inaction. While Toland had indicted prejudice and custom as the chief enemies of reason, divines were not slow to recognize that these two traits, more powerful than formal arguments, might be the Establishment's greatest supports. Much of their strength derived from the operation of informal sanctions. Even when the magistrates did not act against reputed heretics, the hostility of their neighbors worked to make their lives unpleasant. The existence of such pressures led Toland's opponents to appeal openly to prejudice, sometimes subtly, more often crudely. Inadvertently, this appeal facilitated a change in the apologists' conception of what, in fact, they were defending. To conceive of Anglicanism as custom or prejudice might initially require only that it be seen as a self-evidently true system of belief and practice, enjoying a presumptive advantage over the objections of its critics. Nevertheless, it would prove increasingly difficult to avoid identifying a part with the whole, of reducing Anglicanism to the Establishment, an institutional datum whose existence and claim to allegiance were independent of its creed.[6]

Among their arguments apologists had favored one which sanctioned such synecdoche. From the humblest beginnings the Christian church had irresistibly expanded, and its success story amounted to a sign of truth: had a group of obscure Galilean fishermen not enjoyed the divine favor they claimed for themselves, why did their successors prevail over the Roman Empire?[7] Two generations would pass before this argument was answered. In the meantime, clerics had performed such prodigies of doctrinal adaptability as to be able to retain at least the nominal loyalty of the articulate orders.

Although the appeal to prejudice and custom took a variety of forms, the argument that all infidels were immoralists was the most popular. Theologians had long asserted that there might be a connection between immorality and infidelity. From being a possibility, the connection became an inevitability for Augustans. Sceptics like Toland were necessarily evil.[8] By dwelling on moral effects rather than on their putatively doctrinal cause, this generalization fostered the subordination of theory to practice. In addition to promoting the identification of Anglicanism with the Establishment, such a practical emphasis posed a troubling problem. How could the benignity, philanthropy, and churchmanship of Thomas Firmin be reconciled with his inability to subscribe to fundamental Anglican articles? Since Firmin was not unique, the question of whether any good, churchgoing person could be a heretic became unavoidable. In the years following the appearance of *Christianity Not Mysterious,* Anglican apologists would labor successfully to redefine heresy.

The identification of the pope with the Antichrist may have become less frequent by 1700, but the ferocity of English antipopery was far from waning. Examples of this perception occur in later years. More importantly, as Archbishop King's correspondence reveals, for most Englishmen the principal practical and intellectual challenge to their nation and its church seemed to come not from within but from without, not from heretics but from papists. This analysis was not peculiar to the divines. Matthew Tindal had enough confidence in the continuing appeal of anti-Catholicism to use it in *Christianity as Old as the Creation* (1730) much as Toland had a generation earlier. Indirect evidence of the tenacity of this relative evaluation of the seriousness of the two threats lies in the rarity of complaints about freethinkers' use of antipopery to subvert Anglicanism. Occasionally, some divines, usually High-Churchmen, ventured that Protestantism had to mean something more than the rejection of papal pretensions. Nevertheless, Francis Hare was almost unique in recognizing that, by fostering the misrepresentation of Catholic teachings, antipopery had aided the deists' subversion of Anglican doctrines. Daniel Waterland spoke for a wider body of opinion when he urged enforcement of subscription to the Thirty-Nine Articles as a defense against anti-Trinitarians, whose aberrations were almost as enormous as those of the papists.[9]

From this inexhaustible mine of prejudice came the recurrent accusations that Toland was a popish agent. Such charges are less important in themselves than as evidence of the intuition of Anglican polemicists that the redefinition of a threat can offer protection against it. Even professionally antideist clerics like Blackall were obsessed with the Romish menace, and by linking papists and deists, he and others both justified their obsession and sidestepped answering such men as Toland.[10]

When Anglicans reluctantly began to consider how to cope with the varieties of freethought, they depended on these prejudices, assumptions, and impressions. While they did not create a systematic apologetic, they succeeded in engaging the arguments of Toland and other Socinians and deists. By exposing the deficiencies of Toland's scholarship, his critics managed to check him on many specific points. Toland was selective and tendencious in using scriptural texts, and his knowledge of patristic literature proved to be shallow and derivative. Moreover, in answering the *Letters to Serena,* one critic so ruthlessly demonstrated the author's failure to grasp the conclusions of Newtonian science that Toland was scrupulously to avoid scientific affectation in his subsequent encounters with cosmology. However valid, the confutation of a mass of particulars neither disposed of Toland's arguments nor vindicated the Anglican system of belief. If some of his antagonists were inclined to avoid the more demanding tasks by relying on *ad hominem* remarks or retreating to fideism, others endeavored to cope with them.[11]

The assertion that Newtonianism influenced theology during this period is a commonplace, but estimates of the extent of its influence vary. Some Englishmen were preoccupied with natural theology, and the éclat of science led many theologians to attempt to fashion their work in a way which seemed to meet its standards. At the same time the decline of the prestige of metaphysics accelerated. It became increasingly unfashionable to suggest that metaphysical assumptions might affect theological speculations. These conclusions are obvious, and they have led to more venturesome theories. Thus, Margaret C. Jacob has argued that Newtonianism provided the dominant Low-Church party with an innovative world-view suited to the changed political and social situation after the Glorious Revolution.[12]

Whatever the influence of Newtonianism on divinity, it apparently resulted from tensions within Anglicanism rather than from the perception of an external threat. In the first half of the eighteenth century science and theology sustained an armed truce. Toland's uncertain grasp on the findings and principles of the scientific revolution was matched by his deist confreres. But can the same perhaps be said about Anglican apologists? Isaac Newton himself believed in the theological significance of his work, and took an active role in planning some of the Boyle lectures. Occasionally, his zeal led him to structure his scientific works to serve what seemed to him to be pressing theological needs. For their part, the Boyle lecturers sought to exploit the prestige of natural philosophy whenever and however they could. In their hands, mechanism and atomism became charms rather than curses. At the same time their own grasp of what mechanism entailed was frequently precarious. Samuel Clarke, for example, sought both to reject the Aristotelian division of causes into material, formal, and final, and to insist that the efficient causes whose existence he admitted could have a spiritual form.[13]

His confusion illustrates the difficulty in the lecturers' endeavor to baptize mechanism. They could save themselves from the rigorous — and potentially agnostic — Cartesian mechanism only by a series of acts of audacious inconsistency; theological propositions dictated their choice and use of scientific arguments. Matter had to be inert in itself in order that the external infusion of motion might be adduced as evidence of a divinely willed creation. For the lecturers, the existence of self-moved matter was as great a threat to belief in human thought and free will as it was to belief in an unmoved mover.[14] Despite their distaste for the Middle Ages, these writers clung to a vision of the cosmos which Aquinas would have found familiar; man remained the object of God's solicitude.

If the lecturers' vision of an anthropocentric universe let them retain many of the oldest arguments of Christian theology, their self-conscious modernity led them to embellish their formulation with a Newtonian rhetoric. When presenting the arguments from design to "prove" God's existence, Richard Bentley added some allusions to gravity which Newton provided. Aquinas might have been puzzled by them, but he would certainly have recognized the argument — if not its vaunted certitude — as his own. In comparison with Samuel Clarke's Boyle lectures of 1704 and 1705, Bentley's attempt to extend the scientism with which John Wilkins had sought to invest natural theology appears halfhearted. Clarke never quite abandoned the absolute confidence in the attainability of certitude that had marked his youthful Cartesianism. He went so far as to maintain that he was trying to create a *theologia mathematica* combining Christian faith with mathematical certitude. Nonetheless, an examination of the elements of his theological calculus reveals that they conform to the pattern suggested by Bentley's use of the argument from design: a mixture of borrowing and tailoring.[15]

In attempting to adapt mechanism, Clarke became enmeshed in the confusion implicit in his treatment of causality. Having demonstrated that motion cannot inhere in matter, he went on to confess that he had no idea how matter moved.[16] His uncertainty had obvious consequences for his effort to treat scientifically the unmoved mover. While the functions of God were in some instances not incompatible with Newtonian physics, He had no point of contact with it in many others. Clarke was increasingly reduced to using physics as a quarry for illustrations or figures of speech. He seems never to have derived an original argument from it.

Samuel Clarke was perhaps the most Newtonian of the Boyle lecturers. For the most part, his successors shared neither his zeal nor his ability to frame theological arguments scientifically. Those who sought to continue his labors enjoyed mixed success. For example, Brampton Gurdon's effort to prove the existence of providence by appealing to the law of the conservation of motion provided a textbook case of improper inference. Clarke had managed to cast a spell over some of the lesser theological lights of his generation, but their attempts to emulate him often indicated that their minds were untouched by either Newtonian science or Aristotelian logic. Thus, John Witty maintained that self-moved matter cannot produce thought, for if it could, then the whole universe would be able to think. For the antideists who resisted Clarke's spell, motion was still an entity rather than a relation, and the unvarnished cosmological arguments retained their force.[17]

Many historians of science have been disdainful of the scientific competence of Newton's theological admirers. Like Toland himself, these students have concluded that, in their determination to maintain the Cartesian opposition between extended bodies and a thinking spirit, the Newtonian theologians concocted a hodgepodge of physical and metaphysical notions. In treating such subjects as gravity or motion, they tended to harden their master's hypothetical categories into absolute statements. They did not shrink from sacrificing the fundamental principle of the mechanical philosophy, viz., that "all causes in nature after the divine gift of motion are explicable in terms of the action of matter." If Clarke's aspiration to create a *theologia mathematica* bespeaks a misunderstanding of the terms and methods of both Newtonianism and theology, he also exhibited metaphysical limitations during his famous debate with Leibniz. It was perhaps a recognition of this debilitating conjunction which prompted John Henry Newman's definition of natural theology: "a series of pious or polemical remarks upon the physical world viewed religiously."[18]

Even though the attempt of the Boyle lecturers and their admirers to develop a scientific theology did not succeed, it affected the doctrines which they taught. As much as their predecessors, Anglican theologians of this generation were hostile to the notion that, since the traditional articles of Christianity had been formulated in the categories of Neoplatonism and Aristotelianism, they might be conceptually dependent on these philosophies. Directly and indirectly, the lecturers contributed to the intensification of hostility to Scholasticism which took place during the years in which Toland wrote.[19] In contrast, the occasional antideist divines who persisted in recommending the study of the Platonic fathers and Aristotelian Schoolmen failed to convince their fellows that these philosophical traditions provided the only available means of cogently expressing Christian beliefs. When modern apologists were obliged to fall back on the old philosophical divinity to defend received dogmas, they did so grudgingly. Archbishop Wake was expressing the consensus of his church when, three years after Toland's death, he contentedly noted that the universities had rejected Aristotelianism. The concomitant of this rejection was that Locke's name became an intellectual talisman, radiating both novelty and authority, and beguiling even the remaining defenders of school divinity.[20] The issue between Stillingfleet and Locke—whether the future of Latitudinarianism lay with a retreat to tradition or the achievement of further reasonableness—was being decided in Locke's favor.

The other lecturers shared Samuel Clarke's penchant for unacknowledged debts and outright expropriations. Like him, they relied on such old-fashioned notions as final causes and the medieval proofs of God's existence. When they used the first cause argument, they assumed that a necessary existent and a multiform causality were axiomatic. While Aristotle or Aquinas might have plausibly treated these principles as self-evident, those sympathetic to the new epistemology ought to have suspended judgment about them. Instead, the Anglican neologists freely employed these and a number of other axioms which were derived from the classical and medieval constructions of reality. References to the hierarchy of being, uniformitarianism, and the fixity of species recur in their works. On occasion they used formal arguments which one or another of the Schoolmen had judged to be insupportable. For example, Samuel Clarke ignored Aquinas' reservations and adduced the ontological argument for God's existence. More frequently, though, they traveled along one or another of Aquinas' five ways. The partiality of Augustan divines for the argument from design, a restatement of his fifth proof, is notorious. For all that it resembled the first principle of the textbook version of deism, the ontology and teleology which underpinned it were not easily reconcilable with mechanism.[21]

Such instances of a lag between the presuppositions and stated purposes of articulate Anglicans should not be taken as evidence that their postulates were unchanging. Perhaps most evident was the steadily widening, if often quiet, acceptance of the identification of reason with demonstration. As late as 1693, Bentley was still able to presume that reason had a plural nature; in much the same way, the semi-Lockian Synge asserted the claims of right reason and deduction in terms reminiscent of Hooker.[22] Others questioned the prudence of accepting the redefinition. A Malebranchian parson, John Norris, and a Scholastic bishop, Peter Browne—both active opponents of Toland—sought to check the further progress of neologism by presenting reason as something more than demonstration. They found themselves fighting a confused rearguard action. Strongly tempted by Lockianism, Norris seems at times to have been able to resist it only by adopting an irrationalism which made incomprehensibility a measure of truth. Browne felt the same temptation, and it undermined his attempt to offer a systematic critique of scepticism on neo-Aristotelian principles. Since he had to define even elementary terms for the benefit of his predominantly clerical readers, he must have had few illusions about the reception of his effort.[23]

The failure of an alternative epistemology to command allegiance made Lockianism the English theory of knowledge. The works of a number of professedly antideist writers exemplify its triumph. Thomas Beconsall, one of Toland's earliest and harshest critics, unreflectively accepted both the equation of reason and demonstration and the requirement that a proposition produce a clear and distinct idea before it can enjoy a reasonable assent. Among his initial foes Toland had a favorite, William Payne, who was an enthusiastic Lockian. Samuel Clarke was among the most influential Anglican apologists of his time.

In *A Demonstration of the Being and Attributes of God* and *A Discourse concerning the Unchangeable Obligations of Natural Religion,* Clarke assumed the validity of the Lockian system.[24] It is possible that some of John Toland's critics may have avoided grappling with his philosophical method and its implications because they sensed the incompatibility between some of their doctrinal professions and many of their philosophical presuppositions.

The prolongation of this strain had many of the same effects on the theology of those who spoke for the church as it had had on the theology which Toland had adapted from the Socinians. During these years the opinions of many Anglicans about the central topics of *Christianity Not Mysterious* — the nature of religious assent, the place of revelation in forming Christian belief and its relation to natural religion, and the meaning of the Christian mysteries — came to resemble Toland's. The shift is clear in the Augustan theologians' changing conception of the nature of assent. A few of them continued to hold the Scholastic conception of faith as both the acceptance by the mind of a tenet, however imperfectly understood, and an act of will. Because of the decay of the faculty psychology on which this idea depended, other divines tended to reduce faith to an irrational leap.[25] Some Latitudinarians seem to have perceived that the restriction of reason to demonstration would make reasonable assent to most formulas an impossibility. As a result, while they clung to the new definition of reason, they did not object in principle to presenting faith as essentially nonintellectual. While a faith which was exhibited in practice was clear and tangible, a faith bound up with propositions was as unclear and elusive as the propositions themselves. These considerations may help to explain how, in working out the implications of the Lockian epistemology, some of Toland's first critics found themselves accepting his notion of assent. Archbishop Synge had taken much the same line as Toland in *A Gentleman's Religion.* Although later editions contained a "refutation" of the Irishman, it, like *The Reasonableness of Christianity,* was intended as a contribution to the search for an irenicon. As William Molyneux, Locke's intimate, patronizingly remarked:

Tho' the book shows not that freedom of thought you or I perhaps, might expect, yet it shows enough to incense his own herd against him, for there is little of mystery, of Enthusiastic in it and yet the author is a clergyman. And you know that, in a writer on a religious subject, 'tis a high offense even to be silent on those abstruse points.[26]

Synge first presented his full argument in the *Plain and Easy Method* (1715). There he maintained that an individual's primary duty was "to keep his Mind always in a fitting Disposition for the reception of and assenting unto, all such Truths as God shall be pleased to propose unto him." It was unreasonable that any one should give assent without adequate evidence. Properly speaking, therefore, the duty of faith was the maintenance of a fitting disposition to receive whatever truths God chose to make known with such unexceptionable evidence that the individual was incapable of rejecting them. His theory had a number of related implications. First, in order to accept any doctrine, a person had to have an idea of its meaning, and the clearer and more distinct the idea which a doctrine conveyed, the greater its likelihood of being accepted. Secondly, "the formal Act of Assent" could not be considered a duty binding on all men. Thirdly, a good and merciful God was not likely to deem blameworthy a misunderstanding or underestimation of the available evidence. Synge avoided suggesting that the church possessed an authority which was sufficient in itself to command assent to its tenets. His effort reflected the disposition of his party, and with the passage of time there were fewer apologists more assertive than he.[27] The author of *Christianity Not Mysterious* had asked for little else.

The archbishop's analysis seemingly justified the conclusion that God could not demand assent to dogmatic formulations which were often confused. It also suggested that He would account as faith the observance of unmistakably clear rules of conduct. Toland could have taken satisfaction in these conclusions as well. Of course, other divines held out for a starker conception of faith. The Reverend Patrick Middleton's exegesis (1735) of the narrative in Genesis of Abraham's near-sacrifice of Isaac shows that he was one of this group.[28] Middleton's emphasis on the obscurity of the patriarch's faith might have distressed Tillotson and amused Toland. Since he was a nonjuror, his influence on the Walpolian church was limited.

As Toland's notion of assent became prevalent in the church, the conception of mystery which his earliest antagonists had defended faced an uncertain future. Despite their disagreements, most critics at first rejected Toland's assertion that the Bible meant by a mystery something which, though it may once have been hidden or obscure, had become clear through revelation. Peter Browne was almost unique among this group in attempting to give a reasoned defense of the traditional idea that a mystery of faith was a tenet or predicate which would have been incomprehensible without revelation and was imperfectly comprehensible after revelation. In undertaking this task, he once again depended on Scholasticism. Seeking to explore the divine attributes, he distorted Aquinas' analogical method by denying the possibility of affirmations about the divine nature.[29] While Browne did not found a school and had limited influence, he forcefully restated one argument to which many subsequent antideists would resort. Was the incomprehensibility of the controverted teachings of Christianity not analogous to the incomprehensibility of certain universally accepted teachings about nature and her religion? Although a generation would pass before this argument took its classical form in Joseph Butler's *Analogy of Religion* (1736), it had been current a quarter-century before Browne wrote. Its growing popularity was a symptom of Anglican apologists' precarious self-confidence. By the middle of the eighteenth century, those who conceived of themselves as defending the older idea of mystery were often reduced to urging a crudely self-interested argument from agnosticism. If the Christian mysteries could not be proved, neither could they be refuted. Was it not irrational to reject so pleasant and useful a creed?[30]

This agnosticism was the result of the accelerated erosion of assurance in the defensibility of doctrines which were less than clear and distinct. Toland lived long enough to take grim satisfaction in the diminished support for the inherited idea of mystery which was so alarming to the orthodox. Other causes besides the triumph of Lockianism had contributed to the demoralization. The familiar distinction between matters above reason (mysteries) and those contrary to reason (illusions) was precarious, not least because the number of beliefs deemed illusory always seemed to grow at the expense of the number deemed mysterious. Though Synge invoked this distinction, he also encouraged such contraction by dismissing the whole dispute about the meaning of mysteries of faith as "a contention about a word."[31] It was a short step from the conviction that the debate was trivial to the conjecture that the word which had prompted it might also be.

Once again Synge was more precipitate than most of his colleagues, who were inclined to a dilution of the received idea of mystery rather than a repudiation of it. Toland's triple definition of mystery (things not knowable by natural reason without "Express and Immediate Divine Revelation"; things "very obscurely and imperfectly Revealed before the Gospel and the coming of Christ"; and things "eternally incomprehensible") was commonplace when he wrote *Christianity Not Mysterious.* As long as Anglican apologists preserved and applied all three definitions, they could dispute his rejection of the third. When they became attached to the new epistemology, they found its preservation and application difficult. Thus, in a single book Francis Gastrell could condemn the attack on mysteries as a means of striking at the whole of Christianity and, with Synge, maintain that any proposition which had to be accepted as an article of faith could not be mysterious.[32]

Individuals can sometimes succeed in holding two incompatible theses together in a personal tension; with the multiplication of such tensions, more and more individuals will abandon one of them. The way in which Charles Leslie, a nonjuror, and Thomas Halyburton, a leading Scottish divine, received Charles Gildon's retraction of his deism suggests that they were both in the climacteric of such a dilemma. In recanting, Gildon, once Blount's editor, also tried to "Plainly Demonstrate the Reasonableness of the Mysterious Part of Religion." Notwithstanding his approximation of the premise of *Christianity Not Mysterious,* Leslie and Halyburton welcomed Gildon back into the fold.[33] They were presumably more concerned with his profession of loyalty to the church than with his notion of a mystery of faith.

The range of necessary articles which remained mysteries in the sense of being eternally unknowable was quietly contracting. John Conybeare exemplified a common approach in 1723; after having written that a Gospel mystery "was *wholy,* or *in part unknown* 'til deliver'd by our Saviour and his Apostles," he limited the number of those "we are still incapable of comprehending" by a demand for "*plain* and *clear* Proof." Although many theologians continued to treat the Incarnation and the Trinity as dark mysteries, Arianizing divines like Samuel Clarke sought to further the contraction. In his effort, Clarke sometimes used the word *mystery* baldly and exclusively in Toland's sense.[34] It remained for his brother John, the dean of Salisbury, in his Boyle lectures of 1720–1721 explicitly to adopt Toland's definition as uniquely applicable. He did so, of course, without acknowledgment. The apparent absence of contemporary objections to the dean's enterprise suggests that much of the articulate church had acquiesced in the adoption of the Socinian or deist analysis of mysteries of faith. Many churchmen passed from acquiescence to agreement. In the first half of the eighteenth century this analysis had become familiar in Latitudinarian circles; its advocates ranged from associates of Toland to conspicuous opponents of deism. From them it spread to Nonconformists like Edmund Calamy, who had rebuffed the approaches of sceptics like Toland. In light of the growing distaste for the contention that Christianity rested on elusive mysteries, it is understandable that the most thorough catalogue of printed sermons from the period reveals that divines became more and more reluctant to preach on mystery texts.[35]

The changing understanding of faith had profound implications for the treatment of the Bible, the foundation of religion. Augustans who presented themselves as defenders of orthodoxy did not share the belief that the deists' attack on Scripture was superficial. On the contrary, they saw the work of Toland and his fellows as a serious threat to its authority. Nevertheless, the English biblical tradition was sufficiently strong in the eighteenth century that many who abhorred Toland's investigation of the revealed books of the Christian mythical theology felt that they could safely ignore his enterprise. While their silence says nothing about the seriousness of the challenge, it typifies the intellectual somnolence of the Georgian church. Richard Simon's revolutionary researches into Scripture, which had terrified Bossuet, were disseminated in England, but they were regularly ignored or dismissed as a papist artifice. Such general neglect convinced Dean Prideaux in 1716 that he could publish a book on biblical chronology which parroted Archbishop Ussher and still find an audience and be treated as a scholar. This sluggishness courted a rude awakening, since the exposure of the Bible to intense, often jocose scrutiny served to undermine its unquestioned authority.[36]

When churchmen began to consider the task of defending revelation, they faced daunting disadvantages and a few potential assets. Philological and historical backwardness, the most conspicuous of their own handicaps, might have been offset by the deficiencies of some of the deists' categories. An unhistorical cast of mind had led the deists to impose contemporary mores on biblical times, much as their rationalist and voluntarist psychology made them attribute miraculous and other improbable narratives to fraud. Yet these remained latent advantages, since almost all apologists were themselves unhistorical rationalists. As if to compensate for their scholarly backwardness, the church's defenders tried to apply the critical techniques which had been devised for studying classical literature to an examination of the New Testament in light of Toland's objections. In effect, they had forsaken all of the elements of the medieval fourfold concept of hermeneutics except the literal-historical and accepted Toland's thesis that Scripture was a means of information rather than a motive for assent. Few of his theses had been more controversial. Anglican apologists never explicitly abandoned their original objections to it; instead, they tended to acquiesce in Toland's view by no longer repeating them.[37] By remaining silent, churchmen made other, equally sapping concessions to Toland's position. Their distaste for philosophical reasoning contributed to their failure to cope with Toland's reservations about the adequacy of human language to convey purportedly divine truths. Those who felt the strength of such reservations often took steps to accommodate them. Here, too, Dean Clarke pointed the way by proposing to accept as meaningful only those texts which were sensible when read literally. He saw in this strategy a way of minimizing the number of incomprehensible elements in the Bible.[38] He never bothered to catalogue the texts which actually met the criterion.

The redefinition of reason also affected the efforts of Augustan exegetes. Those who had accepted it could no longer consistently hold the inner light theory on which earlier biblicists had depended. Locke's anatomy of the human understanding did not contain a region which, because of peculiar sensitivity to the promptings of the Holy Spirit, would recognize and properly interpret the word of God when confronted with it. Once more churchmen were slow to come to terms with the implications of the epistemology which they had embraced. Throughout Toland's lifetime even apparently Lockian apologists invoked such a faculty as if they had retained Jewel's theory of knowledge. Others indicated that they knew that they had left the sixteenth century. This group sometimes resorted to a defensive argument from prescription: was it reasonable to doubt the authority of a book which had for so long been uniquely honored? Toland had pointed to the Koran as a plausible competitor for the title of God's revelation. In turn, those who sought to defend the Bible by prescriptive means asserted that the miracles recorded there proved its unique status.[39] Another generation would pass before Hume offered his unsettling response to their assertion.

Toland had diagnosed his opponents' fundamental difficulty: how could Protestantism invoke an external guarantee of the received canon and still retain its identity? Although the Socinians had originally raised this point, Toland's reiteration of it kept divines from ignoring it.

Jeremiah Jones, one of the deists' most learned antagonists, saw its force and used a variety of tactics in attempting to deal with it. Central to his case was an appeal to the laity to invest implicit faith in the researches of the erudite and "the authority of the Church." As if he perceived the inherent contradictions of his call—How could Protestants uncritically accept the guidance of an *ecclesia docens*? Why should the learned be any more fit recipients of unquestioning trust than priests?—he also invoked the consciences of all men as witnesses to "the innate evidences of the Scripture, with the testimony of the Spirit."[40] His failure to explain this manner of understanding bespoke resignation to the change in epistemological fashion.

Jones won most of his battles with Toland, only to lose the war. When discussing the history of apocrypha, an amateur like Toland was no match for this scholar; but Jones ignored the significance of his opponent's effort. There was, in fact, not enough uniformity of opinion among the learned to make them creditable repositories of an implicit faith. The history of Nathaniel Lardner, another weighty antagonist of the deists, illustrates the weakness of Jones's case. In the course of his career, Lardner moved from the defense of orthodoxy to an idiosyncratic Socinianism.[41]

Jones was not alone in seeking to invoke the conviction of the church to defend the canon, though most of the lesser figures who followed him were as careful as he not to delve into ecclesiology. There were a few more daring writers, often High-Churchmen, who specified the character and origins of ecclesiastical authority. Usually they cited the binding force of tradition, conciliar decrees, or the apostolic succession embodied in the episcopacy. This was manifestly not a course open to the disciples of Tillotson. Although Toland tactfully refrained from referring directly to the Apocrypha, these deuterocanonical works were an obstacle to presenting the church as the guarantor of the essential contents of the Authorized Version. The majority of those who chose to call themselves Christians—the Greeks and the Romans—considered these fourteen books to be genuine parts of Scripture. In contrast, while the sixth article had honored them, it had not included them in the canon.[42] Even if there had been a solution to this Chinese puzzle, Anglicans would have had to cope with the circularity of any defense of the Bible from the witness of a church whose title deed was the Bible.

The portentous consequences of this imbroglio did not, however, go unnoticed. Francis Hare's *Difficulties and Discouragements Attending the*

Study of Scripture (1713) was the most succinct — if perverse — statement of what the new conception of scriptural authority meant for the effort to derive doctrines from the Bible. Whatever the prelate's design, his logic was remorseless. In effect, he held that in the determination of credenda from the Bible there was no mean between an unfettered right of individual interpretation and complete submission to an external authority. Once it was admitted that only "what is 'plain and clear' in Scripture" had to be believed, then a number of the established church's articles would cease to be binding in faith, since their biblical warrant was neither plain nor clear. Those who sought to maintain an older notion of orthodoxy could invoke tradition, and tradition alone. Most Anglicans, of course, had no precise notion of — much less, loyalty to — a binding traditional authority. Thus, as long as *sola scriptura* remained the religion of Protestants, they would have to cherish their points of agreement and respect their points of disagreement. The former propositions would constitute their articles of religion.[43]

Hare's lucidity was unique. Synge's blandness was more representative of the age. Despite a propensity — understandable in one of his position — for rhetorical embellishments on the necessity of fidelity to the church and its legacy, Synge professed to see the Bible as the fundamental source of his faith. As his was an ethical version of Christianity, he did not know Hare's apprehensions about the effect of the new concept of reason for biblicism. Reason and revelation were ultimately compatible because of the clarity of "all the several *Commands* that God has been pleased to lay upon me."[44] Like Tillotson, Synge suspected that heresy was at root a defect of behavior rather than of belief.

If the Bible did not plainly and clearly sanction a number of dogmatic tenets, it still seemed precise in its moral teachings. As more and more apologists recognized that they could not provide answers to questions about the sources of doctrinal authority, they forcefully reasserted Tillotson's conception of Christianity as morality. In turn, since the identification of religion with morality was a constitutive principle of natural religion, many of them undertook to clarify the relation between natural and revealed religion.

Their speculations usually took one of three forms. They could presume the congruence of the two. They could expatiate on the articles of natural religion inculcated by Christianity, and then casually refer to Christ as the Messiah. Some of them, however, chose to offer a bifurcated religion; they asserted the general sufficiency of belief in the tenets of natural religion, even as they proclaimed their own adherence to the Christian creed. All these approaches presumed that, since God had taught natural religion to Adam and Eve, it was archetypal.[45] Some divines easily moved from this theory to the view that revelation was merely a repetition or accentuation of natural religion. Samuel Clarke, for one, thought that if the discoveries of the two vehicles of religious truth were discordant, then the claims of Christianity would be weakened. Those who dissented from Anglican rationalism knew that they were defending an unfashionable position. Although many shared Berkeley's disdain, few wrote with his perspicuity. He represented Alciphron as having passed from Latitudinarianism through deism to atheism, on the grounds that "a man of courage and sense should follow his argument wherever it leads him, and that nothing is more ridiculous than to be a free-thinker by halves. I approve the man who makes thorough work, and, not content with lopping off the branches, extricates the very root from which they spring."[46]

Ecclesiastical history cannot be treated as an autonomous field of research. This is particularly true of the history of an established church, which must respond to the widest variety of psychological, political, and social stimuli. Throughout Toland's lifetime articulate observers insisted that the English church had to be a force for national unity, if only because England was at war more often than she was at peace. Persuaded that the church itself required peace in order to serve this purpose, Archbishop Tenison, the primate from 1694 to 1715, sought to discourage the lower clergy and laity from undertaking heresy hunts. The most common manifestation of the search for peace and unity continued to be the desire for a formula which would allow all English Christians to adhere to the Establishment. The conviction that latitude of belief was an integral part of Anglicanism was a corollary of this wish. After the signing of the Treaty of Utrecht the flow of sermons — particularly during assizes — inculcating the necessity of peace and unity did not stop. By compounding distrust of the High-Church party so long associated with nonjuring, the Jacobite rising of 1715 strengthened popular acceptance of the necessity of union among real Protestants.[47] Neglected Tory churchmen like Swift might inveigh against what they reckoned to be false irenicism posing as concern for tranquillity, but their sentiments proved to be unappealing. During the reign of George I, most preachers exhibited both a marked distaste for texts which might promote discord between church and state or among

Protestants and a reliance on texts which served the cause of national unity. Walpole's effort to bring stability to England was as successful ecclesiastically as it was politically.[48]

Ingrained prejudices fostered the interpretation of events which prompted these calls for solidarity. They also shaped the responses of most divines to the questions about the nature of the church raised by Toland and other deists. Whether high or low, all churchmen persisted in identifying church and polity; some still maintained that England was the elect nation. The medieval idea of a sacred monarch had been not so much abandoned as altered, so that either the government or the society it protected became hallowed. As a result, the fate of the church was seen as being inextricably bound up with the fate of society and its government.[49] Neither was the idea of the church as, in some sense, an authoritative entity completely lost. Though traces of it appear in the writings of Samuel Clarke, his generation of Latitudinarians had a less certain conception of either the nature of the body or its powers than did that of Tillotson. High-Churchmen sought to invoke the fathers, councils, and apostolic succession as the church's magisterial voices, but they shared an assumption with Low-Churchmen which weakened the plausibility of the appeal.[50] They too were convinced that, however much the government might rely on the church, the church ultimately depended on the government and had to be responsive to it.

Archbishop Laud's putative heirs depicted the church as "a Great and Necessary Branch of our Constitution" at least as frequently as they depicted it as a divine society. To call into question its existence or practices was tantamount to attacking the state.[51] When threatened, the church could reasonably expect succor from the magistrates. High-Churchmen had long posited the adequacy of implicit belief, so that those Englishmen who accepted the national church's will were reckoned as accepting its faith. In most cases, the church's will was identified with its prevailing usage. Although they portrayed authors like Toland as working to destroy binding authority in religion, the members of this party were themselves unable to conceive of a religious jurisdiction higher than the crown. Their prepossessions led them to conclude that the erosion of the church's powers was at least as great a threat as the assault on its dogmas. Even those who emphasized the risk of heresy implicit in permitting men to rely exclusively on their own judgment were concerned to protect the rights of the clerical estate. In fact, High-Churchmen were often more eager to secure the magistrates' intervention to bolster the government's ecclesiastical arm than to refute heretical ideas.[52] They had dealt with occasional conformists in much the same way. Instead of being scandalized at heretics sharing the church's sacramental life, they saw those who exploited loopholes in the Test Act as schismatics whose overt dissent threatened to weaken the Establishment.[53] The prorogation of convocation in 1717 and the repeal of the Schism and Occasional Conformity Acts two years later ratified the failure of their counterrevolution. This reversal not only doomed their attempt to achieve a clerical monopoly of power within the church; it also paved the way for the creation of a new usage, one which their own prejudices would not let them reject.

The Low Church created the new usage. In the course of resisting the lower house of convocation's effort to achieve greater clerical autonomy, the episcopacy renewed its Erastianism. Archbishop Synge ably summarized the sentiments of his order. In his own way, he was as firm an advocate of an inclusive Anglicanism as his High-Church brethren, but he eschewed coercion in favor of accommodation. A zeal for comprehension informed his writings on ecclesiology. He maintained that, in subscribing to the church's formularies, a cleric might freely put on them any construction he found plausible, as long as he was prepared to explain his meaning. Synge proposed a less exacting standard for the laity. For them, conformity to the church's rites and moral injunctions constituted the necessary act of assent.[54]

Like their High-Church competitors, liberal divines had inherited the Anglican distrust of any effort to establish Christian commitment on the basis of dogma. As Elias Sydall, a future bishop of Gloucester, remarked, for clergymen to "affect a Dominion over the Minds and Consciences of Men" by insisting that the laity surrender the right to think independently and give "absolute obedience to their Determinations" was to lay "the very Basis and Ground-Work of Popery." No less than their Laudian confreres, Low-Churchmen were convinced that the well-being of the state depended on the prosperity of the church. They believed that their order was a kind of constabulary charged with inducing their fellow subjects to observe moral regularity, and they acted creatively on their belief. Fostering organizations like the Society for the Reformation of Manners was only one way in which the church might perform her task in new and trying circumstances.[55]

The moralization of the church allowed early eighteenth-century Latitudinarians to undertake the reinterpretation of heresy that became one of their major achievements. Some churchmen persisted in defending the older view of culpable heresy which held that the will and the understanding cooperated in the creation of faith; they could, therefore, consistently argue that formal heresy, the deliberate belief in a tenet which contravened official teachings, resulted from a sinful act of will. In contrast, those divines who redefined assent as acceptance of propositions resting on distinct biblical authority, of which the mind could form clear ideas, came to recognize that heresy would thereby be reduced to a consequence of misunderstanding or misinformation, neither of which was blameworthy.[56]

Yet the New Testament refers to heresy, and as biblicists the Latitudinarians had to develop an alternative meaning for the word. By condensing and reversing the Scholastic theory that sins against the cardinal virtue of temperance could lead to sins against the theological virtue of faith, they concluded that heresy was at root nothing less — nor more — than immorality. This restatement began to take form when apologists chose to pay more attention to the various appetites which prompted heretics than to their defective opinions. It culminated in the equation of such motives with the condition. For those who felt ill at ease with both the reformulation and the older notion, there existed a comfortable evasion. Although references to heresy could not be exorcised, there was no compulsion to preach on them. The available evidence suggests that many clerics took advantage of this tactic. The chronological distribution of the texts of published sermons listed in *The Preacher's Assistant* shows that, in the generation after Toland's death, divines tended to avoid places like Titus 3: 10-11: "A man that is an heretick after the first and second admonition reject; . . . [he] being condemned of himself."[57]

Many reinterpreters of heresy also concluded that opponents of the institutions which promoted both private and public morality were heterodox. Such men were particularly dangerous because their opposition threatened to weaken restraints on the lower orders. The apologists' preoccupation with the threat from below reflects their doubts about their own ability to parry the intellectual thrusts of Toland and his fellow freethinkers. It also suggests that they were slowly coming to the realization that, apart from their belief in the social necessity of Anglicanism, the common ground which they had once shared was dissolving.[58]

Without exception churchmen persisted in seeing belief in a future state of rewards and punishments as a necessary principle. It was crucial to public order because it guaranteed the sanctity of the oaths on which England or any other society presumably depended. Their attachment to belief in personal immortality served to limit their dogmatic suppleness. Despite practical concessions to the fact of doctrinal pluralism, most Augustan clerics were unable to come to terms completely with the idea of freedom of opinion. Therefore, they reacted violently whenever a writer hinted at rejecting the tenets of natural religion which they saw as necessary to popular morality and had succeeded in identifying with Anglicanism.[59]

Since clerics of all parties agreed that their mission was to act as the state's agents in enforcing morals and did not differentiate the state from society, they deemed any challenge to the church to be a challenge to public tranquillity. In general, Toland would have agreed with this assessment, but the civil religion he proposed to raise on the ruins of the Christian poetical theology was deficient in the eyes of even liberal Anglican apologists. They were convinced that Christianity had effected a revolution in the moral condition of the vulgar, that it had made them both better and happier. Thus, when confronted with the virtuous sceptics and pagans whom the deists were wont to invoke as proof of the dispensability of Christianity, Samuel Clarke did not dispute either their existence or their goodness. That there were such men did not make Christianity any less necessary. Through reason, learned and reflective people would always be brought to recognize the self-evident truths of natural religion. Their experience gave no assurance that, when deprived of the support of the Christian redaction of these verities, the majority of their fellows would not lapse into profligacy.[60]

In effect, divines like Clarke thought that the validity of their conception of Christianity could be proved by its utility. It was the same practicality which led some apologists to argue that conformity to Christianity should be seen as a matter of elementary self-interest. Samuel Clarke chose to phrase this appeal to personal advantage as a vulgarization of Pascal's wager argument. While the Frenchman had maintained that human life is meaningful only when man acts as a reasonable being seeking God and that all apparent finite goods are really valueless, the Englishman urged that conformity to Christian ethics promised double happiness: prosperity in this world and felicity in the next.[61] Although some of Clarke's colleagues rejected the notion that men should allow calculations of interest to decide their affairs, most of those who accounted themselves Toland's opponents assumed that such considerations did and should dominate men's lives, including their relations with God.[62] Nevertheless, they did not conclude that individuals' pursuit of their own interests would ever suffice to make men orderly and thus obviate their defense of the tenets of natural religion. The secularization of society was no more a real prospect for Anglican rationalists than it was for deists.

There was, however, nothing in the apologists' conception of Christian ethics which threatened the political and economic interests of most articulate Englishmen. For many Augustan clerics providence had come to be literally "the Nature and Reason of Things"; like Pope, they thought it clear that "whatever *is,* is *right.*" It followed that the Establishment could not challenge the worldly concerns of conforming subjects which did not lead to illegality or sexual irregularity. Among popular preachers, affirmations that the church should seek to curb economic exploitation were as rare as the notion that it could question the moral legitimacy of the crown's actions. They did commend charity, but it too was presumably governed by calculations of self-interest.[63] They had, in any event, scant homiletic concern with the unsettling relations of Dives and Lazarus.

Once the clergy had conceded material self-interest as an encouragement to religious assent, they tended to concern themselves more with the formal act of profession than with its motivation. If apologists admitted that prevailing standards made a considerable measure of private judgment on doctrinal questions unavoidable, they also insisted that this was a personal liberty, not a license to disseminate novel opinions. Taken together, the emphasis on formal profession and the willingness to tolerate private heterodoxy help to explain the increasingly frequent calls to dissemble.[64] The antideists allowed that, while sceptically-inclined gentlemen might believe as little as they wished, they should recognize that their interests obliged them to support the existing social structure. Should the lower orders cease to see it as divinely ordained and to expect the redress of their grievances in the next world, they might revenge themselves on earth. Common sense should lead the articulate classes to hold their tongues. Whatever its immediate attraction, the call to dissemble had a sinister significance for the future of belief. By mid-century, Philip Skelton could write a set of antideist dialogues, *Ophiomaches, or Deism Revealed,* portraying a world like a gallery of distorting mirrors, in which no one was quite what he seemed or believed everything he said or said everything he believed.[65]

At first sight the widespread advocacy of subterfuge may appear to undermine the thesis that, with the passage of time, the Georgian church accepted sincerity as the criterion of true religion. In fact, the outward signs which eighteenth-century divines saw as probable evidence of sincerity were often compatible with dissembling. Although many of them were coming to believe that sincerity (candor in the expression of convictions) rather than faith (assent to a set of credenda) offered salvation, they tended to invest sincerity with much the same causality which had traditionally been imputed to faith. "By their fruits ye shall know them."[66] Consistent moral conduct was a token of inner sincerity. Thus, if one were able to conform to conventions in word and deed, if one behaved morally, then one was evincing the sincere dispositions which were the essence of Augustan Anglicanism.

The redefinition of faith as primarily a matter of practice was crucial to the acceptance of the religion of sincerity. With the exception of a few rigorous determinists like Collins, most English thinkers were attached to the idea that the human will was in some sense free. If they were not thoroughgoing voluntarists, they nonetheless believed that actions usually proceeded from a well-disposed will, rather than from the speculations of the mind. Indeed, one of the objections which reflective Englishmen had to Romanism was that it rested on a consistent but closed system of propositions, enforced by the Inquisition. By systematically extrapolating the corollaries of a number of hypotheses, papists had driven even tepid dissidents to retaliatory feats of intellectual extremism. Since the repressive connivance of Catholic monarchs had made religious discussion impossible, ever larger numbers among their gentle subjects had come secretly to hold sceptical views; the principles of morals were not even safe. Such a polarization of opinion threatened the well-being of civil society, for once the church had lost the support—or at least the acquiescence—of this class, it could no longer perform its central duty, the enforcement of morals.[67]

The Reverend Elisha Smith's *Justifying Sincerity* (1719) provides a convenient exposition of the religion of sincerity, which many Latitudinarians saw as a way of saving England from such polarization. Perhaps the most obvious difficulty Smith had to face was that of defining sincerity. It had several meanings, not all of them easily reconcilable. It might mean purity in the sense of simplicity or uniformity. When Smith wrote of "that *Sincerity,* or Religious Faculty in Man, which shews itself by a conscientious Enquiry after the best Religion," he seems to have been describing a soul which simply (exclusively) desired God. Like generations of Christians before him, he assumed that a soul so disposed would receive the guidance it required to reach salvation.[68] As Smith knew, sincerity might also mean honesty or straightforwardness about convictions. Whether or not he was conscious of the ambiguity of employing both senses of the word without elaboration or distinction, he used them interchangeably, never indicating that the results of candor differed from those of the working of the "Religious Faculty in Man." His analysis of assent suggests that he was, in fact, conscious of the ambiguity and had succeeded in exploiting it to his own ends. To be binding, a doctrine had to have a content that was plain to the understandings of all on whom it was to be imposed. Moreover, Smith thought that the importance of a dogma was to be measured by its effect on the conduct of those who accepted it.[69] While these two propositions allowed him to identify honesty about convictions with justifying sincerity, neither presupposed the existence of souls desiring God exclusively.

Smith wrote in defense of Benjamin Hoadly, the bishop of Bangor, whose assertion that there was no scriptural warrant for a visible ecclesiastical authority had set off the Bangorian controversy. Hoadly's foes realized that, while his partisans had made justifying sincerity a watchword, this idea's future did not depend on the outcome of the controversy.[70] The triumph of the Latitudinarian conviction that Christianity might be reducible to belief in the articles of natural religion and moral regularity had made it normative. Unwittingly, Synge revealed the connection between the two concepts. In *A Plain and Easy Method,* he presented a sceptic who, though "his Mind is not altogether free from Doubt and Hesitation" about some formulas, is resolved to live morally and seeks baptism. The archbishop sought to justify his recommendation that such a person be baptized. Far from consisting of "strength of speculative assent," steadfastness of belief was the "Firmness of Purpose and Resolution which an individual forms within himself." Such determination was integral to that justifying sincerity whose outward signs were moral rather than intellectual. Several years before Synge wrote, Joseph Addison, that eighteenth-century Edmund Wilson, had asserted "the pre-eminence in several respects" of morality over faith in religion. He was convinced both that "the rule of morality is much more certain than that of faith," and that immorality was more dangerous than infidelity. Addison's confidence rested on the successful effort of the rationalist divines to accommodate Anglicanism to one of the central theses of the despised *Christianity Not Mysterious*: that the Bible is primarily a book of ethical rather than of dogmatic instruction.[71]

Although the number of apologists who resisted treating morality as the essence of Christianity and most dogma as accidental diminished with the passage of time, there were some clerics who continued to uphold dogmatism. More often than not, their resistance was prompted by an attachment to the dark view of human nature limned by Paul and completed by Augustine: how could a fallen humanity determine what is moral, let alone act on it without divine aid? They were clearly in a minority; the most persuasive advocates of historical pessimism in the eighteenth century would be philosophical historians, not conservative divines. The triumph of optimistic moralism was so complete that, in 1730, Thomas Rundle, a jealous guardian of the Tillotsonian heritage, was vexed to discover that some Anglicans persisted in clinging to a pessimistic and doctrinal view of religion. A recent study of Augustan preaching suggests that Rundle need not have been alarmed. As perceptive contemporaries, even academic preachers were preoccupied with morality rather than theology.[72]

In their effort to identify Christianity and virtue, some Latitudinarians explained the origins of morality in a way which might have confounded proponents of the Restoration theological accord. Dean Clarke was one of the principal advocates of this etiology. He was so certain that mankind possessed a set of innate moral dispositions that he did not hesitate to minimize the events in Eden and their aftermath. More remarkable, however, was his reliance on a theory of obligation resembling that of the philosophical Shaftesbury. He emphasized the aesthetic element of the earl's hypothesis far more than had Toland in his civil theology. Men could not "avoid seeing the natural obligation they are under to practise Virtue upon account of the native Beauty and Excellency of it."[73]

Clarke's vision was complete without ideas like original sin, the Incarnation, and atonement. Yet he never indicated that he was aware that redefining religion as morality had profound and inescapable implications for theology. Either implicitly or explicitly, many earlier theologians had tended to present God as a kind of cosmic policeman.

Unreflectively, John Clarke himself had created such a figure. This deity had all the attributes of a strong and vigorous magistrate suspicious of defenses based on diminished responsibility.[74] The dean was less subtle than his older brother, who often appeared to worship a God like the deity of natural religion. Profuse in his compliments to the deism of the ancient heathen philosophers, Samuel held that anyone who shared his admiration of them was irresponsible if he sought to separate himself from the church because of uncertainty about "the strength of the Evidence of matter of Fact" (i.e., Christianity's idiosyncratic doctrines). Christianity had proved to be the most practical system for diffusing the principles of natural religion. Accordingly, anyone who sincerely respected these articles was under an obligation to associate himself with the church's promotion of them. His chain of reasoning had considerable appeal. In fact, five years after Clarke wrote, Addison took much the same line in *The Tatler* and thus canonized it as a truism.[75]

Even before Dean Clarke had given his Boyle lectures, some clerics were busy coming to terms with the theological implications of the redefinition of religion as morality. As early as 1697, Toland's sometime opponent, Gastrell, had conceded that it was a matter of indifference how God's nature was conceived, as long as His status as moral legislator was respected. The number who tried to make this adjustment increased with the passage of time. Thus, Arthur Ashley Sykes, a protégé of Samuel Clarke, openly urged the sceptical concern with practicality which underlay Gastrell's position. "Religion is good and useful; it is a Principle of right Action, which all Men at all Times may understand . . . and if any Speculation is proposed, it is only as it may answer this good end." In addition, Sykes accepted and elaborated his patron's depreciation of revelation: "nor is there any one Principle, or *Practice* of *Morality,* which may not be known by natural Reason without Revelation."[76] By restricting God to a distant and indirect superintendence, Sykes had worked out the logic of the Latitudinarians' premises. His logicality was a kind of extremism, and other divines sought a more moderate position. For example, John Leland, the author of the most thorough contemporary treatise on deism, contented himself with reaffirming Tillotson's view of the relation between natural and revealed religions; the two were so compatible as to be almost coincident. Other antideists commended Jean Le Clerc's *Treatise on Incredulity* as a useful work of Christian apologetics.[77] The irony of this recommendation would have delighted the book's translator, John Toland.

The reassessment of the *Treatise on Incredulity* was a manifestation of Le Clerc's rise to respectability in England after 1700, which, in its turn, was indicative of the shift of the center of theological gravity within the church. During the mid-1690s, Gilbert Burnet had feared the possibility that High-Churchmen might exploit his association with Le Clerc to support their charges of heresy against him. Within twenty years Le Clerc was being treated as a patriarch rather than a pariah. At the height of the outcry against Hoadly, Archbishop Wake felt obliged to reassure the elderly Remonstrant that, notwithstanding this unfortunate episode, he presided over a body of exemplary tolerance:

> Whether you regard its ancient, or more properly its apostolic government; or the moderation of its Articles of Religion which the clergy must subscribe; or the liberty allowed to its other members to inquire, determine and even believe in matters of faith (always provided that nothing is publicly set forth which would disturb the peace and tranquility of the church): I doubt if it does not excel greatly all the other reformed churches.[78]

For their part, many laymen were willing to vouch for the primate's contention that they enjoyed the widest latitude of opinion. As an Anglican and a deist, Collins both praised and depended on the church's tolerance. Moreover, he was indiscreet enough to say that the clergy, though bound to subscribe to the Thirty-Nine Articles, held formally heretical opinions at least as frequently as the laity.[79] Collins' observation was acute: the theological diversity among beneficed clergymen could be remarkable.

Richard Roach, the leader of the Philadelphians, a sect of nature pantheists, was the incumbent of St. Augustine's, Hackney, until his death in 1730. He was a curiosity. Most often, advanced theologians continued to labor to reinterpret the meaning and binding force of the dogma of the Trinity. Samuel Clarke was at the hub of this effort, too. He undertook a non-Trinitarian revision of the Book of Common Prayer, which he justified by asserting that subscription required only that individuals make a sincere effort to conform to what they saw as the clear teachings of Scripture. Against his view, Daniel Waterland insisted that the church required "subscription in *her own sense* because she judges no other to be agreeable to Scripture."[80]

In order to differentiate this debate from the Trinitarian controversy which they ended by 1697, historians of Unitarianism have termed it the "Arian controversy." Despite their agreement about periodization, these students have held contradictory views of the influence of the latter dispute. E. M. Wilbur was convinced that the church's refusal to accept Clarke's prayer book finished the anti-Trinitarian movement within Anglicanism but strengthened it among Dissenters. In contrast, J. Hay Colligan, the historian of the Arian movement, believed that the argument between Clarke and Waterland subsided because more and more clergymen came to agree with Clarke. There is considerable circumstantial evidence to support Colligan's thesis. Convocation was unable to move against Clarke in 1714, and he successfully evaded attempts to make him recant. In addition, not only did a number of younger dissenting ministers defect to Anglicanism after the Salters' Hall conferences in 1719 had rejected their Unitarian efforts, but subscription controversies recurred within the church during the next two generations.[81] Whatever the ultimate influence of the new Arianism, it continued to attract many Anglicans after Clarke's death in 1729.

Not all of Archbishop Wake's flock shared his sanguine view of the church's condition. When that pious diarist, the first earl of Egmont, heard of Dr. Rundle's nomination as bishop of Gloucester, he was apprehensive because clerical acquaintances had attributed to the doctor "the principles of Toland." Rundle himself would have summarily rejected the accusation that he was in some sense a deist; his preceptor was Tillotson, not Toland. The bishop's correspondence shows that Egmont was closer to the truth than perhaps he himself knew. When, for example, in 1730 Rundle reviewed the attacks on the deist Thomas Chubb in a letter to his confidante, Mrs. Sandys, he wittily compared the infidel to a David taking on that Goliath, Bishop Gibson; he already abhorred the Philistine who would shunt him off to a wealthy Irish see. Rundle's principles were consistent with his sympathies. He commended John Clarke's Boyle lectures to Mrs. Sandys as a lucid exposition of the philosophical theology to which he and his fellow Tillotsonians were committed. In these lectures Clarke, like Toland in *Christianity Not Mysterious,* had rejected the thesis that a Gospel mystery could be eternally incomprehensible. Far from being unique, Rundle's situation explains why many sober commentators were obsessed with the notion that the church was riddled with priests who dissembled their sceptical beliefs for the sake of their profession.[82] The appeals for subterfuge which apologists had been making since the nineties had been widely heeded.

Notwithstanding Rundle's praise for the younger Clarke brother, churchmen from Archbishop Wake downward had no doubt that it was Samuel to whom they owed the greater debt. A journal like *The History of the Works of the Learned,* whose editors prided themselves on their reasonable and resolute opposition to deism, treated him as the Josiah of Anglicanism; in their opinion, he had devastated the arguments of such infidels as Tindal and Toland. Anticipating the strategy of some ecclesiastical historians, the editors passed over the philosophical foundations of Clarke's theology. Historians of philosophy have not felt free to adopt this approach. They have for the most part grouped the deists and their Latitudinarian opponents together, because, in spite of occasionally differing conclusions, both sides frequently shared the same premises.[83] As the history of the Clarke brothers suggests, many antideists struggled to reconcile their inferences to their assumptions. Superficially, the stillness that follows a difficult adaptation may appear indistinguishable from the quiet that follows a hard-won victory.

The efforts of the Boyle lecturers and other liberal antideists had mellowed, even if they did not devastate, English deism. Their success was primarily due to the suppleness with which they had redefined the terms of theological discussion, but it was eased by their social habits. Traditionally minded clergymen were given to complaining about their rationalist confreres' taste for freethinking company. At first sight their complaints might be dismissed as products of the taste for promiscuous invective which afflicted Augustan polemicists. There is, however, evidence that antideists and deists did fraternize. Samuel Clarke himself appears to have been prone to such behavior. For at least part of his career, he met with freethinkers like Tindal and Collins to discuss religious matters.[84] Although it is impossible to ascertain what effect the discussions had on any of the participants, Tindal's generous citations from Clarke's Boyle lectures in *Christianity as Old as the Creation* suggest that, at the very least, he found the lecturer's ideas comfortable. Similarly, Collins' changing attitude toward the church implies that he judged her increasingly willing to accommodate freethought. Once truculently anticlerical, he had by the early 1720s moderated his hostility.[85]

In contrast, Toland appears to have been a diehard who showed his disdain for the emerging theological consensus by peddling a *démodé* and fissiparous anticlericalism until his death. His decision suggests that temperamentally he had more in common with his countryman, Swift, than with the English deists. As Collins once observed, extreme scepticism and gross superstition are opposing, yet mutually sustaining principles; therefore, both flourish in Roman Catholic countries.[86] By blunting this opposition and cultivating their putative foes, the architects of the new Anglican apologetics helped to promote the peace and unity which all Englishmen eagerly sought.

Students of the period have confirmed Collins' observation. Professor Manuel found that, with the passage of time, "English treatises on theological subjects tended to become more conservative, stereotyped, and orthodox," while in France "the radical temper had possessed society." Anticlericalism was, of course, one of the *philosophes'* principal commodities, and as revolutionary violence in Angers and elsewhere was to show, they did not want for customers. It is also apparent that many of the *philosophes* borrowed liberally from the works of the Anglican rationalists. Voltaire, for example, based the second chapter of his *Traité du métaphysique* on Samuel Clarke's *Demonstration of the Being and Attributes of God;* and in the third he summarized the beginning of Locke's *Essay concerning Human Understanding.* Moreover, the virtually Socinian religious scheme which he once proposed for Geneva resembled Clarke's theological teachings.[87] Taken together, the differences between the French and the English experiences indicate that the search for religious origins of the most famous event which never happened in eighteenth-century England, the second revolution, should be directed to the internal history of Anglicanism.

For many, an irenic reconsideration of the church's exercise of its disciplinary functions complemented this doctrinal retrenchment. Though the episcopacy were charged with applying discipline, they had always been reluctant to initiate firm measures against the deists. In 1701, they responded to the lower house of convocation's appeal to move against the author of *Christianity Not Mysterious* by asserting that a royal writ was necessary before they could act.[88] No such writ was—or would be—forthcoming. While the bishops' irresolution ostensibly resulted from their deference to the civil authorities, it also owed something to their conviction that once the High-Church majority in the lower house had been allowed to begin a heresy hunt, it could not be contained. Burnet's ordeal had shown that the High-Church's quarry would not be limited to lay scribblers. Fear within dissent paralleled fear within the church. As James Shute-Barrington asserted in a paper which he circulated among dissenting ministers in 1718, those outside the Establishment had to regard liberty of belief as indivisible. If, for example, the church succeeded in conquering a group of heretics like the deists, she would be tempted to try to subdue all whom she considered schismatic or heretical.[89] Those who prized domestic peace had strong incentives not to trouble their own house.

The improbable alliance of cathedral and chapel would be sealed during the Bangorian controversy, which, as Professor Sykes recognized, fused all the other religious disputes of the period.[90] The accommodation of Benjamin Hoadly's party turned into policy the widespread indisposition to apply ecclesiastical discipline in cases of doctrinal irregularity. His idea of church government is, therefore, central to understanding the Anglican adjustment to deism.

Hoadly had begun his career as a spokesman for the extreme Latitudinarians, and his subsequent theories were logical extrapolations from some of their central assumptions. In his *Persuasive to Lay Conformity* (1704) he set out to find a means whereby the English church could achieve visible unity, and he does not appear to have been fastidious about how she did so. Since he thought that the union of church and state was indispensable to both parties, he saw no reason to doubt that public tranquillity depended on religious solidarity, particularly in time of war. It was the task of the Establishment to be responsive to the changing demands of the regime. Like Toland, Hoadly believed that whenever the church threatened the government's prerogatives, it deserved curbing or even persecution. He insinuated that the state was the arbiter of its own powers. Accordingly, it could not allow the church to resist its efforts to accommodate the Dissenters' legitimate aspirations, including the practice of occasional conformity on their own terms. Equating catholicity with comprehension, Hoadly hastened to assure Nonconformists who were considering submission that the church would not force them to compromise their beliefs. In return for such tolerance, they should recognize that patriotism sometimes required that they choose dissembling over disunity.[91] Hoadly understandably took pains never to specify any doctrines as necessary. Moral regularity alone was proof of Christianity. He was not slow in recognizing and then embracing the consequences of treating religion as morality. By 1711, he had ceased to recommend dissembling and, like most other Latitudinarians, was using the rhetoric of sincerity in his discussions of justification. A vision of Christianity as sincere virtue animated his sermon on "The Nature of the Kingdom of Christ" which set off the Bangorian controversy.[92]

Notwithstanding Leslie Stephen's judgment that this episode was "one of the most intricate tangles of fruitless logomachy in the language," Hoadly's position was straightforward. He saw no biblical justification for the notion that the clerical order was empowered to fix doctrine. In fact, any individual was free to search Scripture and frame his own articles of belief. Necessarily, there were some things that were binding on all Christians. They constituted pure religion, which Hoadly conceived as entailing fidelity to the moral law, rather than reliance on external observances or theological propositions. He went on to differentiate between the duties of the clerical and the lay estates. The clergy were obliged to support their paymaster, the church, and this responsibility included obedience to the will of the government.[93] The demand for clerical docility was consistent with the bishop's effort to present Anglicanism as essentially an institution for responding to social needs.

The admission of Hoadly's arguments was as important to the success of the church's effort to deal with the deist menace as the arguments themselves. If his allies were diverse, they were markedly less logomachical than his enemies. Veteran Latitudinarians recognized Hoadly as an upholder of their particular notions. For his part, the Reverend Samuel Bold, Locke's friend and advocate, perceived his lordship as fighting to make the church safe for Lockianism. If the bishop prevailed, then the meaning of Christian profession would be clear. "*Professing* Christians do, by their *Profession,* declare, that they believe that *Jesus* is the Christ of God, and that *they* are his Subjects and purpose to govern themselves, under *that* Character, according to the entire Revelation, he hath made of *his* Will, as they shall be *able* to obtain the Knowledge of it."[94]

Bold's perception appears to have been sound, for some of the most accomplished defenders of the religion of sincerity accepted the sufficiency of these two tenets of Locke's version of Christianity. For their part, the bishop's opponents insisted that he enjoyed wide support outside decorously Anglican quarters. An anonymous curate of Middlesex went so far as to compile a roll of testimonials to him from "Deists, Atheists, Arians, Freethinkers, Blasphemers, Church-Levellers, Town-Bully's, Ballad-Makers, &c." However accurate the bulk of this list was, its assertion that deists supported Hoadly had, as his clerical champions knew, a basis in fact. Both publicly and privately, Toland defended the embattled prelate, though he denied any personal connection with him. Moveover, Trenchard and Gordon pleaded Hoadly's cause in *The Independent Whig,* and Tindal eulogized him as "the strenuous Assertor of our religious, as well as civil rights."[95]

The attachment of Hoadly's would-be opponents to assumptions which were reconcilable with his own was crucial to the triumph of his ecclesiology. In taking on the bishop, Thomas Sherlock, who himself became bishop of Bangor in 1728, was primarily concerned to exclude Dissenters from offices of state. Although insisting that officials avoid conventicles, he failed either to present a doctrinal standard for determining what constituted Anglicanism or to define the sacrament whose reception was necessary to hold office. His double failure reflected his reluctance to deal with the problem of authority: what must an Anglican believe, and why must he believe it? Hoadly's partisans were not slow to recognize this logical perplexity, and they suggested that Bangor's enemies were perforce unwitting practitioners of the religion of sincerity.[96]

Men like Sherlock, Hare, and Atterbury tended to be as Erastian as Hoadly.[97] Their dispute with him was not about whether the clergy should be dependent on the state, but rather about the character of this dependence. While Hoadly conceived of his order as the crown's agents in religious or moral affairs, charged with whatever tasks it gave them, his critics saw themselves as its specialists in these matters, who should enjoy substantial autonomy in discharging their duties. Unlike the Trinitarian controversy, the Bangorian controversy was settled by royal writ. By proroguing convocation in 1717 to prevent it from indicting Hoadly's works, the crown resolved the debate in his favor.

Thenceforth, membership in the church was to become an optional consequence of nationality, and divines were to act as the crown's docile and temperate moral police and propagandists. Had clerics and politicians set out to accommodate deism, they could scarcely have achieved a closer approximation of the ends of Toland's civil theology. Privately conceding that their cause was lost, High-Churchmen felt that they were powerless to continue resistance. In 1736, William Warburton, later bishop of Gloucester, published *The Alliance between Church and State,* the most celebrated justification of what had become the Georgian ecclesiastical reality. His guiding principle was that "the more general the terms of communion are, and the wider the bottom is made (consistent with the well-being of a society), the wiser and juster is that institution."[98]

Warburton was describing a compromise which, though it provided for the retention of the Establishment, the Test Act, the Book of Common Prayer, and traditional articles, and left the clergy in possession of their benefices, also allowed Edward Gibbon to be an Anglican. For his part, Gibbon had only to acquiesce "with implicit belief in the tenets and mysteries which are adopted by the general consent of Catholics and Protestants." Despite the embarrassment of having men like Gibbon as coreligionists, most churchmen assured themselves that as long as Anglicanism retained the Test Act and the Prayer Book, it would keep its identity. Historians have ratified the verdict of contemporaries.[99]

By the 1730s two related movements had arisen in opposition to the compromise. As if anticipating the testimony of Henry Dodwell the Younger that the Boyle lectures had converted many to deism, a number of Anglicans concluded that the efforts of theologians like the Clarkes had had indifferent or even harmful results and began to flirt with less rationalist apologetics. The common-sense probabilism of Butler, the immaterialism of Berkeley, and the mysticism of Law were only the most obvious manifestations of the reconsideration, and it engaged lesser partisans as well, especially at Oxford. Among them was John Hutchinson, who influenced both John Wesley and George Whitefield. Although Bishop Gibson, the dominant figure on the episcopal bench, was not an active apologist, he had scant respect for the attempt to exploit the new science in defense of the church and her teachings.[100]

Even the younger generation of Anglican rationalists had doubts about the effectiveness of the apologetics which their predecessors had bequeathed to them. Thus, after confessing that he found formal argumentation to be vain, Sykes, Samuel Clarke's disciple, sought to justify his undoctrinal Christianity by a series of fideistic reflections. However much William Law shared Sykes's reservations about the efficacy of a supposedly demonstrative theology, he saw Christianity as a spiritual communion, whose members were bound together by shared doctrines and regular discipline.[101]

There is little evidence that this attempt at yet another counterrevolution was any more successful than the compromise either in answering the deists' critique or in regaining the adherence of individuals who were attracted to it. At mid-century informed observers were still complaining about declining church attendance among the better orders, and churchmen continued to publish occasional antideist tracts into the 1770s. The most distinguished spokesmen for antirationalism were often sceptical about the success of their own endeavors. When, for example, Butler was offered the primacy in 1747, he reportedly declined because he thought himself too feeble "to try to support a falling church." In retrospect, of course, his judgment seems hasty. Whatever its weaknesses, the Georgian compromise had preserved the Establishment and its temporalities. The rites of the cult of reason were never celebrated in Durham Cathedral.[102]

Among the remarkable effects which have been imputed to Methodism, the second of the religious reactions of the 1730s, few are more striking than its supposed undermining of deism. The theory that Wesley and Whitefield revivified the heart of a people who had fallen into indifference or scepticism may possess dramatic appeal, but it wants proving. Its exponents are vague about how their protagonists convinced Englishmen to discard the conceptions of reason and religion which had been the currency of intellectual exchange for nearly two generations.

Unlike Whitefield, Wesley was a man of considerable personal culture, but he was also quite anti-intellectual. Indeed, he appears to have been under no illusion about his ability to combat deism: "So I am convinced I could not study, to any degree of perfection, either mathematics, arithmetic or algebra without being a Deist, if not an Atheist." While his disciples shared his attitudes, none of them approached his cultivation. Only rarely did Methodism attract the respectability who were most susceptible to reasoned arguments against traditional Christianity. Smollett's account of Mr. Bramble's response to the preaching of his servant, Humphrey Clinker, rings true: " 'In a word, Mr. Clinker, I will have no light in my family but what pays the king's taxes. Unless it be the light of reason, which you don't pretend to follow.' "[103] Whatever effect Methodism may have had on English history, it did not persuade sophisticated Anglicans to abandon the gentlemanly religion which the Latitudinarians had fashioned for them.

Anglicans clung to the Georgian civil religion well into the next century. In 1836, three years after John Keble's assize sermon at Oxford had begun another religious reaction, large numbers of churchmen were concerned about what seemed to be an obscurantist—perhaps even popish—threat to their inherited beliefs. Instinctive Erasmians, many of them sought to defend their creed by returning to its sources. Anticipating Lord Shaftesbury's foundation of the Parker Society, some divines secured royal patronage to edit and publish *The Sacred Classics: Or, Cabinet Library of Divinity* in order to make the great works of Protestantism readily available. Among these classics was John Locke's *Reasonableness of Christianity,* whose message appeared to be urgent. Having discovered the bankruptcy of "the ordinary systems of divinity," Locke turned to the Bible, which taught "doctrines clear and intelligible, and adapted to the apprehension of the bulk of mankind." He scorned clerics who, overlooking the precepts of Christianity, "dwell upon its mysteries, and seem desirous of setting faith and reason in opposition to each other." He had foreseen that they were bound to arrogate infallibility to themselves in order to impose their own point of view.[104]

Locke's anonymous admirer thus depicted him as the engineer of a Protestant *via media,* running between the extremes of scepticism and superstition. This image of moderation proved to be at least as alluring as that which Newman had painted and discarded. A half-century later John Cairns, one of the Kirk's pontiffs, compared the history of eighteenth-century scepticism in England and France and reached a conclusion with which Anthony Collins might have been in sympathy: "A France victoriously unbelieving; a France victoriously Romanist; who dares face either alternative? Must the extremes not almost by this time despair of success? Is not their meeting-point prepared in that evangelical Protestantism, which, alas! they alike despise?"[105]

The deist controversy was an episode in the history of the Latitudinarian endeavor to create a generally acceptable theological position. Though liberal antideists published congruous, if uncoordinated, responses to the writings of men like John Toland, their publications did not constitute a refutation of the deism of the textbooks. They were essentially unoriginal; their elements were either manifest or implicit in works which had appeared during Toland's childhood. In fact, he himself depended on these books both in his critique of the Christian poetical theology and in his own civil theology. Nevertheless, Toland and other freethinkers did affect Anglican thought. By forcing the articulate church to recognize the nature and to accommodate some of the implications of what had become its guiding principles, they helped it to develop a more stable consensus. The Anglican rationalists would inevitably have had to adjust to the consequences of embracing Lockianism, reinterpreting biblicism, and subordinating dogma to morality. Pressure from the deists hastened the period of this adjustment.

Though Mark Pattison attributed unwarranted intellectual coherence to deism, he realized that for two generations Anglican rationalists, Unitarians, and deists were engaged in a theological conversation. Like all conversations, it required of participants a commitment to shared presuppositions and a common discourse. Asperity often marked their exchanges, but they seldom displayed incomprehension and never achieved conclusiveness. Both churchmen and freethinkers were continually changing their minds. Less adaptive disputants increasingly found themselves excluded, and interlopers were usually ignored. Having resigned themselves to the impossibility of victory, those who sustained the enterprise seem to have sensed that convergence should be enjoyed rather than ratified. When speaking of religion, Augustan gentlemen followed the advice which John Toland ascribed to the first earl of Shaftesbury and learned never to tell.[106]

Epilogue

Ce moment capital des définitions et des conventions
nettes et spéciales qui viennent remplacer les significations d'origine confuse et statistique n'est pas ar-
rivé pour l'histoire.

Paul Valéry

The ease with which a projected intellectual portrait of John Toland
has expanded into a crowd scene populated by diverse Augustan
pamphleteers, theologians, and philosophers suggests that *deism* is a
word with an uncertain past. This transformation need not, however,
deny the word a useful future. *Deism* fills a need that historians of the
seventeenth and eighteenth centuries feel as acutely as did the Boyle
lecturers who popularized it. Scholars require a convenient term to
describe the revision of traditional Christian formulas which occupied
so many English writers between the Civil War and the French
Revolution. Habit is powerful enough to ensure that they will continue
to use deism, rather than an alternative like freethinking or rational
theology.

While an attempt to proscribe the word would be futile, Toland's experience implies it must be construed broadly. The history of the diffusion of new ideas about the meaning of theological mysteries and
religious assent illustrates the necessity of such a construction. The
Unitarians who wrote under the patronage of Thomas Firmin were the
first Englishmen to advance these conceptions. They asserted that a
mystery was a proposition which, though it may have been indistinct
before Christianity, was now comprehensible; it followed that a
believer was excused from assenting to any tenet of which he could not
form a clear and distinct idea. Generally ignored, these Socinians have
not been treated as deists. Toland based *Christianity Not Mysterious* on
these two propositions, but his book is still taken as the starting-point of
the deist controversy. In contrast, although John Clarke, the
Latitudinarian dean of Salisbury, used both of them axiomatically in
his Boyle lectures of 1720 and 1721, he is commonly held to have contributed to the church's refutation of the deists.

Remonstrants, Unitarians, and deists may have introduced these notions, but most Anglican rationalists eventually adapted to them. Moreover, liberal churchmen became increasingly convinced that natural religion, a series of propositions and injunctions accessible to unaided human reason, provided the criterion of religious truth. They, too, were participants in an uncoordinated retreat from biblicism and intrusive supernaturalism. Far from weakening their preoccupation with morality, the hostility of their High-Church confreres only strengthened their distaste for clericalism and dogmatism.

Still, convergence is not conjunction. If there are important similarities between Toland and some more reputable writers, there are also irreducible differences between him and his fellow-deists. In his critique of Christian orthodoxy, Toland systematically developed arguments which Socinians had broached and Anglican rationalists were to accommodate. At the same time he was the only putative deist who openly embraced a coherent materialism. The continued use of deism as a category requires that it be divested of excessive analytic pretensions and treated as a flexible verbal convention. Somehow it must allow for a variety of similarities and differences between—and within—the writings of individual deists.

If unchecked by the inventive application of modifiers, such an enterprise would soon deteriorate into the arbitrariness of Humpty-Dumpty: "When I use a word . . . it means what I choose it to mean—neither more nor less." The historiography of Marxism provides a model of the supple application of a philosophical concept to varying situations. It would be unthinkable to exclude Bernstein, Kautsky, or Luxemberg from an account of early twentieth-century Marxist theory. Yet were such a history to overlook either the agreements and disagreements among them on the one hand or their particular evolutions on the other, it would be less than helpful. Whether revisionist, orthodox, or radical, all of them remain Marxists.

Divines such as John and Samuel Clarke may have shared assumptions and propositions with Unitarians and deists, but these points of contact did not interfere with their churchmanship. Engaged in ordering the Tillotsonian heritage, they labored from within to reconcile the church's inherited doctrinal comprehensiveness with what appeared to them to be the requirements of modern thought. While their suggestions did not invariably become writ, by the middle of the eighteenth century the evidence for the success of their effort was overwhelming.

Leslie Stephen sometimes playfully referred to Samuel Clarke as a

"Christian deist." Thereby, he not only coined a *mot juste,* but he may also have anticipated a typology which recognizes the affinities among Unitarians, deists, and Latitudinarians without denying their differences of intention, approach, and style. If Samuel Clarke and the other heirs of Archbishop Tillotson are to be identified as Christian deists, is it not possible to term most of the Socinians, as well as those who acquiesced in the settlement the later Anglican rationalists created, "conforming deists"? Further, might not the simple label *deist* be reserved for Toland and the equally unruly sceptics who followed him? While the last group sometimes conceded that institutional religion was a necessary integument of society, their temperaments led them to chafe under even the gossamer woven by the Christian deists. Increasingly, they chafed alone. Besides ratifying the collapse of the High-Church counterrevolution, Benjamin Hoadly's victory pre-empted the appeal which Toland's successors might otherwise have enjoyed. As long as the leaders of an agrarian and hierarchical society are able to concur, articulate radicals will tend to be ignored.

Such modifications need not exclude the impersonal figures of a watch-universe and its maker which dominate textbook accounts of deism. During the night of 23 November 1654, Pascal conceived a vision of the "God of Abraham and Isaac" which filled him with contempt for the "God of philosophers." Since this experience left Pascal in his body with his mind intact, he had to attempt to reconcile the God of his personal revelation with the God who seemed to be accessible to objective reason. In England throughout the next century Christian, conforming, and unadorned deists faced a similar task, but their sense of the demands of a personal God was usually less urgent than their sense of the obligations which were theirs as reasonable beings. Their deity was less hidden than detached. The theoretical pantheism of John Toland does not undermine this generalization. Since he lacked a compelling vision of the whole, Toland found no immediacy in a deity whose omnipresence required that He be in everything and that everything be in Him.

Final consensus does not preclude intermediate discords. The columns of Toland's works and their refutations in the *British Library Catalogue of Printed Books* are relics of one such controversy. Toland was a gadfly who, by causing temporary discomfort, helped to determine the shape of the succeeding order. Historians ignore such gadflies at their peril. Even though his esoterism was without immediate influence, both his critique of traditional Christianity and his civil theology had some effect. His astute organization and remorseless urging of the Unitarians' arguments so stung those churchmen who were becoming Christian deists that they undertook to size again the fibers which they were weaving into England's new ecclesiastical investment. If the covering was to be adequate — if it was to envelop but not constrict society while itself remaining whole — it had to be flexible enough to adapt to pressures from the articulate orders. Divines had, moreover, to adjust to the goals of Toland's civil theology. Though disinclined to tamper with the church's existing arrangements, many responsible Englishmen shared his desire to identify Christianity with morality and to subjugate the Establishment to the crown. Historians in search of Toland's monument will find it in Georgian Anglicanism.

Abbreviations

Bodl.	Bodleian Library, Oxford.
B.L.	British Library, London.
HMC	Historical Manuscripts Commission.
JT	John Toland.
JT/AG	[John Toland], *The Art of Governing by Partys,* etc. (London, 1701).
JT/AL	John Toland, *Anglia Libera,* etc. (London, 1701).
JT/C	John Toland, *A Collection of Several Pieces of Mr. John Toland,* etc. [ed. Pierre Des Maizeaux], 2 vols. (London, 1726).
JT/CNM	[John Toland], *Christianity Not Mysterious,* etc. (London, 1696).
JT/LM	[John Toland], *The Life of John Milton* [1698], in Helen Darbishire, ed., *The Early Lives of Milton* (London, Constable, 1932).
JT/LS	John Toland, *Letters to Serena,* etc. (London, 1704).
JT/MR	[John Toland], *The Militia Reformed,* etc. (London, 1698).
JT/N	John Toland, *Nazarenus,* etc. (London, 1718).
JT/P	[John Toland], *Pantheisticon, sive formula celebrandae sodalitatis Socraticae,* etc. [1720], Eng. trans. (London, 1751).
JT/SA	[John Toland], *The State-Anatomy of Great Britain,* etc. (London, 1717).
JT/T	John Toland, *Tetradymus,* etc. (London, 1720).
JT/VL	John Toland, *Vindicius Liberius,* etc. (London, 1702).
L.P.L.	Lambeth Palace Library, London.
O.N.B.	Oesterreichische Nationalbibliothek, Vienna.
P.R.O.	Public Record Office, London.
S.U.K.	Spencer Research Library, University of Kansas, Lawrence.
T.C.D.	Trinity College Library, Dublin.

Notes

1. John Toland: A Portrait

1. *Remarks and Collections of Thomas Hearne,* 11 vols. (Oxford, Clarendon Press, 1885-1921), XI, 395 (23 Nov. 1734). John Toland, *Nazarenus,* etc. (London, 1718), p. xvii.

2. [Pierre Des Maizeaux], "Some Memoirs of His [Toland's] Life and Writings," in John Toland, *A Collection of Several Pieces of Mr. John Toland,* etc. [ed. Pierre Des Maizeaux], 2 vols. (London, 1726), I, iv.

3. E.g., JT to Goode, 30 Oct. 1720, B.L. Add. MS. 4295, ff. 39-40.

4. Gardiner to Charlett, 22 Apr. 1701, Bodl. Ballard MSS. XX, f. 16.

5. B.L. Add. MS. 4295, ff. 76-77 (undated fragment).

6. Urban G. Thorschmid, *Vollständige engländische Freydenker Bibliothek,* etc., 3 vols. (Cassel, 1765-1766), III, 6-7. The confusion arises from JT's differing selections for a date of birth. He referred to 30 Nov. 1670 most frequently. Cf. Gibson to Charlett, 21 June 1694, Bodl. Ballard MSS. V, f. 48, and Bodl. Rawlinson MSS. D. 923, f. 317; John O'Donovan, ed. and trans., *Annals of the Kingdom of Ireland, by the Four Masters,* etc., 7 vols. (Dublin, 1851), I, 146-147n.

7. E.g., *Bibliothèque germanique* 6 (1723), 25.

8. Marginal note in JT's copy of Martin Martin, *A Description of the Western Islands of Scotland* (London, 1716), p. 71 (B.L. 806. a. 23); Des Maizeaux, "Some Memoirs," p. vii. [John Toland], *Christianity Not Mysterious,* etc. (London, 1696), p. ix.

9. [Charles Davenant], *Tom Double Return'd Out of the Country,* etc. (London, 1702), pp. 69-71; Gibson to Charlett, 21 June 1694, Bodl. Ballard MSS. V, f. 48.

10. James Coutts, *A History of the University of Glasgow* (Glasgow, J. Maclehose, 1909), pp. 162-212.

11. JT, marginal note in Martin, *Description,* p. 298; *Remarks on the Life of Mr. Milton,* etc. (London, 1699), pp. 9-10; Bodl. Rawlinson MSS. D. 923, f. 317. J. L. Mosheim, *De vita, fatis, et scriptis Joannis Tolandi commentatio,* in *Vindiciae antiquae Christianorum disciplinae,* etc. 2d ed. (Hamburg, 1722), p. 6; Thomas Mangey, *Remarks upon Nazarenus,* etc. (London, 1718), pp. 21-22.

12. Fall to Dunlop, 10 Nov. 1697, National Library of Scotland MS. 9251, ff. 150-151; *A Catalogue of the Graduates in the Faculties of Arts, Divinity, and Law of the University of Edinburgh* (Edinburgh, 1858), pp. 137-138. Gibson to Charlett, 21 June 1694, Bodl. Ballard MSS. V, f. 48. Peter Browne, *A Letter in Answer to a Book,* etc. (Dublin, 1697), p. 148; cf. John Toland, *An Apology for Mr. Toland,* etc. (London, 1697), pp. 11-13.

13. Bodl. Rawlinson MSS. D. 923, f. 317.

14. A. B. Worden, ed., *Edmund Ludlow, A Voyce from the Watch Tower: Part Five, 1660-1662,* Camden ser. 4, vol. 21 (London, Royal Historical Society, 1978), pp. 34-36, attributes four pamphlets published between 1691 and 1693 to JT. Roger Thomas, "Presbyterians in Transition," in C. G. Bolam, Jeremy Goring, et al., *The English Presbyterians: From Elizabethan Puritanism to Modern Unitarianism* (London, G. Allen & Unwin, 1968), pp. 120-126.

15. [John Toland], "An Abstract of Dr. Daniel Williams' *The Gospel Truth,*" *Bibliothèque universelle* 23 (1692), 504–524. Dr. Williams' Library MS. Minutes, M. 82–83, record payments on 12 Dec. 1692 and 19 June 1693.

16. Alexander Gordon, ed., *Freedom after Ejection: A Review (1690–1692) of Presbyterian and Congregational Nonconformity in England and Wales* (Manchester, University Press, 1917), pp. 182–183.

17. John Toland, *Tetradymus,* etc. (London, 1720), p. 160; Olive M. Griffiths, *Religion and Learning: A Study in English Presbyterian Thought* (Cambridge, University Press, 1935), pp. 61–62. [John Toland], *The Description of Epsom,* etc. (London, 1711), p. 9.

18. Mosheim, *De vita,* p. 35. Hendrika J. Reesink, *L'Angleterre et la littérature anglaise dans les trois plus anciens périodiques français en Hollande,* etc. (Zutphen, W. J. Thieme, 1931), p. 106.

19. JT/N, p. iii. Le Clerc to Locke, 25 Aug. 1693, *Lettres inédites de Le Clerc à Locke,* ed. Gabriel Bonno (Berkeley, University of California Press, 1959), pp. 67–68; Locke to Limborch, 13 Jan. 1694 (N.S.), *The Works of John Locke,* ed. Edmund Law, new ed., 10 vols. (London, 1823), X, 35.

20. Lhwyd to Aubrey, 9 Jan. 1694 (N.S.), and to Lister, 13 Mar. 1694 (N.S.), in Robert W. T. Gunther, *Life and Letters of Edward Lhwyd,* Early Science in Oxford, vol. 14 (Oxford, privately printed, 1945), pp. 217, 232. Gibson to Charlett, 23 July 1694, Bodl. Ballard MSS. V, ff. 50, 58.

21. Gibson to Charlett, 23 July 1694, Bodl. Ballard MSS. V, ff. 50, 58. JT to _____, Jan. 1694 [N.S.?], in JT/C, II, 293; John Aubrey, *Miscellanies upon Various Subjects* (London, 1890), pp. 28–29.

22. Gibson to Charlett, 9 Apr. 1694, Bodl. Ballard MSS. V, f. 27, and Charlett to Tenison, 25 Oct. 1695, L.P.L. Cod. MS. Gibson 942, f. 110. _____ to JT, 4 May 1694, in JT/C, II, 295. JT to _____, n.d., *ibid.,* 307; _____ to JT, 4 May 1694, *ibid.,* 296.

23. JT, "The Fabulous Death of Atilius Regulus," JT/C, II, 46. _____ to JT, 30 May 1694, *ibid.,* 312.

24. Charlett to Tenison, 25 Oct. 1695, L.P.L. Cod. MS. Gibson 942, f. 110. Lhwyd commended JT as a hatchet man (Lhwyd to Lister, n.d. [after Jan. 1694/95], in Gunther, *Life and Letters,* p. 278); he discounted rumors of JT's authorship of the *Two Essays.* Anthony à Wood (to Aubrey, n.d. [1695]) mentioned that JT "hath two letters published but never tells me of them" (J. Williams, "An Edition of the Correspondence of John Aubrey with Anthony à Wood and Edward Lhwyd, 1667–1696" [Ph.D. diss., University of London, 1969], p. 610). Cf. Giancarlo Carabelli, *Tolandiana: materiali bibliografici per lo studio dell'opera e della fortuna di John Toland (1670–1722)* (Florence, La nuova Italia, 1975), pp. 20–21, and Joseph M. Levine, *Dr. Woodward's Shield: History, Science and Satire in Augustan England* (Berkeley, University of California Press, 1977), pp. 37–38.

25. Charlett to Tenison, 25 Oct. 1695, L.P.L. Cod. MS. Gibson 942, f. 110; P.R.O. 30/24/21, no. 266. JT to _____, Jan. 1694, in JT/C, II, 294. Hinton to Charlett, 3 Jan. 1695 [N.S.], Bodl. Ballard MSS. XXXVIII, f. 4.

26. Locke to Freke, Feb. 1697, Bodl. Locke MSS. b.1, f. 188; John Toland, trans., *A Discourse upon Coins by Signor Bernardo Davanzati* (London, 1696) is a contribution to this effort; Locke's copy is in the Goldsmith's Library, University of London. Cf. Joyce O. Appleby, *Economic Thought and Ideology in Seventeenth-Century England* (Princeton, University Press, 1978), pp. 199–241.

27. JT to Rev. _____, 12 Sep. 1695, in JT/C, II, 314–317. John C. Biddle, "Locke's Critique of Innate Principles and Toland's Deism," *Journal of the History of Ideas*

37 (1976), 418–422, suggests that it was JT who immediately influenced Locke, if only by forcing him to tighten the exposition of his own thesis.

28. Burnet to Le Clerc, n.d. [ca. 1698], in Annie Barnes, *Jean Le Clerc (1657–1736) et la république des lettres* (Paris, E. Droz, 1938), pp. 256–257; Simpson to JT, 20 Apr. 1697, L.P.L. Cod. MS. Gibson 933, f. 55.

29. JT/CNM, p. 174. *The Post-Man,* no. 101, 28–31 Dec. 1695.

30. JT/CNM, p. xi. *The Post-Man,* no. 178, 27–30 June 1696.

31. Molyneux to Locke, 6 Apr. 1697, *Familiar Letters between Mr. John Locke and Several of His Friends,* etc., 4th ed. (London, 1742), pp. 150–151; Locke to Molyneux, 3 May 1697, *ibid.,* pp. 162–163; Molyneux to Locke, 27 May 1697, *ibid.,* pp. 169–170; Locke to Molyneux, 15 June 1697, *ibid.,* pp. 174–176; Molyneux to Locke, 20 July and 11 Sep. 1697, *ibid.,* pp. 178, 186.

32. Molyneux to Locke, 27 May 1697, *ibid.,* p. 171. "Ballad against Methuen to the Tune of 'Lillebullero,' " n.d., S.P. Dom. (Wm. III), 32/ll/76–77.

33. JT, *Apology,* p. 6; John Toland, *Anglia Libera,* etc. (London, 1701), pp. 164–165.

34. Simpson to JT, 20 Apr. 1697, L.P.L. Cod. MS. Gibson 933, f. 74.

35. *A Letter upon Mr. Toland's Book to I. C. Esquire* (Dublin, 1697), p. 4, cited in Mosheim, *De vita,* p. 76. Browne, *Letter,* p. 169.

36. William Coxe, ed., *Private and Original Correspondence of Charles Talbot, Duke of Shrewsbury,* etc. (London, 1821), pp. 555–557; J. G. Simms, *The Williamite Confiscation in Ireland, 1690–1703* (London, Faber and Faber, 1956), pp. 55–56; J. Roderick O'Flanagan, *The Lives of the Lord Chancellors . . . of Ireland,* 2 vols. (London, 1870), I, 491–494; James A. Froude, *The English in Ireland in the Eighteenth Century,* 3 vols. (London, 1872), I, 250–262.

37. T.C.D. MS. Collection relating to the Irish Convocation, f. 464. Lindesay to Charlett, 19 Oct. 1697, Bodl. Ballard MSS. VIII, f. 76; Leslie Stephen in the *DNB,* s.v. "Toland, John."

38. King to the bishop of Waterford, 5 Oct. 1697, T.C.D. King Papers N.3.1, ff. 96, 98. King to Tenison, 13 Oct. 1697, *ibid.,* f. 86.

39. John Toland, *A Defence of Mr. Toland, in a Letter to Himself* (London, 1697), p. 14; Robert South, *Twelve Sermons upon Several Subjects and Occasions* (London, 1698), dedication. [John Toland], *Pantheisticon, sive formula celebrandae sodalitatis Socraticae,* etc. [1720], Eng. trans. (London, 1751), p. 107.

40. Jean Gailhard, *The Epistle and Preface to the Book against the Blasphemous Socinian Heresie Vindicated,* etc., (London, 1698), p. 5; [Benjamin Gatton], *An Essay toward Comprehension,* etc. (London, 1701), pp. 14–15. [Stephen Nye], *The Agreement of the Unitarians with the Catholick Church* (London, 1697), p. 55.

41. John Toland, *Vindicius Liberius,* etc. (London, 1702), pp. 165–166, 84, 67.

42. Gilbert Burnet, *A History of His Own Time,* 2 vols., consecutive pag. (London, 1840), pp. 690–691.

43. JT to Phillips, 17 Aug. 1703, B.L. Add. MS. 4465, f. 3. The manuscript from which the Aikenhead proceedings were reconstructed belonged to Locke (Thomas B. Howell, ed., *A Complete Collection of State Trials and Proceedings for High Treason and Other Crimes and Dismeanors,* etc., 21 vols. [London, 1809–1828], XIII, 918–939).

44. *Remarks on Life,* p. 18. [John Toland], *The Life of John Milton,* etc. [1698], in Helen Darbishire, ed., *The Early Lives of Milton* (London, Constable, 1932), pp. 150–151. Des Maizeaux, "Some Memoirs," p. xlii. Vernon to the earl of Portland, 29 Apr. 1699, B.L. Add. MS. 40773, f. 333.

45. *Remarks on the Life,* pp. 24–25. H. R. Fox-Bourne, *The Life of John Locke,* 2 vols. (London, 1876), II, 416.

46. Cf. Jean Le Clerc, *Epistolae criticae, et ecclesiasticae,* etc. (Amsterdam, 1700), p. 72, and preface; Coste to Locke, 29 June 1699, Bodl. Locke MSS. c.7, f. 148. George Every, *The High-Church Party, 1688–1718* (London, S.P.C.K., 1956), p. 86. Burnet to Le Clerc, n.d. [1698?], in Fox-Bourne, *John Locke,* II, 416. Limborch to Locke, 3 Aug. 1699, and Locke to Limborch, 5 Sep. 1699, *Works of Locke,* X, 86–87; Gibson to Smith, 8 Apr. 1701, Bodl. Ballard MSS. VI, f. 51; JT/LM, p. 192.

47. Third earl to Ainsworth, 3 June 1709, in *The Life, Unpublished Letters, and Philosophical Regimen of . . . [the] Earl of Shaftesbury,* ed. Benjamin Rand (London, Sonnenschein, 1900), p. 405; fourth earl of Shaftesbury, "A Sketch of the Life of the Third Earl," *ibid.,* pp. xxiii–xxiv. As late as 21 July 1701, Shaftesbury referred to himself as JT's "Best and Truest Friend," (Shaftesbury to JT, P.R.O. 30/24/21, no. 231). See also JT to Shaftesbury, n.d. [1705], *ibid.,* no. 105, explaining how Shaftesbury could visit him "incognito."

48. Shaftesbury to Harley, 30 May 1711, HMC Reports, *Portland MSS.,* IV, 697–698. JT to Mr. _____, 26 June 1705, in JT/C, II, 345. JT, "Another Memorial [1711]," *ibid.,* 227.

49. JT/AL was dedicated to him, and JT trumpeted him at the Hanoverian court (Sophia to Newcastle, 10 Oct. 1710 [*sic*], HMC Reports, *Portland MSS.,* II, 180); Simpson to JT, 20 Apr. 1697, L.P.L Cod. MS. Gibson 933, f. 74. JT to Clayton, 4 Dec. 1698, in JT/C, II, 324. Tanner to Charlett, 6 May 1700, Bodl. Ballard MSS. IV, f. 53; John Toland, "An Exact Account of His [Harrington's] Life," in James Harrington, *The Oceana,* etc., ed. John Toland (London, 1700), pp. ii–iii. Kennett to Charlett, 25 Jan. 1700 [N.S.], Bodl. Ballard MSS. VII, f. 39.

50. J. P. Kenyon, *Revolution Principles: The Politics of Party, 1689–1720* (Cambridge, University Press, 1977), pp. 35–60. Gibson to Charlett, 9 Apr. 1694, Bodl. Ballard MSS. V, f. 27; [John Toland], *The Art of Governing by Partys,* etc. (London, 1701), pp. 149–150; JT, in *Oceana,* p. vii.

51. Henry Horwitz, *Parliament, Policy, and Politics in the Reign of William III* (Manchester, University Press, 1977), pp. 97–98, 214–215, 266, 316–317.

52. JT/AG, pp. 47–48, 112 [cf. the fine analysis, Kenyon, *Revolution Principles,* pp. 53–54], 34.

53. Cf. Horwitz, *Parliament, Policy, and Politics,* pp. 216, 237–238; J. G. A. Pocock, ed., *The Political Works of James Harrington* (Cambridge, University Press, 1977), p. 141; Kenyon, *Revolution Principles,* p. 101.

54. *A Brief Reply to the History of Standing Armies in England* (London, 1698), preface and pp. 24–25. [William Baron], *A Just Defence of the Royal Martyr,* etc. (London, 1699), preface, and Davenant, *Tom Double Return'd,* pp. 69f. [Edward Ward], *A Secret History of the Calves-Head Club,* etc., 2d ed. (London, 1703), p. 11 (cf. Robert J. Allen, *The Clubs of Augustan London* [Cambridge, Mass., Harvard University Press, 1933], pp. 56–69).

55. J. G. A. Pocock, *The Machiavellian Moment: Florentine Political Thought and the Atlantic Republican Tradition* (Princeton, University Press, 1975), p. 449.

56. JT to _____, n.d., in JT/C, II, 415; JT continued to use the Grecian as an address as late as 1703 (JT to Shaftesbury, 10 Mar. 1702 [O.S.], B.L. Add. MS. 7121, f. 62).

57. Worden (*Ludlow, Voyce,* p. 41) opts for collaboration, while Lois G. Schwoerer ("The Literature of the Standing Army Controversy," *Huntington Library Quarterly* 28 [1964–1965], 187–212) suspects not; Lois G. Schwoerer, *"No Standing Armies!": The Antiarmy Ideology in Seventeenth-Century England* (Baltimore, Johns Hopkins University Press, 1974), pp. 173–180.

58. Worden, *Ludlow, Voyce,* pp. 19–22, 38–42. Kenyon, *Revolution Principles,* p. 77.

59. Browne, *Letter,* pp. 176-177. *History of the Works of the Learned* 1 (1699), 737.

60. Pierre Bayle, *Dictionnaire historique et critique,* new augmented ed., 16 vols. (Paris, 1820), II, 1035-1036; Shaftesbury to Furly, 5 Aug. 1700, Thomas Forster, ed., *Original Letters of Locke, Algernon Sidney, and . . . Shaftesbury* (London, 1830), p. 105.

61. "Chapitre General des Chevaliers de la Jubilation," n.d. [ca. 1710], B.L. Add. MS. 4295, ff. 18-19. The best short treatment of the phenomenon is J. M. Roberts, *The Mythology of the Secret Societies* (New York, Scribners, 1972), pp. 15-57. Recent field reports of a pioneer explorer of this world include Margaret C. Jacob, *The Newtonians and the English Revolution, 1689-1720* (Ithaca, Cornell University Press, 1976), pp. 201-250, "Newtonianism and the Origins of the Enlightenment: A Reassessment," *Eighteenth-Century Studies* 11 (1977-1978), 1-25, and *The Radical Enlightenment: Pantheists, Freemasons, and Republicans* (London, G. Allen & Unwin, 1981), pp. 142-181.

62. B.L. Add. MS. 4295, f. 6. Harley to Tenison, 11 Aug. 1701, HMC Reports, *Bath/Longleat MSS.,* I, 53.

63. Shaftesbury to Furly, 21 July 1701, Forster, *Original Letters,* p. 146. JT/AL, pp. 72-73. Narcissus Luttrell, *A Brief Historical Relation of State Affairs from September 1678 to April 1714,* 6 vols. (Oxford, 1857), V, 100-101 (18 Oct. 1701). John Toland, *An Account of the Courts of Prussia and Hanover,* etc. (London, 1705), p. 64. JT/VL, pp. 151-153.

64. [John Toland], *Clito: A Poem on the Force of Eloquence* (London, 1700), p. iv. JT/AL, pp. 11-12. JT/AG, *passim.*

65. *Mr. Toland's Clito Dissected,* etc. (London, 1700), "The Publisher to the Reader." JT announced (The *Post-Man,* no. 902, 18-20 Nov. 1701) that the reports of parliamentary aspirations were false. JT/VL, pp. 82-83. [Edmund Curll], *An Historical Account of the Life and Writings of the Late Eminently Famous Mr. John Toland,* etc. (London, 1722), pp. 66-67. JT/VL, pp. 82-83, 159-160.

66. [John Toland?], *The Principle of the Protestant Reformation Explain'd, in a Letter of Resolution concerning Church-Communion* (London, 1704), pp. 22-23, 20, 24.

67. JT/VL, pp. 135-136. Leibniz to Sophia, 27 Dec. 1701, Onno Klopp, ed., *Correspondance de Leibniz avec l'électrice Sophie de Brunswick-Lunebourg,* 3 vols. (Hanover, 1874), II, 318. Abel Boyer, *The History of Queen Anne,* etc. (London, 1735), p. 20.

68. Thomas Sharp, *Life of John Sharp, D.D.,* etc., ed. T. Newcome, 2 vols. in 1 (London, 1825), 274-275.

69. Sophia to Leibniz, 22 Oct. 1701 and 1 Jan. 1702, Klopp, *Correspondance,* II, 293-294, 320. Leibniz to Burnet, n.d. [late 1701] and 27 Feb. 1702, *ibid.,* 271, 334; Leibniz to Platen, 29 July 1702, *ibid.,* 357-358. Leibniz to Burnet, 27 Feb. 1702, *ibid.,* 334. Sophia to Leibniz, 14 Jan. 1702, *ibid.,* 328.

70. Leibniz to Burnet, n.d., *ibid.,* 276.

71. Leibniz to Sophia, 9 Sep. 1702, *ibid.,* 362. Frances A. Yates, *The Rosicrucian Enlightenment* (London, Routledge and Kegan Paul, 1972), *passim;* Marjorie H. Nicolson, ed., *Conway Letters* (New Haven, Yale University Press, 1930), pp. 454-455; Frances A. Yates, *The Art of Memory* (Chicago, University Press, 1966), pp. 368-389. Margaret C. Jacob has suggested that JT belonged to an international, Masonic, secret society with branches in London, Amsterdam, and The Hague, devoted to the study and propagation of "Brunian" and "Spinozist" principles ("Newtonianism and the Origins of the Enlightenment," 12-25).

72. Cf. Adolphus W. Ward, *The Electress Sophia and the Hanoverian Succession* (London, Goupil, 1903), pp. 341-342, and Ragnhild Hatton, *George I: Elector and King* (Cambridge, Mass., Harvard University Press, 1978), p. 47. Giancarlo Carabelli, "John Toland e G. W. Leibniz: otto lettere," *Rivista critica di storia della filosofia* 29 (1974), 412-431.

73. Schütz to Leibniz, 30 June/11 July 1702, Klopp, *Correspondance*, II, 356–357. Leibniz to Platen, 29 July 1702, *ibid.*, 357–358; Leibniz to Sophia, n.d. [between 21 May and 29 June 1702], *ibid.*, 350–351; cf. Leibniz to Spanheim, 24 June 1702, *ibid.*, 352.

74. Leibniz to Platen, 29 July 1702, *ibid.*, 357–358. Sophia to Schütz, 29 June 1702, Richard Doebner, ed., *Briefe der Königin Sophie Charlotte von Preussen und der Kurfürstin Sophie von Hannover an hannoversche Diplomaten* (Leipzig, Hirzel, 1905), pp. 161–162.

75. Sophia to Leibniz, 16 and 17 Sep. 1702, Klopp, *Correspondance*, II, 367, 369. Leibniz to Sophia, 29 Sep. 1702, *ibid.*, 372. Sophia to Leibniz, 4 Oct. 1702, *ibid.*, 376.

76. Sophie-Charlotte to Bothmer, 30 Sep. 1702, Doebner, *Briefe*, pp. 20–21; J. P. Erman, *Mémoires pour servir à l'histoire de Sophie Charlotte reine de Prusse*, etc. (Berlin, 1801), pp. 203–211. Leibniz to Sophia, 29 Sep. and n.d. [20 Oct.] 1702, Klopp, *Correspondance*, II, 372, 379. Leibniz to Sophia, 29 Sep. 1702, and Sophia to Leibniz, 11 Nov. 1702, *ibid.*, 372, 384. Sophia to Leibniz, 27 Nov. 1702, *ibid.*, 402. Sophia to Leibniz, 4 Apr. 1703, *ibid.*, III, 25.

77. JT to [Harley], 26 June 1704, in JT/C, II, 345. Stratford to the second earl of Oxford, n.d., HMC Reports, *Portland MSS.*, VII, 441.

78. JT to Harley, 26 June 1705, in JT/C, II, 348. JT/AL, pp. 50–51; JT to Harley, 26 June 1705, in JT/C, II, 345–347. JT to Shaftesbury, 10 Mar. 1702 [O.S.?], and Shaftesbury to Halifax, n.d., B.L. Add. MS. 7121, ff. 61–62, 59–60.

79. Sophia to Leibniz, 11 Nov. 1702, Klopp, *Correspondance*, II, 384. JT to Harley, 26 June 1705, in JT/C, II, 346–347.

80. JT, "Project of a Journal," JT/C, II, 201–214. JT, *Principle*, pp. 24–25. JT to Harley, 26 June 1705, in JT/C, II, 338.

81. JT to Shaftesbury, n.d. [after 18 May 1704], P.R.O. 30/24/21, no. 237; JT to Harley, 16 May 1707, HMC Reports, *Portland MSS.*, IV, 408. James Drake, *A Memorial of the Church of England*, etc. (London, 1704), pp. 10–11; [John Toland], *The Memorial of the State of England, in Vindication of the Queen, the Church, and the Administration*, etc. (London, 1705), pp. 65–67. Stephen (*DNB*, s.v. "Toland, John") followed Des Maizeaux ("Some Memoirs," p. lix) in attributing it to Harley's prompting. Cf. [William Stephens?], *A Letter to the Author of the Memorial of the State of England* (London, 1705), p. 29, and JT, *Memorial*, p. 69.

82. Wentworth to Raby, 18 Aug. 1710, John Cartwright, ed., *The Wentworth Papers, 1705–1739* (London, 1883), pp. 136–137; Kenyon, *Revolution Principles*, p. 111. Pocock, *Machiavellian Moment*, p. 365; Geoffrey Holmes, *British Politics in the Age of Anne* (London, Macmillan, 1967), p. 259. Stephens to Shaftesbury, 26 Jan. 1705, P.R.O. 30/24/20, no. 111. _____ to Harley, 5 July 1704, HMC Reports, *Portland MSS.*, IV, 98.

83. JT to Harley, 28 Aug. 1705, B.L. Portland Loan 28/192, f. 269^V. Edmund Calamy, *An Historical Account of My Own Life . . . (1671–1731)*, ed. John T. Rutt, 2d ed., 2 vols. (London, 1830), II, 37–38. [Daniel Defoe], *A Short View of the Present State of the Protestant Religion in Britain*, etc. (Edinburgh, 1707), p. 34. Penn to Harley, 24 Aug. 1705, HMC Reports, *Portland MSS.*, IV, 230.

84. *Remarks on the Life*, p. 44; George Keith, *The Deism of William Penn, and His Brethren, Destructive to the Christian Religion, Exposed*, etc. (London, 1699); cf. William Penn, *The Sandy Foundation Shaken*, etc. (London, 1668), and William Penn, *A Key Opening the Way to Every Capacity*, etc. (London, 1692). Betters to JT, 16 May 1708, B.L. Add. MS. 4465, f. 14. For a tendencious view of Quaker rationalism, see [Charles Leslie], *A Parallel between the Faith and Doctrine of the Present Quakers, and That of the Chief Hereticks in All Ages of the Church* (London, 1700). Cf. JT/AG, p. 20, and JT, *Memorial*,

pp. 26–27. Note the repeated references to "Mr. P.," JT to _____, 14 Dec. 1705, in JT/C, II, 354–356. [John Toland], *The Second Part of the State Anatomy, etc. containing a Short Vindication of the Former Part* (London, 1717), pp. 74–78.

85. [JT] to [Harley], 28 Aug. 1705, HMC Reports, *Portland MSS.,* IV, 235–236. Shower to [Harley], 27 Oct. 1705, *ibid.,* p. 268. Curll *(Historical Account,* p. 40) refers to a suppressed *Defence of Her Majesty's Administration,* etc. (1705). JT to [Harley], 16 May 1707, HMC Reports, *Portland MSS.,* IV, 408.

86. Francis Hare, *The Difficulties and Discouragements Which Attend the Study of Scriptures in the Way of Private Judgment,* etc., 2d ed. (London, 1714), pp. 18–19. Charles Gildon, *The Deist's Manual: or, A Rational Enquiry into the Christian Religion,* etc. (London, 1705). Curll, *Historical Account,* pp. 68, 71.

87. JT, *Principle,* pp. 17–18. JT to Rev. Mr. _____, n.d., in JT/C, II, 375. JT to Tenison, 6 Mar. 1706/07, *ibid.,* p. 373, and 2 May 1707, L.P.L. Cod. MS. Gibson 930, f. 229.

88. Smith to Hearne, 23 Jan. 1706 [O.S.], Bodl. Rawlinson MSS. C. 146, f. 47. Note the silence about JT in [Charles Leslie], *The Second Part of the Wolf Stript of His Shepherd's Clothing* (London, 1707). Ayerst to Charlett, 26 Nov. 1707, Bodl. Ballard MSS. XXVII, ff. 37–38.

89. JT to Harley, 16 May 1707, HMC Reports, *Portland MSS.,* IV, 407–410.

90. Anthony Aufrere, ed., *The Lockhart Papers,* 2 vols. (London, 1817), I, 370–371. Cf. Smith to Hearne, 23 Jan. 1706, Bodl. Rawlinson MSS. C. 146, f. 47, and Edward Harley, "Large Account of the Revolution and Succession," B.L. Portland Loan 29/165, misc. 97. Harley to Tenison, 11 Aug. 1701, HMC Reports, *Bath/Longleat MSS.,* I, 53; cf. James A. Richards, *Party Propaganda under Queen Anne: The General Elections of 1707–1713* (Athens, Ga., University of Georgia Press, 1972), pp. 7–8, and Richard I. Cook, *Jonathan Swift as a Tory Pamphleteer* (Seattle, University of Washington Press, 1967), p. 99.

91. Defoe to Oxford, 19 June, 13 July 1711, and 15 Jan. 1712/13, HMC Reports, *Portland MSS.,* V, 13, 44–45, 263–264. JT, "Scheme, or Practical Model," JT/C, I, 448–474. John Toland, *A Philippick Oration to Incite the English against the French,* etc. (London, 1707), pp. i–ii; Smith to Hearne, 26 Jan. 1706, Bodl. Rawlinson MSS. C. 146, f. 47. JT, "Memorial for the Most Hon.," JT/C, II, 221. *Catalogue of the Harleian Manuscripts in the British Museum,* 4 vols. (London, 1808), II, 230, 235–236. Harley, "Autobiographical Fragment," B.L. Portland Loan, 29/26, f. 5.

92. Des Maizeaux, "Some Memoirs," p. lxi. Cf. Angus McInnes, *Robert Harley, Puritan Politician* (London, Gollancz, 1970), pp. 77–85, and the bishop of London to Harley, 10 Apr. 1707, HMC Reports, *Portland MSS.,* IV, 400. Cf. "Caracteres de plusieurs ministres de la cour d'Angleterre," Cartwright, *Wentworth Papers,* p. 132, and Raby to Harley, n.d. [1708?], and n.d. [attributed to Nov. 1707; probably Jan. 1708], HMC Reports, *Portland MSS.,* IX, 289. _____ to JT, 29 Nov. 1707, B.L. Add. MS. 4295, f. 13, and JT to Harley, 2 Sep. 1710 B.L. Portland Loan 29/196, f. 111.

93. JT, "Memorial for the Most Hon.," JT/C, II, 223–224.

94. Marlborough to Godolphin, 9/20 Dec. 1708, Henry L. Snyder, ed., *The Marlborough-Godolphin Correspondence,* 3 vols., consecutive pag. (Oxford, Clarendon Press, 1975), 1171; Marlborough to Godolphin, 2/13 Aug. 1708, and Godolphin to Marlborough, 8 Aug. 1708, *ibid.,* 1059, 1066; Godolphin to Marlborough, 30 Nov. 1708, *ibid.,* 1165. Compare xlvi–xlvii of the 1707 London edition of JT, *Philippick Oration,* with pp. xxxix–xl of the 1709 Amsterdam edition. Stratford to the 2d earl of Oxford, n.d., HMC Reports, *Portland MSS.,* VII, 441.

95. Worden, *Ludlow, Voyce,* p. 24. Netterville to [Harley], 14 Jan. [1707], HMC

Reports, *Portland MSS.*, VIII, 279. JT to [Oxford], n.d. [1712?], *ibid.*, V, 258–259. JT, "Another Memorial [1711]," JT/C, II, 227–231. Cf. J.A. Downie, *Robert Harley and the Press: Propaganda and Public Opinion in the Age of Swift and Defoe* (Cambridge, University Press, 1979), pp. 19–56, 80–100, 168.

96. JT, marginal note in Martin, *Description,* pp. 166–167. JT/AL, p. 183. Leibniz to Raby, 29 Dec. 1707, John M. Kemble, ed., *State Papers and Correspondence,* etc. (London, 1857), 462–463.

97. Des Maizeaux, "Some Memoirs," p. lxii; B.L. Add. MS. 4295, f. 15; D'Alais to Lewis, 11 Oct. 1707, HMC Reports, *Portland MSS.,* IV, 456. The bishop of Spiga to Sophia, 22 Oct. 1707, Kemble, *State Papers,* pp. 459–460. Howe to [Harley], 11 Oct. 1707, HMC Reports, *Portland MSS.,* IV, 456.

98. Ayerst to Charlett, 26 Nov. 1707, Bodl. Ballard MSS. XXVII, ff. 37–38; Raby to Leibniz, 17 Jan. 1708, Kemble, *State Papers,* p. 465. It lent plausibility to the recurrent charges that JT was a papal agent, e.g., *A Representation of the Present State of Religion,* etc. (Dublin, 1711), p. 4.

99. D'Alais to Lewis, 11 Oct. 1707, HMC Reports, *Portland MSS.,* IV, 456; cf. Leibniz to Raby, 29 Dec. 1707, Kemble, *State Papers,* pp. 462–463, and Des Maizeaux, "Some Memoirs," p. lxii.

100. Des Maizeaux, "Some Memoirs," p. lxv; Giuseppe Ricuperati, "Libertinismo e deismo a Vienna: Spinoza, Toland, e il 'Triregno,'" *Rivista storica italiana* 79 (1967), 630–647; "Varia Doctorum Vivorum de Jordano Bruno," O.N.B. MS. 10390, ff. 374–397; JT, "Catalogue of Books," JT/C, I, 381; JT, "Cicero Illustratus," *ibid.,* p. 231; JT to Höhendorff, 7 Mar. 1711, B.L. Add. MS. 4295, ff. 19–20; "Dissertations Diverses de M. Tolandus," O.N.B. MS. 10325.

101. JT, "Memorial for the Most Hon.," JT/C, II, 225.

102. Pierre-Daniel Huet, *Commentarius de rebus ad eum pertinentibus* (Amsterdam, 1718), pp. 412–413. JT to _____, Jan. 1708, in JT/C, II, 381–382.

103. Ayerst to Charlett, 31 Mar. 1708, Bodl. Ballard MSS. XXVII, f. 41. JT, *Account of the Courts,* pp. 2–3, 10, 49. Ayerst to Charlett, 31 Mar. 1708, Bodl. Ballard MSS. XXVII, f. 41. Raby to [Harley], n.d., HMC Reports, *Portland MSS.,* IX, 289. Raby to Leibniz, 17 Jan. 1708, Kemble, *State Papers,* p. 465. Lewis to Harley, 29 May 1708, HMC Reports, *Portland MSS.,* IV, 491, and Raby to Leibniz, 24 Apr. 1708, Kemble, *State Papers,* pp. 466–467. Leibniz to JT, 30 Apr. 1709, Klopp, *Correspondance,* III, 307.

104. Aubrey Rosenberg, *Tyssot de Patot and His Work, 1655–1738* (The Hague, Nijhoff, 1972), p. 16.

105. Geoffrey Holmes, *The Trial of Doctor Sacheverell* (London, Eyre, Methuen, 1973), p. 27. Cf. John Toland, *Mr. Toland's Reflections on Dr. Sacheverell's Sermon,* etc. (London, 1710), p. 12, and [John Toland], *High Church Display'd: Being a Compleat History of the Affair of Dr. Sacheverell,* etc. (London, 1711), pp. 54f. Cf. JT, *Mr. Toland's Reflections,* p. 15, and Holmes, *Trial of Sacheverell,* p. 78.

106. Holmes, *Trial of Sacheverell,* pp. 45, 101–104.

107. JT to Harley, [22 Aug. –]2 Sep. 1710, HMC Reports, *Portland MSS.,* IV, 572. Molesworth to Harley, 11 Oct. 1710, *ibid.,* p. 613, and Robert Molesworth, *The Principles of a Real Whig* [1711] (London, 1775); Wolfgang Dienemann, "A Bibliography of John Toland (1670–1722)" (Dip. in Librarianship thesis, University of London, 1953), p. 51. JT, *Second Part,* p. 8, and JT/T, pp. xx, xxii. D[rummond] to [Harley], [29 Nov. –]9 Dec. 1710, HMC Reports, *Portland MSS.,* IV, 637.

108. Holmes, *British Politics,* pp. 77, 210, 416. Note the Harley-inspired [Daniel Defoe], *The Secret History of the October Club: From Its Original to This Time* (London, 1711), a

sustained attack on party government; cf. Geoffrey Holmes, "The Attack on 'The Influence of the Crown' 1702–1716," *Bulletin of the Institute of Historical Research* 39 (1966), 62, and *British Politics*, pp. 82–115. JT to [Harley], 7 Dec. 1711, HMC Reports, *Portland MSS.*, V, 126–127.

109. JT, "Memorial for the Most Hon.," JT/C, II, 215–219, and JT to Harley, 3 Dec. 1711, HMC Reports, *Portland MSS.*, V, 120; JT, "Another Memorial [1711]," JT/C, II, 233. JT to [Oxford], n.d. [late 1711?], HMC Reports, *Portland MSS.*, V, 258–260; JT to Oxford, 6 June 1711, B.L. Portland Loan 29/197, ff. 211–211^V. _____ to Oxford, n.d., *ibid.*, 162, f. 5.

110. JT to Oxford, 7 Dec. 1711, B.L. Portland Loan, 29/198, no f. JT to [Oxford], n.d. [late 1711?], HMC Reports, *Portland MSS.*, V, 260; see *The Examiner*, no. 40, 3 May 1711, for Swift's attacks on the Whigs for the "publick Encouragement and Patronage they gave to *Tindall, Toland*, and other atheistical Writers." Molesworth to his wife, 3 May 1712, HMC Reports, *Various MSS.*, VIII, 257.

111. Arminius to JT, 22 Sep. 1712, B.L. Add. MS. 4295, f. 27; JT to Mr. _____, n.d. [late 1712?], in JT/C, II, 428–430; [John Toland], *Dunkirk or Dover*, etc. (London, 1713), p. 14. JT to Mr. _____, 27 Jan. 1713/14, in JT/C, II, 431–433.

112. Pelkum to Oxford, 9–20 Apr. 1714, HMC Reports, *Portland MSS.*, V, 412–413. A diagnosis of this breakdown, *Hannibal Not at Our Gates: or, An Enquiry into the Grounds of Our Present Fears of Popery and the Pre—der*, etc. (London, 1714), manages to be partisan and pertinent. [John Toland], *The Grand Mystery Laid Open*, etc. (London, 1714), pp. 4–6, 26–27; [John Toland], *Characters of the Court of Hannover*, etc. (London, 1714), p. 6. [John Toland], *The Art of Restoring*, etc. (London, 1714), pp. 7–12. JT to Mr. _____, 22 Jan. 1713/14, in JT/C, II, 431. Thomas Bradbury, *Eikon Basilike*, etc. (London, 1715), pp. 20–21. The only extant defense appears to be William Webster, *The Life of General Monk: Late Duke of Albermarle*, etc. (London, 1723) xxiii–xxiv. Boyer, *Queen Anne*, p. 661.

113. JT, *Epsom*, p. 32; JT to Mr. _____, 22 Jan. 1713/14 [*sic*], in JT/C, II, 432.

114. [John Toland], *The State-Anatomy of Great Britain*, etc. (London, 1717), pp. 44–45. JT, "Memorial Presented to a Minister of State," JT/C, II, 257. JT to _____, n.d., in *ibid.*, pp. 429–430; John Dunton, *Mordecai's Memorial: or, There Is Nothing for Him* [1716], in *The Life of Errors and John Dunton*, 2 vols. (London, 1818), II, 730–735. JT/N, p. xiv.

115. *Nouvelles littéraires* 1 (14 Sep. 1715), pp. 167–168; Gwyn to Hearne, 18 June 1718, *Hearne's Collections*, VI, 198. *The Monitor*, no. 2, 24 Apr. 1714.

116. JT/SA, p. 4. JT/T, pp. vii–viii, 199f. [John Toland], *A Short Essay on the Art of Lying*, etc. (London, 1720), pp. 3, 14, 16.

117. JT, *Mr. Toland's Reflections*, p. 13, and [John Toland,] *An Appeal to Honest People against Wicked Priests*, etc. (London, n.d. [1713?], p. 36; JT/SA, p. 43, and JT, *Short Essay*, pp. 6–7. *Reasons against Repealing the Occasional and Test Acts*, etc. (London, 1718), pp. 70–71; [Thomas Dawson], *An Introduction to the Bishop of Bangor's Intended Collection of Authorities*, etc. (London, 1718), pp. vi–vii; Mangey, *Remarks upon Nazarenus*, p. 4; James Paterson, *Anti-nazarenus by Way of Answer to Mr. Toland*, etc. (London, 1718), pp. 70–71. Cf. JT/T, pp. 182–183, and JT to Mr. _____, 21 May 1721, in JT/C, II, 477.

118. [Richard Fiddes], *Remarks on the State Anatomy of Great Britain*, etc. (London, 1717), pp. 5–6, and JT, *Second Part*, p. 9; JT to Mr. C___, 26 Jan. 1718/19, in JT/C, II, 445–448, and Des Maizeaux, "Some Memoirs," p. lxxxviii. B.L. Add. MS. 4295, ff. 34 (29 Mar. 1720), 35 (10 Sep. 1720), and 37–38 (25 Oct. 1720); JT, marginal note in Martin, *Description*, p. 147.

119. Robert M. Adams, "The Mood of the Church and *A Tale of a Tub,*" in *England in the Restoration and Early Eighteenth Century: Essays on Culture and Society,* ed. H. T. Swedenberg (Berkeley, University of California Press, 1972), p. 83.

120. John Nichols, ed., *Literary Anecdotes of the Eighteenth Century,* 9 vols. (London, 1812-1815), VIII, 293-304; Isaac D'Israeli, *The Calamities of Authors,* 2 vols. (New York, 1881), I, 140-141.

121. See the account of 21 Sep. 1720, B.L. Add. MS. 4295, f. 36; Molesworth to JT, 25 June 1720, and JT to Molesworth, 25 June 1720, in JT/C, II, 463, 464-466; JT to Molesworth, [Jan. 1721 (N.S.)], B.L. Add. MS. 4465, f. 23.

122. JT, marginal note in Martin, *Description,* p. 51. Charles B. Realey, *The London Journal and Its Authors* (Lawrence, University of Kansas Press, 1931), pp. 4-5; JT, "Letter Written in the Name," JT/C, II, 469-475.

123. JT/SA, pp. 38, 44-45.

124. JT, *Second Part,* p. 30. JT, "Memorial Presented to a Minister of State," JT/C, II, 256; JT/SA, pp. 40, 10, 95.

125. [John Toland, ed.], *Letters from the R.H. Late Earl of Shaftesbury, to Robert Molesworth,* etc. (London, 1721), and [John Toland and Anthony Ashley-Cooper, earl of Shaftesbury], *The Danger of Mercenary Parliaments* [1698] (London, 1722), were published with Molesworth's assistance; they assert the existence of a kind of Commonwealth apostolic succession. JT to Mr. _____, 16 Mar. 1720, in JT/C, II, 453-457. Molesworth to John Molesworth, HMC Reports, *Various MSS.,* VIII, 312-313; cf. Quentin Skinner, "The Principles and Practice of Opposition: The Case of Bolingbroke versus Walpole," in *Historical Perspectives: Studies in English Thought and Society in Honour of J. H. Plumb,* ed. Neil McKendrick (London, Europa, 1974), pp. 94-110, and Isaac Kramnick, *Bolingbroke and His Circle: The Politics of Nostalgia in the Age of Walpole* (Cambridge, Mass., Harvard University Press, 1968), pp. 252-260.

126. [Daniel Defoe], *An Argument Proving that the Design of Employing and Ennobling Foreigners,* etc. (London, 1717), p. 50; [Daniel Defoe], *A Further Argument against Ennobling Foreigners,* etc. (London, 1717), p. 22.

127. Thoresby to JT, 12 Oct. 1715, in JT/C, II, 439-440; Chamberlayne to JT, 21 June 1718, B.L. Add. MS. 4295, ff. 27-28. Brampton Gurdon, *The Pretended Difficulties in Natural or Reveal'd Religion No Excuse for Infidelity: Sixteen Sermons Preached . . . In the Years 1721 and 1722,* etc., in *A Defence of Natural and Revealed Religion,* etc., [ed. Sampson Letsome and John Nicholl] 3 vols. (London, 1739), III, 315.

128. King to Molesworth, 10 and 29 Sep. 1720, T.C.D. King Papers N.3.6., ff. 117-119, 124-125. JT/P, pp. 98-101.

129. JT/P, preface; JT, *Short Essay,* pp. 18-19. JT, "Physick without Physicians," JT/C, II, 273-291.

130. Molesworth to JT, 5 Jan., n.d., 8 Feb., and 1 Mar. 1722 [N.S.], in JT/C, II, 484-485, 485-486, 489-490; JT to Molesworth, 28 Jan., n.d., and 2 Mar. 1722 [N.S.], *ibid.,* 487-488, 491-492, 494-495. Anon. ltr., 11 Mar. 1721/22, in *The Daily Journal,* no. 355, 13 Mar. 1721/22.

131. *Hearne's Collections,* VII, 343 (27 Mar. 1722). *The Freeholder's Journal,* no. 9, 21 Mar. 1721 [O.S.].

132. Description conflates JT, *Discourse upon Coins,* p. v, and JT, in *Oceana,* p. xliii. Paul Hazard, *European Thought in the Eighteenth Century: From Montesquieu to Lessing,* trans. J. Lewis May (New Haven, Yale University Press, 1954), pp. 249-276.

133. [John Toland, trans.], *The Fables of Aesop* (London, 1704), dedication, and [John Toland, trans.], *The Art of Canvassing at Elections,* etc. (London, 1714), p. v. JT to

Goode, 30 Oct. 1720, B.L. Add. MS. 4295, ff. 39–40; JT, *Second Part,* pp. 47f. JT, "Memorial for the Most Hon.," JT/C, II, 215–219.

134. Apistodemon and Simpson to JT, 1 June and 20 Apr. 1697, L.P.L. Cod. MS. Gibson, 933, ff. 55, 74. Smith to Hearne, 23 Jan. 1706 [O.S.], Bodl. Rawlinson MSS. C. 146, f. 47.

135. JT to _____, n.d., in JT/C, II, 301; JT, *Appeal to Honest People,* p. 43. JT/N, Second letter, p. 57; note his assertion of a thorough knowledge of the ante-Nicene fathers, JT/T, p. xvi; in a footnote (*ibid.,* p. 368 [*sic*]), he tries to pass himself as expert in Italian, German, Dutch, Hebrew, Greek, and Arabic.

136. JT to Southwell, n.d. [1718], B.L. Add. MS. 4465, f. 13; JT to the bishop of London, n.d., L.P.L. Cod. MS. Gibson 943, f. 8. Kennett to Charlett, 2 and 10 Apr. 1701, Bodl. Ballard MSS. VII, ff. 94–98. Ayerst to Charlett, 26 Nov. 1707, *ibid.,* XXVII, ff. 37–38.

137. Cf. JT/P, pp. 9–10, and JT, *Epsom,* pp. 30–31. JT, marginal note in Martin, *Description,* p. 58. JT, "On Reading Mr. Row's Fair Penitent," Apr. 1703, B.L. Add. MS. 4465, f. 4. JT to Mrs. D____, n.d., in JT/C, II, 360–362. JT, "Directions for Breeding," *ibid.,* p. 23.

138. JT to Mr. _____, 9 Feb. 1710 [O.S.], in JT/C, II, 404.

139. JT, *Epsom,* pp. 13–14; JT, marginal note in Martin, *Description,* p. 7.

140. JT/N, Appendix, p. 2; JT, *Account of the Courts,* p. 39. JT, "Account of Jordano Bruno's Book," JT/C, I, 318.

141. JT, *Clito,* p. 7. As the remark that Cicero's writing style flowed like a speech (JT, "Cicero Illustratus," JT/C, I, 291) suggests, he saw writing as an extension of speech by other means. JT/SA, p. 58. JT, "Roman Education," JT/C, II, 4. John Toland, *Christianity Not Mysterious,* etc., 2d ed. (London, 1696), p. 171.

142. Leo Strauss, *Persecution and the Art of Writing* (Glencoe, Free Press, 1952), pp. 22–37. For a recent attempt to adduce JT's work as evidence of the pervasiveness of "secret writing," see Frederick Vaughan, *Political Theory* 4 (1976), 371–372. Günter Gawlick, ed., *Letters to Serena,* by John Toland (Stuttgart, F. Fromann Verlag, 1964), pp. 5*–23*. Bernard to Des Maizeaux, n.d., B.L. Add. MS. 4286, f. 100. John Leland, *A View of the Principal Deistical Writers,* 3 vols. (London, 1754–1756), I, iii.

143. Cf. Thomas Brett, *Tradition Necessary to Explain and Interpret the Holy Scriptures,* etc. (London, 1718), p. ii, and Browne, *Letter,* p. 83; William Carroll, *A Dissertation upon the Tenth Chapter of . . . Mr. Locke's Essay concerning Human Understanding,* etc. (London, 1706), pp. 274–292. *Nouvelles de la république des lettres,* Aug. 1701, pp. 199–200. JT/AG, p. 2.

144. JT/T, pp. vi-vii, 46.

145. Collins to Des Maizeaux, 26 Apr. 1717, B.L. Add. MS. 4282, ff. 127–128.

146. Edmund Wilson, *Axel's Castle: A Study in the Imaginative Literature of 1870–1930* (New York, Scribners, 1931), p. 88. JT, "Specimen of the Critical History," JT/C, I, 30–31. JT/T, p. iv, and JT/N, Appendix, p. 16.

147. JT/CNM, p. iv. JT, *Defence,* p. 8; cf. [John Toland and Anthony Ashley-Cooper, earl of Shaftesbury], *Paradoxes of State,* etc. (London, 1702).

148. JT/SA, p. 23; JT/T, pp. 36–37. JT/LM, p. 195; JT/AG, pp. 43–44. JT/N, First letter, pp. 2–3.

149. JT, "Catalogue of Books," JT/C, I, 350–453. [John Toland], *The Reasons and Necessity of the Duke of Cambridge's Coming,* etc. (London, 1714), p. 15; JT, *Second Part,* p. 17. JT/T, pp. 163–164. [John Toland, trans], *The Agreement of the Customs of the East-Indians, with Those of the Jews, and Other Ancient People,* etc. (London, 1705); [John Toland], *A Letter from an Arabian Physician to a Famous Professor,* etc. (n.p., n.d.; [London,

1706?], p. 6; JT/T, p. 41. A strong statement of the place of ridicule in Augustan intellectual life appears in J. A. Redwood, *Reason, Ridicule and Religion: The Age of Enlightenment in England* (Cambridge, Mass., Harvard University Press, 1976), pp. 14, 25–26, 196. JT, *Letters from the Late Earl of Shaftesbury*, p. xiii.

150. JT/AG averages an anti-Roman reference a page. See John Toland, *Adeisidaemon*, etc. (The Hague, 1709), p. 61, for the assertion that natural portents have no relation to human affairs. JT/T, p. 198.

151. Arnaldo Momigliano, *Studies in Historiography* (London, Weidenfeld and Nicolson, 1966), pp. 40–55. John Toland, *Letters to Serena*, etc. (London, 1704), preface.

152. Toland, marginal note in Martin, *Description*, flyleaf. JT/T, pp. 137–227. JT/N, Second letter, p. 8, and Appendix.

153. Cf. William R. Parker, *Milton's Contemporary Reputation: An Essay* (Columbus, Ohio State University Press, 1940), p. 55, and JT/LM, pp. 100–108; Pocock, *Political Works of Harrington*, pp. xii–xiii; J. G. A. Pocock, "James Harrington and the Good Old Cause: A Study of the Ideological Context of His Writings," *Journal of British Studies* 10 (1970), 30–31. Worden, *Ludlow, Voyce*, esp. pp. 4, 21–34, 51. Much of the second part of Jeremiah Jones, *A New and Full Method of Settling the Canonical Authority of the New Testament*, 3 vols. (1726–1727; reprint, Oxford, 1798), is taken up with a dissection of JT's use of scriptural and patristic sources in *Amyntor* and *Nazarenus*.

154. "Critical Remarks upon Mr. Toland's Book Entitled *Nazarenus*," in JT/C, II, Appendix, 29–59. [John Toland], *Reasons for Naturalizing the Jews*, etc. [1714], in *Pamphlets Relating to the Jews in England during the Seventeenth and Eighteenth Centuries*, ed. Paul Radin (San Francisco, California State Library, 1939), p. 44. JT/N, pp. xviii f. JT/SA, p. 49, and JT, *Art of Restoring*, passim. Cf. Bernard Bailyn, *The Ideological Origins of the American Revolution* (Cambridge, Mass., Harvard University Press, Belknap Press, 1967), pp. 144–159, and G. V. Bennett, "Jacobitism and the Rise of Walpole," *Historical Perspectives*, pp. 70–92. JT, *High-Church Display'd*, p. 105.

155. JT, "Specimen of the Critical History," JT/C, I, 18–19.

156. [John Toland], *Reasons for Addressing His Majesty to Invite into England Their Highnesses*, etc. (London, 1702), p. 9. JT, *Epsom*, p. 29.

157. JT, *Account of the Courts*, pp. 77–78; JT, "Project of a Journal," JT/C, II, 202. JT, "Some Letters," *ibid.*, pp. 48–90. JT/SA, p. 52; JT, "Catalogue of Books," JT/C, I, 388. *Modesty Mistaken: or A Letter to Mr. Toland*, etc. (London, 1702), p. 6.

2. Latitude and Orthodoxy

1. Leslie Stephen, *History of English Thought in the Eighteenth Century*, 3rd ed., 2 vols. (1902; reprint, New York, Harcourt, Brace, and World, 1962), I, 66–68, 93–94.

2. Sermon: Robert South, *Sermons Preached upon Several Occasions*, 5 vols. (Oxford, 1842), I, 182–205. Culture: Rosalie L. Colie, *Light and Enlightenment: A Study of the Cambridge Platonists and the Dutch Arminians* (Cambridge, University Press, 1957), pp. 1–35. Wished: Louis G. Locke, *Tillotson: A Study in Seventeenth-Century Literature* (Copenhagen, Rosenkilde and Bagger, 1954), pp. 58–59.

3. Mistrustful: Henry R. McAdoo, *The Spirit of Anglicanism: A Survey of Anglican Theological Method in the Seventeenth Century* (London, A. and C. Black, 1965), p. 37; ethos: John S. Marshall, "Freedom and Authority in Classical Anglicanism," *Anglican Theological Review* 45 (1963), 55. Erasmian: H. R. Trevor-Roper, "The Religious Origins of the Enlightenment," in *The Crisis of the Seventeenth Century: Religion, the Reformation and Social Change* (New York, Harper and Row, 1968), pp. 193–236, and James K. McConica, *English Humanists and Reformation Politics under Henry VIII and Edward VI*

(Oxford, Clarendon Press, 1965), pp. 13-43; cf. Massimo Firpo, "Recenti studi sul socinianesimo nel sei e settecento," *Rivista storica italiana* 88 (1977), 136-142. Realize: Marjorie O'R. Boyle, *Erasmus on Language and Method in Theology* (Toronto, University of Toronto Press, 1977), 33-57.

4. Jewel: John Jewel, *The Defence of the Apology*, etc., in *Works*, ed. John Ayre, 4 vols. (Cambridge, 1845-1850), III, 199; Laud: William Laud, *Conference with Fisher*, in *Works*, ed. William Scott and John Bliss, 7 vols. (Oxford, 1847-1860), II, 71-72; Chillingworth: William Chillingworth, *The Religion of Protestants*, in *Works*, 3 vols. (Oxford, 1838), I, 404.

5. "It": Jeremy Taylor, *Ductor Dubitantium*, in *The Whole Works*, ed. Reginald Heber, 15 vols. (Oxford, 1828), XI, 442. Disputed: *ibid.*, pp. 446-447.

6. Depicted: Jeremy Taylor, *The Liberty of Prophesying*, in *Works*, VII, ccccxi-ccccxii. Deny: *ibid.*, pp. 491-494. Modified: *ibid.*, p. ccccxxii. Matter: *ibid.*, p. 445. "Heartily": *ibid.*, pp. ccccvii-ccccviii. Maintained: Jeremy Taylor, *Dissuasive from Popery*, in *ibid.*, X, 341-348.

7. *Outré:* Robert Voitle, "The Reason of the English Enlightenment," *Studies on Voltaire* 27 (1963), 1735-1774. Describe: Richard Burthogge, *Organum vetus et novum*, etc., (London, 1678), p. 9, cited in *ibid.*, pp. 1738-1739. Accepted: Thomas Smith, *A Sermon of the Credibility of the Christian Religion*, etc. (London, 1675), pp. 27-28.

8. Henry G. Van Leeuwen, *The Problem of Certainty in English Thought, 1630-1690* (The Hague, Nijhoff, 1963); Robert R. Orr, *Reason and Authority: The Thought of William Chillingworth* (Oxford, Clarendon Press, 1967), pp. 45-70; Richard H. Popkin, "The Philosophy of Bishop Stillingfleet," *Journal of the History of Philosophy* 9 (1971), 303-319; and Robert T. Carroll, *The Common-Sense Philosophy of Religion of Bishop Edward Stillingfleet, 1635-1699* (The Hague, Nijhoff, 1975), pp. 39-79.

9. Van Leeuwen, *Problem of Certainty*. p. 135.

10. Benjamin Whichcote, *Moral and Religious Aphorisms* (London, 1753), nos. 835, 643-645.

11. John Tillotson, *Works*, 10 vols. (Edinburgh and Glasgow, 1748), II, 68.

12. The only full modern account is Martin I. J. Griffin, "Latitudinarianism in the Seventeenth-Century Church of England" (Ph.D. diss., Yale University, 1962); cf. Irène Simon, *Three Restoration Divines: Barrow, South, Tillotson: Select Sermons*, 2 vols. (Paris, "Les belles lettres," 1967-1976), I, 1-148; Philip Harth, *Swift and Anglican Rationalism: The Religious Background of "A Tale of a Tub"* (Chicago, University Press, 1961), pp. 19-51; Barbara J. Shapiro, *John Wilkins, 1614-1672: An Intellectual Biography* (Berkeley, University of California Press, 1969), pp. 148-190.

13. Griffin, "Latitudinarianism," p. 252.

14. Prone: e.g., Offspring Blackall, *The Sufficiency of a Standing Revelation in General*, etc. (London, 1700), (Sermon VIII), pp. 45-48. Use: G. E. Aylmer, "Unbelief in Seventeenth-Century England," in *Puritans and Revolutionaries: Essays in Seventeenth-Century History Presented to Christopher Hill*, ed. Donald Pennington and Keith Thomas (Oxford, Clarendon Press, 1978), p. 24; existence: Tillotson, *Works*, I, 44-45. Offered: Stanley L. Jaki, *The Road of Science and the Ways to God* (Chicago, University Press, 1978), p. 82. Aquinas: Joseph Owens, *An Elementary Christian Metaphysics* (Milwaukee, Bruce, 1963), pp. 341-351. Sought: Edward Stillingfleet, *Reformation of Manners, the True Way of Honouring God*, etc. (London, n.d. [1700]), p. 9. Attracted: Dudley W. R. Bahlmann, *The Moral Revolution of 1688* (New Haven, Yale University Press, 1957), pp. 79-80.

15. Failure: Harth, *Swift and Anglican Rationalism*, pp. 143-144. Grounded: e.g.,

Edward Synge, *A Gentleman's Religion,* etc., 7th ed. (London, 1752), p. 195, and Smith, *Sermon, passim;* cf. J. A. W. Gunn, *Politics and the Public Interest in the Seventeenth Century* (London, Routledge and Kegan Paul, 1969), pp. 266-321. "If": Edward Stillingfleet, *A Letter to a Deist,* etc. (London, 1697), p. 66.

16. Affirmation: Tillotson, *Works,* IV, 161-163. Synge: Synge, *Gentleman's Religion,* pp. 261-262, 299-300. Praised: Tillotson, *Works,* III, 50. "Keep": Humphrey Prideaux, *A Letter to the Deists,* etc. (London, 1697), p. 107.

17. Scholastic theology: cf. Alexandre Koyré, *L'Idée de dieu dans la philosophie de S. Anselme* (Paris, E. Leroux, 1923), pp. 13-34, and Paul Oskar Kristeller, *Renaissance Thought: The Classic, Scholastic, and Humanist Strains* (New York, Harper and Row, 1961), pp. 111-112. "*Plain*": Tillotson, *Works,* VI, 26-27. Gratified: *ibid.,* p. 337.

18. Efforts: Mark H. Curtis, *Oxford and Cambridge in Transition, 1558-1642: An Essay on Changing Relations between the English Universities and English Society* (Oxford, Clarendon Press, 1959), p. 256; declined: cf. William T. Costello, *The Scholastic Curriculum at Early Seventeenth-Century Cambridge* (Cambridge, Mass., Harvard University Press, 1958), pp. 64, 81, and James K. McConica, "Humanism and Aristotle in Tudor Oxford," *English Historical Review* 94 (1979), 315. Dealt: Taylor, *Ductor Dubitantium,* 455-458; S. P., *A Brief Account of the New Sect of Latitude-Men,* etc. (Cambridge, 1662), pp. 22-24. Theologians: Henry R. McAdoo, *The Structure of Caroline Moral Theology* (London, Longmans, 1949), p. 15. Mass: cf. John H. Pruett, *The Parish Clergy under the Later Stuarts: The Leicestershire Experience* (Urbana, University of Illinois Press, 1978), pp. 174-175, and C. F. Allison, *The Rise of Moralism: The Proclamation of the Gospel from Hooker to Baxter* (New York, Seabury, 1966), pp. 200-201. Confident: Edward Stillingfleet, *Several Conferences between a Romish Priest,* etc., in *Works,* 6 vols. (London, 1710), VI, 38.

19. Edward Stillingfleet, *The Bishop of Worcester's Answer to Mr. Locke's Letter,* etc. (London, 1697), pp. 109, 121.

20. Rejecting: Smith, *Sermon,* pp. 51-52. Coupled: Synge, *Gentleman's Religion,* pp. 80, 5. Belief: [Francis Gastrell], *Some Considerations concerning the Trinity,* etc. (London, 1696), p. 52; confusion: Stillingfleet, *Bishop of Worcester's Answer,* pp. 90-91.

21. Realized: Stillingfleet, *Letter to a Deist,* preface. Criterion: *ibid.,* pp. 17-18, 37. Recommendation: *ibid.,* p. 90. Contented: Synge, *Gentleman's Religion,* p. 61. "Suspicion": Stillingfleet, *Letter to a Deist,* p. 36. "I": *A Letter to a Gentleman upon Occasion of Some New Opinions in Religion* (London, 1696), p. 6.

22. "Health": Synge, *Gentleman's Religion,* p. 194. View: Tillotson, *Works,* V, 229, 231; [Richard Willis], *Reflexions upon . . . "An Account of the Growth of Deism,"* etc. (London, 1696), pp. 53-57.

23. Argued: Tillotson, *Works,* X, 74, 134; dismissed: Edward Stillingfleet, *A Discourse in Vindication of the Doctrine of the Trinity,* etc. (London, 1697), pp. lvi-lvii.

24. Seen: William Haller, *Foxe's Book of Martyrs and the Elect Nation* (London, J. Cape, 1963), p. 245. United: Richard Hooker, *Of the Laws of Ecclesiastical Polity,* in *Works,* ed. John Keble, 2 vols. (Oxford, 1865), VIII, 1, 2, and John Milton, *Areopagitica,* in *The Prose Works of John Milton,* ed. J. A. St. John, 5 vols. (London, 1893), II, 91; remained: Gilbert Burnet, *An Exposition of the XXXIX Articles,* etc., 3rd ed. (London, 1705), p. 6. Belief: Every, *High-Church Party,* pp. 19-42. "Such": [Francis Atterbury], *A Letter to a Convocation Man,* etc. (London, 1697), pp. 20-21. Treated: John Sharp, "Against Heresy," in *Works,* 7 vols. (London, 1749), VI, 9. Redirected: H. G. Horwitz, "Comprehension in the Later Seventeenth Century: A Postscript," *Church History* 34 (1965), 343.

25. Achieved: Tillotson, *Works*, II, 331. "Drawn": Humphrey Prideaux, *The True Nature of Imposture Fully Displayed in the Life of Mahomet*, etc. (London, 1697), pp. vi–vii. "Intended": Richard Baxter, *Of National Churches*, etc. (London, 1701), p. 4. Grown: *ibid.*, p. 55. Repeated: William Wake, *The Authority of Christian Princes over Their Ecclesiastical Synods Asserted*, etc. (London, 1697), pp. 94–95.

26. Convinced: John Humfrey, *Mediocria, or a Middle Way between Protestant and Papist*, etc., 2d ed. (London, 1695), p. 1. Refused: *ibid.*, p. 61. Ended: Tillotson, *Works*, VI, 146–149. "There": *ibid.*, V, 9. "None": *ibid.*, IX, 226.

27. Established: Synge, *Gentleman's Religion*, p. 97. Conceived: *ibid.*, p. 42. "Given": *ibid.*, pp. 77–78. "Apprehensions": *ibid.*, p. 259. Exercised: *ibid.*, pp. 233–234. Unable: *ibid.*, p. 73. Assure: Willis, *Reflexions*, pp. 36–37, 29.

28. Termed: Robert Boyle, "Advices in Judging of Things Said to Transcend Reason," in *Works*, ed. Thomas Birch, 6 vols. (London, 1772), IV, 449. Probable: John Williams, *Scripture the Rule of Faith*, etc., (London, 1696), pp. 17–18.

29. "Confused": Stillingfleet, *Letter to a Deist*, pp. 8, 62–63. Began: Edward Stillingfleet, *The Mysteries of the Christian Faith Asserted and Vindicated*, etc. (London, 1696), pp. 6–7.

30. Emphasize: Stillingfleet, *Mysteries*, p. 3. Affirmed: Synge, *Gentleman's Religion*, pp. 53–54.

31. Saw: Tillotson, *Works*, IX, 235–236. Rejecting: *ibid.*, II, 50; "all": *ibid.*, p. 68. Insistence: *ibid.*, V, 8.

32. "Any": *ibid.*, p. 33. Proposition: *ibid.*, pp. 7–8. Confidence: e.g., William Nicholls, *An Answer to an Heretical Book Called the "Naked Gospel"* (London, 1691), pp. 76–77. Realized: Tillotson, *Works*, V, 7–8. Flirt: Synge, *Gentleman's Religion*, pp. 51–52.

33. Relied: cf. Tillotson, *Works*, IX, 230–235, and Synge, *Gentleman's Religion*, p. 61. Insist: Stillingfleet, *Letter to a Deist*, pp. 69–70. Described: J. G. A. Pocock, *Politics, Language, and Time: Essays on Political Thought and History* (New York, Atheneum, 1973), pp. 183–184. "As": Tillotson, *Works*, V, 20.

34. Defined: Tillotson, *Works*, IX, 197. View: *ibid.*, IV, 32–33. Fallibility: *ibid.*, IX, 238; naturalness: *ibid.*, VI, 229. Work: *ibid.*, IX, 243–244, 249. Concluded: Synge, *Gentleman's Religion*, pp. 69–70.

35. "Simplicity": Tillotson, *Works*, II, 1–2. Signs: *ibid.*, pp. 4–5. Presented: cf. *ibid.*, IX, 195, and Synge, *Gentleman's Religion*, p. 171.

36. "For": Tillotson, *Works*, X, 78. Appeal: Stillingfleet, *Letter to a Deist*, preface; Synge, *Gentleman's Religion*, p. 13; *Letter to a Gentleman*, p. 3; Prideaux, *Letter to the Deists*, p. 79. Conformity: Synge, *Gentleman's Religion*, p. 163.

37. Spoke: Willis, *Reflexions*, p. 4. "Beyond": Smith, *Sermon*, p. 12; "curiosity": Stillingfleet, *Mysteries*, p. 39; "Faith": Synge, *Gentleman's Religion*, pp. 4, 54; "wit": Tillotson, *Works*, V, 40.

38. Confident: Tillotson, *Works*, I, 306. Portrayed: *ibid.*, IX, 204. "Positive": *ibid.*, V, 247. Identical: *ibid.*, p. 132; "great": *ibid.*, p. 253. "Our": *ibid.*, I, 115.

39. "That": Tillotson, *Works*, I, 115. Rejected: *ibid.*, pp. 61–62. Subordinated: *ibid.*, V, 255; responsibility: *ibid.*, III, 181. "Second": *ibid.*, VII, 198–199. "Moral": *ibid.*, IX, 72–73. "Greatest": *ibid.*, II, 264.

40. Convinced: John Dryden, *Religio Laici*, in *Works*, ed. Walter Scott and rev. by George Saintsbury, 18 vols. (Edinburgh and London, 1882–1893), X, 13. Endorsements: Tillotson, *Works*, VI, 63, and VIII, 158; cf. Synge, *Gentleman's Religion*, pp. 297–298.

41. Rebuked: Tillotson, *Works*, II, 265, and IX, 6–7. Addressed: *ibid.*, IV, 165–191. "Magnified": *ibid.*, IX, 12. Paradise: *ibid.*, VIII, 176.

42. Ventured: *ibid.,* IX, 286. "Hard": *ibid.,* III, 74.
43. Maintained: *ibid.,* II, 156–157; cf. *ibid.,* X, 85. "Our": *ibid.,* VIII, 160. List: Synge, *Gentleman's Religion,* pp. 99–123; Herbert: Edward, Lord Herbert of Cherbury, *De veritate,* ed. and trans. Meyrick Carré (Bristol, J. W. Arrowsmith, 1937), pp. 289–313. Affirmed: Synge, *Gentleman's Religion,* p. 54.
44. Referred: Tillotson, *Works,* VI, 116–117. Failing: *ibid.,* pp. 105–109; insisting: *ibid.,* p. 130. Paint: *ibid.,* viii, 431. Soteriology: cf. *ibid.,* I, 118, and VI, 32. "Aspire": *ibid.,* III, 120; assurance: *ibid.,* V, 328. Vague: *ibid.,* VII, 359–360. Confident: *ibid.,* V, 224. Identifying: *ibid.,* IX, 298; reduced: *ibid.,* VI, 38–39.
45. Abhorred: Thomas Birch, *The Life of . . . John Tillotson,* etc., 2d ed. (London, 1753), pp. 442–444. "Christian": Ezekiel Hopkins, "The Resurrection of Christ," in *Works* (London, 1701), p. 386.
46. Affirm: Tillotson, *Works,* III, 131. Averred: *ibid.,* p. 134. "Books": *ibid.,* III, 260; "other": *ibid.,* IV, 70; "scriptures": *ibid.,* pp. 119–120. Control: *ibid.,* II, 126; innocent: *ibid.,* p. 121. Assent: *ibid.,* III, 131. Implied: *ibid.,* p. 298.
47. Maintained: [Robert Howard], *The History of Religion,* etc. (London, 1694), pp. 63–64. Priests: *ibid.,* pp. iv–vi. Repudiated: *ibid.,* p. 80; defined: *ibid.,* p. 96. Deny: *ibid.,* pp. 153, 158.
48. Began: [Arthur Bury], *The Naked Gospel,* etc., 2d ed. (London, 1691). Followed: James Parkinson, *The Fire's Continued at Oxford,* etc. (n.p. [London?], 1690), p. 2.
49. Saw: Bury, *Naked Gospel,* p. 15. Proposed: *ibid.,* p. 17. Turned: *ibid.,* pp. 66–73.
50. "Largest": [Arthur Bury], *The Naked Gospel,* etc. (n.p. [Oxford], 1690), pp. 2, 9. Corresponded: Arthur Bury, *The Rational Deist Satisfy'd by a Just Account of the Gospel,* etc., 2d ed. (London, 1703), pp. 2–3, 35. Stated: *ibid.,* p. 48. Asserted: cf. Bury, *Naked Gospel* (1690), preface, and *Rational Deist,* p. 27. Raised: Bury, *Naked Gospel* (1691), pp. 66–69.
51. Found: cf. Bury, *Naked Gospel* (1690), pp. 56–57, and *Rational Deist,* pp. 83–85. Conceding: *ibid.,* p. 122. Assert: *ibid.,* preface. Adopted: *ibid.,* p. 26. Considered: *ibid.,* p. 81. Censuring: Bury, *Naked Gospel* (1690), pp. 34, 37; defined: *ibid.,* p. 1.
52. Hauled: Redwood, *Reason, Ridicule and Religion,* pp. 156–159. Admitting: Bury, *Rational Deist,* dedication.
53. Offered: *Bibliothèque universelle* 19 (1690), 391–435; written: [Jean Le Clerc], *An Historical Vindication of The Naked Gospel,* etc. (n.p., 1690). Beginnings: cf. Lambertus J. van Holk, "From Arminus to Arminianism in Dutch Theology," in *Man's Faith and Freedom: The Theological Influence of Jacobus Arminus* (New York, Abington, 1962), pp. 27–45, and John Tulloch, *Rational Theology and Christian Philosophy in England in the Seventeenth Century,* 2 vols. (Edinburgh, 1872), I, 19–25. Defined: *Bibliothèque universelle* 2 (1686), 27.
54. "Not": Jean Le Clerc, *A Treatise of the Causes of Incredulity,* etc. [trans. John Toland] (London, 1697), pp. 121–122. "His": *ibid.,* pp. 14–15. Believed: *ibid.,* pp. 176–177. Provided: *ibid.,* p. 152. Saw: cf. *ibid.,* pp. 97.
55. Apply: Manlio Iofrida, "Note sul pensiero teologico e filosofico di Jean Le Clerc," *Annali della scuola normale superiore di Pisa* 9 (1979), 1497–1524. Governed: Jean Le Clerc, *Epistolae criticae et ecclesiasticae,* etc. (Amsterdam, 1700), p. 10. Emphasized: "Extrait d'un livre anglois . . . intitulé, 'Essai philosophique concernant l'entendement. . . .' Communiqué par M. Locke," *Bibliothèque universelle* 8 (1688), 83–84. Occurred: *ibid.,* pp. 138–139; command: Jean Le Clerc, *Opera philosophica,* 4 vols. (1692; reprint, Amsterdam, 1722), I, 62. Offered: *ibid.,* p. 115.
56. Maintained: Philipp van Limborch, *Theologia christiana,* etc. (Amsterdam, 1686), VII, xxi. Insisted: *ibid.,* I, xi. Meant: *ibid.,* VII, xx; partook: *ibid.,* xi. Speculation: *ibid.,* xxi. Necessity: *ibid.,* V, ix.

57. "Justification": *ibid.*, VI, iv. Believed: *ibid.*, VI, viii; obeyed: *ibid.*, iv; pagans: *ibid.*, IV, xi. Discounted: Philipp van Limborch, *De veritate religionis christianae*, etc. (Gouda, 1687), pp. 190-228. Refused: Limborch, *Theologia*, V, iii.

58. Accusations: Louis-Anastase Guichard, *Histoire du socinianisme*, etc. (Paris, 1723), pp. 568-581; compliments: *A Brief History of the Unitarians*, etc. (London, 1686), p. 1. Defended: Jean Le Clerc, *Mr. Le Clerc's Extract and Judgment of the Rights of the Christian Church*, etc. (London, 1708).

59. John W. Yolton, *John Locke and the Way of Ideas* (London, Oxford University Press, 1956), p. 180.

60. "If": John Locke, "Reflections upon the Roman Commonwealth" (1660), in Fox-Bourne, *John Locke*, I, 149. "Cause": Locke, "Sacerdos," in *ibid.*, II, 87. Insisting: John Locke, *An Essay concerning Human Understanding*, ed. John W. Yolton, 2 vols. (New York, Everyman Library, 1965), IV, xix, 11. Offensive: John Locke, *The Reasonableness of Christianity*, etc. (London, 1695), pp. 158, 265. Sought: Locke to Molyneux, 22 Feb. 1697, *Familiar Letters*, p. 177.

61. Embodied: William Hull, *Benjamin Furly and Quakerism in Rotterdam* (Swarthmore, Pa., Swarthmore College, 1941), pp. 91-92. Charter: "Rules of a Society," etc., *Works of Locke*, X, 312-313. Collaborated: Popple to Locke, 12 Nov. 1692 and 2 Mar. 1693, Bodl. Locke MSS., c. 17, ff. 201-202, 205-206.

62. Remained: Locke to Limborch, 6 Jan. 1700, *Works of Locke*, X, 197. Believed: Locke, *Reasonableness*, p. 106. "*Reason*": *ibid.*, p. 258.

63. Reaction: See Mario Sina, *L'avvento della ragione: "Reason" e "above Reason" dal razionalismo teologico inglese al deismo* (Milan, Università cattolica del Sacro Cuore, 1976), pp. 408-433. Suppressed: Stillingfleet, *Discourse in Vindication*, pp. iv-v. Violating: *ibid.*, pp. 1-2. Political: Pedro T. Meza, "The Question of Authority in the Church of England, 1689-1717," *Historical Magazine of the Protestant Episcopal Church* 42 (1973), 65. Reveal: cf. *Animadversions on a Late Book Entituled the Reasonableness of Christianity*, etc. (Oxford, 1697), p. 93, and Basnage to Leibniz, 18 June 1696, *Die philosophischen Schriften von G. W. Leibniz*, ed. C. I. Gerhardt, 7 vols. (Berlin, 1875-1890), III, 126.

64. Traced: Stillingfleet, *Discourse in Vindication*, pp. 248, 258, 273. Faithful: *ibid.*, pp. 254-255. Implications: *ibid.*, pp. 230-235. "If": *ibid.*, p. 123.

65. Faced: *ibid.*, p. 27. Manage: *ibid.*, p. li. Appealed: *ibid.*, p. 3. Explicate: *ibid.*, pp. 68, 123, 253; resorted: *ibid.*, p. 108; execrated: *ibid.*, p. xxxvi; cf. Carroll, *Common-Sense Philosophy*, p. 144.

66. Embarrassment: John Locke, *A Letter to the . . . Bishop of Worcester*, etc. (London, 1697), p. 42. "Nothing": *ibid.*, pp. 58-59. Careful: *ibid.*, pp. 17-18. Insisted: *ibid.*, pp. 56-57, 87-88. Allowed: *ibid.*, pp. 13, 54-55.

67. Adverting: *ibid.*, p. 118; "by": *ibid.*, p. 42. Confident: *ibid.*, p. 75. Proved: *ibid.*, pp. 135-136.

68. Locke, *Essay*, IV, x.

69. Efforts: e.g., John Dunn, *The Political Thought of John Locke: An Historical Account of the "Two Treatises of Government"* (Cambridge, University Press, 1969), pp. 188-197. "Holy": Locke, *Letter*, p. 225. Listed: Bodl. Locke MSS. c. 43, ff. 12-13, 26-27. Infallible: Locke, *Essay*, IV, xii, 8. Realized: Yolton, *John Locke*, p. 10.

70. Elicit: Locke, *Essay*, IV, xv, 3; grasp: *ibid.*, III, x, 2-22, 24; cf. J. T. Moore, "Locke's Analysis of Language and the Assent to Scripture," *Journal of the History of Ideas* 37 (1976), 707-714. Enumerated: Locke, *Essay*, IV, xvi, 6-10. "Knowledge": *ibid.*, xviii, 4. "Settled": *ibid.*, xvi, 14. Disproportion: John C. Biddle, "Locke's Critique of Innate Principles and Toland's Deism," *Journal of the History of Ideas* 37 (1976), 416-417. Distinguish: cf. Paul Helm, "Locke on Faith and Knowledge," *Philosophical Quarterly* 23

(1973), 60, and Carroll, *Common-Sense Philosophy,* pp. 96–99. Communicate: cf. Samuel C. Pearson, Jr., "The Religion of John Locke and the Character of His Thought," *Journal of Religion* 58 (1978), 261, and J. T. Moore, "Locke on Assent and Toleration," *ibid.,* p. 32.

71. Admit: Locke, *Essay,* IV, xviii, 7. "Capable": *ibid.,* xii, 8. "It": *ibid.,* 11; cf. Locke, *Reasonableness,* pp. 17–18. Secure: Helm, "Locke on Faith," p. 65.

72. Toyed: Stillingfleet, *Bishop of Worcester's Answer,* pp. 90–91. Rehash: cf. *ibid.,* p. 109, and Aquinas, *Summa Theologiae,* I, 2, 3; denounce: Stillingfleet, *Bishop of Worcester's Answer,* p. 121. Invited: *ibid.,* p. 4. Asserted: John Locke, *Mr. Locke's Reply to the . . . Bishop of Worcester's Answer,* etc. (London, 1697), pp. 9–19, 98.

73. Reproaching: Locke, *Mr. Locke's Reply,* pp. 84–85. "Voluntary": John Locke, *A Letter concerning Toleration* (1689), in *Works of Locke,* V, 13. Determine: *ibid.,* pp. 14, 19. Extended: Locke, *Reasonableness,* pp. 191–192, 298.

74. Attempts: e.g., Nicholls, *Answer,* p. 42; [Richard Willis], *The Occasional Paper, Number III,* etc. (London, 1697), p. 10; Nathaniel Taylor, *A Preservative against Deism,* etc. (London, 1698), pp. viii–x; *A Letter to a Member of Parliament, Shewing the Necessity of Regulating the Press,* etc. (London, 1699), p. 36. "Instrument": South, *Sermons,* II, 185–186.

75. Maintained: South, *Sermons,* II, 190. Demanded: *ibid.,* pp. 194–195. "Men": *ibid.,* p. 201.

76. *Ibid.,* p. 186.

3. The Varieties of Socinianism

1. Noted: Gilbert Burnet, *A History of His Own Time,* 2 vols., consecutive pag. (London, 1840), p. 651. Rebuked: Burnet to Limborch, 18 Nov. 1694, Bodl. MS. Eng. Theo., c. 23, f. 12.

2. Accused: Barnes, *Jean Le Clerc,* p. 164. Begun: Every, *High-Church Party,* pp. 77–79.

3. Pursued: cf. Drake, *Memorial,* p. 14, George Hickes, preliminary discourse to William Carroll, *Spinoza Reviv'd,* etc. (London, 1709), and Jean Gailhard, *The Blasphemous Socinian Heresie Disproved and Confuted,* etc. (London, 1697), pp. 6–7. Left: [Stephen Nye], *The Life of Thomas Firmin,* etc. (London, 1698), p. 14. Recognizing: J. C. Van Slee, *De Geschiedenis van het Socinianisme in de Nederlanden* (Haarlem, F. Bohn, 1914), pp. 119–135; inquiring: Firmin to Locke, 25 July 1694, Bodl. Locke MSS. c. 8, f. 109; grateful: Le Clerc to Locke, 19 Apr. 1689, *ibid.,* c. 13, f. 35.

4. Charles Leslie, *The Socinian Controversy Discuss'd,* etc. (London, 1708), Dialogue VI, preface.

5. Maintained: Edward Stillingfleet, *A Discourse concerning the Doctrine of Christ's Satisfaction,* etc. (1675; reprint, London, 1696); cf. Jonathan Edwards, *A Preservative against Socinianism,* etc. (1693; reprints, London, 1697, etc.). Concluded: Smith, *Sermon,* p. 11.

6. Patronage: B.L. Add. MS. 24478 ("Grounds and Occasions of the Controversy concerning the Unity of God"); pamphlets: Herbert McLachlan, *The Story of a Nonconformist Library* (Manchester, University Press, 1923), pp. 53–87. Ascribed: *ibid.,* p. 85. Saw: Nye, *Agreement of the Unitarians,* pp. 54–55. Survived: Bodl. Rawlinson MSS. D. 1152, ff. 57–57^V (Diary of John Roach).

7. Ignored . . . skirted: H. Lismer Short, "The Importance of the Seventeenth Century in Unitarian History," *Transactions of the Unitarian Historical Society* 9 (1950), 188–200; H. John McLachlan, *Socinianism in Seventeenth-Century England* (London, Oxford University Press, 1951), pp. 317–335; Earl M. Wilbur, *A History of Unitarianism,* 2 vols. (Cambridge, Mass., Harvard University Press, 1946–1952), II, 216–235. Affirm: Stephen, *History of English Thought,* I, 93–94; Roland N. Stromberg, *Religious Liberalism*

in Eighteenth-Century England (London, Oxford University Press, 1954), pp. 50–52; and Zbigniew Ogonowski, "Le 'Christianisme sans mystères' selon John Toland et les sociniens," *Archiwum historii filozofii i myśli społecznej* 12 (1966), 205–223; deny: Massimo Firpo, "Il rapporto tra socinianesimo e primo deismo inglese negli studi di uno storico polacco," *Critica storica* 10 (1973), 243–297, "Recenti studi sul socinianesimo," pp. 106–152, and "John Locke e il socinianesimo," *Rivista storica italiana* 92 (1980), 35–124; Gerard Reedy, "Socinians, John Toland, and the Anglican Rationalists," *Harvard Theological Review* 70 (1977), 285–304. Written: Peter Gay, ed., *Deism: An Anthology* (Princeton, Van Nostrand, 1968), p. 47. "When": Wilbur, *History of Unitarianism*, II, 222.

8. Denial: cf. Nye, *Agreement of the Unitarians*, p. 3, and "An Account of Mr. Firmin's Religion," in Nye, *Life*, p. 4; assertion: Nye, *Agreement of the Unitarians*, p. 1. Believed: Francis Falwood, *The Socinian Controversy Touching the Son of God*, etc. (London, 1693). Charging: John Edwards, *The Socinian Creed*, etc. (London, 1697), pp. 23–46.

9. Identifying: Stephen Nye, *A Discourse concerning Natural and Revealed Religion*, etc. (London, 1696), p. 96. Affirmation: Nye, *Agreement of the Unitarians*, pp. 50–52. List: Nye, *Discourse*, pp. 2, 61–62. Corresponded: *ibid.*, pp. 123–125. Worked: *ibid.*, pp. 98, 108.

10. "Thoughts": Bayle, *Dictionnaire historique et critique*, XIII, 342. Found: Edwards, *Socinian Creed*, pp. 23–46. Strengthened: Gailhard, *True Character*, pp. 170–171. Distance: Nye, *Discourse*, p. 45; recourse: [Thomas Emlyn], *A Vindication of the Remarks upon Mr. Charles Leslie's First Dialogue*, etc. (London, 1708), p. 1.

11. Form: McLachlan, *Socinianism*, p. 336.

12. Pointed: *The Judgment of the Fathers concerning the Doctrine of the Trinity*, Part I (London, 1695), p. 32; cf. Nye, *Agreement of the Unitarians*, pp. 52–53. "But": [Stephen Nye], *A Brief History of the Unitarians*, etc., 2d ed. (London, 1691), pp. 10–12. "Who": Nye, "Account of Mr. Firmin's Religion," pp. 8–9.

13. Assumption: Ludwik Chmaj, "Wkłady Rakowskie Fausta Socyna," in Ludwik Chmaj, ed., *Studia nad arianizmem* (Warsaw, PWN, 1959), pp. 168–198 (I owe this reference to George H. Williams). Imbibed: George H. Williams, *The Radical Reformation* (Philadelphia, Westminster, 1962), pp. 22–26, 753; Aldo Stella, *Anabattismo e antitrinitarismo in Italia nel XVI secolo: nuove ricerche storiche* (Padua, Liviana, 1969), pp. 100–103, 111n; Zbigniew Ogonowski, *Socznianizm a oświecenie: Studia nad myśla filozoficzno-religijna arian w Polsce XVII w.* (Warsaw, PWN, 1966), pp. 140–146 (I owe this reference to George H. Williams).

14. This paragraph rests on John H. Randall, Jr., *The School of Padua and the Emergence of Modern Science* (Padua, Editrice Antenore, 1961).

15. Foreseen: W. Owen Chadwick, *From Bossuet to Newman: The Idea of Doctrinal Development* (Cambridge, University Press, 1957), p. 89. Held: Stanislaus Kot, "Le mouvement antitrinitaire au XVI ème et au XVII ème siècle," *Humanisme et renaissance* 4 (1937), 120–121. Thought: *Bibliotheca fratrum polonorum, Opera Socini*, cited in Ogonowski, "Le 'Christianisme sans mystères,' " p. 214. Found: Antal Pirnát, *Die Ideologie der Siebenbürger Antitrinitarier in den 1570er Jahre* (Budapest, Verlag der Ung. Akademie der Wissenschaften, 1961), pp. 78–79.

16. Abandon: Ogonowski, "Le 'Christianisme sans mystères,'" pp. 214–215. Concluded: *Bibliotheca fratrum polonorum, Opera Crelli*, IV, 114b, cited in *ibid.*, p. 216. Positing: Joachim Stegmann, *De iudice et norma controversarum fidei*, etc. (Eleutheropoli [Amsterdam], 1644), cited in *ibid.*, p. 218.

17. Approved: Pirnát, *Ideologie*, pp. 68–69, 160, 182; numbered: Kot, "Le mouvement antitrinitaire," pp. 113–114. Discerned: Zygmut Jedryka, "Le socinianisme et les lumières," *Studies on Voltaire* 88 (1972), 809–829. Assumed: *Epitome colloquii Racoviae*

habiti anno 1601, ed. Lech Szczucki and Janusz Tazbir (Warsaw, PWN, 1966), pp. 31–42. Held: *ibid.,* p. 26. Pointed: Kot, "Le mouvement antitrinitaire," p. 121.

18. Circulating: Thomas Long, *An Answer to a Socinian Treatise, Call'd "The Naked Gospel,"* etc. (London, 1691), preface. Sent: Kot, "Le mouvement antitrinitaire," p. 136. Observed: Samuel Przypkowski, *Cogitationes sacrae ad initium evangelii Matthaei et omnes epistolas apostolicas,* etc. (Eleutheropoli [Amsterdam], 1692), preface. Grasped: Pierre Jurieu, *Le Tableau du socinianisme,* etc. (The Hague, 1690), pp. 87–88.

19. Divisions: [Stephen Nye?], *A Letter of Resolution concerning the Doctrines of the Trinity,* etc. (London, n.d. [1691]), pp. 7–8. Accepted: Nye, *Discourse,* p. 105. Invoking: *Faith of One God . . . Asserted and Defended* (London, n.d. [1691]), p. 1; alluring: William Sherlock, *The Present State of the Socinian Controversy,* etc. (London, 1698), p. 53. Insistence: Nye, *Discourse,* p. 87.

20. Saw: cf. Sherlock, *Present State,* p. 53; [Thomas Tenison], *The Creed of Mr. Hobbes Examined,* etc., 2d ed. (London, 1671), p. 39; [Peter Allix], *A Defence of the Brief History of the Unitarians,* etc. (London, 1691), p. 8; and [Matthew Tindal], *A Letter to the Reverend the Clergy of Both Universities,* etc. (London, 1694), p. 32. "Meaning": Battista Mondin, *The Principle of Analogy in Protestant and Catholic Theology,* 2d ed. (The Hague, Nijhoff, 1968), p. 187.

21. Exploited: Nye, *Letter of Resolution,* p. 7. Subjected: *ibid.,* p. 12.

22. Persisted: [Thomas Tenison], *The Difference betwixt the Protestant and Socinian Methods,* etc. (London, 1687), pp. 9–10. Wrote: Nye, *Agreement of the Unitarians,* p. 7. Knew: Edwards, *Socinian Creed,* pp. 73–101. Nye's: Nye, *Agreement of the Unitarians,* pp. 9–10. Compounded: Nye, *Discourse,* pp. 3–8. Thought: Stillingfleet, *Discourse in Vindication,* p. 230.

23. Imputing: John Norris, *An Account of Reason of Faith,* etc. 13th ed. (London, 1740), p. 12. "Pretended": *The Unreasonableness of the Doctrine of the Trinity Briefly Demonstrated,* etc. (London, 1692), p. 6.

24. Remains: cf. Firpo, "John Locke e il socinianesimo," pp. 111–112; Zbigniew Ogonowski, "Wiara i rozain w doktrynych religynych Socynian i Locke'a," in Chmaj, *Studia nad arianizmem,* pp. 425–450 (I owe this reference to George H. Williams); and Nicholas Jolley, "Leibniz on Locke and Socinianism," *Journal of the History of Ideas* 39 (1978), 233–250. Popple: [William Popple], *A Rational Catechism,* etc. (London, 1687). Sensed: Sherlock, *Present State,* pp. 90–91. Rebuked: Nye, *Discourse,* pp. 231–232. Invoke: e.g., *The Reflections concerning the XXVIII Propositions touching the Doctrine of the Trinity,* etc. (London, 1695), and *The Exceptions of Mr. Edwards,* etc. (London, 1695).

25. Concluded: McLachlan, *Socinianism,* pp. 11–12. Maintained: H. H., "A Letter to the Author," in Nye, *Discourse,* pp. 218–220; confident: Allix, *Defence,* pp. 9–10.

26. Professed: [Stephen Nye], *Reflections on Two Discourses concerning the Divinity of Our Saviour,* etc. (London, 1693), p. 5. Rejection: Nye, *Discourse,* pp. 144–150. Repudiation: [Stephen Nye?], *The Acts of the Great Athanasius,* etc. (n.p., n.d. [London, 1690?]). "Improper": Gailhard, *True Character,* pp. 177–178; cf. [Peter Browne], *Things Divine and Supernatural Conceived by Analogy with Things Natural and Human* (London, 1723), p. 372. Suggested: Daniel P. Walker, *The Decline of Hell: Seventeenth-Century Discussions of Eternal Torment* (London, Routledge and Kegan Paul, 1964), p. 16.

27. Found: Tenison, *Difference,* p. 45; consoled: Synge, *Gentleman's Religion,* pp. 299–300. Depends: Nye, *Discourse,* p. 1. Maintained: Nye, *Agreement of the Unitarians,* p. 41. Held: *ibid.,* p. 45. "What": Nye, *Letter of Resolution,* p. 1.

28. This paragraph summarizes Tindal, *Letter to the Reverend,* pp. 33–34.

29. Made: Gailhard, *Blasphemous Socinian Heresie,* pp. 146–147. Followed: *ibid.,* p. 143. Dismissed: *Some Thoughts upon Dr. Sherlock's Vindication of the Doctrine of the Holy*

Trinity, etc., 2d ed. (London, 1691), p. 13.

30. Preserving: Tenison, *Difference,* pp. 29–33. Defined: John Williams, *The Perfection of the Evangelical Revelation,* etc. (London, 1696), p. 7. Make: John Williams, *Of the Perspecuity of Scripture and Rules for Interpretation of It,* etc. (London, 1696), pp. 14–16. Interpret: Williams, *Scripture the Rule of Faith,* pp. 23, 19–20, 12.

31. Dismissed: Edwards, *Socinian Creed,* p. 10. Appropriate . . . accusing: Stillingfleet, *Discourse in Vindication,* pp. 153–156. Contrast: Mangey, *Remarks upon Nazarenus,* p. 34.

32. Contented: *Some Thoughts,* p. 15. Avowed: Nye, *Reflections,* pp. 23–24. Answered: Nye, *Agreement of the Unitarians,* pp. 4–5.

33. Simon: *Considerations on the Explication of the Doctrine of the Trinity,* etc. (London, 1694), p. 30; insinuated: Nye, *Agreement of the Unitarians,* pp. 28–29; averred: [Stephen Nye], *An Accurate Examination of the Principal Texts Usually Alleged for the Divinity of Our Saviour,* etc. (London, 1692). Undertook: Nye, *Agreement of the Unitarians,* pp. 28–29. Favored: Nye, *Discourse,* p. 201.

34. Eschewing: [Stephen Nye], *The Trinitarian Scheme of Religion,* etc. (London, 1692), p. 27. Assaulted: Nye, *Letter of Resolution,* p. 2. Insistence: *ibid.,* p. 5.

35. This paragraph summarizes Tindal, *Letter to the Reverend,* p. 34.

36. This paragraph summarizes *Some Thoughts,* p. 14; cf. *Considerations,* p. 4.

37. "Term": *Unreasonableness of the Doctrine,* p. 4. "There": Nye, *Trinitarian Scheme,* p. 5. "It": *Unreasonableness of the Doctrine,* p. 7.

38. Allowed: Allix, *Defence,* pp. 9–10. Clarify: *An Impartial Account of the Word MYSTERY,* etc. (London, 1691), pp. 13, 18. Believe: cf. Tindal, *Letter to the Reverend,* pp. 3–4, and Nye, *Letter of Resolution,* p. 3. Suggested: *Impartial Account,* p. 20. "Mystery": Allix, *Defence,* p. 49; cf. *Impartial Account,* p. 5.

39. "Question": Gilbert Burnet, *Four Discourses Deliver'd to the Clergy of the Diocess of Sarum,* etc. (London, 1694), p. 26; cf. Every, *High-Church Party,* pp. 102–103.

40. Seen: Smith, *Sermon,* pp. 25–26. Described: Stillingfleet, *Discourse in Vindication,* pp. xlix–l. Maintained: Norris, *Account of Reason and Faith,* pp. 167–168. Accused: Sherlock, *Present State,* p. 81. Gave: Leslie, *Socinian Controversy,* Dialogue V, p. 11.

41. [Charles Leslie], "A Supplement upon Occasion of a History of Religion," in *The Charge of Socinianism against Dr. Tillotson,* etc. (London, 1695), p. 28.

42. Ventured: Burnet, *Four Discourses,* pp. 26, 31. "Men": Sherlock, *Present State,* pp. 55–56.

43. Attack: *The Doctrine of the Catholick Church, and of the Church of England,* etc. (London, 1697), pp. 22–24. Castigated: [Robert South], *Animadversions upon Dr. Sherlock's Book,* etc. (London, 1693), pp. xvi–xviii. Aggravated: Leslie, "Supplement upon Occasion," pp. 27–28.

44. Ascribed: William Payne, *The Mystery of the Christian Faith and of the Blessed Trinity Vindicated,* etc. (London, 1697), pp. 57–96. Complained: Leslie, *Charge of Socinianism,* pp. 29–30.

45. Confident: *Impartial Account,* p. 23. "Given": *ibid.,* p. 22.

46. Denounced: cf. *Remarks on the Life,* p. 33, and Mangey, *Remarks upon Nazarenus,* p. 49. Asserted: [William Freke], *A Vindication of the Unitarians,* etc., 2d ed. (London, 1690), p. 29. Outraged: Nye, *Agreement of the Unitarians,* p. 17. Described: Nye, *Brief History,* p. 3.

47. Burnet to Limborch, 27 May [1698?], Bodl. MS. Eng. Theo., c. 23, f. 13.

48. More to Lady Conway, 29 Aug. 1662, in Marjorie H. Nicolson, ed., *Conway Letters* (New Haven, Yale University Press, 1930), p. 208. Accused: Leslie, *Socinian Controversy,* Dialogue V, p. 10. Noted: JT, *Principle,* p. 23.

49. Wondered: Stillingfleet, *Discourse in Vindication,* p. 60. Integral: Matthias Earberry, *Deism Examin'd and Confuted,* etc. (London, 1697), pp. 119–120. Guaranteed: *ibid.,* p. 118.

50. Aware: Nye, *Trinitarian Scheme,* p. 5. "All": Nye, *Discourse,* p. 7. Restatement: *ibid.,* pp. 5–13. Conceded: *ibid.,* pp. 6–7. "Easily": *ibid.,* p. 37.

51. Nye, *Discourse,* pp. 38–45.

52. Described: Nye, *Agreement of the Unitarians,* pp. 5–6. Accepted: Nye, *Reflections,* p. 16; cf. Nye, *Discourse,* p. 20. Refuted: *Considerations,* pp. 31–33.

53. "Most": Nye, *Discourse,* p. 3. Worked . . . useless: *ibid.,* pp. 27, 110.

54. Made: *ibid.,* p. 37. Appeared: See Randall, *School of Padua,* pp. 107–112. Avoided: Tindal, *Letter to the Reverend,* p. 33.

55. "Pillar": Holmes, *Trial of Sacheverell,* p. 26. Explained: Nye, *Life,* pp. 20–21.

56. Treated: Nye, *Life,* p. 21. " 'Tis": *ibid.,* p. 51. "Like": *ibid.,* pp. 77–78. "Not": *ibid.,* p. 63.

57. Stigmatizing: Edwards, *Socinian Creed,* pp. 176–201. Wrote: Nye, *Reflections,* p. 7. Diminish . . . prompt: Nye, *Discourse,* pp. 108, 115–122. Admitted: Nye, *Trinitarian Scheme,* pp. 25–26. "True": Nye, *Discourse,* pp. 58–59. "Lust": Nye, *Agreement of the Unitarians,* p. 14.

58. Task: Nye, *Reflections,* p. 3. Anglicanism: Nye, *Trinitarian Scheme,* p. 28. Appeal: [Robert Howard], *A Twofold Vindication of the Late Arch-Bishop of Canterbury,* etc. (London, n.d. [1696]), pp. 47–48; disposed: cf. John Edwards, *A Brief Vindication of the Fundamental Articles of the Christian Faith,* etc. (London, 1697), p. 114, and Gailhard, *Epistle and Preface,* pp. 24–25.

59. Saw: Burnet to Limborch, 18 Nov. 1694, Bodl. MS. Eng. Theo. c. 23, f. 12; subsided: cf. Wilbur, *History of Unitarianism,* II, 230–231, and McLachlan, *Socinianism,* p. 333. Propagating: Prideaux to Tenison, 2 Oct. 1696, L.P.L. Cod. MS. Gibson 930, f. 56; concern: Stillingfleet, *Discourse in Vindication,* p. xlviii. Expressed . . . refuting: Hippolyte De Luzancy, *Remarks on Several Late Writings, Publish'd in England, by the Socinians,* etc. (London, 1696), and *A Conference between an Orthodox Christian and a Socinian,* etc. (London, 1698).

60. Ends: Robert Wallace, *Antitrinitarian Biography,* etc., 3 vols. (London, 1850), I, 192–319. Observed: JT to Phillips, 17 Aug. 1703, B.L. Add. MS. 4465, f. 3. Induce: [John Toland], *Socinianism Truly Stated,* etc. (London, 1705). Driven: Burnet to Limborch, 18 Nov. 1694, Bodl. MS. Eng. Theo. c. 23, f. 12. Presenting: Thomas Halyburton, *Natural Religion Insufficient, and Reveal'd Necessary to Man's Happiness,* etc., 2 pts. in 1 vol., (Edinburgh, 1714), I, 17, 59–61. Persisted: e.g., [Phillip Skelton] *Ophiomaches, or Deism Revealed,* etc., 2d ed., 2 vols. (London, 1751), a series of dialogues in which a deist squire and a Unitarian clergyman work hand in glove.

61. Hoped: John Tillotson, *A Sermon concerning the Unity of the Divine Nature,* etc. (London, 1693), pp. 16–17; urgency: This account summarizes Edward Carpenter, *Thomas Tenison, Archbishop of Canterbury: His Life and Times* (London, S.P.C.K., 1948), pp. 297–300. Turned: Nye, *Acts of the Great Athanasius;* clarifications: e.g., William Sherlock, *An Apology for Writing against the Socinians,* etc. (London, 1693). Provided: *A Discourse concerning the Nominal and Real Trinitarians,* etc. (n.p., n.d. [1695]). Preached: Joseph Bingham, "On the Trinity," in *The English Sermon,* vol. II, 1650–1750, ed. C. H. Sisson (Cheadle Hulme, Carcanet Press, 1976), 222–240.

62. F. B., *A Free but Modest Censure on the Late Controversial Writings and Debates,* etc. (London, 1698), p. 15.

63. Robert Jenkin, *The Reasonableness and Certainty of the Christian Religion,* etc., 5th ed., 3 vols. (London, 1721), I, xi.

302 Notes to Pages 106–110

64. Concede: Stillingfleet, *Discourse in Vindication,* pp. xlviii–l. Discerned: Sherlock, *Apology,* p. 18. Differed: Charles Blount, *The Oracles of Reason,* etc. (London, 1693), p. 91. Insisted: JT, *Apology,* p. 41.

65. "Deist": Nye, *Letter of Resolution,* p. 18. Wrote: *Some Thoughts,* p. 21. Sought: Nye, *Agreement of the Unitarians,* p. 55. Identified: Prideaux to Tenison, 2 Oct. 1696, L.P.L. Cod. MS. Gibson 930, f. 56. Appreciation: McLachlan, *Socinianism,* p. 323; bombarded: Nye to Tenison, 6 Dec. 1699 and 4 Nov. 1703, L.P.L. Cod. MS. Misc. 953, ff. 64, 79.

66. Burnet to Le Clerc, n.d. [1698?], in Barnes, *Jean Le Clerc,* p. 256.

67. Labored: [Peter Browne], *The Procedure, Extent, and Limits of Human Understanding,* etc. (London, 1728), p. 40. Absolved: Leslie, *Charge of Socinianism,* p. 16, and Edwards, *Socinian Creed,* cf. pp. 138–144, 150. Chary: Browne, *Procedure,* p. 40.

68. "Work": Bernard J. F. Lonergan, *Method in Theology* (New York, Herder and Herder, 1972), p. 132.

69. Fashioned: John P. Donnelly, "Calvinist Thomism," *Viator: Medieval and Renaissance Studies* 7 (1976), 441–455, and "Italian Influences on the Development of Calvinist Scholasticism," *Sixteenth Century Journal* 7 (1976), 81–101. Proved: e.g., John Wallis, *The Doctrine of the Blessed Trinity Briefly Explain'd,* etc. (London, 1690).

4. The Task of Criticism

1. Conviction: _____ to Toland, 4 and 7 May 1694 in JT/C, II, 295–298, 298–300; Edwards, *Socinian Creed,* pp. 150, 214; Gailhard, *Blasphemous Socinian Heresie,* p. 102, and *Epistle and Preface,* pp. 49–51; Payne, *Mystery of the Christian Faith,* cf. pp. 61, 96; Norris, *Account of Reason and Faith,* 305–306, 334; Willis, *Occasional Paper,* p. 20; [Thomas Beconsall], *The Christian Belief,* etc. (London, 1696), pp. 12, 40–41. Divinity: *A Letter to I. C. Esq; upon Mr. Toland's Book,* etc. (Dublin, 1697), p. 4; Creed: *Nouvelles de la république des lettres,* Oct. 1699, pp. 367–368; "Branch": Browne, *Letter,* p. 205. Link: Edmund Elys, *Letter to the Hon. Sir Robert Howard,* etc. (London, 1696), pp. 8–16. Professed: Stillingfleet, *Discourse in Vindication,* pp. 2, 231, 272, and *Bishop of Worcester's Answer,* p. 5. Reluctant: Locke, *Mr. Locke's Reply,* p. 56. Welcomed: [Thomas Beverley], *Christianity the Great Mystery,* etc. (London, 1696), pp. 2–4, 49–53. "Indifferency": Edwards, *Socinian Creed,* preface.

2. Cf. [Daniel Defoe], *Animadversions on the Succession to the Crown of England Consider'd,* etc. (London, 1701), p. 28, and *Argument,* p. 51. *Remarks on the Life,* preface; *Nazarenus:* "A Letter from Mr. T–l____d to Master R–ch____d B____ley," *The Spy,* no. 13, 8 Feb. 1721; *Tetradymus:* Thomas Lewis, *The History of Hypatia,* etc. (London, 1721), p. 3. Presented: *Applebee's Original Weekly Journal,* 17 Mar. 1722, p. 2318.

3. Recognized: [William Stephens?], *An Apology for the Parliament, Humbly Representing to Mr. J G,* etc. (London, 1697), pp. 4–5. Hope: [Stephen Nye], *An Historical Account, and Defence of the New Testament,* etc. (London, 1700), p. 109. Wrote: _____ to JT, n.d., B.L. Add. MS. 4465, f. 55–56, and Eagle to JT, 20 June 1720, *ibid.,* f. 20.

4. Disavowal: JT, *Apology,* pp. 36–37, and JT/N, First letter, p. 77. Differentiated: JT, *Defence,* p. 11; quoted: JT, *Apology,* pp. 45–46. Separate: JT/CNM-2, p. 50; intended, JT/CNM, p. xvii. Realized: JT, *Apology,* pp. 31–32, and JT, *Defence,* p. 2. Alive: JT to Phillips, 17 Aug. 1703, B.L. Add. MS. 4465, f. 3. Ventured . . . knew: JT, *Socinianism Truly Stated,* pp. 9–10; JT/T, p. 190; defend: JT/LM, p. 139. Firmin: *ibid.,* p. 191; dismissed: JT, *Memorial,* p. 84. Statement: JT to _____, n.d., in JT/C, II, 303–304. Evasiveness: e.g., JT/VL, p. 82, and JT, *Second Part,* p. 22. Sensitive: *Remarks on the Life,* p. 55; George Smalridge, *A Sermon Preach'd before the Honourable House of Commons,* etc. (London, 1702), p. 11.

5. Tended: Ogonowski, "Le 'Christianisme sans mystères,' " pp. 205–223. Emphasizing . . . assumed: Firpo, "Il rapporto tra socinianesimo e primo deismo inglese," pp. 271, 274, and "John Locke e il socinianesimo," pp. 100, 107–108.

6. Maintain: Reedy, "Socinians, John Toland," pp. 294–298. "Reason": Tindal, *Letter to the Reverend,* pp. 33–34.

7. Arthur O. Lovejoy, *The Great Chain of Being: A Study of the History of an Idea* (Cambridge, Mass., Harvard University Press, 1936), p. 4.

8. "One": Denzinger-Schönmetzer, *Enchiridion Symbolorum,* 36th ed., no. 75. "Individual": Aquinas, *Summa Theologiae,* I, 29, 1. Descartes: René Descartes, *The Principles of Philosophy,* in *The Philosophical Works of Descartes,* ed. and trans. E. S. Haldane and G. R. T. Ross, corr. ed., 2 vols. (Cambridge, University Press, 1931), I, 302, 222. "Thinking": Locke, *Essay,* II, xxvii, 9. Sherlock: William Sherlock, *Vindication of the Doctrines of the Trinity and of the Incarnation* (London, 1690), p. 47. Socinians: *Brief Notes on the Creed of St. Athanasius* (n.p., n.d. [London, 1690?]), p. 2. "Trifle": JT, *Letter from an Arabian,* p. 6; unscriptural: JT/T, pp. 133–134; "barbarous": JT/N, p. xx.

9. Appears: Redwood, *Reason, Ridicule and Religion,* pp. 29, 108. Fideist: Günter Gawlick, ed., *Letters to Serena,* by John Toland (Stuttgart, F. Fromann Verlag, 1964), pp. 5*–23*; Marxist: Erwin Pracht, ed., *Briefe an Serena,* by John Toland, trans. G. Wickmann (Berlin, Akademie Verlag, 1959), pp. vii–lxviii.

10. Presented: Stephen, *History of English Thought,* I, 87–93. Reformulation: Sina, *L'avvento della ragione,* pp. 501–505.

11. Proponents: F. H. Heinemann, "John Toland and the Age of the Enlightenment," *Review of English Studies* 20 (1944), pp. 125–146; Margaret C. Jacob, "John Toland and the Newtonian Ideology," *Journal of the Warburg and Courtauld Institutes* 32 (1969), 307–331; *Newtonians and the English Revolution,* pp. 201–250; "Newtonianism and the Origins of the Enlightenment," pp. 1–25; rev. of Worden, ed., *Ludlow, Voyce, American Historical Review* 85 (1980), 389–390; *Radical Enlightenment,* pp. 83–84, 152–154; James R. Jacob and Margaret C. Jacob. "The Anglican Origins of Modern Science: The Metaphysical Foundations of the Whig Constitution," *Isis* 71 (1980) 251–267; Chiara Giuntini, *Panteismo e ideologia repubblicana: John Toland (1670–1722)* (Bologna, Il Mulino, 1979); Massimo Firpo, "John Toland e il deismo inglese," *Rivista storica italiana* 90 (1978), 327–380, and Alfredo Sabetti, *John Toland, un irregolare della società e della cultura inglese tra seicento e settecento* (Naples, Liguori editore, 1976). Conceding: Jacob, "John Toland," p. 312. Acquainted: *ibid.,* pp. 309–311; fabricated: *ibid.,* pp. 313, 316. Affected: Jacob and Jacob, "Anglican Origins," p. 266. Adhering: cf. *ibid.,* pp. 264–265, and Jacob, rev. of Worden, p. 390; opposed: Jacob, "Newtonianism and the Enlightenment," pp. 20–22. Changing: Giuntini, *Panteismo e ideologia,* p. 62n.; enlighten: *ibid.,* p. 491. Follower: *ibid.,* pp. 74, 82; ideologist: *ibid.,* pp. 185–187. Introduced: *ibid.,* p. 291; became . . . grew: *ibid.,* pp. 203–204; inability: *ibid.,* pp. 9–10. Transformed: *ibid.,* pp. 307–310. Complemented: *ibid.,* pp. 265, 279. Resorted: *ibid.,* pp. 439–440.

12. Presenting: Jacob, rev. of Worden, p. 390. Dot: e.g., JT/VL, pp. 119–120; JT/LS, preface; [John Toland, ed. and trans.], *A Letter against Popery,* etc. (London 1712), p. 22; JT/N, p. xi, (First letter) 67; JT/T, pp. 182–183, 221–222. Deny: Giuntini, *Panteismo e ideologia,* p. 40n. Lucretius: Lucretius, *De rerum natura,* II, 8; series: Adeisidaemon, the main figure of *Clito,* gave his name to the volume of 1709, just as *Clito* itself ("The Key") was followed by the essay "Clidophorus" ("The Key-Bearer") in *Tetradymus.* Toland coined the word *pantheist* in *Socinianism Truly Stated* and wrote *Pantheisticon.* Recapitulate: cf. L.P., Master of Arts [John Toland], *Two Essays Sent in a Letter from Oxford,* etc. (London, 1695), pp. 8, 13–14, and JT/P, pp. 46, 53–54. *Jovis:* JT, *Two Essays,* p. 43.

13. Albert Lantoine, *Un précurseur de la franc-maçonnerie: John Toland, 1670-1722* (Paris, E. Nourry, 1927), pp. 105, 155; Eugene I. Dyche, "The Life, Works, and Philosophical Relations of John (Janus Junius) Toland, 1670-1722" (Ph.D. diss., University of Southern California, 1944), pp. 241-254; Wolfgang Dienemann, "A Bibliography of John Toland (1670-1722)" (Dip. in librarianship thesis, University of London, 1953), p. ii; H. F. Nicholl, "The Life and Work of John Toland" (M. Litt. thesis, Trinity College, Dublin, 1962), pp. 49, 54, 110-111, 142; Robert R. Evans, "John Toland's Pantheism: A Revolutionary Ideology and Enlightenment Philosophy" (Ph.D. diss., Brandeis University, 1965), pp. 12, 26-28, 121, 168, 194; Stephen H. Daniel, "The Philosophic Methodology of John Toland" (Ph.D. diss., St. Louis University, 1977), pp. 48-49, 82, 303, 308, 356-357.

14. Defined: cf. Dominick La Carpa, "Rethinking Intellectual History and Reading Texts," *History and Theory* 19 (1980), 255. Using: JT, *Clito*, pp. 5-6: "Who": *ibid.*, pp. 8-9. "Fatal": *ibid.*, pp. 11-12. "But": *ibid.*, pp. 16-17.

15. "Varro's": JT/T, p. 91. Reflecting: [Jean Le Clerc], "Opscula mythologica, ethica, et physica graece et latine," *Bibliothèque universelle* 7 (1687), 97-116; cf. JT/VL, p. 6; JT, "Primitive Constitution," JT/C, II, 121, and JT/LS, p. 56. Augustine, *The City of God*, trans. Marcus Dods, et al (New York, Random House, 1950), VI, 5. "Fault": *ibid.* "That": *ibid.*, 7.

16. This paragraph depends on Frank E. Manuel, *The Eighteenth Century Confronts the Gods* (Cambridge, Mass., Harvard University Press, 1959), pp. 24-40, and Gianfranco Cantelli, "Myth and Language in Vico," in *Giambattista Vico's Science of Humanity*, ed. Giorgio Tagliacozzo and Donald P. Verene (Baltimore, Johns Hopkins University Press, 1976), pp. 47-63. Treated: cf. Pierre Bayle, *Continuation des pensées diverses*, etc. [1704], in *Oeuvres diverses*, 3 vols. (The Hague, 1727), III, 254-256, and Le Clerc, "Opscula," pp. 102-103.

17. Adopted: JT/LS, pp. 30, 128; exploit: JT, *Adeisidaemon*, pp. 117, 156-157. Relied: cf. JT/LS, pp. 85, 56; judged: JT/T, p. 93; commended: *ibid.*, p. 91; cf. J. Tate, "Cornutus and the Poets," *Classical Quarterly* 23 (1929), 41-45. Believing: cf. JT/CNM, p. 13, and JT/LS, pp. 1-14; assumed: JT/T, pp. 3-4, 87-88, 94; cf. JT/CNM, pp. iv-vii, xiv, and JT/P, preface. Mask: JT/T, pp. 77-79. Proposed: B.L. Add. MS. 4295, f. 71 ("Superstition Unmasked"); found: cf. JT/LS, pp. 88-91, and JT/T, p. 77.

18. Maintained: Cicero, *Tusculanae disputationes*, I, 26, 65, and IV, 33, 71. "Was": JT/SA, p. 80. Belief: cf. Cicero, *Tusculanae disputationes*, I, 12, 49, 117, and JT/LM, p. 127. "Designedly": JT/P, preface; doubted: Cicero, *Tusculanae disputationes*, II, 4. Identified: R. J. Goar, *Cicero and the State Religion* (Amsterdam, Hakkert, 1972), p. 94; cf. JT, "Primitive Constitution," JT/C, II, 120-121.

19. "Nation": JT to _____, n.d., B.L. Add. MS. 4465, f. 59. Adhere: JT/CNM, pp. xvii-xviii. Differentiating: JT to Leibniz, 14 Feb. 1710 (O.S.), in JT/C, II, 391; silent: JT, "Fabulous Death," *ibid.*, II, 39-40. Moses: JT, *Two Essays*, pp. 15, 29.

20. Maintained: JT/CNM, pp. 147-148; JT/T, pp. 223-224. Meant: JT/CNM, pp. xix-xx; JT, *Defence*, p. 5; JT, *Second Part*, pp. 21-22; avoided: JT/CNM, p. 108. Held: JT/T, p. 96. Portrayal: JT/VL, p. 106. Recognized: JT/N, p. vii. "Reconciling": JT/T, pp. 224-225.

21. "Universal": JT, *Two Essays*, p. i; seeing: JT, "Primitive Constitution," JT/C, II, 139. Provided: from "The Excellence of Abraham's Faith and Obedience" (1686). Dissembling: B.L. Add. MS. 4295, f. 67 ("Church by Law Established"). Borne: JT and Shaftesbury, *Paradoxes of State*, p. 4. Seized: JT/VL, pp. 92-94; suggestion: Willis, *Occasional Paper*, p. 26. Pleasure: JT/AL, pp. 65-66.

22. Envisioned: cf. JT/CNM, pp. xxvi–xxvii, and JT, *Defence,* pp. 6–7; conclusion: JT to Baldwin, 24 Feb. 1697 (O.S.), B.L. Add. MS. 4295, f. 4. Reconcile: JT, "Primitive Constitution," JT/C, II, 169–170.

23. Subject: Evans, "John Toland's Pantheism," p. 137. Conviction: JT, *Socinianism Truly Stated,* p. 5; division: JT, *Agreement of the Customs,* p. 92; denial: JT, *Principle,* pp. 19–20. Thought: JT, *Socinianism Truly Stated,* p. 7. Obliged: JT/P, p. 98; retained: cf. *ibid.,* p. 62, and preface.

24. Metaphor: cf. John Miller, *Popery and Politics in England, 1660–1698* (Cambridge, University Press, 1973), p. 71, and Joseph T. Huston, "Aspects of English Anti-Catholic Propaganda, 1667–1692" (Ph.D. diss., University of Michigan, 1965), pp. 194–195. Mean: JT, *Memorial,* pp. 101–102. Allowed: JT/VL, pp. 92, 100–101. Defended: JT/CNM, pp. 23–25.

25. Explain: [John Toland], *A Letter to a Member of Parliament,* etc. [1698], in *State Tracts . . . of William III,* 3 vols. (London, 1706), II, 618. Attribute: JT, *Appeal to Honest People,* pp. 31–32. Lash: JT/VL, p. 75. Attacked: Beverley, *Christianity the Great Mystery,* preface.

26. Seems: JT, "Abstract," pp. 506–508. Recover: JT/CNM, p. 61. Anticipated: JT/LM, pp. 182–183. Endow: JT/CNM, p. 174, and JT/N, p. xx. Critical: JT/P, p. 62, and JT, *Letter to an M. P.,* p. 615. Asserted: JT/CNM, p. 19.

27. Condemn: JT/CNM, pp. 98–99, 125. Locke: Basil Willey, *The Seventeenth-Century Background: Studies in the Thought of the Age in Relation to Poetry and Religion* (New York, Columbia University Press, 1935), pp. 276–277. Denied: S. G. Hefelbower, *The Relation of John Locke to English Deism* (Chicago, University Press, 1918), p. 18. Observers: Browne, *Letter,* pp. 2–33, and [John Witty], *The Reasonableness of Assenting to the Mysteries of Christianity,* etc. (London, 1708), pp. 34, 37. Eventually: JT/T, p. 190. Once: JT, *Letter to an M. P.,* p. 626.

28. Logicians: Wilbur S. Howell, *Logic and Rhetoric in England, 1500–1700* (Princeton, University Press, 1956), p. 3; cf. JT, "Primitive Constitution," JT/C, II, 128. Admitted: JT, *Defence,* p. 9; relied: e.g., JT/CNM, pp. 83, 87; "Men": JT/LS, p. 226.

29. Straightforward: JT/CNM, pp. 75–80. Expanded: *ibid.,* p. 7; cf. Locke, *Essay,* IV, xvii, 23. Held: JT/CNM, pp. 14–16; cf. Locke, *Essay,* II, i, 3–4; IV, xvi, 5. Constitute: JT/CNM, p. 16. Idea: *ibid.,* pp. 17–18: cf. Locke, *Essay,* IV, ii, 14–15. Toland: cf. JT/CNM, pp. 15–16, and Locke, *Essay,* IV, xv, 4.

30. Endued: JT/CNM, pp. 9–10; cf. Locke, *Essay,* II, vi–vii. Defines: JT/CNM, pp. 14–15; cf. Locke, *Essay,* IV, ii, 1–2. Classes: JT/CNM, pp. 17–18; cf. Locke, *Essay,* II, i, 1–2. Probability: JT/CNM, p. 13, and JT/CNM-2, p. 15; cf. Locke, *Essay,* IV, xv, 3. Explanation: *ibid.,* IV, ii, 1; insistence: *ibid.,* iii, 5; effort: *ibid.,* xviii. "What": JT/CNM, p. 23; cf. Locke, *Essay,* IV, xvii, 23; took: JT/CNM, pp. 12–13.

31. Construing: cf. JT/CNM, pp. 14–15, and Locke, *Essay,* IV, ii, 4. Defined: JT/CNM, pp. 12–13; cf. Locke, *Essay,* IV, xvii, 2. That: (1) JT/CNM, pp. 42–43, 160–161, 151; (2) p. 7; (3) pp. 130, 174; (4) p. 137; (5) pp. 9, 173; (6) p. 145; (7) p. 126; (8) pp. 38, 115; (9) pp. 57, 146–147.

32. Accepting: cf. JT/CNM, p. 87, and Locke, Essay, III, vi, 9, and IV, iii, 6. Distinguished: *ibid.,* III, iii, 15–18. Understood: JT/CNM, pp. 83–85. Men: *ibid.,* pp. 82–83.

33. Incomprehensible: Beconsall, *Christian Belief,* pp. 149–150. Challenge: Browne, *Letter,* p. 146. Relied: cf. JT/CNM, p. 16, and Locke, *Essay,* IV, xvi, 14. Affirmed: cf. JT/CNM, pp. 4–6, and Locke, *Essay,* IV, xviii, 6. Treated: cf. *ibid.,* IV, xvi, 14, and xix, 14–16. Simplified: JT/CNM, p. 109; cf. JT/VL, p. 104. "Prophetical": JT/CNM, p. 109. Judged: *ibid.,* p. 15. Rejected: *ibid.,* pp. 49–50.

34. Admitted: JT, *Defence,* pp. 4-5. Proposed: JT/CNM, p. 90; blend: JT/VL, pp. 92-93. "Nothing": JT/CNM, pp. 75-76. Presumed: *ibid.,* p. 91.

35. Distinguished: JT/CNM, pp. 95-97; cf. G. Bornkamm, in *Theological Dictionary of the New Testament,* s.v. *"mustērion."* Dismissed: JT/CNM, p. 111, 102-103. Allowed: *ibid.,* p. 142. Held: JT/N, First letter, p. 33. Amounted: JT/T, p. 79.

36. Interpreted: cf. JT/CNM, p. 141, and Locke, *Essay,* IV, xvi, 14; treated: cf. JT/CNM, p. 145, and Locke, *Essay,* IV, xviii, 5. Concede: JT/CNM, p. 133. Heresy: *ibid.,* p. 80. Indicted: JT, *Defence,* p. 2.

37. Impart: JT/N, p. v. Exposition: JT/CNM, pp. 136-137. Verdict: Rom. 4:20.

38. Professed: JT/CNM, pp. 93-94. Treated: *ibid.,* p. xiii. "Curious": JT, "Primitive Constitution," JT/C, II, 132-133; cf. JT/T, p. 224. Messiah: JT/CNM, pp. 47-48; died: JT, "Primitive Constitution," JT/C, II, 130. Musings: B.L. Add. MS. 4295, ff. 69-70 ("Christopaedia").

39. "Inveterate": Browne, *Letter,* p. 96. Publish: JT/CNM, pp. 88, 134. Voltaire: Peter Gay, *Voltaire's Politics: The Poet as Realist* (Princeton, University Press, 1959), p. 241.

40. Suggests: Robert M. Burns, "David Hume and Miracles in Historical Perspective" (Ph.D. diss., Princeton University, 1971), pp. 21-33. "Operation": Browne, *Letter,* pp. 182-183. Stressed: JT, *Two Essays,* pp. 4, 8, 13-14; mocked: JT, marginal note in Martin, *Description,* p. 49. Maintained: JT/CNM, p. 152. Proofs: *ibid.,* pp. 150-157. Related: JT/T, p. 5; reported: B.L. Add. MS. 4465, f. 69^v (undated fragment). Holding: JT, "Primitive Constitution," JT/C, II, 188.

41. JT, "Primitive Constitution," JT/C, II, 165, 128.

42. Quest: JT/T, p. 142. Socinians: *Faith of One God . . . Asserted and Defended* (London, n.d. [1691]), p.1; adopted: JT/N, First letter, p. 83. Placing: JT/CNM, p. 176.

43. Linked: JT/CNM, p. 54. Recovered: JT, *Appeal to Honest People,* p. 41. Assumed . . . dismiss: JT, "Primitive Constitution," JT/C, II, 142. Intimated: JT/CNM, p. 75. Invoked: JT/T, title page (Ps. 78:2). References: JT/CNM, pp. 115-117.

44. Encompassed: JT, *Letter against Popery,* p. 5. Critics: Gailhard, *Blasphemous Socinian Heresie,* p. 316. Maintained: JT, "Primitive Constitution," JT/C, II, 122-123, 154. "Subject": *ibid.,* p. 163. Informing: JT, *Letter against Popery,* pp. 22-23.

45. Progenitors: cf. JT, "Primitive Constitution," JT/C, II, 192, and JT, *Letter against Popery,* pp. 10-11. Represented: JT, *Second Part,* p. 20. Variety: JT/CNM, pp. 123, 3. Doomed: JT/T, p. 172. Disdained: JT, *Letter against Popery,* pp. 8-9. Represent: cf. *ibid.,* pp. 9-10, and JT/CNM, p. 26.

46. Pursued: JT, *Letter against Popery,* pp. 18-19, 7-8.

47. Convinced: [John Toland], *Amyntor: or, a Defence of Milton's Life,* etc. (London, 1699), p. 23. Jerome: JT/N, First letter, p. 59. Defender: JT/T, pp. 133-134. Sympathizers: *ibid.,* pp. vii-viii. Embellish: Charles Kingsley, *Hypatia: or, New Foes with an Old Face,* 2 vols. (London, 1890), II, 321-323.

48. Believed: JT, "Primitive Constitution," JT/C, II, 173. Bishops: JT/N, Second letter, p. 37. Assert: JT, "Primitive Constitution," JT/C, 194-195. Exemplified: JT/T, p. 97. Expanded: [John Toland], *The Destiny of Rome,* etc. (London, 1718), p. 22, and JT, "Primitive Constitution," JT/C, II, 195. Amounted: *ibid.,* p. 157. Props: JT/LM, p. 95.

49. Fruit: JT/LS, pp. 104-105. Degradation: JT/N, First letter, p. 70; divisions: JT, "Primitive Constitution," JT/C, II, 123-124. Known: cf. *ibid.,* pp. 149-150, and JT/T, p. viii. Ridicule: B.L. Add. MS. 4295, ff. 64-65 (two "psalms"). Obstacle: JT, *Mr. Toland's Reflections,* p. 8. Ceremony: cf. JT/CNM, pp. 172-173, and JT to Mr. ———, ca. 16 Mar. 1720, in JT/C, II, 457. Adopted: cf. JT/CNM, pp. 159-160, and Nye, *Agreement of the Unitarians,* pp. 11-12. Insisted: JT/LS, p. 3.

50. Appropriating: JT/VL, pp. 119–120. Priestcraft: JT/N, First Letter, pp. 54–76. Infected: JT/CNM, p. 161. Suggested: JT, *Appeal to Honest People,* pp. 39–40.

51. JT/CNM, pp. 90–91, 41, 92–93.

52. Conditions: JT/CNM, pp. 42, 50. Forged: JT, *Letter against Popery,* p. 18. "Sacred": JT, *Two Essays,* p. 31; cf. JT, "Primitive Constitution," JT/C, II, 146. "Establish": JT, *Two Essays,* p. ii.

53. Presented: JT/T, p. 31; cf. JT, *Two Essays,* p. 23. "Expert": JT, "Catalogue of Books," JT/C, I, 383; disposed: JT, marginal note in Martin, *Description,* p. 5. Portray: JT/CNM, pp. 119, 158–159. Scholarship: *Journal des savants,* supplement, Sept. 1708; Le Clerc, Simon: cf. JT, *Two Essays,* p. 33, and JT/N, First letter, p. 56; Spinoza: cf. Giuntini, *Panteismo e ideologia,* pp. 420–423, and Piergiorgio Grassi, "Il *Christianity Not Mysterious* di John Toland," *Studi urbanati di storia, filosofia e letteratura,* n.s. B, 49 (1975), 250–251, 256–259; question: e.g., JT to Rev. Mr. _____, 12 Sept. 1695, in JT/C, II, 314–317. Delineate: JT, *Agreement of the Customs,* p. 20. "Jews": JT, *Reasons for Naturalizing,* p. 41.

54. Denied: JT, *Adeisidaemon,* p. 160. Uncertain: *ibid.,* pp. 155–156. Led: *ibid.,* pp. 146–148. Invoked: *ibid.,* p. 104; theocracy: *ibid.,* p. 126. Barren: *ibid.,* pp. 138–139. Subject: *ibid.,* p. 158. Insinuate: *ibid.,* p. 117. Oracles: *ibid.,* pp. 164–168.

55. Renunciation: JT/T, p. xi, 13, 87; jabs: e.g., JT/CNM, pp. xxv–xxvi, and JT, *Destiny of Rome,* p. 24; determination: JT/T, p. 3. Written: Blaise Pascal, *Pensées,* ed. Louis Lafuma (Paris, Garnier-Flammarion, 1973), no. 600.

56. Concluded: JT, "Fabulous Death," JT/C, II, 46–47. Discerned: JT, *Apology,* p. 33. Ended: JT/LM, pp. 150–151.

57. Cited: Offspring Blackall, *A Sermon Preached . . . Jan. 30th, 1698–9* (London, 1699), p. 16. Replied: JT, *Amyntor,* p. 42. Asserted: *ibid.,* pp. 15, 23. Deployed: JT's principal sources were Richard Simon, *Histoire critique des versions du Nouveau Testament,* etc. (Rotterdam, 1690), and *Histoire critique des principaux commentateurs du Nouveau Testament* (Rotterdam, 1690); Louis Ellies Du Pin, *Nouvelle bibliothèque des auteurs ecclésiastiques,* vol. I, *Auteurs des trois premières siècles* (Paris, 1686); Johannes Ernst Grabe, *Spicilegium ss. patrum, ut et haereticorum,* vol. I (Oxford, 1698); William Cave, *Scriptorum ecclesiasticorum historia literaria,* pt. I (London, 1688); and Henry Dodwell, *Dissertationes in Irenaeum* (Oxford, 1689). Retracted: Offspring Blackall, *Reasons for Not Replying to a Book Lately Published,* etc. (London, 1699), pp. 6, 3. Others: *ibid.,* pp. 8–9.

58. This account follows Erman, *Mémoires,* pp. 203–211.

59. Cf. JT to Arminius, 1 Aug. 1710, B.L. Add. MS. 4465, f. 11, and to Höhendorff, 7 Mar. 1711, B.L. Add. MS. 4295, ff. 19–20.

60. Pursuing: B.L. Add. MS. 4465, ff. 61–62 ("Certain Sayings"), and B.L. Add. MS. 4295, f. 72 (undated fragment); reconsidering: JT, *Amyntor,* pp. 56–57, and JT/N, Second letter, p. 8; Socinian: cf. Max Wiener, "John Toland and Judaism," *Hebrew Union College Annual* 16 (1941), 217, and Leo Strauss, *Spinoza's Critique of Religion,* trans. E. M. Sinclair (New York, Schocken, 1965), pp. 64–85. Suggested: JT, *Amyntor,* p. 64. Attribute: cf. JT/CNM, p. 152, and JT/N, pp. vi, (First letter) 24. Assumed: *ibid.,* p. iii. Added: *ibid.,* p. iv; cf. Isaac de La Peyrère, *Du rappel des Juifs* (n.p., 1643). Allowed: JT/N, pp. vii–viii. Depended: *ibid.,* First letter, pp. 44, 16, 71–72.

61. Contended: JT/N, p. iii. Regarded: Prideaux, *Letter to the Deists,* p. 11. Renewed: JT/N, First letter, pp. 10–11. Taunt: Leslie, *Socinian Controversy,* Dialogue IV, pp. 25–26.

62. JT/CNM, p. 146. L.P.L. Cod. MS. Gibson 933, f. 8 ("Copy of Mr. Toland's Ltr."). JT/CNM, p. 142, and JT, "Primitive Constitution," JT/C, II, 178. JT, *Principle,* p. 26.

63. Criterion: JT/CNM, p. 79, and JT/T, p. 224; JT, "Primitive Constitution," JT/C, II, 145-146; cf. JT, *Principle,* pp. 3-4, and JT/LS, p. 19. Achieved: JT/N, First letter, p. 14. "They": JT/CNM, p. 55. Insisted: JT/N Second letter, p. 16. Buttressed: cf. JT, "Primitive Constitution," JT/C, II, 138, and Harry A. Wolfson, *The Philosophy of the Church Fathers,* I (Cambridge, Mass., Harvard University Press, 1956) 17-18.

64. Championing: cf. JT, "Abstract," pp. 517-519, and Daniel Williams, *The Gospel-Truth Stated and Vindicated,* etc. (London, 1692), preface. Deferred: JT/CNM, p. 95; JT/N, First letter, p. 68. Sustained: JT to Mr. _____, n.d., in JT/C, II, 427-428. Maintained: JT, *Memorial,* p. 85. Ventured: JT, "Primitive Constitution," JT/C, II, 135. Judged: JT to _____, n.d., B.L. Add. MS. 4465, f. 59.

65. Professed: JT to Clayton, 4 Dec. 1698, in JT/C, II, 323. Affirmed: cf. JT/CNM, p. xvii, and JT, "Primitive Constitution," JT/C, II, 134. Treated: JT/LS, preface. Emphasized: JT to –, n.d., B.L. Add. MS. 4465, ff. 55-56. Chose: JT to Clayton, 7 Dec. 1698, in JT/C, II, 325. "Cicero": Augustine, *City of God,* xix, 4. "Imprudence": JT, *Agreement of the Customs,* pp. 155-156.

66. Seen: Augustine, *City of God,* I, 15; cf. II, 23; III, 18. Identified: *ibid.,* XVIII, 51; XXI.

67. JT, *Two Essays,* p. 38; JT/CNM-2, pp. 170-171.

5. The Quest for Civic Virtue

1. Types: JT/N, Appendix, p. 57; confront: *ibid.,* p. 6. Idea: Pocock, *Political Works of Harrington,* p. 17.

2. Rationalism: cf. JT/AL, pp. 44-45, and JT, in *Oceana,* p. xix. Prosperity: JT and Shaftesbury, *Danger of Mercenary Parliaments,* p. 8.

3. Tyranny: JT, *Apology,* p. 15. Prejudice: JT, *Reasons for Naturalizing,* p. 50; superstition: JT/P, preface; mystery: JT, *Art of Restoring,* p. 28; expression: JT, *Letter against Popery,* p. 5.

4. Rome: JT/LM, p. 172. Rise: [John Toland], *The Militia Reformed,* etc. (London, 1698), p. 62. Associations: JT/LM, p. 92.

5. Lists: JT, *Second Part,* pp. 24-25, JT/T, p. 223, and JT, "Another Memorial [1711]," JT/C, II, 227, 231. Constantine: JT, *Appeal to Honest People,* pp. 1, 16-23.

6. Rummaged: [John Toland], *A Letter from General Ludlow to Dr. Hollingworth* (Amsterdam [*sic*], 1692), pp. 28-29; JT, *Appeal to Honest People,* pp. 36-38; JT, "Memorial Presented to a Minister of State," JT/C, II, 242-243; civil: cf. JT/LS, p. 116, and JT, *Appeal to Honest People,* p. 6.

7. Characteristics: JT, *Agreement of the Customs,* p. 8, and JT, *Reasons for Naturalizing,* p. 49. Policy: JT/SA, pp. 53, 58. Innocuousness: JT, *Memorial,* p. 44; conscience: [John Toland], *The Declaration Lately Published by the Elector Palatine,* etc. (London, 1707), p. 3. Disdained: JT to _____, n.d. [1694], in JT/C, II, 307; proclaimed: JT, *Clito,* p. 11. Party: [John Toland], *A Defence of the Parliament of 1640,* etc. (London, 1698), preface, and JT/SA, pp. 14-18; standing: JT/LM, p. 133, and JT/SA, pp. 59-60; frequent: cf. JT/AG, pp. 70-73, and JT/SA, p. 38; social: JT/AL, pp. 11-12, and JT/SA, pp. 39-40.

8. "Game": Pocock, *Political Works of Harrington,* p. 142. "Inducements": Worden, *Ludlow, Voyce,* pp. 29-30.

9. Quentin Skinner, "Motives, Intentions, and the Interpretation of Texts," *New Literary History* 3 (1972), 406-407.

10. Cf. Pocock, *Machiavellian Moment,* pp. 419-423, 460-461, and Worden, *Ludlow, Voyce,* pp. 39-42.

11. Pocock, *Machiavellian Moment*, pp. 478, 486–488, 446.

12. Cf. Locke, *Essay*, III, x, 34, and David Hume, "Of Eloquence," in *Essays Moral, Political, and Literary*, ed. T. H. Green and T. H. Grose, 2 vols. (London, 1898), I, 172–173.

13. Considerable: JT, *Art of Canvassing*, p. v. Repudiation: JT, "Roman Education," JT/C, II, 2; tradition: Kristeller, *Renaissance Thought*, pp. 11–13. Principle: Hanna H. Gray, "Renaissance Humanism: The Pursuit of Eloquence," in *Renaissance Essays from the "Journal of the History of Ideas,"* ed. P. O. Kristeller and P. P. Wiener (New York, Harper and Row, 1968), p. 203.

14. Models: JT, *Adeisidaemon*, pp. i–ii. Anticipator: JT/AG, pp. 178–179.

15. The following paragraphs depend on Alain Michel, *Rhétorique et philosophie chez Cicéron: essai sur les fondements philosophiques de l'art de persuader* (Paris, Presses universitaires de France, 1960), pp. 3–30, and Jerrold E. Siegel, " 'Civic Humanism' or Ciceronian Rhetoric? The Culture of Petrarch and Bruni," *Past and Present* 34 (1966), 3–48, and *Rhetoric and Philosophy in Renaissance Humanism: The Union of Eloquence and Wisdom, Petrarch to Valla* (Princeton, University Press, 1968). Ends: Cicero: *De oratore*, II, xxviii, 121, and lxxvii, 310.

16. Joining: Cicero, *De oratore*, II, xxx, 120; shaped: *ibid.*, I, xxxiv, 157. Occasions: *ibid.*, III, xxvii, 107. Obligation: *ibid.*, I, xxiii, 108.

17. Eugenio Garin, *Italian Humanism: Philosophy and Civic Life in the Renaissance*, trans. Peter Munz (New York, Harper and Row, 1965), pp. 5–7, 50–66.

18. Cicero, *De oratore*, I, viii, 33, and II, lxxxii, 337.

19. Quentin Skinner, *The Foundations of Modern Political Thought*, 2 vols. (Cambridge, University Press, 1978), I, 175, 44–45.

20. Cicero, *De oratore*, II, ix, 35.

21. Preference: JT/LS, preface. Culling: JT/LM, p. 127.

22. Flux: cf. JT, *Destiny of Rome*, p. 7, and JT, *Memorial*, p. 5. Prudence: JT, *Philippick Oration*, p. 2n.

23. Focus: John Toland, *Cicero Illustratus*, etc. (London, 1712), pp. 11–12. Inconstant: JT/AG, p. 5. Notion: Tacitus, *Dialogus de oratoribus*, cc. 36–41, and pseudo-Longinus, *On the Sublime*, c. 44. Principles: JT/AG, p. 54.

24. JT, *Clito*, pp. 4–6.

25. Deal: JT, *Philippick Oration*, pp. vii–viii. "Nature": JT, *Art of Canvassing*, p. iv. Immutable: JT, *Philippick Oration*, pp. vii–viii. Accepted: JT/LM, p. 83, and JT, *Letter to an M.P.*, p. 625; cf. George H. Nadel, "Philosophy of History before Historicism," *History and Theory* 3 (1964), 291–315. "Endeavor": JT/MR, p. 64.

26. Fissiparous: [John Toland], *Propositions for Uniting the Two East-India Companies*, etc. (London, 1701), p. 1; endure: JT, in *Oceana*, p. xl. Great: JT, *Philippick Oration*, p. xl. Stentorian: JT/AL, p. 189; uproot: JT, *Adeisidaemon*, pp. 77–78. Recommended: JT, "Roman Education," JT/C, II, 6–7. Required: Add. to French MS. of JT/LS, O.N.B., MS. 10325, f. 94^{v}.

27. Prevail: JT/AG, p. 11. Worked: *ibid.*, p. 7, and JT/SA, p. 28. Forced: JT, *Art of Canvassing*, pp. 2, 37. Orator's: JT, *Clito*, p. 6.

28. Carried: JT/LS, pp. 98–99. View: JT, *Reasons for Addressing*, p. 9, and JT, *Mr. Toland's Reflections*, pp. 2–3; cult: cf. Helen Randall, "The Rise and Fall of a Martyrology: Sermons on Charles I," *Huntington Library Quarterly* 10 (1947), 155, and Byron D. Stewart, "The Cult of the Royal Martyr," *Church History* 38 (1968), 183–184. Admitted: Kenyon, *Revolution Principles*, pp. 61–62.

29. Dented: Jennifer Carter, "The Revolution and the Constitution," in *Britain after the Glorious Revolution*, ed. Geoffrey Holmes (New York, St. Martin's Press, 1969), p.

42; interpreted: Holmes, *Trial of Sacheverell*, p. 32. Create: H. T. Dickinson, *Liberty and Property: Political Ideology in Eighteenth-Century England* (New York, Holmes and Meier, 1977), p. 60, and Kenyon, *Revolution Principles*, pp. 35–60.

30. Provided: Kenyon, *Revolution Principles*, p. 51. Undermine: [John Toland, ed.], Algernon Sidney, *Discourses concerning Government*, etc. (London, 1698), p. 437; offer: cf. *ibid.*, pp. 130, 152; consent: *ibid.*, pp. 24–27, 74–75, 243–249; parliament: *ibid.*, pp. 377, 412.

31. "Such": JT, "Another Memorial [1711]," JT/C, II, 227–228. Three: JT, *Memorial*, p. 76.

32. Distinguished: JT/VL, p. 125. Acceptance: *ibid.*, pp. 127–128; cf. JT/AL, p. 92, and JT, in *Oceana*, p. viii. Usurper: JT, *High Church Display'd*, p. 13, and JT, in *Oceana*, p. xvii. Charge: [Charles Davenant], *The Old and Modern Whig Truly Represented*, etc. (London, 1702), p. 2. Synonym: *ibid.*, pp. 17–18.

33. Discard: Shaftesbury to Van Twiddie, 17 Jan. 1705 [O.S.], in Shaftesbury, *Life, Unpublished Letters*, p. 351; shrink: Wake to Nicolson, 23 Jan. 1700 [O.S.], in *Letters on Various Subjects, Literary, Political, and Ecclesiastical*, etc., ed. John Nichols, 2 vols., consecutive pag. (London, 1809), p. 217. Disappearance: Caroline Robbins, *The Eighteenth-Century Commonwealthman* (Cambridge, Mass., Harvard University Press, 1961), p. 31; blunting: Holmes, *British Politics*, p. 60. Vulnerable: Caroline Robbins, ed., *Two English Republican Tracts* (Cambridge, University Press, 1969), pp. 40–42.

34. Parallels: JT, in *Oceana*, p. x; permanence: [John Toland], *Her Majesty's Reasons*, etc. (London, 1712), in *A Collection of Scarce and Valuable Tracts*, etc. ["Somers Tracts"], ed. Walter Scott, 2d ed., 13 vols. (London, 1809–1815), XIII, 216. Debt: JT, in *Oceana*, p. viii. Offered: JT/LM, p. 174. "Such": JT/MR, p. 23.

35. Invading: [John Toland], *A Letter from Major General Ludlow to Sir E[dward] S[eymour]* (Amsterdam [*sic*], 1691), p. 25; cf. JT, *Defence of the Parliament*, p. 39.

36. Complemented: JT, *Defence of the Parliament*, preface, and JT, *Ludlow to Seymour*, pp. 1–2. Suspect: Kenyon, *Revolution Principles*, pp. 7, 16. Owed: JT/AL, pp. 1–6.

37. Lifeblood: Holmes, *British Politics*, p. 6. Solidified: *ibid.*, pp. 7, 221. Reign: Kenyon, *Revolution Principles*, pp. 100–101, and Dennis A. Rubini, "Party and the Augustan Constitution, 1694–1716: Politics and the Power of the Executive," *Albion* 10 (1979 [*sic*]), 193–208. Shifted: Horwitz, *Parliament, Policy, and Politics*, pp. 97–98, 214–215, 266, 316–317; cf. JT/MR, pp. 8–9. Regularly: Holmes, *British Politics*, pp. 221–222; identifiable: Dickinson, *Liberty and Property*, pp. 102–104.

38. Cf. Pocock, *Politics, Language, and Time*, p. 143, and Lawrence Stone, "The Results of the English Revolutions of the Seventeenth Century," in *Three British Revolutions: 1641, 1688, 1776*, ed. J. G. A. Pocock (Princeton, University Press, 1980), pp. 32–34.

39. Originated: Pocock, *Machiavellian Moment*, pp. 406–407. Imagination: [Charles Davenant], *True Picture of a Modern Whig* (London, 1701), pp. 32–33. Partners: Dickinson, *Liberty and Property*, pp. 94–95, 164. Insisted: Shaftesbury to Molesworth, 6 Jan. 1708 [O.S.], JT, *Letters from the Late Earl of Shaftesbury*, pp. 20–21. Ridiculed: Shaftesbury to John Molesworth, 30 Aug. 1712, in Shaftesbury, *Life, Unpublished Letters*, p. 512.

40. Captured: Davenant, *Tom Double Return'd*, pp. 69–71. Anticipated: JT/AG, pp. 98–99. Recognized: John Trenchard and Thomas Gordon, *Cato's Letters*, 3d ed., 4 vols. (London, 1733), III, 258–259 (no. 96), and *London Journal*, no. 787, 27 July 1734.

41. Pocock (*Machiavellian Moment*, pp. 426–427) would insert a fourth during the last years of Anne, in which Swift for the Tories and Addison for the Whigs used these two

rhetorics in aid of their respective parties. Holmes (*British Politics*, pp. 221) sees a revival of Country Whig efforts in Commons between 1705 and 1708. Harley directed a Country propaganda effort against the ministry after the 1708 general election (Downie, *Robert Harley*, pp. 104–114). None of these exhibits the concert of rhetoric and parliamentary activity which marked the other three. Echoed: Trenchard to Simpson, 25 Oct. and 8 Nov. [1721], S.U.K., MS. 623, ff. 30–31, 34–35.

42. Appropriated: Skinner, "Principles and Practice of Opposition," p. 113. Essence: Pocock, *Machiavellian Moment*, p. 478. Incompatibility: cf. *ibid.*, p. 409, and John Brewer, "English Radicalism in the Age of George III," in *Three British Revolutions*, pp. 342–348. Office: Dickinson, *Liberty and Property*, p. 122.

43. Pocock, *Political Works of Harrington*, pp. 144–145.

44. Trepidation: Dickinson, *Liberty and Property*, pp. 79–80. Collaborate: Holmes, *British Politics*, p. 224.

45. Congenial: Lee Horsley, "*Vox Populi* in the Political Literature of 1710," *Huntington Library Quarterly* 38 (1975), 335–353. Maneuvers: Kenyon, *Revolution Principles*, pp. 201–202. Language: *ibid.*, p. 170; cf. Downie, *Robert Harley*, p. 4, and Kramnick, *Bolingbroke and His Circle*, pp. 115–136, 197–200. Ascendancy: W. A. Speck, "The General Election of 1715," *English Historical Review* 90 (1975), 518–519, 521.

46. JT, *Discourse on Coins*, and JT, *Propositions for Uniting*.

47. JT/P, pp. 105–106.

48. Occasioned: JT to Mr. _____, 26 June 1705, in JT/C, II, 340–341. Somers: Shaftesbury to Furly, 19 Apr. 1701, Forster, *Original Letters*, pp. 93–94. Harley: Shaftesbury to Furly, 17 Feb. 1702 and 30 Jan. 1703, *ibid.*, pp. 128, 192.

49. Successes: Dickinson, *Liberty and Property*, pp. 108, 81. Undaunted: Holmes, *British Politics*, p. 259. Evolution: Angus McInnes, "The Political Ideas of Robert Harley," *History* 50 (1965), 321.

50. Truism: Skinner, *Foundations*, I, 158. Statement: Pocock, *Machiavellian Moment*, pp. 365–366. Summary: Molesworth, *Principles*, pp. 6–7.

51. Praise: cf. JT, in *Oceana*, p. viii, and JT/AG, pp. 32–33. Maintained: *ibid.*, pp. 31–32. Whigs: Dickinson, *Liberty and Property*, pp. 82–83. Advocate: [John Toland], *Limitations for the Next Foreign Successor*, etc. (London, 1701), p. 14. Flirted: *ibid.*, pp. 22–23. Control: JT/SA, p. 10; equated: Joyce O. Appleby, "The Social Origins of American Revolutionary Ideology," *Journal of American History* 64 (1977–1978), 939–940. View: JT/SA, p. 71.

52. Suspicion: H. T. Dickinson, "The Eighteenth-Century Debate on the Sovereignty of Parliament," *Transactions of the Royal Historical Society*, 5th ser., 26 (1976), 189–210, with citations. Citizens: JT/MR, p. 6. Portrayed: JT/AG, p. 174.

53. List: JT and Shaftesbury, *Danger of Mercenary Parliaments*, p. 1. Nominating: JT/AG, p. 110.

54. System: JT/AG, pp. 94–115; arrogation: JT/AL, p. 165. Lingua franca: Dickinson, *Liberty and Property*, p. 187.

55. JT/AG, pp. 75–78.

56. Disregard: JT and Shaftesbury, *Danger of Mercenary Parliaments*, pp. 6–7. Trumpeted: JT, *Letters from the Late Earl of Shaftesbury*, p. xviii. Clique: William Coxe, *Memoirs of the Life and Administration of Sir Robert Walpole*, 3 vols. in 4 (London, 1798), II, 62–63. Push: Dickinson, "Eighteenth-Century Debate," p. 201.

57. Depicted . . . located: JT/AL, pp. 53, 23–26, and JT, *Her Majesty's Reasons*, p. 214. Treated: JT/MR, pp. 50–51, and JT/AG, p. 41. Eulogized: JT/SA, p. 9. Confine: JT, *Limitations*, pp. 7–8. Indicting: JT/LM, p. 86; excusing: JT, *Second Part*, p. 16.

58. Abhorred: JT to _____, 26 June 1705, in JT/C, II, 338-339; distinguished: JT/VL, p. 134; vindicated: JT, in *Oceana*, pp. xxiii-xxiv. Rome: cf. *ibid.*, p. x, and JT to Mr. _____, n.d., in JT/C, II, 376-377. Governors: JT, in *Oceana*, pp. ix-x, and JT, "Memorial Presented to a Minister of State," JT/C, II, 249.

59. Virtually: N.B. the warning about oligarchy, [John Toland], *Reasons Most Humbly Offer'd*, etc. (London, 1720), pp. 26-27. Demarcate: JT/AG, p. 74. Measures: JT/SA, p. 41.

60. Cherished: JT/AL, pp. 11-12, and JT/MR, pp. 30-31. Contemplated: JT/LM, p. 85. Differentiating: JT/AL, pp. 57-58; insisted: JT, *Philippick Oration*, p. 6n.

61. Men: JT/AL, dedication. Warned: JT/AG, pp. 100-101.

62. Described: JT, *Limitations*, p. 10; presented: JT/LM, p. 128. Standard: JT/AL, pp. 178-179; imply: JT, *Reasons for Naturalizing*, p. 57.

63. Orientals: JT, *Agreements of the Customs*, p. 8; Irish: JT, *Limitations*, p. 18. Appeals: JT, *Reasons and Necessity*, p. 28; call: JT, *Characters of the Court*, p. 15; hostility: JT/AG, p. 104. Nature: JT, *Letter to an M.P.*, pp. 614-616; self-interest: JT, *Memorial*, p. 48.

64. Distinction: JT/MR, pp. 18-19. "Fairest": JT/AG, p. 173. Identify: JT, *Defence of the Parliament*, pp. 4, 14; JT, in *Oceana*, p. i; JT, *Reasons for Naturalizing*, p. 46; JT, *Reasons Most Humbly Offer'd*, p. 5.

65. Interplay: Isaiah Berlin, "Two Concepts of Liberty," in *Four Essays on Liberty* (London, Oxford University Press, 1969), pp. 118-172; cf. Pocock, *Political Works of Harrington*, p. 146, and J. H. Hexter, rev. of Pocock, *Machiavellian Moment, History and Theory* 16 (1977), 334-335. Championed: JT, *Memorial*, p. 43; embraced: JT, in *Oceana*, pp. xix, xxxix. Advocated: JT/LM, p. 122; committed: JT/MR, pp. 26, 30-31, 56, 74 n.90.

66. Interpenetrate: JT/VL, p. 146. Described: JT/AG, p. 3; cf. John Fortescue, *The Governance of England*, ed. Charles Plummer (Oxford, 1885), pp. 113-116. Participation: JT/SA, p. 12. Exercise: cf. JT/MR, p. 4, and JT, *Letter to an M.P.*, p. 623.

67. Director: JT, *Appeal to Honest People*, p. 52; provided: JT/AG, p. 79. Category: cf. JT, *High-Church Display'd*, pp. 52-53, 109, and JT, *Reasons for Naturalizing*, pp. 57-58. "England": JT, "Memorial Presented to a Minister of State," JT/C, II, 252. Proposed: *ibid.*, pp. 255-256. Presentiment: JT, in *Oceana*, p. i.

68. Diagnosed: Skinner, *Foundations*, I, 42-43. Machiavelli: *ibid.*, pp. 164, 183.

69. Adapted: Pocock, *Machiavellian Moment*, p. 389. Participate: Pocock, *Political Works of Harrington*, p. 145. Authors: [John Trenchard, Walter Moyle, and John Toland], *A Short History of Standing Armies*, etc. [1698] (London, 1773), pp. vii-ix, 58-59, 63, 70. Accepted: JT/MR, p. 12; cf. [John Trenchard, Walter Moyle, and John Toland], *An Argument Shewing that a Standing Army*, etc. (London, 1697), pp. 17-18.

70. Located: JT/MR. pp. 33-36, and JT, *Philippick Oration*, p. 60n. Contemplated: JT/AG, pp. 100, 165-166. Appealing: John Toland, *An Account of the Courts of Prussia and Hanover*, etc., 2d ed. (London, 1706), p. 6.

71. Neo-Harringtonians: Pocock, *Political Works of Harrington*, p. 138. Correlation: J. G. A. Pocock, "England," in *National Consciousness, History, and Political Culture in Early-Modern Europe*, ed. Orest Ranum (Baltimore, Johns Hopkins University Press, 1975), p. 116; N.B. the caution in Pocock, *Machiavellian Moment*, p. 446. Praised: JT, in *Oceana*, p. iii. Reject: JT/SA, p. 43. Toyed: Charles Davenant, "Essays upon the Probable Methods of Making a People Gainers in the Balance of Trade," [1699] in *Political and Commercial Works of . . . Dr. Charles D'Avenant*, ed. Charles Whitworth, 5 vols. (London, 1771), II, 275; writers: John Trenchard, *Some Considerations upon the State of Our Publick Debts*, etc. (London, 1720), pp. 6-7, 15.

72. Advertised: JT, "Scheme, or Practical Model," JT/C, I, 448–474. Denunciation: JT, "Memorial Presented to a Minister of State," JT/C, II, 250–251.

73. Asserted: Gary S. DeKrey, "Trade, Religion, and Politics in London in the Reign of William III" (Ph.D. diss., Princeton University, 1978), pp. 15, 17, 103. Growing: *ibid.*, pp. 251–252; forfeited: *ibid.*, p. 324.

74. Furthered: JT, marginal note in Martin, *Description*, flyleaf. Clung: JT/MR, p. 17. Words: Sidney, *Discourse concerning Government*, p. 209. Insisted: JT, *Clito*, p. 13; cf. JT/AL, pp. 140–141; JT/AG, pp. 161, 175, 194; JT, *Reasons for Naturalizing*, p. 44. Tories: Downie, *Robert Harley*, pp. 7–8.

75. Innocent: JT/AG, p. 8. Nurtured: *ibid.*, p. 7. "Calculated": *ibid.*, p. 32; brought: *ibid.*, p. 51. King: *ibid.*, pp. 42–43.

76. Rushed: cf. Joseph Addison, *Spectator*, no. 125, 24 July 1711, and Jonathan Swift, *The Sentiments of a Church-of-England Man* [1708], in *Prose Works*, ed. Herbert Davis, 16 vols. (Oxford, Blackwell, 1939–1974), II, 13–14. Reality: JT, *Memorial*, pp. 63–64. Berated: JT to _____, 26 June 1705, in JT/C, II, 340–341. Identified: *ibid.*, p. 345, and JT, "Another Memorial [1711]," *ibid.*, p. 221.

77. Davenant, *Old and Modern Whig*, p. 3.

78. Traitors: JT and Shaftesbury, *Paradoxes of State*, pp. 2–3. True . . . convinced: conflates JT/AG, pp. 54, 34, 48–49.

79. Meant: Holmes, *British Politics*, pp. 369–370. Mouthed: cf. JT, *Reasons and Necessity*, p. 6, and JT/SA, p. 98. Separate: JT, *Mr. Toland's Reflections*, pp. 2–3, and JT/SA, p. 14. Discovered: JT, *Grand Mystery*, pp. 14–15, and JT/SA, p. 18. Urging: JT, "Memorial Presented to a Minister of State," JT/C, II, 245, and JT/SA, p. 94. Trimmers: cf. JT/AG, p. 118, and JT/SA, p. 103.

80. Resting: JT/MR, p. 21; Gothic: *ibid.*, p. 92. Punctuates: JT, *Philippick Oration*, p. 23n; sneer: JT, *Reasons for Naturalizing*, p. 50. Disclosure: Defoe, *Argument*, pp. 52–65. Proposed: JT/SA, p. 59; protested: JT, *Second Part*, pp. 33–35. Molesworth: cf. Molesworth, *Principles*, pp. 16–17, and William Cobbett, ed., *Parliamentary History of England*, 36 vols. (London, 1806–1820), VII, 536–537.

81. Fabricators: JT, in *Oceana*, p. xxiii; ancients: JT, *Adeisidaemon*, pp. 7, 19; survival: *ibid.*, pp. 77–78.

82. Demands: cf. JT, *Reasons for Naturalizing*, p. 55, and JT, marginal note in Martin, *Description*, p. 97. Preserved: JT, *Letters from the Late Earl of Shaftesbury*, p. vii. Vindicate: Ernest L. Tuveson, "Origins of the Moral Sense," *Huntington Library Quarterly* 11 (1948), 259.

83. Presented: JT to Rev. Mr. _____, n.d., in JT/C, II, 373. Indulged: JT, "Project of a Journal," *ibid.*, 202. "He": JT, *Letter to an M.P.*, p. 614. Granted: JT to Clayton, 4 Dec. 1698, in JT/C, II, 318–320.

84. Bias: JT/MR, p. 11; cf. Cicero, *De officiis*, I. Conscience: JT/MR, p. 3. Trusted: JT/AG, p. 80. Identified: *ibid.*, dedication, cf. Trenchard, Moyle, and JT, *Short History*, pp. iii–v. Distasteful: JT/AG, pp. 21–22; connected: JT, *Mr. Toland's Reflections*, p. 10; determined: JT/SA, p. 19.

85. Time: Christopher Hill, "From Oaths to Interest," in *Society and Puritanism in Pre-Revolutionary England* (London, Secker and Warburg, 1964), pp. 382–419; affirmed: JT, *Reasons for Addressing*, p. 19. Suggestion: JT, *Adeisidaemon*, pp. 68–69. Fulminated: JT/T, pp. 63–64; tolerate: JT, *Adeisidaemon*, pp. 77–78. Living: JT, *Agreement of the Customs*, p. 159. Depended: JT/AL, pp. 95–96. Function: JT, *Appeal to Honest People*, pp. 10–11, and JT, "Memorial Presented to a Minister of State," JT/C, II, 239–240, 253.

86. Attributing: Pocock, *Politics, Language, and Time*, p. 128; cf. Pocock, *Political*

Works of Harrington, p. 143. Assumed: Rosalie L. Colie, "Spinoza and the Early English Deists," *Journal of the History of Ideas* 20 (1959), 23–46. Endowed: Harrington, *Oceana,* p. 110. Head: Harrington, *A System of Politics,* in *ibid.,* p. 500. Functioning: *ibid.,* pp. 507–508.

87. Professed: JT, *Second Part,* p. 23. Criterion: JT/LS, p. 19. Noninterference: JT/SA, p. 75; asserted: JT/T, p. xxi. Certainty: JT, *Second Part,* pp. 67, 74. Paramount: JT, *Epsom,* pp. 14–15. Divided: JT and Shaftesbury, *Paradoxes of State,* p. 2; JT, "Primitive Constitution," JT/C, II, 121, 133–134. Broadening: JT, *Letter to an M.P.,* p. 620; urging: JT/N, First letter, p. 40; unchurching: JT, *Second Part,* p. 15.

88. Machiavelli: Pocock, *Machiavellian Moment,* pp. 202, 214–215. Muster: JT/MR, pp. 26–27; camps: *ibid.,* p. 37. NCO: *ibid.,* p. 28. Extension: *ibid.,* pp. 27–28. Possess: *ibid.,* p. 47. Bolster: *ibid.,* p. 26.

89. Ascribed: JT, *Account of the Courts,* p. 16. Amounted: JT, "Directions for Breeding," JT/C, II, 18–19; endeavored: JT, "Roman Education," *ibid.,* p. 8. Boys: JT, "Directions for Breeding," *ibid.,* p. 23. Obstacle: JT/N, First letter, pp. 73–74. Reorganize: JT, "Memorial Presented to a Minister of State," JT/C, II, 241. Changed: *ibid.,* p. 248.

90. Refrained: JT, *Memorial,* p. 58. Judged: Henry Neville, *Plato Redivivus, or A Dialogue concerning Government* [ca. 1681], in Robbins, *Two Republican Tracts,* pp. 153–155; aspired: JT/AL, p. 97. Invoke: JT, "Primitive Constitution," JT/C, II, 120–122. Promote: JT, "Memorial Presented to a Minister of State," *ibid.,* p. 246. Convinced: JT, marginal note in Martin, *Description,* p. 312.

91. Maintained: JT, *Reasons for Naturalizing,* p. 62. Reformed: JT/N, First letter, p. 30. Lost: JT/T, p. 215. Degenerate: JT, "Another Memorial [1711]," JT/C, II, 229–230.

92. Invoking: JT, *Clito,* p. 19. Rejected: *ibid.,* pp. 17–18. Convinced: JT, *Letter to an M.P.,* p. 623. Hope: Pliny to Tacitus, in JT, "Some Letters," JT/C, II, 83–84. Depended: JT/MR, 49–50, 83. Omitting: JT, *Clito,* p. 16.

6. The Philosophia Perennis

1. Arrive: cf. Smith to Hearne, 23 Jan. 1706 (O.S.), Bodl. Rawlinson MSS. D. 401, f. 30, and Cuper to Le Clerc, 15 Jan. 1709 (N.S.), in Gisbertus Cuper, *Lettres de critique, d'histoire, de littérature,* etc. (Amsterdam, 1742), p. 367; uncertain: Chamberlayne to JT, 21 June 1718, B.L. Add. MS. 4295, ff. 27–28; Leibniz to JT, 30 Apr. 1709, in Giancarlo Carabelli, "John Toland e G. W. Leibniz: otto lettere," *Rivista critica di storia della filosofia* 29 (1974), 417–420. Recognition: Le Clerc, *Treatise of the Causes,* pp. 5–6. Accused: Browne, *Things Divine,* p. 98, and [William Wotton], *A Letter to Eusebia,* etc. (London, 1704), p. 37.

2. Denied: JT/N, First letter, p. 8. Incapable: JT to Lord_____,n.d., B. L. Add. MS. 4465, ff. 34–35. Depended: JT/LS, preface. Insist: *ibid.,* p. 160, and preface.

3. Dismissed: Stephen, *History of English Thought,* I, 87. Presented: Norman L. Torrey, "The English Critical Deists and Their Influence on Voltaire" (Ph.D. diss., Harvard Univerity, 1926), pp. 153–161; seen: e.g., Evans, "John Toland's Pantheism," p. 188; Jacob, *Newtonians and the English Revolution,* pp. 232–248; Giuntini, *Panteismo e ideologia,* pp. 313, 333–334. Read: Heinemann, "John Toland," pp. 125–46.

4. Cf. Heinemann, "John Toland," p. 140.

5. Argued: JT, *Two Essays,* p. 30. Moses: ibid., pp. ii–iii. Rejecting: *ibid.,* p. 25. "Power": *ibid.,* p. 41; conviction: *ibid.,* p. 43.

6. Written: *ibid.,* pp. ii, 7–8. Reconcile: Thomas Burnet, *The Sacred Theory of the*

Earth, ed. Basil Willey (Carbondale, Southern Illinois University Press, 1965), pp. 407-408; Marjorie Hope Nicolson, *Mountain Gloom and Mountain Glory: The Development of the Aesthetics of the Infinite* (Ithaca, N. Y., Cornell University Press, 1959), pp. 184-270, for a summary of the Burnet controversy.

7. Thomas Burnet, *Archaeologiae philosophicae: sive doctrina antiqua et rerum originibus* (London, 1692), pp. 184-186. Blount, *Oracles of Reason,* p. 2. Cf. Joseph M. Levine, *Dr. Woodward's Shield: History, Science, and Satire in Augustan England* (Berkeley, University of California Press, 1977), pp. 34-36.

8. "History": JT, *Two Essays,* p. 15. Meaningless: *ibid.,* pp. 13-14. Reflected: *ibid.,* pp. 2-3. Acquit: *ibid.,* pp. 34-35. Herring: *ibid.,* pp. iv-v. Held: *ibid.,* pp. ii-iii; expressed: *ibid.,* p. 31.

9. Convinced: JT, *Principle,* p. 20. Sense: JT to Molesworth, n.d. [1720], in JT/C, II, 492.

10. Agreed: JT/LS, pp. 66-67. Set: Wolfgang Von Leyden, *Seventeenth-Century Metaphysics: An Examination of Some Main Concepts and Theories* (London, Gerald Duckworth & Co., 1968), pp. xiv-xv. Problem: cf. Anthony Flew, "Locke and the Problem of Personal Identity," in C. B. Martin and P. M. Armstrong, eds., *Locke and Berkeley: A Collection of Critical Essays* (Notre Dame, Ind., University Press, 1968), pp. 155-178.

11. Locke, *Essay,* III, vi; cf. JT/LS, p. 227, and Locke, *Essay,* III, vi, 35, 9.

12. Conceded: Locke, *Essay,* III, vi, 12. "Creature": John N. Deck, "St. Thomas Aquinas and the Language of Total Dependence," in Anthony Kenny, ed., *Aquinas: A Collection of Critical Essays* (Garden City, N. Y., Doubleday, 1969), p. 240. Recognized: Leibniz to Bayle, 5 Dec. 1702, Leibniz, *Die philosophischen Schriften,* III, 68. Hinted: Bayle, *Dictionnaire historique et critique,* V, 512-514.

13. Described: Collins to Locke, 16 Feb. 1704 (N.S.), Bodl. Locke MSS. c. 7, ff. 16-17. Criticism: Leibniz to Sophia, n.d. [ca. 16 Oct. 1702], Klopp, *Correspondance,* II, 364-365; "Serena": JT, *Adeisidaemon,* p. 13.

14. Exceptions: *Letter to a Gentleman,* pp. 12-13; convinced: Stillingfleet, *Mysteries,* p. 20; Gildon, *Deist's Manual,* p. 49. "Those": Samuel Clarke, *A Discourse concerning the Unchangeable Obligations of Natural Religion,* etc., 4th ed. corr. (London, 1716), p. 18. Felt: Samuel Clarke, *A Demonstration of the Being and Attributes of God,* etc. (London, 1705), p. 198, and John Harris, *The Atheistical Objections against the Being of God and His Attributes,* etc. (London, 1698) (Sermons IV-V), pp. 5-6. Sure: e.g., John Howe, *The Living Temple,* etc., 2 parts (London, 1702), I, 199-200, II, 58. "Mere": Richard Bentley, *A Confutation of Atheism,* etc. (London, 1692) (Sermon III), p. 18.

15. "Activity": JT/LS, p. 165. "Certain": JT/P, p. 58. "Several": JT/LS, p. 159. "Motion": *ibid.,* p. 176. Impenetrability: *ibid.,* preface. Place: *ibid.,* pp. 180-182. "Prime": JT/P, pp. 18-19.

16. "Seed": JT/P, pp. 32-33. Rejected . . . relied: cf. JT/LS, p. 210, and JT, *Account of the Courts,* p. 9. Excluded: JT/N, Appendix, p. 3. Unwillingness: Giuntini, *Panteismo e ideologia,* p. 464; attempts: e.g., Sieur C. P., *Historie de la machine du monde, ou physique mechanique* (Marseilles, 1704).

17. Space . . . motion: JT/LS, pp. 180-182, 212-213, 219-220, and JT/P, pp. 15, 20; cf. Brian P. Copenhaver, "Jewish Theologies of Space in the Scientific Revolution: Henry More, Joseph Raphson, Isaac Newton, and Their Predecessors," *Annals of Science* 37 (1980), 546-548. Denied: JT/LS, p. 175. Opponents: Edward Grant, "Medieval and Seventeenth-Century Conceptions of an Infinite Void Space beyond the Cosmos," *Isis* 60 (1969), 39-60. Seemed: Clarke, *Demonstration of the Being,* p. 49. Description: JT/P, p. 15.

18. Seemed: cf. Ralph Cudworth, *The True Intellectual System of the Universe*, ed. Thomas Birch, 4 vols. (1743; reprint, London, 1820), I, 292–295, and Clarke, *Demonstration of the Being*, pp. 114–115. Devoted: e.g., Stillingfleet, *Bishop of Worcester's Answer*, p. 55, and Humphrey Ditton, *A Discourse concerning the Resurrection of Jesus Christ in Three Parts* (London, 1712), p. 474. Observation: Locke, *Essay*, IV, iii, 6.

19. Held: Leibniz to Sophia, 9, 13 Sep. 1702 and n.d., Klopp, *Correspondance*, II, 361–362, 363–364, 364–365. Insisted: Leibniz to Bayle, 5 Dec. 1702, Leibniz, *Die philosophischen Schriften*, III, 68. Assert: JT to Sophie-Charlotte, n.d., *ibid.*, VI, 508–514.

20. Presented: JT/P, pp. 16–17. Depicted: JT/LS, pp. 173–174. Dispose: JT/P, p. 26. "Peculiar": *ibid.*, p. 22. Ideas . . . actions: cf. *ibid.*, p. 24, and JT/LS, pp. 232–233.

21. "Ethereal": JT/P, pp. 22–23; suffused: *ibid.*, p. 15. Convinced: JT/LS, p. 232. Fellows: B.L. Add. MS. 4465, f. 54 ("Fen to Fil Greeting").

22. JT/LS, p. 54, and preface.

23. Cf. Gildon, *Deist's Manual*, dedication, and Jacob Viner, *The Role of Providence in the Social Order: An Essay in Intellectual History* (Philadelphia, American Philosophical Society, 1972), p. 13. Conformed: Francis Hare, *Scripture Vindicated from the Misinterpretations of the Lord Bishop of Bangor* (London, 1721), p. xxi.

24. Portrayed: JT/LS, p. 192. Denied . . . hint: cf. *ibid.*, pp. 157, 160–161. Reproved . . . rebuked: *ibid.*, p. 220. Relegate: *ibid.*, pp. 234–236.

25. Meant: JT, *Socinianism Truly Stated*, p. 7. Alluded: *ibid.* Used: JT, *Adeisidaemon*, p. 117. "Pantheistick": JT to Leibniz, 14 Feb. 1710, in JT/C, II, 394. "Finally": JT/P, pp. 17–18; cf. *ibid.*, pp. 15, 70. Created: Elie Benoist, *Mélange de remarques critiques, historiques, philosophiques*, etc. (Delft, 1712), pp. 252, 256; using: Hare, *Scripture Vindicated*, p. xxi.

26. Treating: Roger L. Emerson, "English Deism, 1670–1755: An Enlightenment Challenge to Orthodoxy" (Ph.D. diss., Brandeis University, 1962), p. 83. Attributing . . . describing: JT/P, p. 61. Idea . . . belief: cf. Aquinas, *Summa contra Gentiles*, III, 116, and *Summa Theologiae*, II–II, 23–1. Contained: JT/P, p. 14.

27. Suggested: JT, *Adeisidaemon*, p. 18. Distinguished . . . admit: JT/P, p. 14. Sceptical: Leibniz to JT, 30 Apr. 1709, Klopp, *Correspondance*, III, 307–309; reject: Arthur Ashley Sykes, *The Principles and Connexion of Natural and Reveal'd Religion*, etc. (London, 1740), p. 75.

28. John Locke, *A Third Letter for Tolerance* [1693], in *Works of Locke*, VI, 416–417; JT, *Adeisidaemon*, pp. 68, 76–77.

29. E.g., JT, "Physick without Physicians," JT/C, II, 285, and JT, marginal note in Martin, *Description*, pp. 175, 196.

30. "All": JT/T, p. 85. Laboring: JT/N, First letter, p. 7. Confident . . . sure: cf. JT/T, p. 85, and JT, *Agreement of the Customs*, p. 136.

31. Clear: JT, *Adeisidaemon*, pp. 67–68. Syncretism: Paolo Casini, *L'universo-macchina: origini della filosofia newtoniana* (Bari, Editori Laterza, 1969), pp. 205–238. Mean: cf. JT, *Two Essays*, pp. 29–32, and JT/T, pp. 74–76. Mutilated: JT/P, pp. 56–57, and JT, *Adeisidaemon*, p. 80. Embellished: JT/T, pp. 83, 77, and JT, *Agreement of the Customs*, p. 102; compile: JT/P, pp. 56–57.

32. Partiality: JT/P, p. 64. Noted: JT/LS, pp. 115–116. Resembled . . . grasping: *ibid.*, p. 7. Demonstrate: JT, *Adeisidaemon*, p. 155.

33. Attribute . . . present: cf. JT, *Agreement of the Customs*, pp. 13, 95, and JT/P, p. 34. Moses: *ibid.*, p. 47. Object: JT, *Adeisidaemon*, pp. 117–118, 155–156. Singled: JT/P, p. 18. Establish: rev. of John George Wachterus, *Der Spinozismus in Judentumb* (Amsterdam, 1699), in *History of the Works of the Learned* 2 (1700), 76–78.

34. Derivative: Stuart Piggott, *The Druids* (London, Thames and Hudson, 1968), p. 131. Suggestion: Jean-Félix Nourrison, *Philosophies de la nature: Bacon, Boyle, Toland, Buffon* (Paris, 1887), p. 132; solicitude: e.g., JT, marginal note in Martin, *Description,* p. 154. Dedicated: JT/P, pp. 95–96. Held: JT, "Specimen of the Critical History," JT/C, I, 46.

35. Undertook: JT to Leibniz, 28 Dec. 1709, B.L. Add. MS. 4465, ff. 7–8. Deified: JT/LS, p. 72. Representations: JT, "Specimen of the Critical History," JT/C, I, 40–41. Dominated: Manuel, *Eighteenth Century Confronts the Gods,* p. 66.

36. Considered . . . undergo: JT/P, p. 21. "Motion" . . . "equinoctial": *ibid.,* pp. 39–40. "All": JT/LS, p. 188. Maintained: JT/P, p. 55. Led: JT/LS, pp. 190–191; recur: JT/P, pp. 28, 42. Immune: JT/LS, p. 191. Controlled: JT/P, pp. 39–40.

37. Rejected: JT, marginal note in Martin, *Description,* pp. 336–337. Argued: JT, *Destiny of Rome,* p. 5, citing Eccles. 1:9. Conformed: cf. JT/LS, p. 171, and JT, *Agreement of the Customs,* p. 151. Amounted: JT, "Specimen of the Critical History," JT/C, I, 47.

38. Despair: For the possibility of optimism resulting from such an outlook, Karl Löwith, *Meaning in History* (Chicago, University Press, 1957), pp. 214–222, and John A. Bernstein, "Beauty and the Law: Shaftesbury's Relation to Christianity and the Enlightenment" (Ph.D. diss., Harvard University, 1970), p. 175. Gave: JT/P, pp. 39–40. Systematized: cf. *ibid.,* p. 33, and JT, *Clito,* p. 16.

39. Accusing: Benoist, *Mélange,* pp. 29–30. Profess . . . equate: cf. JT/N, First letter, p. 60; JT, "Specimen of the Critical History," JT/C, I, 15; and JT/P, pp. 73–74, 84. Hopes: cf. *ibid.,* p. 102, and JT/LS, preface.

40. JT/LS, preface; JT/N, p. iv; JT/P, preface; JT/T, p. 94.

41. Thought: Leland, *View,* I, 398. Accept: JT/P, pp. 88, 33.

42. Abandoning . . . transcending: JT/LS, pp. 13, 164. Appreciate: JT, *Clito,* pp. 10–11. Freed: JT/P, pp. 73, 82.

43. Resignation: JT/P, preface and pp. 66, 73.

44. Included: JT, *Adeisidaemon,* pp. 72–73. Eschewed: JT/P, p. 57. Behaved: B.L. Add. MS. 4465, f. 69^V (undated fragment); impressed: JT/P, p. 51. Standard: *ibid.,* p. 86.

45. Essential: JT/P, pp. 107, 57, 63–64, 66. Accorded: e.g., JT, *Letter from an Arabian,* p. 10. Depicted: JT, *Clito,* pp. 20–21.

46. Donald Greene, "Augustinianism and Empiricism: A Note on Eighteenth-Century Intellectual History," *Eighteenth-Century Studies* 1 (1967–1968), 67.

47. Richard H. Popkin, "Scepticism in the Enlightenment," *Studies on Voltaire* 26 (1963), 1321–1345; JT/T, p. xvii.

48. Leibniz to Sophia, 9 Sep. 1702, Klopp, *Correspondance,* II, 363. Cf. Paolo Casini, "Toland e l'attività della materia," *Rivista critica di storia della filosofia* 22 (1967), 45.

49. Maintained: Leibniz to Sophia, 9 Sep. 1702, Klopp, *Correspondance,* II, 362–363. Differentiating . . . insisted: Thomas Hobbes, *Concerning Body,* in *The English Works of Thomas Hobbes,* ed. William Molesworth, 11 vols. (London, 1839–1845), I, 10–11. "One": *ibid.,* p. 102; "variety": *ibid.,* pp. 69–70. Local: *ibid.,* p. 109. Dismissed: Thomas Hobbes, *Leviathan,* in *English Works,* III, 27. Evade: *ibid.,* p. 97. "Most": Thomas Hobbes, *An Answer to a Book,* etc. in *English Works,* IV, 306; extension: *ibid.,* p. 313. Identical: Hobbes, *Concerning Body,* p. 3; permitted: *ibid.,* p. 123. Phantasms: *ibid.,* pp. 94–95.

50. Puzzled: Giuntini, *Panteismo e ideologia,* p. 361.

51. Held: e.g., Bentley, *Confutation of Atheism* (Sermon VI). Belittle: cf. JT/LS, p.

152, and JT/N, p. viii; correct: JT/LS, pp. 165–239. Obsession: Samuel I. Mintz, *The Hunting of Leviathan: Seventeenth-Century Reactions to the Materialism and Moral Philosophy of Thomas Hobbes* (Cambridge, University Press, 1962), pp. 147–156.

52. Exponent: Clarke, *Demonstration of the Being*, p. 33. Contended: Aram Vartanian, *Diderot and Descartes: A Study of Scientific Naturalism in the Enlightenment* (Princeton, University Press, 1953), p. 124.

53. Physics: This summary draws on Wallace E. Anderson, "Cartesian Motion," in *Motion and Time, Space and Matter: Interrelations in the History of Philosophy and Science,* ed. Peter K. Machamer and Robert G. Turnbull (Columbus, Ohio State University Press, 1976), pp. 200–223. Discerned: cf. Voltaire, *Mélanges,* in *Oeuvres complètes,* ed. Louis Moland, 52 vols. Paris 1877–1883), XXII, 404, and James Collins, *God in Modern Philosophy* (London, Routledge and Kegan Paul, 1960), p. 146. Separated: Norman Kemp Smith, *Studies in the Cartesian Philosophy* (London, Macmillan, 1902), pp. 39–40. Allow: Von Leyden, *Seventeenth-Century Metaphysics,* pp. 230–233. Criticized: JT/LS, p. 225; cf. Casini, *L'universo-macchina,* p. 226.

54. Attributed: Rosalie L. Colie, "Spinoza and the Early English Deists," *Journal of the History of Ideas* 20 (1959), 23–46. Undermine: Giuntini, *Panteismo e ideologia,* pp. 347–354. Accepted: F. H. Heinemann, "Toland and Leibniz, *Philosophical Review* 54 (1945), 452. Objected: JT/LS, p. 139; refusal: Benedict Spinoza, *Ethics,* in *Chief Works,* trans. R. H. M. Elwes, 2 vols. (reprint, New York, Dover, 1951), II, 93–95. Familiar: Howe, *Living Temple,* I, 74–75; disinclined: Clarke, *Demonstration of the Being,* p. 49.

55. Method: JT/LS, p. 153. Shrunk: *ibid.,* pp. 134–135, 136, 139, 143–144. Used: JT, *Adeisidaemon,* p. 117. Held: Christopher Hill, *The World Turned Upside Down: Radical Ideas during the English Revolution* (London, Temple Smith, 1972), pp. 231–246, and William C. Diamond, "Natural Philosophy in Harrington's Political Thought," *Journal of the History of Philosophy* 16 (1978), 387–398.

56. Observed: JT, *Adeisidaemon,* pp. 59–60. Borelli: JT, in *Oceana,* p. xxxviii. Struggled: Edward G. Ruestow, *Physics at Seventeenth and Eighteenth-Century Leiden: Philosophy and the New Science in the University* (The Hague, Nijhoff, 1973), pp. 71, 107, 130–131.

57. Denying: JT/LS, p. 166, and JT/P, p. 70. Rejected: Locke, *Essay,* II, xv, and III, iv, 7–10.

58. Styled: JT/LS, pp. 182–183. Before: Christina M. Eagles, "David Gregory and Newtonian Science," *British Journal of the History of Science* 10 (1977), 216–225; cf. Jacob, *Newtonians and the English Revolution,* pp. 211, 229. Reaction: Jacob and Jacob, "Anglican Origins of Modern Science," 264–265; attempt: Casini, *L'universo-macchina,* p. 207.

59. Oblivious: [John Toland], "Remarques critiques sur la système de M. Leibnitz . . . où l'on recherche en passant pourquoi les systêmes metaphysiques de mathematiciens ont moins de clarté, que ceux des autres," *Histoire critique de la république des lettres* 11 (1716), 128–131; quantification: Robert Kargon, *Atomism in England from Hariot to Newton* (Oxford, Clarendon Press, 1966), p. 124. "Estimation": J. E. McGuire and P. M. Rattansi, "Newton and the 'Pipes of Pan,' " *Notes and Records of the Royal Society of London* 21 (1966), 125.

60. Argued: Jacob, "Toland and the Newtonian Ideology," pp. 308–309, 323. Treated: R. Harré, *Matter and Method* (London, Macmillan, 1964), pp. 57–59.

61. Attack: e.g., JT/LS, pp. 216–220. Invoke: *ibid.,* pp. 233–234. Hope: *ibid.,* p. 183. Materialize: David Kubrin, "Newton and the Cyclical Cosmos: Providence and the Mechanical Philosophy," *Journal of the History of Ideas* 28 (1967), 339. Required: Isaac Newton, *Mathematical Principles of Natural Philosophy,* ed. Florian Cajori (Berkeley, University of California Press, 1934), p. 545. Literal: W. G. Hiscock, ed., *David*

Gregory, Isaac Newton and Their Circle: Extracts from David Gregory's Memoranda, 1677–1708 (Oxford, privately printed, 1937), p. 30.

62. Maintained: Harris, *Atheistical Objections* (Sermon I), p. 19. Meditated: Gianni Paganini, "Tra Epicure e Stratone: Bayle e l'imagine di Epicuro dal sei al settecento," *Rivista critica di storia della filosofia* 33 (1978), 95–104; provided: Cicero, *De finibus*, I, vi; Augustine, *City of God*, VII, 6; Leibniz to JT, 1 Mar. 1710 (N.S.), in JT/C, II, 401; Thomas F. Mayo, *Epicurus in England (1659–1725)* (Dallas, Southwest Press, 1934), p. 111. Defined: Aristotle, *Physics*, VIII, 1, trans. R. P. Hardie and R. K. Gaye, in Richard McKeon, ed., *The Basic Works of Aristotle* (New York, Random House, 1941), p. 355; cf. JT/LS, p. 165. Praised: JT/P, p. 25; eager: *ibid.*, p. 58. Coincided: cf. Günter Gawlick, "Cicero and the Enlightenment," *Studies on Voltaire* 25 (1963), 671.

63. "Nature": F. M. Cornford, *The Laws of Motion in Ancient Thought* (Cambridge, University Press, 1931), p. 47.

64. Parallel: Hélèné Metzger, *Attraction universelle et religion naturelle chez quelques commentateurs anglais de Newton*, 3 vols. consecutive pag. (Paris, Hermann et Cie, 1938), p. 195; presents: Jacob, "Toland and the Newtonian Ideology," p. 309. Trace: Frances A. Yates, *Giordano Bruno and the Hermetic Tradition* (London, Routledge and Kegan Paul, 1964), *The Art of Memory* (Chicago, University Press, 1966), and *Rosicrucian Enlightenment*.

65. Architect: Yates, *Giordano Bruno*, pp. 144–156. Bacon: Yates, *Rosicrucian Enlightenment*, pp. 119–125; Descartes: Yates, *Giordano Bruno*, pp. 452–455; Newton: cf. Yates, *Rosicrucian Enlightenment*, pp. 200–202, 204–205, and Richard S. Westfall, "Newton and the Hermetic Tradition," in Allen G. Debus, ed., *Science, Medicine, and Society in the Renaissance*, 2 vols. (New York, Science History Publications, 1972), II, 183–198.

66. Question: Mary Hesse, "Hermeticism and Historiography: An Apology for the Internal History of Science," in *Historical and Philosophical Perspectives of Science*, ed. Russell H. Stuewer (Minneapolis, University of Minnesota Press, 1970), pp. 134–162. Ignore: Robert S. Westman, "Magical Reform and Astronomical Reform: The Yates Thesis Reconsidered," in *Hermeticism and the Scientific Revolution* (Los Angeles, William Andrews Clark Memorial Library, 1977), pp. 11–12. Showed: *ibid.*, pp. 20, 69, 72. Abandoning: *ibid.*, pp. 21–24; owed: Edward A. Gosselin and L. S. Lerner, eds. and trans., *The Ash-Wednesday Supper: La cena de le ceneri*, by Giordano Bruno (Hamden, Ct., Archon, 1977), p. 42. Emerges: Hélène Vedrine, *La conception de la nature chez Giordano Bruno* (Paris, J. Vrin, 1967), pp. 37–38, 346–355. Argued: J. E. McGuire, "Neoplatonism and Active Principles: Newton and the *Corpus Hermeticum*," in *Hermeticism and the Scientific Revolution*, p. 106.

67. Kept . . . referred: B.L. Add. MS. 4295, ff. 41–42 ("Books in My Room," Oct. 1720); JT/P, pp. 24, 38, 46, and JT, *Fables of Aesop*, preface. Portraying: Walter Scott, trans. and ed., *Hermetica: The Ancient Greek and Latin Writings which Contain Religious and Philosophical Teachings Ascribed to Hermes Trismegistus*, 4 vols. (Oxford, Clarendon Press, 1924–1936), I, 175. Stuff: *ibid.*, pp. 177, 139. Discerned: JT, *Fables of Aesop*, preface; unwilling: JT, "Catalogue of Books," JT/C, I, 395.

68. Possession: Giovanni Aquilecchia, "Nota su John Toland traduttore di Giordano Bruno," *English Miscellany* 9 (1958), 77–86; judged: O.N.B. MS. 10390, f. 391^V. Produced: JT, "Account of Jordano Bruno's Book," JT/C, I, 316–349. Essayed: B.L. Add. MS. 4295, ff. 64–65 ("A Psalm before Sermon, in Praise of Assinity"). Enlightened . . . eluded: JT to Mr. _____, n.d. [1707?], in JT/C, II, 377, 380. Distributing: cf. Erman, *Mémoires*, p. 198, and Leibniz to JT, 30 Apr. 1709, Klopp, *Correspondance*, III, 309, published: Giovanni Aquilecchia, "Scheda bruniana: la traduzione 'tolandiana' dello Spaccio," *Giornale storico della letteratura italiana* 152 (1975), 311–313. Ex-

coriated: [Thomas Brett], *Discourses concerning the Ever-Blessed Trinity* (London, 1720), pp. 8–9; Skelton, *Ophiomaches,* I, 60; expression: Eustace Budgell, *Spectator,* no. 389, 27 May 1712.

69. Confident: Giordano Bruno, *Spaccio della bestia trionfante,* etc. [ed. and trans. John Toland?] (London, 1713), p. 4; based: Yates, *Giordano Bruno,* pp. 257–274. Appreciated: JT, "De genere, loco, et tempore mortis Jordani Bruni," JT/C, I, 313. Concluded: JT, "Account of Jordano Bruno's Book," JT/C, I, 332; cf. Paul-Henri Michel, *La Cosmologie de Giordano Bruno* (Paris, Hermann, 1962), pp. 101–103, 139, and Gosselin and Lerner, *Ash-Wednesday Supper,* pp. 30–33. Obliged: JT, "Account of Jordano Bruno's Book," JT/C, I, 328; cf. Michel, *Cosmologie,* pp. 104–107. Participated: JT, "Account of Jordano Bruno's Book," JT/C, I, 324–325. Contrariety: Bruno, *Spaccio,* pp. 4–5.

70. Saw: cf. JT, "Account of Jordano Bruno's Book," JT/C, I, 322, and Bruno, *Spaccio,* pp. 73–74. Catalogued: Giordano Bruno, *The Expulsion of the Triumphant Beast,* ed. and trans. Arthur D. Inerti (New Brunswick, N. J., Rutgers University Press, 1964), pp. 76–77 [from the "Explanatory Epistle" omitted in the 1713 translation]. Partook: Bruno, *Spaccio,* p. 229. Kept: Vedrine, *Conception de la nature,* pp. 104, 141–146.

71. Exemplified: Bruno, *Spaccio,* p. 45. Reach: JT, "Account of Jordano Bruno's Book," JT/C, I, 342–345.

72. Closed: cf. JT, "Account of Jordano Bruno's Book," JT/C, I, 316–317, and Bruno, *Expulsion,* p. 76. Pointed . . . rebuked: Bruno, *Spaccio,* pp. 102, 93–95; intrinsic: *ibid.,* p. 205. Advised . . . insisted: *ibid.,* pp. 90–92, 96–97. Protestations: JT, "Account of Jordano Bruno's Book," JT/C, I, 326–327.

73. Discriminated: JT, "Account of Jordano Bruno's Book," JT/C, I, 319–320. Transmigration: cf. Bruno, *Spaccio,* pp. 9–10, and Michel, *Cosmologie,* p. 121. Exception: cf. Bayle, *Dictionnaire historique et critique,* IV, 175, 177, and Giuntini, *Panteismo e ideologia,* pp. 296–301, 353.

74. Insistence: JT, "Account of Jordano Bruno's Book," JT/C, I, 346; theorized: Yates, *Giordano Bruno,* pp. 312–313, 407–414. Recognized: JT to Leibniz, n.d., JT/C, II, 395. Dedicated: JT/P, p. 13. Shared: *ibid.,* pp. 94–95.

75. Used: JT, "Memorial Presented to a Minister of State," JT/C, II, 243. Referred: JT to Goode, 30 Oct. 1720, B.L. Add. MS. 4295, ff. 39–40. Winking: JT/P, pp. 108–109; "Let": *ibid.,* p. 64. Evinced: B.L. Add. MS. 4295, f. 18 ("Extrait"), and JT to Höhendorff, 7 Mar. 1711 (N.S.), *ibid.,* ff.19–20.

76. Prosper: C. H. Josten, ed., *Elias Ashmole (1617–1692): His Autobiographical and Historical Notes,* etc., 5 vols. (Oxford, Clarendon Press, 1966), II, 395. Accused: Gibson to Charlett, 21 June 1694, Bodl. Ballard MSS. V, f. 48; belonged: *The History and Constitution of the Most Ancient and Honourable Fraternity of Free and Accepted Masons* (London, 1746), p. 106. Received: Apistodemon to JT, 1 June 1697, L.P.L. Cod. MS. Gibson 933, f. 55; Philocles to JT, 13 Nov. 1718, B.L. Add. MS. 4465, ff. 17–18.

77. Accepted: Des Maizeaux, "Some Memoirs," p. lxxxvi; assertion: JT/P, pp. 57–58. Informed: Albert Lantoine, *Un précurseur de la franc-maçonnerie: John Toland, 1670–1722* (Paris, E. Nourry, 1927). Point: Paul Dudon, "John Toland fut-il un précurseur de la franc-maçonnerie?," *Etudes* 204 (1930), 51–61.

78. Contention: Piggott, *Druids,* p. 181. Interest: cf. Thomas Paine, *The Origin of Freemasonry,* in *The Life and Works of Thomas Paine,* ed. William Van der Weyde, 10 vols. (New Rochelle, N.Y., Thomas Paine National Historical Association, 1925), IX, 167–189, and G. Adolf Koch, *Republican Religion: The American Revolution and the Cult of Reason* (New York, H. Holt and Co., 1933), pp. 118–119. Feast . . . functioning: Douglas Knoop and G. P. Jones, *The Genesis of Freemasonry: An Account of the Rise and*

Development of Freemasonry in Its Operative, Accepted, and Early Speculative Phases (Manchester, University Press, 1947), p. 168, and "Freemasonry and the Idea of Natural Religion," *Ars Quatuor Coronatorum* 56 (1946), 47. Transformed: Roberts, *Mythology of the Secret Societies* pp. 20–21; unaware: *ibid.,* p. 18n. Unknown: Knoop and Jones, "Freemasonry and the Idea," p. 46. Catechisms: Douglas Knoop, G. P. Jones, and Douglas Hamer, eds. and trans., *The Early Masonic Catechisms,* 2d ed. (Manchester, University Press, 1963); absolved: cf. Knoop and Jones, *Genesis of Freemasonry,* p. 180, and "Freemasonry and the Idea," pp. 38–43.

79. Lay: Dorothy Schlegel, "Freemasonry and the *Encyclopédie* Reconsidered," *Studies on Voltaire* 90 (1972), 1433–1460. Generated: Ira O. Wade, *The Clandestine Organization and Diffusion of Philosophical Ideas in France from 1700 to 1750* (Princeton, University Press, 1938), p. 17. Reconstructed: Jacob, *Newtonians and the English Revolution,* pp. 220–227; "Newtonianism and the Origins of the Enlightenment," pp. 11–25; *Radical Enlightenment,* pp. 118–119, 144, 156–159; Jacob and Jacob, "Anglican Origins," pp. 264–267. Possessed: B.L. Add. MS. 4295, f. 18 ("Extrait").

80. Describe: Jacob, "Newtonianism and the Origins of the Enlightenment," pp. 15–16; greeted: Giuntini, *Panteismo e ideologia,* pp. 483–485; cf. Jacob, *Radical Enlightenment,* pp. 119, 156–159.

81. Tradition: Arthur O. Lovejoy, "The Dialectic of Bruno and Spinoza," *University of California Publications in Philosophy* 1 (1904), 149, 166.

7. The Elusiveness of Deism

1. Evans, "John Toland's Pantheism," p. 193.

2. "With": Robert Burton, *The Anatomy of Melancholy* [1621], 3 vols. (London, G. Bell and Sons, 1926–1927), III, 440. Excerpted: *OED,* s. v. "Deist." Distinguish: Günter Gawlick, "Der Deismus als Grundzug der Religionsphilosophie der Aufklärung," in *Hermann Samuel Reimarus (1694–1768), ein "bekannter Unbekannter" der Aufklärung in Hamburg* (Göttingen, Vanderhoeck & Ruprecht, 1973), pp. 19–22. Indicated: *ibid.,* p. 40, n.21. "Term": Günter Gawlick, "Hume and the Deists: A Reconsideration," in *David Hume: Bicentenary Papers,* ed. G. P. Morice (Edinburgh, University Press, 1977), p. 130.

3. Using: Blaise Pascal, *Pensées,* ed. Louis Lafuma (Paris, Garnier-Flammarion, 1973), no. 17. Presented: John Dryden, *Religio Laici,* in *Works,* ed. Walter Scott and rev. George Saintsbury, 18 vols. (Edinburgh and London, 1882–1893), X, 39–40; identified: Clement Walsh, "A Note on the Meaning of 'Deism,' " *Anglican Theological Review* 38 (1956), 160–165. "They": Clarke, *Concerning the Unchangeable Obligations,* pp. 302–303. Identifying: *Catalogus Bibliothecae Harleianae,* 3 vols. (London, 1743), I, 154–158.

4. Postulate: Edwards, *Socinian Creed,* p. 122; JT, *Principle,* p. 23; Norris, *Account of Reason and Faith,* p. 5. Portrayed: Browne, *Procedure,* pp. 27–29; assert: Browne, *Things Divine,* p. 62. Dissolve: Browne, *Procedure,* pp. 114–115. Subordinated: Gailhard, *Epistle and Preface,* pp. 52–53; H. De Luzancy, *A Sermon Preached at Colchester 2 June 1697,* etc. (London, 1697), p. 10. Saw: Charlett to Tenison, Oct. 1695, B.L. Add. MS. 4229, f. 21; reckoned: Edmund Calamy, *Thirteen Sermons concerning the Doctrine of the Trinity,* etc. (London, 1722), preface.

5. Matthew Tindal, *Christianity as Old as the Creation,* etc. (London, 1730), pp. 368–369.

6. Anticipated: John Conybeare, *The Mysteries of the Christian Religion Credible,* etc. (London, 1723), pp. 3–4; Earbery, *Deism Examin'd,* p. 1; [William Stephens], *An Ac-*

count of the Growth of Deism in England, etc. (London, 1709), pp. 1–2; maintained: Norris, *Account of Reason and Faith,* p. 312; Jones, *New and Full Method,* III, 8–9. Held: JT, *Memorial,* p. 103; cf. JT, *Defence,* p. 16. Saw: [Anthony Collins], *A Discourse of the Grounds and Reasons of the Christian Religion,* 2d ed. (London, 1737), ("Letter to the Author"), pp. 88–89. Depicted: *ibid.,* p. 90. Reported: [Peter Annet], *Deism Fairly Stated, and Fully Vindicated,* etc. (London, 1746), p. 16.

7. Tindal, *Christianity,* p. 371; Nye, *Discourse,* pp. 46, 182.

8. Deemed: John Edwards, *A Free Discourse concerning Truth and Error,* etc. (London, 1701), pp. 423–424. Conceding: Stillingfleet, *Letter to a Deist,* preface.

9. William Whiston, *Memoirs of the Life and Writings of Mr. William Whiston,* etc., 2 vols. in 1 (London, 1749), pp. 105 ff.; Bentley, *Confutation of Atheism* (Sermon I), pp. 5–6.

10. Charles Blount, *Anima Mundi: or, An Historical Narration of the Opinions of the Ancients concerning Man's Soul after This Life,* etc. (London, 1679), preface. Repeating: Halyburton, *Natural Religion,* preface. Used: JT/CNM, p. 176. "Indifference": JT, *Agreement of the Customs,* pp. 152–153; "impotent": JT to _____, n.d., in JT/C, II, 303–304. Include: *Remarks on the Life,* p. 6. Certain: *Mr. Toland's Clito,* pp. 11, 17. Exploited: JT, *Apology,* p. 20.

11. Hobbes: [Thomas Tenison], *The Creed of Mr. Hobbes Examined,* etc., 2d ed., (London, 1671), dedication; Spinoza: Earberry, *Deism Examin'd,* p. 108. "Those": Popple to Locke, 15 Jan. 1695. (O.S.) Bodl. Locke MSS. c. 17, f. 221. Used: Thomas Burnet, *Third Remarks concerning an "Essay concerning Humane Understanding,"* etc. (London, 1699), pp. 22–23. "Speak": Hickes, "Preliminary Discourse"; cf. [John Witty], *The First Principles of Modern Deism Confuted,* etc. (London, 1707), pp. i–iv, 162–163.

12. Postulated: *Modesty Mistaken: or, A Letter to Mr. Toland,* etc. (London, 1702),pp. 1–10; believed: Earberry, *Deism Examin'd,* preface; included: Hickes, "Preliminary Discourse"; compiled: Halyburton, *Natural Religion;* viewed: Joannes F. Buddeus, *Traité de l'athéisme et de la superstition,* etc. (Amsterdam, 1740), pp. 51–53, 87–92; wrote: Taylor, *Preservative,* pp. xxx, 255, and [Charles Leslie], *A Short and Easie Method with the Deists,* etc. (London, 1698), p. 19; treated: *Remarks on the Life,* pp. 12, 19; included: Harris, *Atheistical Objections* (Sermon I), p. 20; named: J. A. Fabricius, *Delectus argumentorum et syllabus scriptorum,* etc. (Hamburg, 1725), p. 479; equated: Paterson *Antinazarenus,* p. 69, and Norris, *Account of Reason and Faith,* p. 326; presented: Gurdon, *Pretended Difficulties,* pp. 315, 367.

13. Yolton, *John Locke,* p. 170.

14. Clarke, *Concerning the Unchangeable Obligations,* pp. 13–25. William Berriman, *The Gradual Revelation of the Gospel, from the Times of Man's Apostasy,* etc., in *A Defence of Natural and Revealed Religion,* etc., [ed. Sampson Letsome and John Nicholl], 3 vols. (London, 1739), III, 595–596.

15. T. E. Jessop, introduction to *Alciphron, or the Minute Philosopher* [1732], by George Berkeley, in *The Works of Bishop Berkeley,* ed. A. A. Luce and T. E. Jessop, 9 vols. (London, Nelson, 1948–1957), III, 6.

16. [_____ Herbert], *The Establishment Vindicated against the Advocates for Licentiousness* (London, 1730), p. 21. Skelton, *Ophiomaches,* whose subtitle lists Herbert, Shaftesbury, Hobbes, Toland, Tindal, Collins, Mandeville, Dodwell, Woolston, Morgan, and Chubb; for Hume, *ibid.,* II, 20–22. Think: *ibid.,* p. 83. Linked: *ibid.,* I, 264. Held: *ibid.,* pp. 34–35.

17. Saw: Leland: *View,* I, 1; infer: *ibid.,* III, 43. Belonged: *ibid.,* I, 62–63; mounted: *ibid.,* p. 149. Introduced: *ibid.,* p. 388.

18. Organized: Peter Gay, ed., *Deism: An Anthology* (Princeton, Van Nostrand, 1968), pp. 12–13. Clung: cf. Giancarlo Carabelli, "Deismo inglese e dintoni: alcuni studi recenti," *Rivista critica di storia della filosofia* 33 (1978), 418–451. Offered: G. V. Lechler, *Geschichte des englischen Deismus* (Stuttgart, 1841), p. 460. Philosophical: cf. Arthur R. Winnett, "Were the Deists 'Deists'?" *Church Quarterly Review* 161 (1960), 70–77.

19. Emerson, "English Deism," pp. 42–43.

20. J. A. Redwood, "Charles Blount (1654–93), Deism, and English Free Thought," *Journal of the History of Ideas* 35 (1974), 498.

21. Arthur O. Lovejoy, "The Parallel of Deism and Classicism," in *Essays in the History of Ideas* (1948; reprint, New York, G. P. Putnam's Sons, 1960), p. 78.

22. Roland Stromberg, "Lovejoy's 'Parallel' Reconsidered," *Eighteenth-Century Studies* 1 (1967–1968), 383–384; cf. Leonard P. Wessell, "Rejoinder to Stromberg's 'Reconsideration,'" *ibid.*, 2 (1968–1969), 439–449. Maintained: Stromberg, "Lovejoy's 'Parallel,'" pp. 383–384; see also his *Religious Liberalism*, pp. 52–69.

23. Gawlick, "Hume and the Deists," p. 133.

24. Blount, *Oracles of Reason*, p. 92; Tindal, *Christianity*, pp. 363–365; Annet, *Deism Fairly Stated*, pp. 4, 16, 70–71, 97.

25. Herbert, *De veritate*, p. 308; Thomas Woolston, *The Old Apology for the Truth of the Christian Religion*, etc. (London, 1705), p. 382.

26. Blount, *Oracles of Reason*, p. 201; [Charles Blount], *Religio Laici: Written in a Letter to John Dryden* (London, 1683), p. 20.

27. Charles Blount, *The First Two Books of Philostratus, concerning the Life of Apollonius Tyaneus*, etc. (London, 1680), p. 82; Blount, *Religio Laici*, pp. 30–32, 41–42, 46, and *First Two Books*, p. 95. Outrageous: e.g., Blount, *Oracles of Reason*, pp. 36, 40–41; cf. Ugo Bonanante, *Charles Blount: libertinismo e deismo nel seicento inglese* (Florence, La nuova Italia, 1972), pp. 168–169.

28. Expressions . . . differentiated: Collins, *Discourse of the Grounds* ("Letter to the Author"), p. 90. Insisted: *ibid.*, pp. xi–xii. Denied: *ibid.*, p. 101. Defended: *ibid.*, p. 213.

29. Hugo Grotius, *Annotationes in libros evangeliorum* (Amsterdam, 1641), and *Annotationes in vetus testamentum* (Paris, 1664).

30. Collins, *Discourse of the Grounds*, pp. xii, 234–235. Confident: [Anthony Collins], *A Discourse of Free-Thinking*, etc. (London, 1713), p. 37. Meant: *ibid.*, p. 40; conform: *ibid.*, p. 10. Borrowed: Collins, *Discourse of the Grounds*, p. 20. Thesis: cf. *ibid.*, p. 13, and Collins, *Discourse of Free-Thinking*, pp. 98–99.

31. Raised: Tindal, *Christianity*, pp. 11–12. Designated: *ibid.*, p. 31. Thought: *ibid.*, pp. 179–180. "Unchangeable": *ibid.*, p. 3.

32. Riddled: *ibid.*, pp. iii–iv, 2–12, 59–64. Immutable: *ibid.*, pp. 31, 200. Shared: *ibid.*, pp. 327–328, 375, 9. Measured: *ibid.*, pp. 243–272. Unlikely: *ibid.*, pp. 327–328. "Existed": *ibid.*, p. 4.

33. Blount, *Religio Laici*, dedication; cf. Bonanante, *Charles Blount*, pp. 74–79.

34. Tindal, *Christianity*, pp. 13–21; Annet, *Deism Fairly Stated*, pp. 10–12. Present: John Hunt, *Religious Thought in England from the Reformation to the End of the Last Century*, 3 vols. (London, 1870–1873), II, 105.

35. Assigned: Emerson, "English Deism," pp. 46–48. Epicurus: Blount, *Oracles of Reason*, pp. 106–110; Spinoza: [Charles Blount], *Miracles, No Violations of the Laws of Nature*, etc. (London, 1683); played: Blount, *Oracles of Reason*, pp. 158–168; Burnet: John Wilmot, earl of Rochester, *A Letter to Dr. Burnet from . . . the Earl of Rochester as He Lay on His Death-Bed*, etc. (London, 1680).

36. Connect: Blount, *Oracles of Reason*, pp. 88–106. Adopted: Blount, *Anima Mundi*,

p. 3. Prove: JT/N, First letter, p. 16; Tindal, *Christianity*, p. 2; Collins, *Discourse of Free-Thinking*, pp. 12–14, 171–173; indifferent: Bonanante, *Charles Blount*, p. 74. Gainsaid: cf. James O'Higgins, "Archbishop Tillotson and the Religion of Nature," *Journal of Theological Studies*, n.s. 24 (1973), 122–142.

37. Herbert, *De Veritate*, pp. 289–313. Accepted: Blount, *Religio Laici*, p. 88; [Matthew Tindal], *The Rights of the Christian Church*, etc., 4th ed. (London, 1708), p. 223; [Anthony Collins], *Essay on the Use of Reason in Propositions*, etc. (London, 1707), p. 3. Concerned: Blount, *Oracles of Reason*, preface. Mean: Collins, *Discourse of Free-Thinking*, p. 5. Shared: [Anthony Collins], *A Philosophical Inquiry concerning Human Liberty*, 3d ed. (London, 1735), p. iii; Tindal, *Christianity*, p. 294. Content: Annet, *Deism Fairly Stated*, p. 51.

38. Tindal, *Christianity*, pp. 159, 182. Efforts: e.g., *ibid.*, pp. 180–181. "Foundation": Collins, *Discourse of Free-Thinking*, p. 3.

39. Assigned: Blount, *Oracles of Reason*, p. 91; Tindal, *Christianity*, p. 191; Collins, *Discourse of Free-Thinking*, p. 26; Annet, *Deism Fairly Stated*, p. 14. Blount, *Religio Laici*, pp. 27–28. Collins, *Discourse of Free-Thinking*, p. 125; cf. David Berman, "Anthony Collins' Essays in the *Independent Whig*," *Journal of the History of Philosophy* 13 (1975), 463–469. Tindal, *Christianity*, p. 231. Thomas Chubb, *An Enquiry concerning Faith and Mysteries*, in *A Collection of Tracts on Various Subjects*, etc., 2d ed., 2 vols. (London, 1754), I, 256; Annet, *Deism Fairly Stated*, p. 27. Collins, *Essay on the Use*, p. 3, and *Philosophical Inquiry*, p. 11; Tindal, *Christianity*, pp. iii, 48.

40. Blount, *Oracles of Reason*, pp. 100–104. Tindal, *Christianity*, pp. 278, 390–391, 419, and Matthew Tindal, *Christianity as Old as the Creation*, part 2 (London, 1730 [*sic*; 1732]), p. xxv. Depended: Tindal, *Christianity*, pp. 322–327. Owned: James O'Higgins, *Anthony Collins: The Man and His Works* (The Hague, Nijhoff, 1970), p. 33; dealt: Collins, *Discourse of the Grounds*, p. 133. Defended: *ibid.*, pp. iv–v.

41. Thomas Chubb, *The Supremacy of the Father Vindicated*, etc. (London, 1718); used: Thomas L. Bushell, *The Sage of Salisbury: Thomas Chubb, 1679–1747* (New York, Philosophical Library, 1967), pp. 129–146. Thomas Morgan, *A Refutation of the False Principles . . . with a Postscript concerning the Real Argument between the "Athanasians" and "Socinians" in the Trinitarian Controversy* (London, 1722); Thomas Morgan, *Physico-Theology*, etc. (London, 1741), p. 297. Annet, *Deism Fairly Stated*, pp. 57–58.

42. Cf. Laurens Laudan, "The Clock Metaphor: The Impact of Descartes on English Methodological Thought, 1650–1665," *Annals of Science* 22 (1966), 73–104. Used: e.g., JT/LS, pp. 184–185. Contented: Blount, *Oracles of Reason*, p. 12; Collins, *Discourse of the Grounds*, pp. 28, 196, and *Discourse of Free-Thinking*, pp. 21–25; Tindal, *Christianity*, p. 327; rejected: Peter Annet, *The Resurrection of Jesus Considered: In Answer to the Tryal of the Witnesses*, 3d ed. (London, 1744), pp. 51–52.

43. Blount, *Oracles of Reason*, pp. 178, 55, 222. Defined: Blount, *Religio Laici*, pp. 58–59. Intrigued: *ibid.*, p. 68. Trace: Blount, *Anima Mundi*, pp. 7–8. Defining: cf. Bonanante, *Charles Blount*, p. 21; Blount, *Anima Mundi*, p. 7; Vergil, *Eclogues*, III, 60. Augustine, *City of God*, VII, 9. Blount, *Oracles of Reason*, p. 213. Charles Gildon, preface to *ibid.*; and cf. Bonanante, *Charles Blount*, pp. 24–25, 77–78.

44. Collins, *Discourse of Free-Thinking*, pp. 104–105; [Anthony Collins], *A Vindication of the Divine Attributes*, etc. (London, 1710), p. 4. Univocal: e.g., *ibid.*, p. 10; cf. James O'Higgins, "Hume and the Deists: A Contrast in Religious Approaches," *Journal of Theological Studies*, n.s. 22 (1971), 488. David Berman, "Anthony Collins: Aspects of His Thought and Writings," *Hermanthea* 97 (1975), 49–70, and "Anthony Collins and the Question of Atheism in the Early Part of the Eighteenth Century," *Proceedings of the Royal Irish Academy* 75, sec. C (1975), 85–102. Possible: cf. O'Higgins, *Anthony Collins*, p. 15.

45. Dismay: Halyburton, *Natural Religion,* I, 220; professing: Blount, *Religio Laici,* dedication; [Matthew Tindal], *A Defence of Our Present Happy Establishment and Administration Vindicated,* etc. (London, 1722); O'Higgins, *Anthony Collins,* p. 22; Andrew Kippis, *Biographia Britannica,* etc., 2d ed., 5 vols. (London, 1773–1780), s.v. "Chubb, Thomas." Held: Emerson, "English Deism," pp. 237–251. Professed: e.g., Collins, *Discourse of Free-Thinking,* pp. 131–137. Termed: cf. Blount, *Religio Laici,* pp. 26–27, and Tindal, *Rights of the Christian Church,* pp. 321–323.

46. Shared: e.g., Tindal, *Rights of the Christian Church,* pp. 283, 408–409. Denial: Tindal, *Christianity,* pp. 285, 315; [Anthony Collins], *An Historical and Critical Essay on the Thirty-Nine Articles,* etc. (London, 1724), pp. viii–x. Fathers: Tindal, *Christianity,* pt. 2, p. xxxii; councils: Tindal, *Rights of the Christian Church,* pp. 192–193; bishops: *ibid.,* pp. 143, 160–162.

47. Made: e.g., Tindal, *Rights of the Christian Church,* pp. 406–407. Defend: Collins, *Discourse of the Grounds* ("Letter to the Author"), pp. 63–64; curb: Tindal, *Rights of the Christian Church,* pp. 12–13. "Perfect": *ibid.,* pp. iv–v; regulate . . . determine: *ibid.,* pp. 80–84, 125, and Collins, *Essays on the Thirty-Nine Articles,* pp. 6–7. Presented: Tindal, *Rights of the Christian Church,* p. 213, and Collins, *Discourse of Free-Thinking,* p. 27. Agreed: Tindal, *Rights of the Christian Church,* pp. 295–296.

48. Blount, *Oracles of Reason,* pp. 88–89, and Tindal, *Rights of the Christian Church,* p. 116. Tindal, *Christianity,* p. 2.

49. Presented: Collins, *Discourse of Free-Thinking,* p. 18. Convinced: *ibid.,* pp. 15, 177. Invoked: cf. Collins, *Discourse of the Grounds,* pp. xxxix–xl, and Tindal, *Rights of the Christian Church,* p. 186, and *Christianity,* p. 45. Paying: *ibid.,* pp. 10, 32, 45, 75, 77, 136, 147, 170–172, 216, 221, 267. "Whom": Collins, *Discourse of Free-Thinking,* p. 171.

50. Provided: O'Higgins, *Anthony Collins,* pp. 8–11. "Whose": Collins, *Philosophical Inquiry,* p. 94. Infer: Tindal, *Christianity,* pp. 292, 396–399, 416; Collins, *Discourse of Free-Thinking,* pp. 47–49. Receive: entry of 31 Oct. 1733, HMC Reports, *Egmont MSS.,* I, 405–406; became: Tindal, *Christianity,* pp. 16–17.

51. Becoming: Gildon, in Blount, *Oracles of Reason,* p. 199; Collins, *Discourse of Free-Thinking,* p. 171; Tindal, *Christianity,* pp. 298, 366.

52. Assertion: Blount, *Religio Laici,* pp. 14–15. Division: cf. Tindal, *Rights of the Christian Church,* pp. 112–113. Socrates: Collins, *Discourse of Free-Thinking,* pp. 123–124; Confucius: Tindal, *Christianity,* p. 342.

53. Assert: Blount, *Religio Laici,* pp. 47–48. "Extant": Blount, *Oracles of Reason,* p. 88. Rejection: Blount, *Anima Mundi,* p. 20; cf. Bonanante, *Charles Blount,* pp. 167–169.

54. Tindal, *Rights of the Christian Church,* p. 114, and *Christianity,* pp. 59–60.

55. Collins, *Discourse of the Grounds* ("Letter to the Author"), pp. 64–65, 67.

56. Portraying: Gildon, preface to Blount, *Oracles of Reason;* Annet, *Deism Fairly Stated,* p. 35; Tindal, *Christianity,* pt. 2, p. ii. Freethinking: Collins, *Discourse of Free-Thinking,* p. 178; pulling down: Tindal, *Christianity,* p. 421.

57. Blount, *Oracles of Reason,* pp. 106–110. Imply: Frederick Copleston, *A History of Philosophy,* 9 vols. (London, Burns, Oates & Washbourne, 1946–1975), I, 406–411. Link: Blount, *Oracles of Reason,* p. 88. Indicate: Tindal, *Christianity,* pp. 345–346. Rejected: *ibid.,* pp. 122–129, 170, 175; Christian: *ibid.,* p. 99.

58. Blount, *First Two Books,* pp. 28, 151, 243; Tindal, *Christianity,* p. 281; Collins, *Discourse of Free-Thinking,* p. 30; Collins to Sophia, quoted in Kemble, *State Papers,* pp. 51–52. Partial: Tindal, *Rights of the Christian Church,* preface; presented: Tindal, *Christianity,* p. 165.

59. Blount, *Religio Laici,* pp. 49–50; Tindal, *Christianity,* p. 22. Entailed: *ibid.,* pp. 16, 113.

60. Collins, *Discourse of Free-Thinking,* pp. 33–34; [Anthony Collins], *Reflections on Mr. Clarke's Second Defence,* etc., 2d ed. (London, 1711), pp. 22–23; Collins, *Philosophical Inquiry,* pp. 16–17.

61. Sceptical: Halyburton, *Natural Religion,* I, 30–39, and Earberry, *Deism Examin'd,* p. 157. Balancing: Blount, *Anima Mundi,* pp. 9–10.

62. Tindal, *Christianity,* p. 76, and Collins, *Discourse of Free-Thinking,* p. 38. Professions: Tindal, *Rights of the Christian Church,* p. 146, and *Christianity,* p. 26. O'Higgins, *Anthony Collins,* p. 234; Collins, *Discourse of Free-Thinking,* p. 148.

63. Tindal to Locke, n.d. [1697], Bodl. Locke MSS. c. 20, f. 210; J. H. Broome, "An Agent in Anglo-French Relationships: Pierre Des Maizeaux, 1673–1745" (Ph.D. diss., University of London, 1949), pp. 294–295.

64. Targets: O'Higgins, *Anthony Collins,* p. 51. Thought: cf. JT/N, p. xxiii. Dedicating: JT, *Fables of Aesop,* and *Adeisidaemon;* corresponded: O'Higgins, *Anthony Collins,* p. 14; houseguest: JT to Goode, 30 Oct. 1720, B.L. Add. MS. 4295, ff. 39–40. Avoided: Collins to Des Maizeaux, n.d. [1718], B.L. Add. MS. 4282, f. 226. Referred: JT, *Philippick Oration,* pp. xi–xii.

65. Professed: Blount, *Anima Mundi,* preface; affected: Blount, *First Two Books,* p. 5; twitting: *ibid.,* preface. Allow: cf. Bonanante, *Charles Blount,* pp. 172–173.

66. James Foster, *The Usefulness, Truth, and Excellency of the Christian Revelation Defended,* etc., 2d ed. (London, 1731), pp. 4, 23–24, 273–274. Issue: *ibid.,* p. 8.

8. A Religion Fit for Gentlemen

1. Holds: Norman Sykes, *The English Religious Tradition: Sketches of Its Influence on Church, State, and Society* (London, SCM Press, 1953), p. 61. Sees: Hugh D. McDonald, *Ideas of Revelation: An Historical Study, 1700 to 1860* (London, Macmillan, 1959), p. 112. Maintained: E. C. Moore, *An Outline of the History of Christian Thought since Kant* (London, Duckworth, 1909), p. 24. Mark Pattison, "Tendencies of Religious Thought in England, 1688–1750," in *Essays and Reviews,* 3d ed. (London, 1860), p. 257; cf. Richard S. Westfall, *Science and Religion in Seventeenth-Century England* (New Haven, Yale University Press, 1958), pp. 217–218, and Jacob, *Newtonians and the English Revolution,* p. 171.

2. Perplexed: e.g., William Carroll, *A Dissertation upon . . . Mr. Locke's Essay concerning Humane Understanding,* etc. (London, 1706), pp. 276–289. "I": Charles Wheatly, *Fifty Sermons on Several Subjects and Occasions,* 3 vols. (London, 1746), II, 236–237. Dilatory: Norman Sykes, *Edmund Gibson, Bishop of London, 1669–1748: A Study in Politics and Religion in the Eighteenth Century* (London, Oxford University Press, 1926), pp. 249–250. Advised: Warburton to Birch, 22 Apr. 1741, in John Nichols, ed., *Literary Anecdotes of the Eighteenth Century,* 9 vols. (London, 1812–1815), V, 570; cf. Norman Sykes, *William Wake, Archbishop of Canterbury,* 2 vols. (Cambridge, University Press, 1957), I, 57–58; Burnet to Tenison, 18 June 1706, B.L. Add. MS. 4229, f. 63; Mangey, *Remarks upon Nazarenus,* preface.

3. Presented: Jacob, *Newtonians and the English Revolution,* pp. 143–200; John J. Dahm, "Science and Apologetics in the Early Boyle Lectures," *Church History* 39 (1970), 172–186; William Coleman, "Providence, Capitalism, and Environmental Degradation: English Apologetics in an Era of Revolution," *Journal of the History of Ideas* 37 (1976), 27–44; Larry Stewart, "Samuel Clarke, Newtonianism, and the Factions of Post-Revolutionary England," *ibid.* 42 (1981), 53–72. Preoccupied: Bentley, *Confutation of Atheism* (Sermon I), pp. 12–13, 14. Convert: Richard Kidder, *Demonstration of the Messias in Which the Truth of the Christian Religion Is Proved, against All the Enemies Thereof, but Especially against the Jews,* etc. (London, 1694–1700). Applied: Blackall, *Sufficiency of a*

Standing Revelation. Endeavored: Harris, *Atheistical Objections* (Sermon II), p. 4. Making: Clarke, *Demonstration of the Being*, p. 1. Played: Clarke, *Concerning the Unchangeable Obligations*, pp. 13–35, 147; cf. James E. Force, "Whiston Controversies: The Development of 'Newtonianism' in the Thought of William Whiston" (Ph.D. diss., Washington University, 1977), pp. 185–191, 308–311.

4. Urban: Earberry, *Deism Examin'd*, p. 1. Convinced: Willis, *Occasional Paper*, p. 12. Saw: Halyburton, *Natural Religion*, I, 15. Insistence: [Jonathan Swift], *A Letter to a Young Gentleman, Lately Enter'd into Holy Orders*, etc. (London, 1721), p. 26. Chubb: cf. Thomas L. Bushell, *The Sage of Salisbury: Thomas Chubb, 1679–1747* (New York, Philosophical Library, 1967), pp. 3–10. Disappear: Blackall, *Sufficiency of a Standing Revelation* (Sermon VIII), pp. 34–35. Tolerate: Halyburton, *Natural Religion*, I, 5; depended: Alan D. Gilbert, *Religion and Society in Industrial England: Church, Chapel, and Social Change, 1740–1914* (London, Longmans, Green, 1976), p. 13.

5. Self-evident: Skelton, *Ophiomaches*, II, 47. Counseled: Synge, *Gentleman's Religion*, pp. 51–52. Written: e.g., Prideaux, *Letter to the Deists*.

6. Recognize: cf. Browne, *Procedure*, p. 233, and Gurdon, *Pretended Difficulties*, p. 284. Derived: Hare, *Difficulties and Discouragements*, p. 18; Defoe, *Argument*, p. 74; Leland, *View*, III, 641–660. Led: cf. Skelton, *Ophiomaches*, II, 134–135, 298–299, and Bentley, *Confutation of Atheism* (Sermon I), pp. 24–35. Identifying: cf. Blackall, *Sufficiency of a Standing Revelation* (Sermon V), p. 58, and Paterson, *Anti-nazarenus*, pp. 61–62.

7. Amounted: Prideaux, *Letter to the Deists*, p. 33; Leland, *View*, I, 422–423; Skelton, *Ophiomaches*, II, 1–58.

8. Argument: Smith, *Sermon*, pp. 8–9; Swift, *Letter*, p. 29; Taylor, *Preservative*, p. iii; Gailhard, *Blasphemous Socinian Heresie*, dedication; Harris, *Atheistical Objections* (Sermon I), p. 14; Blackall, *Sufficiency of a Standing Revelation* (Sermon II), p. 6; Clarke, *Demonstration of the Being*, pp. 2–3; John Clarke, *An Enquiry into the Cause and Origin of Evil*, etc. (London, 1720), pp. 24–25; Halyburton, *Natural Religion*, I, 53; Gildon, *Deist's Manual*, p. iv; Brett, *Discourses*, pp. 10–11. Toland: Browne, *Letter*, p. 98; [William Baron], *Regicides No Saints nor Martyrs*, etc. (London, 1700), p. 134; Mangey, *Remarks upon Nazarenus*, p. 2; Skelton, *Ophiomaches*, II, 261.

9. Waning: John Miller, *Popery and Politics in England, 1660–1688* (Cambridge, University Press, 1973), p. 88. Occur: Sykes, *Principles and Connexion*, pp. 179–199. Use: Tindal, *Christianity*, p. 414. Complaints: e.g., Fiddes, *Remarks on the State Anatomy*, p. 42. Ventured: *ibid.*, p. 33, and Thomas Lewis, *An Historical Essay upon the Consecration of Churches*, etc. (London 1719), pp. viii–ix. Recognizing: Hare, *Scripture Vindicated*, p. xxxi. Urged: Daniel Waterland, *The Case of Arian-Subscription Considered*, etc. (London, 1721), p. 7.

10. Accusations: cf. Fiddes, *Remarks on the State-Anatomy*, p. 51, and *A Representation of the Present State of Religion*, etc. (Dublin, 1711), p. 4. Justified: Offspring Blackall, *Works*, 2 vols., consecutive pag. (London, 1723), p. 179; Gailhard, *Blasphemous Socinian Heresie*, dedication; *Remarks on the Life*, pp. 49–51; Payne, *Mystery of the Christian Faith*, p. 95; Leslie, *Socinian Controversy*, Dialogue IV, pp. 38–41; Halyburton, *Natural Religion*, I, 20–21; Skelton, *Ophiomaches*, II, 308–311.

11. Scriptural: Benoist, *Mélange*, p. 219, and [John Jebb], "A Discourse concerning the Pillar of Fire and Cloud," etc., in *Bibliotheca Litteraria* 5 (1723), 15–16; patristic: John Richardson, *The Canon of the New Testament Vindicated*, etc., 2d ed. (London 1701), pp. 27–28; Beconsall, *Christian Belief*, pp. 103–115; Browne, *Letter*, pp. 210–222. Demonstrated: Humphrey Ditton, *The General Laws of Nature and Motion*, etc. (London, 1705). Relying: Mangey, *Remarks upon Nazarenus*, pp. 2, 85, 122; retreating: Synge,

Gentleman's Religion, p. 283; Gailhard, *Blasphemous Socinian Heresie*, dedication; Oliver Hill, *A Rod for the Backs of Fools*, etc. (London, 1702), dedication.

12. Preoccupied: N.B. the caution of Geoffrey Holmes, rev. of Jacob, *Newtonians and the English Revolution*, in *The British Journal for the History of Science* 11 (1978), 169; fashion: H. R. McAdoo, *The Spirit of Anglicanism: A Survey of Anglican Theological Method in the Seventeenth Century* (London, A. and C. Black, 1965), p. 311. Accelerated: François Russo, "Théologie naturelle et secularisation de la science au XVIIIème siècle," *Recherches de science religieuse* 66 (1978), 27–62. Argued: cf. Margaret C. Jacob, "The Church and the Formation of the Newtonian World-View," *Journal of European Studies* 1 (1971), 128–148, and "Newtonian Science and Radical Enlightenment," *Vistas in Astronomy* 22 (1979), 545–555.

13. Sustained: cf. Stromberg, *Religious Liberalism*, pp. 26–33, and Westfall, *Science and Religion*, pp. 49–69. Matched: e.g., O'Higgins, *Anthony Collins*, p. 43. Believed: Isaac Newton, *Mathematical Principles of Natural Philosophy*, ed. Florian Cajori (Berkeley, University of California Press, 1934), p. 545, and *Opticks*, 4th ed. (1730; reprint, New York, Dover, 1952), pp. 381, 405–406; took: Henry Guerlac and Margaret C. Jacob, "Bentley, Newton, and Providence (The Boyle Lectures Once More)," *Journal of the History of Ideas* 30 (1969), 307–318. Structure: Kubrin, "Newton and the Cyclical Cosmos," p. 334; Jacob, "Toland and the Newtonian Ideology," p. 321. Became: e.g., Bentley, *Confutation of Atheism* (Sermon II), p. 4, and (Sermon VII), p. 6, and Harris, *Atheistical Objections* (Sermon IV), p. 26. Grasp: Jacob, *Newtonians and the English Revolution*, p. 178. Reject: J. H. Gay, "Matter and Freedom in the Thought of Samuel Clarke," *Journal of the History of Ideas* 24 (1963), 99.

14. Dictated: Westfall, *Science and Religion*, p. 51. Inert: Bentley, *Confutation of Atheism* (Sermon II), p. 17, and (Sermon VI), p. 34; Harris, *Atheistical Objections* (Sermon IV), p. 32; Clarke, *Enquiry into the Cause*, pp. 88–89. Threat: Bentley, *Confutation of Atheism* (Sermon II), p. 23, and Clarke, *Demonstration of the Being*, pp. 180–182.

15. Design: William L. Rowe, *The Cosmological Argument* (Princeton, University Press, 1975); added: Bentley, *Confutation of Atheism* (Sermon II), p. 29, and (Sermon VI), p. 20. Recognized: Aquinas, *Summa Theologiae*, I, 2, 3. Marked: Eugenio Garin, "Samuel Clarke e il razionalismo inglese del secolo XVIII," *Sophia* 2 (1934), 295. Maintain: Clarke, *Demonstration of the Being*, preface. Reveals: James P. Ferguson, "The Image of the Schoolmen in 18th Century English Philosophy, with Reference to the Philosophy of Samuel Clarke," *Arts libéraux et philosophie au moyen âge* (Montreal, Institut d'études mediévales, 1969), pp. 1199–1206.

16. Demonstrated: cf. Clarke, *Demonstration of the Being*, pp. 45–47, and *A Third and Fourth Defense of an Argument Made Use of in a Letter to Mr. Dodwel*, 2d ed. (London, 1712), pp. 86–87.

17. Gurdon, *Pretended Difficulties*, pp. 314–317. Witty, *First Principles*, pp. ix–x, 183. Resisted: e.g., William Nicholls, *A Conference with a Theist*, 3d ed., 2 vols. (London, 1723), II, 204–206.

18. Concluded: Hélène Metzger, *Attraction universelle et religion naturelle chez quelques commentateurs anglais de Newton*, 3 vols., consecutive pag. (Paris, Hermann et Cie, 1938), p. 110. Harden: Kubrin, "Newton and the Cyclical Cosmos," p. 339. "All": Robert Kargon, *Atomism in England from Hariot to Newton* (Oxford, Clarendon Press, 1966), p. 138. Bespeaks: Robert H. Hurlbutt, *Hume, Newton, and the Design Argument* (Lincoln, University of Nebraska Press, 1965), p. 32; exhibited: Margula R. Perl, "Physics, and Metaphysics in Newton, Leibniz, and Clarke," *Journal of the History of Ideas* 30 (1969), 507–526. John H. Newman, *The Idea of a University*, 4th ed. (London, 1875), p. 461.

19. Hostile: Mangey, *Remarks upon Nazarenus,* pp. 125-126. Contributed: Clarke, *Concerning the Unchangeable Obligations,* p. 246.

20. Persisted: Hare, *Scripture Vindicated,* p. xxxiii. Obliged: Witty, *First Principles,* pp. vi-vii, 194, 288; Clarke, *Demonstration of the Being,* pp. 80-81, 85-86. Noted: Wake to de Crousaz, 11 Oct. 1725, in Sykes, *Wake,* II, 169; cf. [William Wotton], *A Letter to Eusebia,* etc. (London, 1704), pp. 10-11. Talisman: Halyburton, *Natural Religion,* II, 7-8; beguiling: Yolton, *John Locke,* p. 123.

21. Relied: cf. Clarke, *Demonstration of the Being,* p. 141, and Bentley, *Confutation of Atheism* (Sermon III), p. 8. Used: *ibid.,* (Sermon I), pp. 23, 33, and Blackall, *Sufficiency of a Standing Revelation* (Sermon VIII), pp. 47-52. Although Clarke argued against the eternity of the universe and for a necessary existent (*Demonstration of the Being,* pp. 42-43, 20-21), he, like Aristotle, seems to have thought of creation as an ordering rather than as a making *ex nihilo* (cf. *ibid.,* pp. 120-121, 158, and Aristotle, *Metaphysics,* XI, 6). Hierarchy: Bentley, *Confutation of Atheism* (Sermon III), p. 4; uniformitarianism: Clarke, *An Enquiry into the Cause and Origin of Moral Evil,* etc. (London, 1721), p. 11; fixity: Bentley, *Confutation of Atheism* (Sermon IV), pp. 30-31, and Clarke, *Demonstration of the Being,* pp. 120-121. Reservations: Aquinas, *Summa contra Gentiles,* I, x; adduced: Clarke, *Demonstration of the Being,* p. 35. Partiality: e.g., Nicholls, *Conference with a Theist,* II, 437-486, and Bentley, *Confutation of Atheism* (Sermon VIII), p. 41; restatement: Hurlbutt, *Hume, Newton,* p. 135. Resembled: Herschel Baker, *The Wars of Truth: Studies in the Decay of Christian Humanism in the Earlier Seventeenth Century* (Cambridge, Mass., Harvard University Press, 1952), p. 350, n.164; ontology: Clarke, *Demonstration of the Being,* p. 108; teleology: Clarke, *Moral Evil,* pp. 103-104.

22. Bentley, *Confutation of Atheism* (Sermon III), p. 37; Synge, *Gentleman's Religion,* pp. 279-281.

23. Cf. Norris, *Account of Reason and Faith,* pp. 16-17, and Browne, *Procedure,* p. 244. Tempted: Norris, *Account of Reason and Faith,* p. 22; adopting: *ibid.,* pp. 98-99, 145-146. Felt . . . undermined: Browne, *Procedure,* pp. 29-30, 62; cf. James O'Higgins, "Browne and King, Collins and Berkeley: Agnosticism or Anthropomorphism?", *Journal of Theological Studies,* n.s. 27 (1976), 102-103, and Arthur R. Winnett, *Peter Browne: Provost, Bishop, Metaphysician* (London, S.P.C.K., 1974), pp. 132, 148-149. Define: Browne, *Things Divine,* p. 89.

24. Accepted: Beconsall, *Christian Belief,* pp. 27, 54, 59. Lockian: Payne, *Mystery of the Christian Faith,* pp. 33-34. Assumed: James P. Ferguson, *The Philosophy of Dr. Samuel Clarke and Its Critics* (New York, Vantage Press, 1974), pp. 248-249; cf. G. A. J. Rogers, "Locke's *Essay* and Newton's *Principia,*" *Journal of the History of Ideas* 39 (1978), 217-232.

25. Hold: Elys, *Letter to Howard,* p. 6; Browne, *Letter,* pp. 154-155, and *Procedure,* p. 254. Reduce: Norris, *Account of Reason and Faith,* pp. 37-38.

26. Found: Willis, *Occasional Paper,* p. 21, and Gastrell, *Some Considerations,* p. 11. Molyneux to Locke, 24 Dec. 1695, *Familiar Letters,* p. 105.

27. Edward Synge, *A Plain and Easy Method,* etc. (London, 1715), preface, pp. 98, 12, preface. Fewer: cf. Gailhard, *Blasphemous Socinian Heresie,* pp. 328-329, and George Stanhope, *A Paraphrase and Comment upon the Epistles and Gospels,* etc., 4th ed., 4 vols. (London, 1726), III, 154-155.

28. Suggested: Samuel Clarke, *Three Practical Essays, viz., on Baptism, Confirmation, Repentance,* etc. (London, 1699), pp. 135-136. [Patrick Middleton], *The Case of Abraham,* etc. (London, 1735), pp. 16-17, 22.

29. Rejected: Willis, *Occasional Paper,* p. 16; Witty, *First Principles,* pp. ix-x; Beconsall, *Christian Belief,* pp. 58-59, 78; Beverley, *Christianity the Great Mystery,* pp. 37-48;

Gailhard, *Blasphemous Socinian Heresie,* p. 320; Elys, *Letter to Howard,* p. 12. Give: cf. Browne, *Letter,* pp. 13, 57, 106, and *Things Divine,* p. 203. Explore: Browne, *Letter,* pp. 41–43, and *Things Divine,* p. 310; method: Aquinas, *Summa Theologiae,* I, 13; cf. Anders Jeffner, *Butler and Hume on Religion: A Comparative Analysis* (Stockholm, Diakonistyrelsens Bokförlag, 1966), pp. 184–185.

30. Analogous: Browne, *Procedure,* p. 247, and *Things Divine,* pp. 403–405. Current: Smith, *Sermon,* pp. 15–24; Stillingfleet, *Mysteries,* pp. 20–21; Synge, *Gentleman's Religion,* p. 298; cf. Don Cupitt, "The Doctrine of Analogy in the Age of Locke," *Journal of Theological Studies,* n.s. 19 (1968), 186–202. Urging: Leland, *View,* I, 455.

31. Take: JT/N, p. ix; alarming: B. Regis, *The Mystery of Godliness Consider'd,* etc. (London, 1721), and Norris, *Account of Reason and Faith,* p. 3. Invoked: Synge, *Gentleman's Religion,* pp. 292–293, 297–298.

32. Commonplace: Payne, *Mystery of the Christian Faith,* pp. 6–7. Gastrell, *Some Considerations,* pp. 4–5, 49–50.

33. Gildon, *Deist's Manual,* pp. xi–xii, 239; Leslie, appendix, *ibid.,* pp. 1–24, and Halyburton, *Natural Religion,* II, 30.

34. Written: John Conybeare, *The Mysteries of the Christian Religion Credible,* etc. (Oxford, 1723), pp. 5–6, 25. Treat: Brett, *Discourses,* p. 117, and Skelton, *Ophiomaches,* II, 78. Used: Clarke, *Three Practical Essays,* pp. 116–117.

35. Adopt: Clarke, *Moral Evil,* pp. 91–93. Ranged: [William Stephens], *An Account of the Growth of Deism in England* (London, 1709), p. 17; Thomas Wheatland, *Twenty-Six Practical Sermons on Various Subjects* (London, 1739), pp. 266–267; Isaac Terry, *Sixteen Sermons upon Select Subjects* (Canterbury, 1746), pp. 261–312; Sykes, *Principles and Connexion,* p. 248. Edmund Calamy, *Thirteen Sermons concerning the Doctrine of the Trinity,* etc. (London, 1722), pp. 102–103; cf. James Foster, *Sermons,* 5th ed., 4 vols. (London, 1755), I, 159–184. Reveals: Sampson Letsome, ed., *The Preacher's Assistant, in Two Parts.* Pt. I: *A Series of the Texts of All the Sermons and Discourses Preached upon and Published since the Restoration to the Present Time* (London, n.d. [1753]). I have examined the references under every text in the Authorized Version containing the word *mystery.*

36. Dismissed: Gailhard, *Blasphemous Socinian Heresie,* p. 159, and Nicholls, *Conference with a Theist,* II, 5–6. Convinced: Humphrey Prideaux, *The Old and New Testament Connected,* etc., 3 pts. in 2 vols. (London, 1716–1718), II, 553, 364–365. Served: Alan Richardson, "The Rise of Modern Biblical Scholarship and Recent Discussion of the Authority of the Bible," in *The Cambridge History of the Bible,* ed. P. R. Ackroyd, C. F. Evans, et al. 3 vols. (Cambridge, University Press, 1963–1970), III, 243.

37. Faced: Hans W. Frei, *The Eclipse of Biblical Narrative: A Study in Eighteenth and Nineteenth Century Hermeneutics* (New Haven, Yale University Press, 1974), pp. 51–65. Backwardness: e.g., Paterson, *Anti-nazarenus,* p. 67. Unhistorical: Leland, *View,* I, 153–159; psychology: Mangey, *Remarks upon Nazarenus,* p. 37. Apply: Jones, *New and Full Method,* and Nathaniel Lardner, *The Credibility of the Gospel History,* 2d ed., 3 vols. (London, 1730). Objections: Stillingfleet, *Bishop of Worcester's Answer,* pp. 42–43; Browne, *Letter,* pp. 20–21, 94–95; Beconsall, *Christian Belief,* p. 15; Payne, *Mystery of the Christian Faith,* p. 60.

38. Failure: Blackall, *Sufficiency of a Standing Revelation* (Sermon V), p. 36; Earberry, *Deism Examin'd,* p. 18; Browne, *Things Divine,* pp. 30–34. Saw: Clarke, *Moral Evil,* p. 289.

39. Invoked: Blackall, *Sufficiency of a Standing Revelation* (Sermon I), p. 19; Paterson, *Anti-nazarenus,* pp. 79–80; Halyburton, *Natural Religion,* II, 160; Edmund Calamy, *An Historical Account of My Own Life . . . (1671–1731),* ed. John T. Rutt, 2d ed., 2 vols. (London, 1830), II, 170. Resorted: Skelton, *Ophiomaches,* II, 33–34; Blackall, *Sufficiency*

of a Standing Revelation (Sermon III), p. 7. Asserted: Paterson, *Anti-nazarenus,* pp. 8, 38–39; Skelton, *Ophiomaches,* I, 19–24; Leland, *View,* I, 420–422; cf. Nola J. Wegman, "Argument and Satire: The Christian Response to Deism, 1670–1760" (Ph.D. diss., Northwestern University, 1967), p. 43.

40. Kept: cf. Stillingfleet, *Letter to a Deist,* p. 11. Saw: Jones, *New and Full Method,* I, 7–10, 152, 56.

41. Alexander Gordon in the *DNB,* s.v. "Lardner, Nathaniel."

42. Followed: Samuel Smeaton, *Christian Zeal Recommended,* etc., 2d ed. (London, 1705), pp. 8–9. Cited: Francis Hare, *Church-Authority Vindicated,* etc. (London, 1720), p. 8; Brett, *Tradition Necessary,* pp. i, xv; Richardson, *Canon of the New Testament,* preface, and p. 31. Included: cf. Skelton, *Ophiomaches,* II, 20.

43. Hare, *Difficulties and Discouragements,* pp. 46, 12, 10, 46.

44. Edward Synge, *The Authority of the Church in Matters of Religion* (London, 1718), pp. 24–25, and *Plain and Easy Method,* pp. 11–12.

45. Presume: Gailhard, *Blasphemous Socinian Heresie,* p. 308. Expatiate: Bentley, *Confutation of Atheism* (Sermon I), p. 12. Chose: Synge, *Gentleman's Religion,* pp. 95–273. Archetypal: Prideaux, *Letter to the Deists,* pp. 143–150; Sykes, *Principles and Connexion,* pp. 434–507; Samuel Jones, *The Most Important Question, What is Truth,* etc., 2d ed. (London, 1720), pp. 12–13; Leland, *View,* I, 31; cf. Wegman, "Argument and Satire," pp. 42–43.

46. Clarke, *Concerning the Unchangeable Obligations,* pp. 164–165, 12. Knew: Halyburton, *Natural Religion,* I, 17, 30; Nicholls, *Conference with a Theist,* I, 164–167. "Man": Berkeley, *Alciphron, Works,* III, 44.

47. Discourage: Edward Carpenter, *Thomas Tenison, Archbishop of Canterbury: His Life and Times* (London, S.P.C.K., 1948), p. 297. Desire: [Benjamin Gatton], *An Essay towards Comprehension,* etc. (London, 1701), pp. 5–7, and Stanhope, *Paraphrase and Comment,* I, 56–58. Conviction: Drake, *Memorial,* pp. 29–30. Flow: Robert Ham, *The Duty and Advantages of National Unity . . . in a Sermon, Preach'd 16 April 1713,* etc. (Exeter, n.d.). p. 2l; Samuel Berdmore, *The Love of Our Country,* etc. (Nottingham, 1717); Richard Derby, *Love to Our Church and Nation Recommended and Enforced,* etc. (London, 1717); R. Sherret, *Peace and Loyalty Recommended,* etc. (London, 1720), pp. 15–16. Strengthened: G. V. Bennett, *The Tory Crisis in Church and State, 1688–1730: The Career of Francis Atterbury, Bishop of Rochester* (Oxford, Clarendon Press, 1975), pp. 205–222.

48. Inveigh: Jonathan Swift: *Brotherly Love: A Sermon* [1717] (London, 1754). Exhibited: e.g., Letsome, *Preacher's Assistant,* I, 118–123, 191–192 (for Matt. 10:34, and Rom. 14). Ecclesiastically: Thomas J. F. Kendrick, "The Church-Whig Alliance, the Anti-Clericals, and the Government of Sir Robert Walpole, 1727–1737" (Ph.D. diss., University of Toronto, 1961), pp. 1–96; J. H. Plumb, *The Growth of Political Stability in England, 1675–1725* (London, Macmillan, 1967); Geoffrey Holmes, *Religion and Party in Late Stuart England* (London, Historical Association, 1975), pp. 29–30.

49. Persisted: Beconsall, *Christian Belief,* pp. 146–147; Henry Downes, *The Necessity and Usefulness of Laws and the Excellency of Our Own,* etc. (London, 1708); Synge, *Authority of the Church,* p. 5; [William Baron], *A Just Defence of the Royal Martyr,* etc. (London, 1699), preface; maintained: Browne, *Things Divine,* p. 162. Altered: *Letter to an M. P.,* pp. 3–4; *Remarks on the Life,* p. 35; Gildon, *Deist's Manual,* p. 224; cf. Gerald M. Straka, *Anglican Reaction to the Revolution of 1688* (Madison, State Historical Society of Wisconsin, 1962), p. 83. Seen: Sherret, *Peace and Loyalty,* p. 28, and R. Altham, *A Charge Deliver'd to the Clergy of the Arch-Deaconry of Middlesex,* etc. (London, 1717), p. 5.

50. [Samuel Clarke], *Some Reflections on That Part of a Book Called AMYNTOR,* etc. (London, 1699), pp. 35–37. Invoke: Mangey, *Remarks upon Nazarenus,* pp. 124–125;

Richardson, *Canon of the New Testament*, p. 67; [Charles Leslie], *A Short and Easie Method with the Deists*, etc. (London, 1698), p. 76.

51. "Great": Drake, *Memorial*, p. 14. Tantamount: *Remarks on the Life*, preface, and *The Establishment of the Church, the Preservation of the State*, etc. (London, 1702), pp. 1–2, 20.

52. Unable: Brett, *Tradition Necessary*, p. xxi. Conclude: Drake, *Memorial*, p. 20; Hare, *Scripture Vindicated*, p. xvii; Leslie, appendix to Gildon, *Deist's Manual*, pp. 23–24. Secure: Hare, *Difficulties and Discouragements*, p. 14; Lewis, *History of Hypatia*, pp. 29–30.

53. Mangey, *Remarks upon Nazarenus*, p. 122; *Remarks on the Life*, p. 75; Lewis, *History of Hypatia*, pp. 12–13; Francis Higgins, *A Sermon Preach'd at the Royal Chappel at White-hall*, etc. (London, 1707), pp. 9–11, 13.

54. Renewed: [Richard West], *The True Character of a Church-Man, Shewing the False Pretences to that Name*, etc. (London, 1711), pp. 2–4, 31. Synge, *Plain and Easy Method*, pp. 52–53, 49–50; cf. Synge, *Authority of the Church*, pp. 28–29.

55. Elias Sydall, *The True Protestant and Church of England Clergy Vindicated*, etc. (London, 1715), pp. 21–22. Fostering: *Occasional Paper*, n.s., 2:9 (1717), pp. 8, 24–25.

56. Argue: Norris, *Account of Reason and Faith*, pp. 68, 159. Recognize: Williams, *Scripture the Rule of Faith*, p. 25.

57. Lead: Aquinas, *Summa Theologiae*, I, 87, 4, and II–II, 15, 3; concluded: John March, *Sermons Preach'd on Several Occasions*, 2d ed. (London, 1699), pp. 100–124; John Warren, *Sermons upon Several Subjects*, etc., 2 vols. (London, 1739), I, 32; Edward Bullard, *There Must be Heresies: A Sermon Preach'd before the University of Oxford* (London, 1734); Wheatly, *Fifty Sermons*, I, 236–268; Septimus Turton, *A Sermon Preached at St. Margaret's Church, Westminster* (London, 1749). Avoid: Letsome, *Preacher's Assistant*, I, 244.

58. Cf. Wegman, "Argument and Satire," p. 7–8, 83, 226.

59. Guaranteed: Witty, *First Principles*, p. i; Taylor, *Preservative*, p. 78; Clarke, *Concerning the Unchangeable Obligations*, pp. 184–185; Gildon, *Deist's Manual*, p. 200; *Mr. Toland's Clito*, p. 5; Blackall, *Sufficiency of a Standing Revelation* (Sermon II), p. 25; Halyburton, *Natural Religion*, I, 5–6; Skelton, *Ophiomaches*, II, 64–65. Unable: John Rogers, *Seventeen Sermons on Several Occasions* (London, 1736), pp. 334–336. Reacted: Earberry, *Deism Examin'd*, pp. 94–95, 116; Skelton, *Ophiomaches*, I, 31–32; Leland, *View*, II, 655; succeeded: Bury, *Rational Deist*, p. 11; Clarke, *Concerning the Unchangeable Obligations*, pp. 165–166; Paterson, *Anti-nazarenus*, p. 4; Robert Leeke, *No Act of Religion Acceptable to God Without Faith*, etc. (London, 1730), pp. 16–17.

60. Deemed: Bentley, *Confutation of Atheism* (Sermon I), pp. 34–35. Convinced: Halyburton, *Natural Religion*, I, 213–214; Clarke, *Concerning the Unchangeable Obligations*, pp. 9–10. Assurance: *ibid.*, pp. 154–159, 212–213.

61. Clarke, *Concerning the Unchangeable Obligations*, pp. 208–209. Argue: Gailhard, *Blasphemous Socinian Heresie*, dedication; *Letter to an M. P.*, pp. 59–60; Sykes, *Principles and Connexion*, pp. 250–251. Maintained: Lucien Goldmann, *The Hidden God: A Study of Tragic Vision in the "Pensées" and the Tragedies of Racine*, trans. Philip Thody (London, Routledge and Kegan Paul, 1964), p. 302; Clarke, *Demonstration of the Being*, p. 6.

62. *A Confutation of the Reasons for Naturalizing the Jews*, etc. (London, 1715), pp. 32–33; Bentley, *Confutation of Atheism* (Sermon I), p. 20; William Fleetwood, *A Compleat Collection of the Sermons, Tracts and Pieces of All Kinds*, etc. (London, 1737), p. 100; Blackall, *Works*, pp. 730–741; Halyburton, *Natural Religion*, I, 34–35; Skelton, *Ophiomaches*, II, 52–55.

63. Thought: Clarke, *Demonstration of the Being*, p. 256. Challenge: Bentley, *Confutation of Atheism* (Sermon I), p. 17; Blackall, *Works*, pp. 158, 699. Commend: *ibid.*, p. 168.

64. Tended: Skelton, *Ophiomaches*, I, 45–46. Admitted: R. Altham, *Church Authority Not an Universal Supremacy*, etc. (London 1720), p. 10. Blackall, *Sufficiency of a Standing Revelation* (Sermon VIII), pp. 53–56, 59–60; Gurdon, *Pretended Difficulties*, p. 285; Hare, *Scripture Vindicated*, p. 129; Joseph Addison, *The Tatler*, no. 135, 16–18 Feb. 1709.

65. E.g., Skelton, *Ophiomaches*, I, 15.

66. Accepted: JT/T, p. 158; Collins, *Discourse of the Grounds*, p. xiv; Gilbert Dalrymple, *A Letter from Edinburgh to Dr. Sherlock*, etc., 2d ed. (London, 1718), pp. 19–24. Invest: Clarke, *Concerning the Unchangeable Obligations*, p. 335.

67. Believed: Payne, *Mystery of the Christian Faith*, p. 68. Duty: Bury, *Rational Deist*, p. 119.

68. "Sincerity": Elisha Smith, *Justifying Sincerity Stated and Reconciled to the Light of Nature, the Word of God, the Rule of Our Faith and to a National Church*, etc. (London, 1719), pp. 4–5.

69. *Ibid.*, pp. 18–19; *ibid.*, pp. 24–25; *ibid.*, pp. 18–19.

70. Hare, *Scripture Vindicated*, pp. 98–99; cf. Dalrymple, *Letter from Edinburgh*, p. 17.

71. Synge, *Plain and Easy Method*, preface and p. 51. Joseph Addison, *The Spectator*, no. 459, 16 Aug. 1712. Accommodate: Clarke, *Demonstration of the Being*, pp. 13–14; Blackall, *Sufficiency of a Standing Revelation* (Sermon II), p. 4; Clarke, *Moral Evil*, p. 58.

72. Continued: Luke Milbourne, *A False Faith Not Justified by Care for the Poor*, etc. (London, 1698); Norris, *Account of Reason and Faith*, p. 327; Halyburton, *Natural Religion*, I, 23, 26; Browne, *Things Divine*, p. 327. Prompted: Halyburton, *Natural Religion*, I, 23, 200; Browne, *Procedure*, pp. 334–335, 378; Skelton, *Ophiomaches*, I, 88–89, 106–108, and II, 152–153, 212. Vexed: Rundle to Mrs. Sandys, 16 Mar. 1729 (O.S.), James Dallaway, ed., *Letters of the Late Thomas Rundle, L.L.D.*, etc., 2 vols. (Gloucester, 1789), II, 112–115; cf. O. F. Christie, ed., *The Diary of William Jones of Broxbourne, 1771–1821* (London, Brentano's, 1929), p. 58. Preoccupied: James Downey, *The Eighteenth-Century Pulpit: A Study of the Sermons of Butler, Berkeley, Sterne, Whitefield, and Wesley* (Oxford, Clarendon Press, 1969), pp. 12–17.

73. Clarke, *Moral Evil*, pp. 113–115, 208–223. Cf. [Anthony Ashley-Cooper, earl of Shaftesbury], *An Inquiry concerning Virtue*, etc. [ed. John Toland] (London, 1699), p. 3. "Avoid": Clarke, *Moral Evil*, p. 158.

74. Clarke, *Moral Evil*, pp. 66–67, 90, 132–133.

75. Clarke, *Concerning the Unchangeable Obligations*, pp. 71, 14–15, 222. Took: Joseph Addison, *The Tatler*, no. 135, 16–18 Feb. 1709.

76. Francis Gastrell, *The Certainty and Necessity of Religion in General*, etc. (London, 1697), p. 18; Sykes, *Principles and Connexion*, pp. 99, 108.

77. Leland, *View*, I, 428, 438. Commended: Nicholls, *Conference with a Theist*, I, 330.

78. Wake to Le Clerc, 25 Oct. 1717, in Sykes, *Wake*, II, 262.

79. Collins, *Discourse of the Grounds*, p. xvii, and *Discourse of Free-Thinking*, pp. 61–75.

80. Roach: Daniel P. Walker, *The Decline of Hell: Seventeenth-Century Discussions of Eternal Torment* (London, Routledge and Kegan Paul, 1964), p. 270. Undertook . . . insisted: Gerald R. Cragg, *Reason and Authority in the Eighteenth Century* (Cambridge, University Press, 1964), pp. 250–252.

81. Differentiate: But N.B. David Hume, *The Natural History of Religion* [1757], in *Philosophical Essays on Morals, Literature, and Politics*, ed. Thomas Ewell, 2 vols. (Philadelphia, 1817), II, 469, n.30. Wilbur, *History of Unitarianism*, II, 236–237. J. Hay Colligan, *The Arian Movement in England* (Manchester, University Press, 1913), p. 65; cf. Eamon Duffy, " 'Whiston's Affair': The Trial of a Primitive Christian, 1709–1714," *Journal of Ecclesiastical History* 27 (1976), 129. Defect: Roger Thomas, "Presbyterians in

Transition," in C. G. Bolam, Jeremy Goring, et al., *The English Presbyterians: From Elizabethan Puritanism to Modern Unitarianism* (London, G. Allen & Unwin, 1968), p. 173.

82. Heard: Entry of 6 Feb. 1733 (O.S.), HMC Reports, *Egmont MSS.*, II, 23. Rundle to Mrs. Sandys, n.d. [1730], Dallaway, *Letters*, II, 157–158, and n.d. [winter 1719/20], *ibid.*, 13–14. Obsessed: West, *True Character*, pp. 2, 6; *A Detection of the True Meaning and Wicked Design of a Book*, etc. (London, 1710), p. 5; Nicholls, *Conference with a Theist*, I, v; Skelton, *Ophiomaches*, I, xii, 36–37.

83. Doubt: Sykes, *Wake*, II, 155. Prided: *The History of the Works of the Learned* 2 (1737), 375; treated: *ibid.*, pp. 87–88. Grouped: cf. Emile Bréhier, *The History of Philosophy*, 7 vols., trans. J. Thomas and Wade Baskin (Chicago, University Press, 1963–1969), V, 15–16, and D. L. Le Mahieu, *The Mind of William Paley: A Philosopher and His Age* (Lincoln, University of Nebraska Press, 1976), p. 39.

84. Given: George Smalridge, *A Sermon Preach'd before the Honourable House of Commons*, etc. (London, 1702). Met: William Whiston, *Memoirs of the Life and Writings of Mr. William Whiston*, etc., 2 vols. in 1 (London, 1749), p. 182.

85. Tindal, *Christianity*, pp. 54, 214, 382; O'Higgins, *Anthony Collins*, p. 143.

86. Collins, *Discourse of Free-Thinking*, p. 104.

87. Manuel, *Eighteenth Century Confronts the Gods*, p. 73. Violence: John McManners, *French Ecclesiastical Society under the Ancien Régime* (Manchester, University Press, 1960), pp. 26–56. Cf. W. H. Barber, "Voltaire and Samuel Clarke," *Studies on Voltaire* 179 (1979), 47–61; R. E. Florida, *Voltaire and the Socinians, ibid.* 122 (1974), 173–245.

88. Responded: Norman Sykes, *From Sheldon to Secker: Aspects of English Church History, 1660–1768* (Cambridge, University Press, 1959), p. 58.

89. Succeeded: Secker to Fox, 20 May 1719, in *Monthly Repository and Review of Theology* 16 (1821), 633.

90. Sykes, *Wake*, II, 165.

91. Benjamin Hoadly, *A Persuasive to Lay Conformity: or, the Reasonableness of Constant Communion with the Church of England*, etc. (London, 1704), pp. 2, 21, 36, 23. Believed: cf. *ibid.*, p. 4, and Benjamin Hoadly, *A Preservative against the Principles and Practices of the Nonjurors Both in Church and State*, etc. (London, 1716), pp. 61–62. Hoadly, *Persuasive to Lay Conformity*, pp. 27, 33.

92. Benjamin Hoadly, *Several Discourses concerning the Terms of Acceptance* (London, 1711), pp. 249–250, 277, 298–299, and *The Nature of the Kingdom, or Church of Christ*, etc., 12th ed. (London, 1717), p. 25.

93. Stephen, *History of English Thought*, II, 132. Free: Hoadly, *Preservative*, preface. Conceived: Hoadly, *Nature of the Kingdom*, pp. 5–6. Obliged: Benjamin Hoadly, *A Serious Enquiry into the Present State of the Church in England*, etc. (London, 1711), p. 13.

94. Samuel Bold, *Some Thoughts concerning Church Authority*, etc. (London, 1724), p. 21; cf. Henry D. Rack, " 'Christ's Kingdom Not of This World': The Case of Benjamin Hoadly versus William Law Reconsidered," *Studies in Church History*, vol. 12, ed. Derek Baker (Oxford, Blackwell, 1975), 278–280, 290–291.

95. Accepted: Smith, *Justifying Sincerity*, pp. 19–20. Compile: *A Muster-Roll of the B. of B-ng-r's Seconds*, etc. (London, 1720); cf. Paterson, *Anti-nazarenus*, pp. 70–71. Knew: Dalrymple, *Letter from Edinburgh*, pp. 34–35. Defended: JT to Mr. _____, 21 May 1721, B.L. Add. MS. 4295, ff. 44–47, and JT/N, pp. xxiv–xxv. John Trenchard and Thomas Gordon, *The Independent Whig*, no. 5, 17 Feb. 1720; Tindal, *Christianity*, p. 215.

96. Thomas Sherlock, *An Answer to the Lord Bishop of Bangor's Late Book*, etc. (London, 1719). Suggested: Dalrymple, *Letter from Edinburgh*, p.20.

97. Cragg, *Reason and Authority*, p. 189.

98. Consequence: Gilbert, *Religion and Society*, pp. 11–12; act: *ibid.*, pp. 75–76. Felt:

Maittaire to Charlett, 23 May 1718, Bodl. Ballard MSS. XVII, f. 110. William War-burton, *The Alliance between Church and State,* etc., 3d ed. (London, 1748), p. 38; cf. R. W. Greaves, "The Working of the Alliance: A Comment on Warburton," in *Essays in Modern Church History in Honor of Norman Sykes,* ed. G. V. Bennett and J. D. Walsh (New York, Oxford University Press, 1966), pp. 163–180.

99. Edward Gibbon, *Memoirs of My Life and Writings* (London, Oxford University Press, 1907), p. 63. Assured: *A Plea for the Sacramental Test; as a Just Security to the Church Established, and Very Conducive to the Welfare of the State* (London, 1736). Ratified: cf. Nor-man Sykes, *Church and State in England in the Eighteenth Century* (Cambridge, University Press, 1934), p. 90, and *From Sheldon to Secker,* pp. 57, 67, 211.

100. [Henry Dodwell], *Christianity Not Founded on Argument,* etc. (London, 1734), pp. 85–86. Manifestations: cf. Stromberg, *Religious Liberalism,* pp. 88–109. Hutchinson: John Hunt, *Religious Thought in England from the Reformation to the End of the Last Century,* 3 vols. (London, 1870–1873), III, 316. Scant: Gibson to Berkeley, 9 July 1735, in *The Works of Berkeley,* ed. A. C. Fraser, 4 vols. (Oxford, 1871), IV, 238–239.

101. Sykes, *Principles and Connexion,* p. 246. Cf. William Law, *An Appeal to All That Doubt . . . the Gospel, whether They be Deists, Arians, Socinians, etc., or Nominal Christians,* 3d ed. (London, 1768), and Berkeley, "Sermon on the Mystery of Godliness," *Works,* VII, 89–102.

102. Complaining: Skelton, *Ophiomaches,* I, 12; cf. Gilbert, *Religion and Society,* p. 27; continued: Wegman, "Argument and Satire," p. 13. Declined: Thomas Bartlett, *Memoirs of the Life, Character, and Writings of Bishop Butler* (London, 1839), p. 96. Celebrated: cf. Norman Ravitch, *Sword and Mitre: Government and Episcopate in France and England in the Age of Aristocracy* (The Hague, Mouton, 1966), pp. 153, 212–213.

103. John Wesley, "The Use of Money," *Works,* 5th ed. (London, 1860), VI, 128, cited in Bernard Semmel, *The Methodist Revolution* (New York, Basic Books, 1973), p. 214n. Tobias Smollett, *The Expedition of Humphrey Clinker,* 2 vols. (London, Oxford University Press, 1925), I, 195.

104. Preface to *The Reasonableness of Christianity,* The Sacred Classics or, Cabinet Library of Divinity, ed. Richard Cattermole and Henry Stebbing (London, 1836), pp. xlix–l.

105. John Cairns, *Unbelief in the Eighteenth Century as Contrasted with Its Earlier and Later History* (Edinburgh, 1881), p. 169.

106. N. Boyle, "Shaftesbury's Religion of the Wise," *Notes and Queries,* n.s. 26 (1979), 25–26.

Selected Bibliography

A. *Manuscript Sources*

Bodleian Library, Oxford: Ballard Manuscripts; English Theological Manuscripts; Locke Manuscripts; Rawlinson Manuscripts.

British Library, London: Additional Manuscripts 4229, 4282, 4286, 4295, 4465, 7121, 24478, 40773; Portland Loan Manuscripts; Toland's annotated copy of Martin Martin, *A Description of the Western Islands of Scotland.* London, 1716 (806. a. 23).

Dr. Williams' Library, London: Manuscript Minutes of the Presbyterian Fund.

Lambeth Palace Library, London: Gibson Manuscripts; Miscellaneous Manuscripts.

National Library of Scotland, Edinburgh: Manuscript 9251.

Oesterreichische Nationalbibliothek, Vienna: Autographen XLV; Manuscripts 10325, 10390.

Public Record Office, London: Shaftesbury Papers; State Papers Domestic (William III).

Spencer Research Library, University of Kansas, Lawrence: Trenchard-Simpson Correspondence.

Trinity College Library, Dublin: King Papers; Manuscript Collection relating to the Irish Convocation.

B. *Works of John Toland Arranged Chronologically*

A Letter from Major General Ludlow to Sir E[dward] S[eymour]. Amsterdam [*sic*], 1691. (Anonymously).

"An Abstract of Dr. Daniel Williams' 'The Gospel Truth.' " *Bibliothèque universelle et historique* 23 (1692), 505–509. (Anonymously).

A Letter from General Ludlow to Dr. Hollingworth, etc. Amsterdam [*sic*], 1692. (Anonymously).

Two Essays Sent in a Letter from Oxford, etc. London, 1695. (Pseudonym: L. P., Master of Arts).

Christianity Not Mysterious, etc. London, 1696. Second edition, signed, London, 1696. (Anonymously).

A Discourse on Coins, by Signor Bernardo Davanzati, etc. London, 1696. (Translator).

An Apology for Mr. Toland, etc. London, 1697.

An Argument Shewing that a Standing Army, etc. London, 1697. (Attributed to Toland, with John Trenchard and Walter Moyle).

A Defence of Mr. Toland, in a Letter to Himself. London, 1697.

The Danger of Mercenary Parliaments. [1698]. 2d ed. London, 1722. (Attributed to Toland, with Anthony Ashley-Cooper, earl of Shaftesbury).

A Defence of the Parliament of 1640, etc. London, 1698. (Anonymously).

Discourses concerning Government, etc. By Algernon Sidney. London, 1698. (Presumed editor).

A Letter to a Member of Parliament, etc. [1698]. In *State Tracts . . . of William III.* 3 vols. London, 1706, II, 614–626. (Anonymously).

The Life of John Milton, etc. [1698]. In Helen Darbishire, ed. *The Early Lives of Milton.* London, Constable, 1932, pp. 83–197. (Anonymously).

Memoirs of Edmund Ludlow, Esq., etc. 2 vols. Vivay [*sic*], 1698. (Anonymously).

The Militia Reform'd, etc. London, 1698. (Anonymously).

A Short History of Standing Armies, etc. [1698]. London, 1773. (Attributed to Toland, with John Trenchard and Walter Moyle).

Amyntor: or, a Defence of Milton's Life, etc. London, 1699. (Anonymously).

An Inquiry concerning Virtue, etc. [By Anthony Ashley-Cooper, earl of Shaftesbury]. London, 1699. (Presumed editor).

The Memoirs of Denzil, Lord Holles, etc. London, 1699. (Presumed editor).

Clito: A Poem on the Force of Eloquence. London, 1700. (Anonymously).

"An Exact Account of His [Harrington's] Life." In James Harrington, *The Oceana,* etc. Ed. John Toland. London, 1700.

Anglia Libera, etc. London, 1701.

The Art of Governing by Partys, etc. London, 1701. (Anonymously).

Limitations for the Next Foreign Successor, etc. London, 1701. (Anonymously).

Propositions for Uniting the Two East-India Companies, etc. London, 1701. (Anonymously).

Paradoxes of State, etc. London, 1702. (Attributed to Toland, with Anthony Ashley-Cooper, earl of Shaftesbury).

Reasons for Addressing His Majesty to Invite into England Their Highnesses, etc. London, 1702. (Anonymously).

Vindicius Liberius etc. London, 1702.

The Fables of Aesop, etc. London, 1704. (Presumed translator).

Letters to Serena, etc. London, 1704.

The Principle of the Protestant Reformation Explain'd, in a Letter of Resolution concerning Church Communion, etc. London, 1704. (Anonymously).

An Account of the Courts of Prussia and Hanover, etc. London, 1705.

The Agreement of the Customs of the East-Indians with Those of the Jews and Other Ancient People, etc. London, 1705. (Presumed translator).

The Memorial of the State of England, in Vindication of the Queen, the Church, and the Administration, etc. London, 1705. (Anonymously).

Socinianism Truly Stated, etc. London, 1705. (Anonymously).

A Letter from an Arabian Physician to a Famous Professor, etc. N.p., n.d. [London, 1706?]. (Anonymously).

The Declaration Lately Published by the Elector Palatine, etc. London, 1707. (Anonymously).

A Philippick Oration to Incite the English against the French, etc. London, 1707.

Oratio Philippica ad excitandos contra Galliam Britannos, etc. Amsterdam, 1709.

Adeisidaemon, etc. The Hague, 1709.

The Jacobitism, Perjury, and Popery of High-Church Priests, etc. London, 1710. (Anonymously).

Mr. Toland's Reflections on Dr. Sacheverell's Sermon, etc. London, 1710.

The Description of Epsom, etc. London, 1711. (Anonymously).

High-Church Display'd: Being a Compleat History of the Affair of Dr. Sacheverell, etc. London, 1711. (Anonymously).

Cicero Illustratus, etc. London, 1712.

Her Majesty's Reasons, etc. London, 1712. In *A Collection of Scarce and Valuable*

Tracts, etc. ["Somers Tracts"]. Ed. Walter Scott. 2d ed. 13 vols. London, 1805–1815, XIII, 215–216. (Anonymously).

A Letter against Popery, etc. London, 1712. (Presumed editor and translator).

An Appeal to Honest People against Wicked Priests, etc. London, n.d. [1713?]. (Anonymously).

Dunkirk or Dover, etc. London, 1713. (Anonymously).

The Art of Canvassing at Elections, etc. London, 1714. (Presumed translator).

The Art of Restoring, etc. London, 1714. (Anonymously).

Characters of the Court of Hannover, etc. London, 1714. (Anonymously).

The Funeral Elogy and Character of H.R.H., the Late Princess Sophia, etc. London, 1714.

The Grand Mystery Laid Open, etc. London, 1714. (Anonymously).

The Reasons and Necessity of the Duke of Cambridge's Coming, etc. London, 1714. (Anonymously).

Reasons for Naturalizing the Jews, etc. [1714]. In *Pamphlets Relating to the Jews in England during the Seventeenth and Eighteenth Centuries.* Ed. Paul Radin. San Francisco, California State Library, 1939, pp. 40–65. (Anonymously).

"Remarques critiques sur la systême de M. Leibnitz . . . où l'on recherche en passant pourquoi les systêmes metaphysiques ont moins de clarté, que ceux des autres." *Histoire critique de la république des lettres* 11 (1716), 115–133. (Anonymously).

The State-Anatomy of Great Britain, etc. London, 1717. (Anonymously).

The Second Part of the State Anatomy, etc., Containing a Short Vindication of the Former Part, etc. London, 1717. (Anonymously).

The Destiny of Rome, etc. London, 1718. (Anonymously).

Nazarenus, etc. London, 1718.

Pantheisticon, sive formula celebrandae sodalitatis Socraticae, etc. [1720]. Eng. trans. London, 1751. (Anonymously).

Reasons Most Humbly Offer'd, etc. London, 1720. (Anonymously).

A Short Essay on the Art of Lying, etc. London, 1720. (Anonymously).

Tetradymus, etc. London, 1720.

Letters from the R.H. the Late Earl of Shaftesbury, to Robert Molesworth, etc. London, 1721. (Presumed editor).

A Collection of Several Pieces of Mr. John Toland, etc. [Ed. Pierre Des Maizeaux]. 2 vols. London, 1726.

C. *Other Printed Primary Sources*

Addison, Joseph, Richard Steele, et al. *The Spectator.*
————. *The Tatler.*

[Allix, Peter]. *A Defence of the Brief History of the Unitarians,* etc. London, 1691.

[Annet, Peter]. *Deism Fairly Stated, and Fully Vindicated,* etc, London, 1746.

Aquinas, Thomas. *Summa Theologiae.* Eng. trans. 3 vols. New York, Benziger, 1948.

Ashley-Cooper, Anthony, earl of Shaftesbury, *The Life, Unpublished Letters, and Philosophical Regimen of [the] Earl of Shaftesbury.* Ed. Benjamin Rand. London, Sonnenschein, 1900.

Augustine. *The City of God.* Trans. Marcus Dods, et al. New York, Random House, 1950.

Bayle, Pierre. *Dictionnaire historique et critique.* New, augmented ed. 16 vols. Paris, 1820.

[Beconsall, Thomas.] *The Christian Belief*, etc. London, 1696.

Benoist, Elie. *Mélange de remarques critiques, historiques, philosophiques*, etc. Delft, 1712.

Bentley, Richard. *A Confutation of Atheism*, etc. London, 1692.

Berkeley, George. *The Works of Bishop Berkeley*. Ed. A. A. Luce and T. E. Jessop. 9 vols. London, Nelson, 1948–1957.

[Beverley, Thomas]. *Christianity the Great Mystery*, etc. London, 1696.

Blackall, Offspring. *The Sufficiency of a Standing Revelation in General*, etc. London, 1700.

_____. *Works*. 2 vols., consecutive pag. London, 1723.

Blount, Charles. *Anima Mundi: or, An Historical Narration of the Opinions of the Ancients concerning Man's Soul after This Life*, etc. London, 1696.

_____. *The First Two Books of Philostratus, concerning the Life of Apollonius Tyaneus*, etc. London, 1680.

_____. *The Oracles of Reason*, etc. London, 1693.

[_____]. *Religio Laici: Written in a Letter to John Dryden.* London, 1683.

[Brett, Thomas]. *Discourses concerning the Ever-Blessed Trinity*. London, 1720.

_____. *Tradition Necessary to Explain and Interpret the Holy Scriptures*, etc. London, 1718.

Browne, Peter. *A Letter in Answer to a Book*, etc. Dublin, 1697.

[_____]. *The Procedure, Extent, and Limits of the Human Understanding*. London, 1728.

[_____]. *Things Divine and Supernatural Conceived by Analogy with Things Natural and Human*. London, 1723.

Bruno, Giordano. *Spaccio della bestia trionfante*, etc. [Ed. and trans. John Toland?]. London, 1713.

[Bury, Arthur]. *The Naked Gospel*, etc. N.p. [Oxford], 1690. 2d ed. London, 1691.

_____. *The Rational Deist Satisfy'd by a Just Account of the Gospel*, etc. 2d ed. London, 1703.

Cicero. *De oratore*. Trans. E. W. Sutton and H. Rackham. 2 vols. Loeb Classical Library. Cambridge, Harvard University Press, 1942.

Clarke, John. *An Inquiry into the Cause and Origin of Moral Evil*, etc. London, 1721.

Clarke, Samuel. *A Demonstration of the Being and Attributes of God*, etc. London, 1705.

_____. *A Discourse concerning the Unchangeable Obligations of Natural Religion*, etc. 4th ed., corr. London, 1716.

[Collins, Anthony]. *A Discourse of Free-Thinking*, etc. London, 1713.

[_____]. *A Discourse of the Grounds and Reasons of the Christian Religion*, etc. 2d ed. London, 1737.

[_____]. *A Philosophical Inquiry concerning Human Liberty*. 3d ed. London, 1735.

Considerations on the Explication of the Doctrine of the Trinity, etc. London, 1694.

[Curll, Edmund]. *An Historical Account of the Life and Writings of the Late Eminently Famous Mr. John Toland*, etc. London, 1722.

Dallaway, James, ed. *Letters of the Late Thomas Rundle, L.L.D.*, etc. 2 vols. Gloucester, 1789.

Dalrymple, Gilbert. *A Letter from Edinburgh to Dr. Sherlock*, etc. 2d ed. London, 1718.

[Davenant, Charles]. *Tom Double Return'd Out of the Country*, etc. London, 1702.

[Defoe, Daniel]. *An Argument Proving that the Design of Employing and Ennobling Foreigners*, etc. London, 1717.

[Des Maizeaux, Pierre]. "Some Memoirs of His [Toland's] Life and Writings." In John Toland, *A Collection of Several Pieces of Mr. John Toland*, etc. [Ed. Pierre Des Maizeaux], I, iii–xcii. 2 vols. London, 1726.

Drake, James. *A Memorial of the Church of England*, etc. London, 1704.

Earberry, Matthias. *Deism Examin'd and Confuted*, etc. London, 1697.

Edwards, John. *The Socinian Creed*, etc. London, 1697.

Elys, Edmund. *Letter to the Hon. Sir Robert Howard*, etc. London, 1696.

[Fiddes, Richard]. *Remarks on the State Anatomy of Great Britain*, etc. London, 1717.

Forster, Thomas, ed. *Original Letters of Locke, Algernon Sidney, and . . . Shaftesbury*. London, 1830.

Foster, James. *The Usefulness, Truth, and Excellency of the Christian Revelation Defended*, etc. 2d ed. London, 1731.

Gailhard, Jean. *The Blasphemous Socinian Heresie Disproved and Confuted*, etc. London, 1697.

_____. *The Epistle and Preface to the Book against the Blasphemous Socinian Heresie Vindicated*, etc. London, 1698.

[Gastrell, Francis]. *Some Considerations concerning the Trinity*, etc. London, 1696.

Gildon, Charles. *The Deist's Manual: or, A Rational Enquiry into the Christian Religion*, etc. London, 1705.

Gurdon, Brampton. *The Pretended Difficulties in Natural or Revealed Religion No Excuse for Infidelity: Sixteen Sermons Preached . . . in the Years 1721 and 1722*, etc. In *A Defence of Natural and Revealed Religion*, etc., III, 277–399. [Ed. Sampson Letsome and John Nicholl]. 3 vols. London, 1739.

Halyburton, Thomas. *Natural Religion Insufficient, and Reveal'd Necessary to Man's Happiness*, etc. 2 pts. in 1 vol. Edinburgh, 1714.

Hare, Francis. *The Difficulties and Discouragements Which Attend the Study of Scriptures in the Way of Private Judgement*, etc. 2d ed. London, 1714.

_____. *Scripture Vindicated from the Misinterpretations of the Lord Bishop of Bangor*, etc. London, 1721.

Harris, John. *The Atheistical Objections against the Being of God and His Attributes*, etc. London, 1698.

Herbert of Cherbury, Edward, Lord. *De veritate*. Ed. and trans. Meyrick Carré. Bristol, J. W. Arrowsmith, 1937.

Hickes, George. Preliminary discourse to *Spinoza Reviv'd*, etc. By William Carroll. London, 1709.

Historical Manuscripts Commission Reports. Portland Manuscripts.

Hoadly, Benjamin. *A Persuasive to Lay-Conformity: or, The Reasonableness of Constant Communion with the Church of England*, etc. London, 1704.

Hobbes, Thomas. *The English Works of Thomas Hobbes*. Ed. William Molesworth. 11 vols. London, 1839–1845.

[Howard, Robert]. *The History of Religion*, etc. London, 1694.

An Impartial Account of the Word MYSTERY, etc. London, 1691.

Jones, Jeremiah. *A New and Full Method of Settling the Canonical Authority of the New Testament*. 3 vols. [1726–1727]. Oxford, 1798.

Kemble, John M., ed. *State Papers and Correspondence*, etc. London, 1857.

Klopp, Onno, ed. *Correspondance de Leibniz avec l'électrice Sophie de Brunswick-Lunebourg*. 3 vols. Hanover, 1874.

Le Clerc, Jean. *A Treatise of the Causes of Incredulity*, etc. [Trans. John Toland]. London, 1697.

Leibniz, Gottfried Wilhelm. *Die philosophischen Schriften von G. W. Leibniz*. Ed. C. I. Gerhardt. 7 vols. Berlin, 1875–1890.

Leland, John. *A View of the Principal Deistical Writers*, etc. 3 vols. London, 1754–1756.

[Leslie, Charles]. *The Charge of Socinianism against Dr. Tillotson*, etc. London, 1695.

_____. *The Socinian Controversy Discuss'd*, etc. London, 1708.

Letsome, Sampson, ed. *The Preacher's Assistant, in Two Parts.* Part I: *A Series of the Texts of All the Sermons and Discourses Preached upon and Published since the Restoration to the Present Time.* London, n.d. [1753].

A Letter to a Gentleman upon Occasion of Some New Opinions in Religion. London, 1696.

A Letter to a Member of Parliament, Shewing the Necessity of Regulating the Press, etc. London, 1699.

Lewis, Thomas, *The History of Hypatia,* etc. London, 1721.

Locke, John. *An Essay concerning Human Understanding.* Ed. John W. Yolton. 2 vols. New York, Everyman Library, 1965.

―――. *Familiar Letters between Mr. John Locke and Several of His Friends,* etc. 4th ed. London, 1742.

―――. *A Letter to the . . . Bishop of Worcester,* etc. London, 1697.

―――. *Mr. Locke's Reply to the . . . Bishop of Worcester's Answer,* etc. London, 1697.

―――. *The Reasonableness of Christianity,* etc. London, 1695.

―――. *The Works of John Locke.* Ed. Edmund Law. New ed. 10 vols. London, 1823.

Mangey, Thomas. *Remarks upon Nazarenus,* etc. London, 1718.

Molesworth, Robert. *The Principles of a Real Whig.* [1711]. London, 1775.

Mosheim, J. L. *De vita, fatis, et scriptis Joannis Tolandi commentatio.* In *Vindiciae antiquae Christianorum disciplinae,* etc. 2d ed. Hamburg, 1722.

Mr. Toland's Clito Dissected, etc. London, 1700.

Nicholls, William. *A Conference with a Theist.* 3d ed. 2 vols. London, 1723.

Norris, John. *An Account of Reason and Faith,* etc. 13th ed. London, 1740.

[Nye, Stephen]. *The Agreement of the Unitarians with the Catholick Church.* London, 1697.

―――. *A Discourse concerning Natural and Revealed Religion,* etc. London, 1696.

[―――?]. *A Letter of Resolution concerning the Doctrines of the Trinity,* etc. London, n.d. [1691].

[―――]. *The Life of Thomas Firmin,* etc. London, 1698.

[―――]. *Reflections on Two Discourses concerning the Divinity of Our Saviour,* etc. London, 1693.

[―――]. *The Trinitarian Scheme of Religion,* etc. London, 1692.

Paterson, James. *Anti-nazarenus by Way of Answer to Mr. Toland,* etc. London, 1718.

Payne, William. *The Mystery of the Christian Faith and of the Blessed Trinity Vindicated,* etc. London, 1697.

Prideaux, Humphrey. *A Letter to the Deists,* etc. London, 1697.

Remarks and Collections of Thomas Hearne. 11 vols. Oxford, Clarendon Press, 1885–1921.

Remarks on the Life of Mr. Milton, etc. London, 1699.

Richardson, John. *The Canon of the New Testament Vindicated,* etc. 2d ed. London, 1701.

Scott, Walter, trans. and ed. *Hermetica: The Ancient Greek and Latin Writings Which Contain Religious and Philosophical Teachings Ascribed to Hermes Trismegistus.* 4 vols. Oxford, Clarendon Press, 1924–1936.

Sherlock, William. *The Present State of the Socinian Controversy,* etc. London, 1698.

[Skelton, Philip]. *Ophiomaches, or Deism Revealed,* etc. 2 vols. London, 1751.

Smith, Elisha. *Justifying Sincerity Stated and Reconciled to the Light of Nature, to the Word of God, the Rule of Our Faith, and to a National Church,* etc. London, 1719.

Smith, Thomas. *A Sermon of the Credibility of the Christian Religion,* etc. London, 1675.

Some Thoughts upon Dr. Sherlock's Vindication of the Doctrine of the Holy Trinity, etc. 2d ed. London, 1691.

South, Robert. *Sermons Preached upon Several Occasions.* 5 vols. Oxford, 1842.

Stillingfleet, Edward. *The Bishop of Worcester's Answer to Mr. Locke's Letter,* etc. London, 1697.

Bibliography

_____. *A Discourse in Vindication of the Doctrine of the Trinity*, etc. London, 1697.
_____. *A Letter to a Deist*, etc. London, 1697.
_____. *The Mysteries of the Christian Faith Asserted and Vindicated*, etc. London, 1696.
Sykes, Arthur Ashley. *The Principles and Connexion of Natural and Reveal'd Religion*, etc. London, 1740.
Synge, Edward. *The Authority of the Church in Matters of Religion*. London, 1718.
_____. *A Gentleman's Religion*, etc. 7th ed. London, 1752.
_____. *A Plain and Easy Method*, etc. London, 1715.
Taylor, Jeremy. *The Whole Works*. Ed. Reginald Heber. 15 vols. Oxford, 1828.
[Tenison, Thomas]. *The Difference betwixt the Protestant and Socinian Methods*, etc. London, 1687.
Tillotson, John. *Works*. 10 vols. Edinburgh and Glasgow, 1748.
Tindal, Matthew. *Christianity as Old as the Creation*, etc. London, 1730.
[_____]. *A Letter to the Reverend the Clergy of both Universities*, etc. London, 1694.
[_____]. *The Rights of the Christian Church*, etc. 4th ed. London, 1708.
The Unreasonableness of the Doctrine of the Trinity Briefly Demonstrated, etc. London, 1692.
Van Limborch, Philip. *Theologia christiana*, etc. Amsterdam, 1686.
Williams, John. *Scripture the Rule of Faith*, etc. London, 1696.
[Willis, Richard]. *The Occasional Paper, Number III*, etc. London, 1697.
[_____]. *Reflexions upon . . . "Account of the Growth of Deism,"* etc. London, 1696.
[Witty, John]. *The First Principles of Modern Deism Confuted*, etc. London, 1707.

D. Secondary Works

Barnes, Annie. *Jean Le Clerc (1657–1736) et la république des lettres*. Paris, E. Droz, 1938.
Berman, David. "Anthony Collins and the Question of Atheism in the Early Part of the Eighteenth Century." *Proceedings of the Royal Irish Academy*, 75, sec. C (1975), 85–102.
Bonanante, Ugo. *Charles Blount: libertinismo e deismo nel seicento inglese*. Florence, La nuova Italia, 1972.
Carabelli, Giancarlo. *Tolandiana: materiali bibliografici per lo studio dell'opera e della fortuna di John Toland (1670–1722)*. Florence, La nuova Italia, 1975.
Carroll, Robert T. *The Common-Sense Philosophy of Bishop Edward Stillingfleet, 1635–1699*. The Hague, Nijhoff, 1975.
Casini, Paolo. *L'universo-macchina: origini della filosofia newtoniana*. Bari, Editori Laterza, 1969.
Dickinson, H. T. *Liberty and Property: Political Ideology in Eighteenth-Century Britain*. New York, Holmes and Meier, 1977.
Downie, J. A. *Robert Harley and the Press: Propaganda and Public Opinion in the Age of Swift and Defoe*. Cambridge, Cambridge University Press, 1979.
Emerson, Roger L. "English Deism, 1670–1755: An Enlightenment Challenge to Orthodoxy." Ph.D. dissertation, Brandeis University, 1962.
Erman, J. P. *Mémoires pour servir à l'histoire de Sophie Charlotte reine de Prusse*, etc. Berlin, 1801.
Evans, Robert R. "John Toland's Pantheism: A Revolutionary Ideology and Enlightenment Philosophy." Ph.D. disertation, Brandeis University, 1965.
Every, George, *The High-Church Party, 1688–1718*. London, S.P.C.K., 1956.
Firpo. Massimo. "John Locke e il socinianesimo." *Rivista Storica italiana* 92 (1980), 35–124.
_____. "Il rapporto tra socinianesimo e primo deismo inglese negli studi di uno storico polacco." *Critica storica* 10 (1973), 243–297.
_____. "Recenti studi sul socinianesimo nel sei e settecento." *Rivista storica italiana* 88

(1977), 106-152.

Fox-Bourne, H. R. *The Life of John Locke.* 2 vols. London, 1876.

Gilbert, Alan D. *Religion and Society in Industrial England: Church, Chapel, and Social Change, 1740-1914.* London, Longmans, Green, 1976.

Giuntini, Chiara. *Panteismo e ideologia repubblicana: John Toland (1670—1722).* Bologna, Il Mulino, 1979.

Heinemann, F. H. "John Toland and the Age of the Enlightenment." *Review of English Studies* 20 (1944), 125-146.

Holmes, Geoffrey. *British Politics in the Age of Anne.* London, Macmillan, 1967.

_____. *The Trial of Doctor Sacheverell.* London, Eyre, Methuen, 1973.

Horwitz, Henry. *Parliament, Policy, and Politics in the Reign of William III.* Manchester, Manchester University Press, 1977.

Jacob, James R. and Margaret C. "The Anglican Origins of Modern Science: The Metaphysical Foundations of the Whig Constitution." *Isis* 71 (1980), 252-267.

Jacob, Margaret C. "John Toland and the Newtonian Ideology." *Journal of the Warburg and Courtauld Institutes* 32 (1969), 307-331.

_____. "Newtonianism and the Origins of the Enlightenment: A Reassessment." *Eighteenth-Century Studies* 11 (1977-1978), 1-25.

_____. *The Newtonians and the English Revolution, 1689-1720.* Ithaca, Cornell University Press, 1976.

_____. *The Radical Enlightenment: Pantheists, Freemasons, and Republicans.* London, G. Allen & Unwin, 1981.

Kenyon, J. P. *Revolution Principles: The Politics of Party, 1689-1720.* Cambridge, Cambridge University Press, 1977.

Knoop, Douglas and G. P. Jones. "Freemasonry and the Idea of Natural Religion." *Ars Quatuor Coronatorum* 56 (1946), 38-57.

Kot, Stanislaus. "Le Mouvement antitrinitaire au XVIème et au XVIIème siècle." *Humanisme et renaissance* 4 (1937), 16-58, 109-156.

Kramnick, Isaac. *Bolingbroke and His Circle: The Politics of Nostalgia in the Age of Walpole.* Cambridge, Harvard University Press, 1968.

Kristeller, Paul Oskar. *Renaissance Thought: The Classic, Scholastic, and Humanist Strains.* New York, Harper and Row, Harper Torchbooks, 1961.

Kubrin, David. "Newton and the Cyclical Cosmos: Providence and the Mechanical Philosophy." *Journal of the History of Ideas* 28 (1967), 325-346.

Manuel, Frank E. *The Eighteenth Century Confronts the Gods.* Cambridge, Harvard University Press, 1959.

McGuire, J. E. "Neoplatonism and Active Principles: Newton and the *Corpus Hermeticum.*" In *Hermeticism and the Scientific Revolution,* pp. 93-142. Los Angeles, William Andrews Clark Memorial Library, 1977.

McLachlan, H. John. *Socinianism in Seventeenth-Century England.* London, Oxford University Press, 1951.

Michel, Paul-Henri. *La Cosmologie de Giordano Bruno.* Paris, Hermann, 1962.

Ogonowski, Zbigniew. "Le 'Christianisme sans mystères' selon John Toland et les sociniens." *Archiwum historii filozofii i myśli spolecznej* 12 (1966), 205-223.

O'Higgins, James. *Anthony Collins: The Man and His Works.* The Hague, Nijhoff, 1970.

Pocock, J. G. A. *The Machiavellian Moment: Florentine Political Thought and the Atlantic Republican Tradition.* Princeton, Princeton University Press, 1975.

_____, ed. *The Political Works of James Harrington.* Cambridge, Cambridge University Press, 1977.

_____. *Politics, Language, and Time: Essays on Political Thought and History.* New York, Atheneum, College Editions, 1973.

_____, ed. *Three British Revolutions: 1641, 1688, 1776.* Princeton, Princeton University Press, 1980.

Redwood, John. *Reason, Ridicule and Religion: The Age of Enlightenment in England, 1660–1750.* Cambridge, Harvard University Press, 1976.

Reedy, Gerard. "Socinians, John Toland, and the Anglican Rationalists." *Harvard Theological Review* 70 (1977), 285–304.

Roberts, J. M. *The Mythology of the Secret Societies.* New York, Scribners, 1972.

Sina, Mario. *L'avvento della ragione: "Reason" e "above Reason" dal razionalismo inglese al deismo.* Milan, Università cattolica del Sacro Cuore, 1976.

Skinner, Quentin. *The Foundations of Modern Political Thought.* 2 vols. Cambridge, Cambridge University Press, 1978.

_____. "The Principles and Practice of Opposition: The Case of Bolingbroke versus Walpole." In *Historical Perspectives: Studies in English Thought and Society in Honour of J. H. Plumb,* ed. Neil McKendrick, pp. 94–110. London, Europa, 1974.

Stephen, Leslie. *History of English Thought in the Eighteenth Century.* 3d ed. 2 vols. [1902]. Reprint, New York, Harcourt, Brace, and World, Harbinger Books, 1962.

Stromberg, Roland. *Religious Liberalism in Eighteenth-Century England.* London, Oxford University Press, 1954.

Sykes, Norman. *William Wake, Archbishop of Canterbury.* 2 vols. Cambridge, Cambridge University Press, 1957.

Wegman, Nola J. "Argument and Satire: The Christian Response to Deism, 1670–1760." Ph.D. dissertation, Northwestern University, 1967.

Westfall, Richard. *Science and Religion in Seventeenth-Century England.* New Haven, Yale University Press, 1958.

Westman, Robert S. "Magical Reform and Astronomical Reform: The Yates Thesis Reconsidered." In *Hermeticism and the Scientific Revolution,* pp. 1–91. Los Angeles, William Andrews Clark Memorial Library, 1977.

Wilbur, Earl M. *A History of Unitarianism.* 2 vols. Cambridge, Harvard University Press, 1946–1952.

Worden, A. B., ed. *Edmund Ludlow, A Voyce from the Watch Tower: Part Five, 1660–1662.* Camden ser. 4, vol. 21. London, Royal Historical Society, 1978.

Yates, Frances A. *Giordano Bruno and the Hermetic Tradition.* London, Routledge and Kegan Paul, 1964.

_____. *The Rosicrucian Enlightenment.* London, Routledge and Kegan Paul, 1972.

Yolton, John W. *John Locke and the Way of Ideas.* London, Oxford University Press, 1956.

Index

91, 139; as theological language, 112–113, 243; JT's rejection of, 144; theocentricity of, 177

The Second Part of the State Anatomy (1717), 35

Secret Societies, JT's involvement in, 3, 15–16, 19, 39, 201–203

Self-image, JT's, 1, 40, 42

Self-interest: Anglican appeals to, 56, 59, 257–258; JT's attitude toward, 168

Seneca, 232

Septennial Act (1716), 37, 142, 153, 156, 157

Servetus, Michael, 7, 85

Settlement, Act of (1701), 16, 156, 157

Shaftesbury, Anthony Ashley-Cooper, 1st earl of, 151, 273

Shaftesbury, Anthony Ashley-Cooper, 3rd earl of, 16, 38, 143, 151, 154, 261; JT's relations with, 6, 12, 14, 15, 21, 22–24; relations with Harley, 23; influence on JT, 167–168, 171

Shaftesbury, Anthony Ashley-Cooper, 4th earl of, 12

Shaftesbury, Anthony Ashley-Cooper, 7th earl of, 272

Sharp, John, 18, 20, 25, 40, 60

Sherlock, Thomas, 269

Sherlock, William, 97, 98, 105, 106, 112–113

A Short History of Standing Armies (1698), 15

Shute-Barrington, James, 267

Sidney, Algernon, 12, 148, 164

Simon, Richard, 47, 57, 94, 133, 249

Sincerity: as mark of faith, 64, 226, 259–260; Socinian insistence on, 89, 103; JT's invocation of, 132, 137; Bruno on, 200; deists' appeals to, 226, 227; Hoadly's use of, 267–268

Skelton, Philip, 212, 258–259

Skinner, Quentin, 143

Smith, Elisha, 259–260

Smith, Thomas, 53, 58, 97

Smollett, Tobias, 271

Social contract, JT on, 150

Society for the Reformation of Manners, 67, 103, 255

Socinianism, 7, 10, 23, 43, 82–108 passim, 110–112, 115, 250, 251; JT accused of, 5, 8, 10, 11, 51, 109–110, 210–211; JT's relation to, 6–7, 10, 17, 104, 106, 110–113,

115–116, 122–123, 124, 125, 127, 128, 130, 132, 134, 136–137, 138, 139–140, 174, 176, 233, 245, 275, 277; Anglican opposition to, 52–53, 56–57, 76, 97, 104, 106; Latitudinarian convergence with, 69, 71, 103–104, 115–116, 245, 248–249, 264; and Remonstrants, 73, 82–83; connection of with deism, 83, 85, 88, 94, 104, 105–108, 222–223, 235

Socinianism Truly Stated (1705), 104, 182

Socinus, Faustus, 86–87, 88, 89, 93

Socinus, Lællius, 85

Socrates, 138, 222, 228

Socratic Society, 182, 201–202

Somers, John, baron, 154

Sophia, Electress-Dowager of Hanover, 18, 31, 158; and JT, 16, 19, 20, 23, 29, 34

Sophie-Charlotte, Queen of Prussia, 20, 135, 178

South, Robert, 51, 80–81, 98, 105, 110

South Sea Bubble, 37, 152, 165

South Sea Company, 36

Spaccio della bestia trionfante (trans., 1712), 198–199

Spanheim, Frederick ("the Younger"), 4, 19, 20

Spinoza, Baruch, 92, 94, 106, 133, 185, 220; and JT, 30, 113, 191, 193, 201, 204; accused of deism, 209, 210; accused of atheism, 193, 210, 236

Spy, JT as, 5–6, 23, 27, 33

Stanhope, James, 1st earl of, 37

Standing army, 150, 154; JT's attitudes toward, 14–15, 142, 149, 152, 166–167

The State-Anatomy of Great Britain (1717), 35, 37, 38

Stegmann, Joachim, 88

Stephen, Leslie, 51, 113, 114, 174, 211, 268, 275–276

Stephens, William, 13, 15

Stillingfleet, Edward, 10, 54, 55, 58, 84, 107; moralism of, 56, 59, 170; and exegesis, 61–62; versus Locke, 74–80, 100, 104, 109, 122, 124, 243; on Socinianism, 76, 97, 104, 106; on deism, 208

Strabo, 185

Stratford, William, 20

Strauss, Leo, 43

Stromberg, Roland N., 215

Style, JT's, 49–50, 214, 217, 219

Harvard Historical Studies

88. *Angeliki E. Laiou.* Constantinople and the Latins: The Foreign Policy of Andronicus, 1282–1328. 1972.
89. *Donald Nugent.* Ecumenism in the Age of the Reformation: The Colloquy of Poissy. 1974.
90. *Robert A. McCaughey.* Josiah Quincy. 1772–1864: The Last Federalist. 1974.
91. *Sherman Kent.* The Election of 1827 in France. 1975.
92. *A. N. Galpern.* The Religions of the People in Sixteenth-Century Champagne. 1976.
93. *Robert G. Keith.* Conquest and Agrarian Change: The Emergence of the Hacienda System on the Peruvian Coast. 1976.
94. *Keith Hitchins.* Orthodoxy and Nationality: Andreiu Şaguna and the Rumanians of Transylvania, 1846–1873. 1977.
95. *A. R. Disney.* Twilight of the Pepper Empire: Portuguese Trade in Southwest India in the Early Seventeenth Century. 1978.
96. *Gregory D. Phillips.* The Diehards: Aristocratic Society and Politics in Edwardian England. 1979.
97. *Alan Kreider.* English Chantries: The Road to Dissolution. 1979.
98. *John Buckler.* The Theban Hegemony, 371–362 BC. 1980.
99. *John A. Carey.* Judicial Reform in France before the Revolution of 1789. 1981.
100. *Andrew W. Lewis.* Royal Succession in Capetian France: Studies on Familial Order and the State. 1982.
101. *Robert E. Sullivan.* John Toland and the Deist Controversy: A Study in Adaptations. 1982.